Cyril Hopkins'

Marcus Clarke

Cyril Hopkins'

Marcus Clarke

edited from the manuscript in the
Mitchell Library
by

Laurie Hergenhan,
Ken Stewart and
Michael Wilding

Australian Scholarly Publishing
in association with the
State Library of Victoria

© Laurie Hergenhan,
Ken Stewart and
Michael Wilding 2009

First published 2009
Australian Scholarly Publishing Pty Ltd
7 Lt Lothian St Nth, North Melbourne, Vic 3051
TEL: 03 9329 6963 FAX: 03 9329 5452
EMAIL: aspic@ozemail.com.au
WEB: scholarly.info

The publication of this work has been kindly assisted by the Australian Academy of the Humanities.

ISBN 978 1 921509 12 4

Copyediting and indexing by Diane Carlyle
Design and typesetting by Sarah Anderson
Printing and binding by BPA Print Group Ltd
Cover Photograph of Marcus Clarke aged 20 before he left Ledcourt Station. SLV H81.204/2 : mp013422

Contents

Introduction

Cyril Hopkins wrote his life of Marcus Clarke over a century ago,[1] but until now it has never been published in whole or in part. Although known to a few scholars, it has not been readily accessed, partly because of copyright restrictions, and partly because of its handwritten state.

Cyril and his brother, the poet Gerard Manley Hopkins, were close friends of Marcus Clarke from before, and throughout, their school days in London, and Cyril corresponded with Clarke during his early years in Melbourne. He is the only known person with whom Clarke kept in close contact by letters. The biography contains not only unique factual material, interpretations, and research undertaken by Hopkins, but also lengthy extracts from many unpublished pieces and letters written by Clarke himself, the originals of which have not survived.

It is a fascinating story of a colonial emigrant's life and times in its portrayal of both up-country colonial life, and of Bohemian life in 'Marvellous Melbourne' in the post-gold rush era. Clarke's letters give memorable pictures of the mercurial emigrant's ups and downs as a jackaroo, as a traveller in remote rural and gold-mining areas of the colonies, as a struggling journalist, as librarian, as a theatre critic, and as a *bon viveur* in Melbourne café society; and also of the bustling and variegated life of a thriving colonial city. It is of particular interest as the only known source of information concerning Clarke's early life in London, and his first years in Australia, where he struggled to stay afloat as a journalist and writer. The reader comes to see Clarke gradually detaching himself from England and aspects of British culture, identifying with his new country both as a man and as a writer, and perhaps painting a rosier picture for his distant friend than his colonial vicissitudes warranted. Although Cyril the Victorian gentleman was inclined to apologise for Clarke's bohemianism, the biographer's perspective itself brings into relief the rebellion against Victorian conventionality that characterised Clarke's life and work.

When Hamilton Mackinnon published the first biography of Clarke in 1884, to accompany the *Marcus Clarke Memorial Volume*,[2] he remarked:

> Of his school days little is known, save what can be gathered from a note-book – a kind of diary – kept by him at that period; and even in this the information is most fragmentary as, like other and subsequent attempts of his in keeping records, he adhered to no system and was by no means regular in noting down passing occurrences. According to this book he seems to have had only two friends, with whom he was upon terms of great intimacy. They were brothers, Cyril and Gerald [sic] Hopkins, and they appear, judging from jottings and sketches of theirs in his scrap album, to have been talented both as versifiers and pen and ink sketchers; in both of which their schoolfellow was equally good. Among other jottings to be found in this school record is one bearing the initials G. H., and referring to one 'Marcus Scrivener' as a 'Kaleidoscopic, Parti-colored, Harlaquinesque [sic] Thaumatropic being'. (15–16)

The notebook or diary seems now to be lost. But Cyril Hopkins' manuscript provides much of the information on Clarke's school days, and his friendship with Cyril and Gerard Manley Hopkins, that Mackinnon lacked.[3]

Marcus Clarke's connections with the Manley Hopkins family, in particular with Gerard the eldest son, and his younger brother Cyril, began in a chance meeting, memorably described by Cyril in Chapter 2 of his biography, when they were young boys on holiday on the Isle of Wight. Clarke's father, newly a widower, was in deep mourning, and Clarke himself was at that time a delicate boy with a disability in one arm. The boys made friends and played together. Later they went to the same London school, Sir Roger Cholmeley's Grammar School, sometimes spelled Cholmondeley, pronounced Chumley but usually called Highgate School from the suburb where it is situated. Thus began a close friendship important to the three of them and assisted by some family contact.

Manley Hopkins senior left school at fifteen, later becoming an average adjuster or marine insurance broker and setting up his own firm, with a branch in every major British port. It is still in business today (Martin, Manley Hopkins and Cooks

Ltd). Manley's brothers, Charles and Edward, held significant government positions
in Hawaii and he himself became its Consul-General in the United Kingdom for
forty years (1856–96), a position putting him in contact with important people
of the day. Bishop Wilberforce wrote a preface to Manley's history of Hawaii and
when Queen Emma of Samoa visited London she called on the Hopkins family.[4]
Cyril in turn became British Vice-Consul (1896–1900), something that perhaps
helped bring a wider, extra-British dimension to his perspective on Clarke in
Australia. Norman White comments that Gerard's 'lifelong silence on his father's
Hawaiian connections is remarkable. (Manley often exaggerated the importance
of his largely honorary position, which had comic embarrassing aspects.)'[5] Again,
Gerard never mentioned in his letters the nature of his father's job which made
possible 'a comfortable social position' (White (2004) 54).

Cyril as second son was perhaps overshadowed in the family by Gerard as the
talented eldest and by gifted siblings. It was not assumed that Gerard would follow in
his father's footsteps, this being left to Cyril. Biographies of Gerard generally reflect
this positioning, while in his professional life Cyril was overshadowed by his father.
Cyril clearly had his artistic and literary interests too, but made finance his career. A
few anecdotes survive. A family story records that when they were children, Gerard
was once found crying 'because Cyril has become so ugly'.[6] There was a certain rivalry
between the brothers. Gerard wrote to his school friend Ernest Hartley Coleridge
(grandson of the poet Samuel Taylor Coleridge), 3 September 1862:

> Cyril is now, if you want to write, 'chez M. Le pasteur Monchatre, Elbeuf, Près de
> Rouen, France'; he left Esslingen when my father and brother went over to fetch him in
> August, he will stay in France till Xmas. He has not grown a moustache (caze why? caze
> he would if he could, but he can't) but he has shaved twice!! There is not a vestige of hair
> on his face, they say. He is still mad about the army and indeed cares for nothing else.
> He smoke furiously and is utterly unpatriotic.[7]

'While Cyril cultivated manliness in the City Office', writes White, 'Gerard
developed other friendships'.[8]

When Manley sought a school for his two eldest sons, he did so as one
'moving uneasily between a trade and profession'.[9] His choice of school may
have been influenced by the connection with Clarke's father, whose family was
firmly entrenched in professions and public service, especially the army. Sir
Roger Cholmeley's Grammar School catered for sons of lawyers (as Clarke was),

clergymen, bankers, army officers and those wanting to move up the social scale. The headmaster, Dr Dyne, raised the academic achievement and enrolment of the school, the curriculum emphasising the classics in typical Victorian style, but he also placed an unusual emphasis on the ability to write English well.

The school had something of a literary tradition. One young master, R. W. Dixon, a poet, was intimate with the Pre-Raphaelites. Gerard later developed a friendship with him. Former pupils included the philologist, W. W. Skeat, Philip Worsley, who won the Newdigate Prize at Oxford and translated the *Odyssey* into Spenserian stanzas (Martin 13, 19), and two of Dickens' young protégés, the novelist and editor Edmund Yates, and G. A. Sala, an exponent of the 'new journalism' whom the young Clarke admired. Works by both of Yates and Sala feature in Clarke's correspondence with Cyril. Later pupils include the politician Anthony Crosland, Sir Martin Furnival Jones, Director of MI5, 1965–72, Alex Comfort, Owen Barfield, Sir John Betjeman, and Stephen Ward (of the Profumo affair). T. S. Eliot taught there for a short time; so did Arthur Waugh (father of Alec and Evelyn Waugh) after his retirement during World War II.

Gerard Manley Hopkins was two years older than his brother Cyril, who was the same age as Clarke. 'The two brothers got along well enough but seem never to have been close' (Martin 9). From Cyril's biography it is clear, however, that at school they moved as siblings in a common circle with Clarke, an important friend of each. One Hopkins biographer (Eleanor Ruggles) says Clarke was Gerard's best friend. Another, Norman White, comments that 'a major influence at school was an unconventional boy, Marcus Clarke, a high-spirited and gifted writer who passed on to Hopkins his enthusiasm for contemporary English artists especially Frederick Walker and J. E. Millais'.[10] All three boys belonged to the school's Elgin House, which catered for boarders. According to one commentator, Gerard won so many prizes 'one can only feel sorry for Cyril who entered school in 1856, two years after Gerard, had an absolutely consistent record of never winning a prize, and left in 1861, two years before Gerard, to take a position in his father's business' (Martin 14). Cyril records that a literary prize was withheld from Clarke by Dyne because he had neglected his other studies.

In his biography, Cyril is self-effacing, maintaining a typical Victorian reticence and propriety, amounting to self-censorship, so he gives no indication of how he may have felt about this intellectual disparity with his brother or about sibling rivalry. Cyril simply presents Gerard as a companion to himself and Clarke. The latter achieved a measure of fame long before Gerard became recognised as a poet and before Cyril wrote his biography, so in recording the school years Cyril naturally saw Clarke as the successful artist.

Cyril's memories of friendship with Clarke and Gerard illuminate the context of school life at Highgate: of conditions and activities, curricular and extra-curricular, of pastimes and escapades. Compared with Gerard or Clarke, Cyril seems prosaic. Indeed his very typicalness as a middle-class gentleman makes his a valuable and unusual testimony concerning Gerard's school days and throws into relief Clarke's unconventionality.

Cyril records that the three boys shared an interest in wide reading: of romances, mystery and adventure stories, Gothic tales. Gerard won the school poetry prize at Easter 1860 with a poem on 'The Escorial' and showed early promise as an artist. His family thought that he might make art his career. He had been taught painting and drawing by his Aunt Annie Hopkins before he went to school and had shown some promise; Mackinnon's *Memorial Volume* refers to 'sketches' by Cyril and Gerard in Clarke's scrap album (16); the younger brothers Arthur (1847–1930) and Everard (1860–1928) were both professional artists – Arthur won a gold medal at the Royal Academy and for twenty-five years contributed to the *Graphic*; Everard held a Slade scholarship for three years and contributed illustrations to London magazines; both contributed to *Punch*.[11] Another brother, Lionel, became a distinguished Sinologist, translator of *The Six Scripts on the Principles of Chinese Writing* by Tai T'ung (Cambridge, 1954).

C. N. Luxmoore recalled in a letter to Arthur Hopkins (from whom he took art lessons) that Gerard as a schoolboy 'was full of fun, rippling over with jokes, and chaff, and facile with pencil and pen, with rhyming jibe or cartoon'.[12] Gerard illustrated Clarke's first literary endeavours. He drew a frontispiece to Clarke's Gothic poem, 'The Lady of Lynn', a cover for one of Clarke's earliest tales, 'Prometheus', and an illustration of 'The Alchemist' for another. Gerard himself 'produced his poetic variations on the theme of arcane knowledge in "The Alchemist in the City"' (White (2004) 31). Clarke had a lifelong interest and reading in alchemy, and Cyril Hopkins is especially useful in indicating something of both its origins and continuance.

Cyril does not discuss Gerard's writing. His brother Gerard's high opinion of Clarke's poetry, however, is on record. Gerard wrote to Ernest Hartley Coleridge, 3 September 1862:

> Secondly I must tell you that Clarke writes very good poetry. He and I compare notes and ideas. I think I shewed you his 'Lady of Lynn'. I suppose you do not mind;

I told him about your writing and two of your ideas, the 'abyss of green' and 'the incandescence of those hues' etc; also since there was nothing private I read him your last letter. He would like to write to you, but does not know if you would like it.[13]

Cyril records that Clarke sent home to England the verses of this poem, 'The Lady of Lynn', 'for which he requested my brother, Gerard, to do an illustration … This was accordingly supplied and some slight alterations … were suggested at the time. These were adopted and two more verses added. Soon after his arrival in Melbourne, Marcus posted me a copy of the poem with a view to its insertion in *Once a Week*, a periodical then at the zenith of its popularity …' (Chapter 5). Cyril adds that this literary and artistic periodical was edited by a friend of the Hopkins family, Edward Walford, and that the three schoolboys had taken out a joint subscription to it. Manley Hopkins had published in *Once a Week* and one of Gerard's earliest poems, 'Winter with the Gulf Stream', was published there in 1863, one of the very few poems published in his lifetime. Clarke's poem was not accepted.[14]

One Hopkins biographer suggests that Clarke's prose may have influenced Gerard's early style and with two such eager and youthful creative minds the possibility of cross-fertilisation is likely, even if the influence was not lasting. White, quoting from Cyril's biography, cites a description of a sunset, which Clarke observed on his way to Australia and which he sent in a letter to Cyril (presumably to be read by the Hopkins family), as evidence of the exchange of ideas and images between Gerard and Clarke. He suggests that the passage had much in common with 'the undisciplined description in Gerard's "A Vision of Mermaids"' (White (1992) 30). Cyril compares it to the style of Robert Louis Stevenson; Brian Elliott[15] dismisses Clarke's description as 'Ruskinesque'. White argues that the early Hopkins was influenced by Ruskin; so, probably, was the young Clarke. Both writers are noted for the dramatic and visual immediacy of their writings. Clarke's interest in the visual arts inspired one of his first essays in Australia, 'Popular Art and Gustave Doré', published in the *Australasian*, 28 September 1867, a copy of which he sent to Cyril.

Gerard's and Clarke's temperaments also helped to draw them together. Cyril describes Clarke's oral storytelling powers, his wit and liveliness, his 'gift of laughter' and a daredevil quality as making him an entertaining companion. But he stresses that to Clarke's intimates, including the Hopkins boys, Clarke was no 'butterfly', showing a serious and darker side that emerged in the stories Gerard illustrated and to which his own nature would have responded. Clarke gave Gerard a volume of

Edgar Allan Poe's poems which the latter passed on to Cyril when he joined the Jesuits (White (1992) 30).

Clarke features in two stories about Gerard's school days. The first incident involves Clarke and Gerard as co-victims in a flogging by the headmaster, Dyne, whom both boys detested (Martin 16–18). Hopkins wrote to his friend C. N. Luxmoore, 7 May 1862: 'Clarke my co-victim was flogged, struck off the confirmation list and fined £1; I was deprived of my room for ever, sent to bed at half past nine till further orders, and ordered to work *only* in the school room, not even in the library and might not sit on a window sill on the staircase to read.'[16] Elliott (1958) remarks:

> Gerard's account of the trouble, in a letter to a school friend, is not fully explicit and the cause remains obscure; but it is open to conjecture that the two boys had offended Dyne upon some point of religious orthodoxy. A later remark of Clarke's may have some bearing upon the incident. When he was informed of Gerard's conversion he wrote to Cyril that he considered the Roman Catholic 'the most picturesque and splendid form of belief', which he had once (and the reference must be to his school days) been tempted to adopt himself, although he had not done so because he rather 'inclined to the mystical in religion.' By 'mystical' Clarke seems to mean mysterious; if the reference was to schoolboy occultism or any form of 'Roman' experimentalism Dyne would certainly not have approved of it. (14)

Clarke later wrote his own account of being flogged, in the *Australasian*, 24 July 1869:

> When I was at school I was flogged twice a week, and did not like it. The gentlemanly headmaster – he was cousin to an earl, a D. D., and strictly orthodox – was noted for his use of the birch, and used to smack his lips over a flogging with intense glee. He was a left hander (there was a legend extant to the effect that he had broken his right arm in flogging a boy, but I always doubted it myself), and the way he used to 'draw' the birch was astonishing. He used always to stop after ten strokes, if the victim cried out, but as I was under the impression that he flogged me from purely personal motives, and wanted to show my indifference and skey-orn, I would have died rather than whimper ... I was regarded as a small hero by the whole of the fourth form, and when my particular friend picked out the buds with a pen knife that night, and

related a complimentary remark made by Bluggins ma. [major], head of the "sixth"
and a Triton among schoolboy minnows, I felt almost happy.

Elliott (1958) remarks 'we may, if we care to, imagine that the particular friend
was Cyril Hopkins, and the Triton Gerard (who was at one time 'Cock of the Walk
at Elgin')' (255). It is also tempting to see such episodes as sources of the famous
flogging scene in *His Natural Life*. In a day of formidable flogging headmasters,
writes Martin, 'Dyne was a rival for the honours with Dr Keate of Eton'; Edmund
Yates recalled him as 'a swisher';[17] 'a man whose logic was comprised in the birch,
to whom an answer however respectful was at least mutiny, if not rank blasphemy',
Luxmoore described him to Arthur Hopkins.[18] Clarke's sense that he was being
flogged 'from purely personal motives' was shared by Gerard, who also felt a personal
vindictiveness in Dyne's treatment of him.[19]

   The second enigmatic episode involving Clarke is recorded by Gerard in the
same letter to C. N. Luxmoore, 7 May 1862, though had apparently taken place
earlier. (Gerard's nickname was 'Skin'.)

> The last blow was this. I extract the account from my journal. 'April 13.' (Sunday).
> * * 'After prayers Alexander Strachey came up to the bedroom at my request to have
> a last talk at the end of the quarter. I had found out from Clarke who had walked to
> Finchley with him the day before that on Clarke making some mention of me as 'your
> friend Skin', he said, 'He is not my friend'. 'O yes he is' said Clarke, and afterwards
> asked why he went no walks with me. 'Because he never asks me' said Strachey. Not
> wishing to compromise Clarke, I first asked him the same question, to which he
> gave at once the same ungrateful answer. Being thus master of the situation, I told
> him I had not expected so ungrateful an answer. He knew, I said, the reason; at least
> he might have appreciated the sacrifice; that he had not spoken except on the most
> trivial subjects and on some days not even that, that he had taken no notice of me,
> and that I had been wretched every time I saw or thought of it, was only what I had
> bargained for, I sowed what I now reaped; but after this sacrifice to be told he did not
> walk with me because I never asked him was too much. I put a parallel case to him; I
> told him he might find many friends more liberal than I had been but few who would
> make the same sacrifice I had; but I could not get him to see it: after I had said all,
> the others came up to bed. I asked him if he had anything more to say. He objected
> that the others had come up to interrupt it. 'But should you have had anything if
> they had not?' I asked. 'No, I don't think so' he said with a cool smile, and I left him.

Perhaps in my next friendship I may be wiser.' When I got the exhibition my mother thought I might in civility write to him. He did not answer however, and, with the exception of a cold 'How do you do?', we have not spoken this quarter. Yet it is still my misfortune to be fond of and yet despised by him. If ever hereafter you should have any intercourse with him *expert crede* and do not believe in his unselfishness, his sincerity, or his gratitude, for he has little of either. Now you know my case.[20]

Clarke 'passed on to Hopkins his enthusiasm for contemporary British artists especially Frederick Walker and J. E. Millais. Hopkins started writing [at school] poetic descriptions of nature and weather effects.'[21] Cyril records that Clarke preserved from the sale of his father's effects a fine engraving of Millais' picture, *A Huguenot*, and cherished it until he died. White adds that as late as 1881, Hopkins was still using *A Huguenot* as a critical illustration in an argument with Bridges.[22]

Clarke sensed this sympathetic bond of budding fellow artists and later treated it in a story, 'Holiday Peak'.[23] Written in Australia, it is a fantasy set in the Australian bush about 'what might have been', ostensibly an extravagant fable but one where Gothic romance is combined with insights into alternative destinies lurking in everyone. Clarke knew from Cyril that Gerard had become a Jesuit. Gerard was received into the Roman Catholic Church, 21 October 1866, and became a novitiate of the Society of Jesus at Manresa, in Roehampton, in 1868. He was at St Mary's Hall seminary at Stonyhurst in Lancashire from 1870 until August 1873. In 'Holiday Peak', published in the *Australasian*, 18 and 25 January 1873, Clarke writes an alternative scenario for both of them:

Passing by an old house which stood back from the others in the terrace, my attention was caught by a crimson scarf trailing from one of the upper windows. 'An artist lives there,' was my first thought, for nowhere in the world save in the pictures of Prout do we see bits of colour floating about in that fashion. 'Yes, you are right,' said a young man, emerging from the well-dressed crowd which throngs in spring the steps of the Academy.

It was Gerard? Gerard my boy friend, who fled from Oxford to Stonyhurst, and embraced the discipline of Loyola. 'Gerard, what means this?'

'Dear old fellow,' said he, putting his arm round my neck in the fond old schoolboy fashion, 'it means that I thought better of my resolve, and followed out the natural bent of my talents. My picture, the "Death of Alcibiades," is the talk of the year. I shall soon be as famous as you.'

'As I! You jest. A poor devil banished to Bush Land, tied neck and heels in debt, soon slips out of the memory even of his friends.'

'So you persist in that dream about Australia! Surely you know that the fortune was recovered; that your year of poverty but served to correct your boyish extravagances, and that in easy circumstances you banished Poins and Pistol, and settled down to the career you chose!'

'Gerard, you are laughing at me!'

'Come into your own house, then, and be convinced,' said Gerard.

My house, it appeared, was a villa at Richmond; the railway station was sufficiently near to take me into town when town-talk was needed, and yet the cottage in its charm of park and river was sufficiently far from London smoke to suffer one's soul to breathe freely.

'I wonder,' said Gerard, 'that with the horses you keep you *ever* travel by the train?'

'My horses, then, are considered good?'

'Horses and books are your only extravagance. It is lucky that your income is not sufficiently large to suffer you to indulge a taste for pictures. You had better put down your yacht, and buy my "Death of Cromwell."'

'No, no,' I said dreamily, accepting this novel position; 'I always had a taste for yachting – but come in and let us converse.'

'You dine with Carabas tonight, remember,' said Gerard; 'Balthazar Claës and Byles Gridley will be there. I know you affect to dislike dinners, but the Marchioness is a good soul, and you must not disappoint her.'

'True,' said I, 'she is; and after presenting my eldest daughter, too. I shall certainly come.'

'The *Superfine Review* has cut up your last book, as usual,' remarked Gerard, turning over the papers on the horseshoe-table; 'but to an author whose readers are counted by millions, and to whom Chapman and Hall give £5,000 a volume, a sneer in the *Superfine* is not of much consequence.'

'No, indeed,' I replied, feeling much as if someone had taken away my head and left me a bubble of air in place of it. 'Besides, I write for the *Slaughterer*, and the two papers are at daggers drawn.'

'Ah! lucky fellow,' said Gerard, throwing open the window to inhale the perfume of my rose-garden. 'How different things *might have been* if you hadn't taken your uncle's advice.'

And after an assurance from Gerard that the young Clarke had never been introduced to the dubious pleasures of Armida-gardens, in a passage Cyril quotes in Chapter 1, the episode concludes with the news that Thackeray has not died.

'Nonsense! He is as hearty as you or I. I met him at Dickens's (they are great friends now, you know) the other day, and he never looked better. If it had not been for his excellent constitution, and the attention of Dr Lydgate, however, he might have been dead long ago.'

'Gerard, my dear fellow,' said I, rising, 'I – I feel a little confused; leave me for a while. We will meet at dinner.'

'Very well,' said Gerard. 'I will take Constantia for a drive.'

'Constantia! What, not the girl we –?'

'The same, dear old fellow.'

'And she did not marry Count Caskowisky?'

'Count Caskowisky be confounded! No; she married me. We have three children. *Sans adieu!*'

I fell back in my easy chair, *my* easy chair, stupefied. I must be dreaming! But no, the well-bred presence of my Swiss valet, as he laid out my dress clothes, was too palpable a reality!

Gerard, no surname attached, is re-imagined as a successful painter and a contented, indeed happy man with his wife Constantia and three children. His house catches attention because of a crimson scarf drifting out of a window, suggesting the sensuality and vigour of the artist. Clarke as a fellow artist (in the story, he is a prosperous, successful writer) is here suggesting not only with hindsight, but with a critical insight as well, the tensions he would have sensed at school within the younger Gerard and something of the conflicts to come – though these proved more creative than Clarke or anyone else realised at the time. Apparently no one had put these contradictions on record at the time Clarke published 'Holiday Peak', three years before Hopkins broke his poetic silence with 'The Wreck of the Deutschland', written in Spring 1876 (White (1992) 276).

Clarke knew of Gerard's literary interests during his school days, but, like most people (Cyril apparently amongst them), seems unaware of the continuation of his vocation as a poet. In 1884 Hopkins wrote that only eleven friends had been given his poetry to read (Martin xiii). The first collection of his poetry, edited by Robert Bridges, did not appear until 1918 – a dozen years after Cyril had written his biographical study of Marcus Clarke. Marcus, as far as Cyril knew at the time of writing, was his closest literary acquaintance. It is not known whether Gerard was ever aware of Clarke's successful career as writer of fiction.

Perhaps it was Clarke's rewriting in 'Holiday Peak' of Gerard's celibacy as well as of his religious vocation that prompted Cyril to keep silent about that part of the reference to Gerard, observing a propriety constantly present in his biography. In this story Clarke seems surprised and disappointed, if not shocked at the direction Gerard's career as Jesuit took, a reversal of his spiritedness and artistic ambitions as a fellow schoolboy. In the story of 'what might have been', Gerard renounces the church to 'follow the natural bent of my talents', and become a respected member of the Royal Academy. For a while Gerard indeed had considered painting as a career. He wrote to A. W. M. Baillie in 1868, 'You know I once wanted to be a painter. But even if I could I wd. not I think, now, for the fact is that the higher and more attractive parts of the art put a strain upon the passions which I shd. think it unsafe to encounter.'[24]

While Clarke was perhaps critical of Gerard's choice of a religious career, in writing about the Jesuits in the *Australasian*, 20 December 1867, and elsewhere in his writings, he showed sympathy for the Jesuits – recognising that they had been grossly caricatured in literature. When Cyril wrote to tell him of Gerard's conversion, Clarke replied: 'I am not surprised … I always thought he had a leaning that way. Indeed, for an imaginative, clever *and yet timid mind*, the Romish church is the only one which satisfies … Happy is the man who *can* believe! I cannot. But am no desperate destroyer; no denier of God and Heaven!'[25]

'Poor Clarke is on the voyage out to Australia, his father having met with a paralysis of the brain', Gerard wrote in a postscript to a letter to Ernest Hartley Coleridge, 22 March 1863 (Abbott, ed., 16). Neither Gerard nor his family, who invited Clarke to stay a couple of days before he left, and who had a long-standing friendship with him, sympathetic as they were, could really have appreciated how deeply the father's sudden and distressing illness disturbed his son. Thus Clarke passed out of Gerard's life but not Cyril's. Clarke himself was 'bewildered' by his situation as he wrote to Cyril, and having no real confidant to turn to he retreated into reticence, being 'subdued and reserved' as Cyril records in Chapter 5, even swearing him to secrecy on one confessional occasion. Cyril is the main source of information about Clarke's state of mind and experiences in his first years in Australia, but tantalisingly he draws on Clarke's letters selectively. Clarke himself was reticent: 'I will not detail the sad events which took place on his [father's] illness'. And he goes on to dwell on the financial chaos and disappointment rather than his suffering. 'Imagine – if you can – my position before I left England', following the collapse of his expectations of 'going into the Foreign Office after spending three years in France'. He fled 'the pity' of friends and relations. We must look in Clarke's later works for glimpses of what he must have endured.

Cyril, who was always associated by Clarke with his youthful life and hopes, is the one main link he maintained with England from Australia, writing numerous letters to him. Clarke wanted to let Cyril know, and to leave a diary-like record of his strange new life in Australia, to share his hopes of getting on in the colonial world, paving the way for his return. Thoughts of return gradually faded after Clarke became a successful journalist and writer in Melbourne. Nevertheless, he still nursed hopes of achieving recognition as a writer back in England. 'How did you like *His Un-Natural Life*? I mean *really* you know?' (The word 'really' strongly underlined.) 'Tell me in thy reply!' he wrote to Cyril, probably the only friend 'at home' with whom he could discuss literary matters.[26] Clarke wrote disparagingly to Cyril about letters from his army cousins with whom he apparently had nothing in common. Cyril's memories of their schoolboy friendship and of Clarke's vibrant personality and talent grew stronger and probably rosier as he himself aged so that in writing the biography in his later life Cyril was coping with the shadow of his own mortality, combining affection and nostalgia.

Little is recorded of Cyril's adult life. In 1872 he married Harriet Bockett (1845–1928). Gerard noted in his diary that he wrote to Cyril on his wedding day.[27] His brother, Arthur, married her sister Isabella (1850–1919). They were daughters of Daniel Bockett of Heath House, Hampstead, the suburb where the Hopkins family lived (House, ed., 382). Cyril, who had no children, did not marry again after his wife's death in 1928. Cyril's will (Somerset House, filed under 25/6/1932) shows that he was living in retirement at 'Colaba', 45 Festing Road, Southsea, Hampshire, when he died in 1932. He is buried in the cemetery of that town.

Cyril's memoir is the primary source of the information we have about Marcus's outback experience, on two stations, Swinton and Ledcourt, in Western Victoria, in which his uncle, James Langton Clarke, held a financial interest.[28] This has been variously interpreted as a false start, a wrong turning, an unlikely attempt at an inappropriate career. It perhaps more properly should be seen as jackarooing, that colonial rite of passage of upper middle-class Englishmen. A year or so spent on an outback station was the traditional gap year activity of English young men of the class to which the Clarkes and the Hopkins belonged, or aspired. A year out roughing it in the colonies, and then back home to be a landowner or go to university or take up a career in the army, or in the city, or in publishing. It is a class issue, as with so many things English and colonial. Marcus's stint should be seen in this context. Even if it wasn't quite like that in reality, this was the context in which he chose to present it. An upper-class lark.

Hopkins records some of Clarke's plans to take up land. Anthony Trollope's son tried that and failed financially time after time, refinanced by his father. Marcus had little money and no father. In the end he treated the experience as a colonial service finishing school, as if he were just one more upper middle-class young Englishman out for a year or so's toughening.

But Marcus never went back. There was nothing to go back to. He stayed in Melbourne and became a journalist, a playwright, a short story writer and, most famously of all, a novelist.

From the perspective of later commentators, Clarke's life has been associated mainly with his experiences as a Bohemian and journalist in post-gold rush Melbourne. Cyril Hopkins' memoir reveals how his previous spell travelling around the goldfields as a bank officer and as a jackeroo in the Wimmera were important to him; he wrote vividly about them in letters to Cyril, later recalling these days in his short stories, sketches and the latter part of the unabridged *His Natural Life*. Indeed Clarke was honing his literary style from his first letters as a New Chum onwards, drawing upon keen observation and transforming it into vibrant pictures through his luminous and adaptable style. These unpublished impressions are valuable in their own right. Visiting goldfields towns, Clarke used minute details in painting general pictures. He carefully noted technical details of mining and recorded colloquialisms, some of these details reappearing later in his fiction. It is as though Clarke were using his letters to Cyril if not as a notebook then as a kind of *aide mémoire*. Clarke was never one to waste literary material; rather, he conserved and recycled it.

Clarke recorded the varied phases of his work and moods on the Wimmera station: the exuberance of hard stock-riding and cattle-hunting on fine days, periods of intolerable heat, the attractions of neighbouring scenery of plain, river and ranges – for he did not write much of its 'weird melancholy' though he once called it '*toujours gum*' – roughing it in out-station huts, physical clashes with recalcitrant ex-convict workers, bushfire, days of intolerable heat and days of weather heady like champagne, the demanding work, and the leisure hours back at the station when he could read and write. Along with other bush workers he also experienced the boredom born of isolation and work routines which would drive many to escape through benders lasting days, or longer, as they drank their cheques out. Clarke entered into this new life with exuberance and curiosity, as he generally entered into new ventures. He worked hard here and later in Melbourne, his letters giving the lie to those who posthumously and perhaps condescendingly liked to picture him as a dilettante and devil-may-care, granted that like many artists he did not always act responsibly. Clarke's landmark description, 'the keynote of Australian scenery', was called up not only by the paintings with which it was originally associated but also by vivid memories of bush life. Though the description is a bravura piece in a Gothic mode, it draws on sharp observation, as in 'from the melancholy gums, strips of white bark hang and rustle'.

Clarke's unpublished up-country pictures that Hopkins preserved, in their vivid colour, their mixture of observation and lively imagination, contrast with the work of most of his predecessors. They had tended to write with documentary realism, 'travel books in disguise' as Frederick Sinnett put it in *The Fiction Fields of Australia* (1856); others such as Henry Kingsley used romance to tint their pictures. In *The Recollections of Geoffry Hamlyn*, published some six years before Clarke arrived in Australia, Kingsley depicted up-country life as largely conducted by English ladies and gentlemen on vine-covered verandas or on so-called sporting excursions such as kangaroo hunts. This turning of bush life into a picnic was to earn Joseph Furphy's scorn and stimulated new approaches by Ada Cambridge, Lawson and others.

Clarke mentions two gruelling overland excursions into the outback, to Fort Bourke in north-west New South Wales, and to Queensland, in which one of his companions died. He experienced at first hand then a variety of Australian terrain. If he did not choose to extend his time in the bush but instead took advantage of a gregarious life in a prosperous colonial city, his bush experience – for which Cyril Hopkins' memoir provides the main source – contributed importantly to his literary output. As Clarke put it in a letter: 'And having done all the cattle-hunting, stock-riding etc., I want to fall back on cultivated society, books, music, "Cigars and Chat / Chicken, champagne and all that"'.

The Hopkins family had provided 'cultivated society, books, music' back in England. Its members were literary and artistic. Cyril's father Manley Hopkins was a prolific writer. His books include two relating to his profession, *A Handbook of Averages* and *A Manual of Marine Insurance*, a history of Hawaii, three volumes of poetry and an unpublished novel. He contributed regularly to the *Times*, *Cornhill Magazine* and *Once a Week*. Cyril shared the family's cultural interests. His memoir of Clarke is studded with quotations from contemporary writers and references to painters. He has tended to be categorised by commentators on Clarke and Hopkins as a literary amateur, but he is an amateur only in the sense that he deals with a very different range of writers from those the professional literary scholars were later to institutionalise, which makes it an invaluable, otherwise irretrievable, context. The canonical writers from F. R. Leavis's 'Great Tradition' for instance, – Jane Austen, George Eliot, Henry James, Joseph Conrad – are never mentioned; though it was of course Leavis who was largely responsible for the critical acceptance of Gerard Manley Hopkins' poetry with his *New Bearings in English Poetry* (1932).

Many of the writers Cyril refers to in his biography are part of the English diaspora, the imperial spread of English writers, some expatriates, some travellers, and some colonials settled in the metropolis, writers who came from or went to the outreaches of empire. They include Robert Louis Stevenson, Rudyard Kipling, Samuel Butler, W. H. Hudson, Fergus Hume, E. W. Hornung, Mrs Campbell Praed, Tasma, Miles Franklin, Henry Lawson, and Grant Allen.

In this he reflects the actual circumstances of the Hopkins and Clarke families, scattered around the globe. Manley Hopkins' brothers Edward and Charles both lived in Hawaii;[29] his son Lionel served as a Consul in China and Gerard spent the last five years of his life in Ireland as Professor of Greek at University College, Dublin. Marcus Clarke's father and two uncles, of Anglo-Irish heritage, were both born in the West Indies; his cousin Sir Andrew Clarke spent most of his life in Australia, India and the Straits Settlements, where he was Governor; in Singapore today a road and a quay are named after him. Marcus's uncle, Sir Andrew Clarke Snr, was Governor of West Australia; another uncle, James Langton Clarke, was a county court judge in Victoria, later retiring to the south of France; Marcus's father-in-law, the actor John Dunn, was born in Ireland and worked in England and the United States before settling in Australia.

Hopkins was trying to establish a setting for Clarke's life and work from contemporary writers, as well as to fill in descriptions of places when Clarke himself had not provided them. The quotations have a documentary utility. They set the scene, both topographical and cultural. They provide a literary context. They show the sort of context in which Clarke was read in the 1890s when five of his works were reissued from London publishers.

Clarke's letters from Melbourne deal with the very beginnings of his literary and journalistic career. They are a unique record. They fill in the context of what was a meteoric rise in the Melbourne press. Clarke had begun to submit to the Melbourne *Punch* and other journals soon after his arrival and during his first year when employed at the Bank of Australasia. After spending nearly two years in the bush, he returned to Melbourne mid-1867. In his obituary of Alfred Telo a dozen years later, Clarke recalled that time:

> Alfred Telo was the first literary man whose acquaintance I made in Melbourne, and
> we lived in chambers together. I had just abandoned the elegant occupation of working

overseer on a station in the mallee at £40 a year and 'my tucker,' for the scarcely less cheerful situation of reporter on a Melbourne daily at 30s. a week. Alfred Telo lived over a sewing machine shop in Collins-street, the proud possessor of a suite of three rooms. I flung my 30s. a week into the ménage, and sent my modest trunk into the back attic.[30]

Clarke sent Cyril copies of two of his earliest essays published in the *Australasian* – 'Balzac and Modern French Literature', 3 August 1867, and 'Popular Art and Gustave Doré', 28 September 1867. They were unsigned, and it is only through Clarke's letter to Cyril that we can be confident of their authorship. In the covering letter he announces that he is now on the staff of the *Argus*: 'The *Argus* people were in want of a theatrical critic and I accepted the post at a salary of three hundred a year' (Chapter 20). This is twice the salary he gives in the Telo obituary: either his memory was faulty, or he exaggerated to Cyril, or being theatrical critic was a promotion from being a reporter. According to Mackinnon's *Memorial Volume*, however, he lost this staff position when he 'took upon himself to criticise a performance ... which, unfortunately ... did not come off' (27). On 23 November 1867 he began his 'Peripatetic Philosopher' column in the *Australasian*. It proved immediately popular, and a selection from it was to make his first book in 1869. Soon – March 1868 – he was part-owner and editor of the *Colonial Monthly* and began serialising his first novel, *Long Odds*, in its pages. The magazine was not a financial success and Clarke relinquished the editorship in September 1869. He then established the magazine *Humbug*, which ceased publication four months later in January 1870, at the same time as the *Colonial Monthly* collapsed.

Long Odds was published by Clarson, Massina, of Melbourne, in 1869. H. M. Hyndman reviewed it in the *Argus*, 2 July 1869, 5–6. In the 1880s Hyndman became one of the first English Marxists, founding the Social Democratic Federation, whose members included William Morris (before leaving to found the Socialist League) and Bernard Shaw (who left to join the Fabian Society). An upper-class Cambridge educated radical, he was a model for Jack Tanner in Shaw's *Man and Superman* (1903). In 1869 he visited Australia, where he became a member of the establishment Melbourne Club, which Clarke had joined a year earlier. In his *The Record of an Adventurous Life*, Hyndman records that

the manager of the *Argus*, who was a member of the club, an old Lincoln College, Oxford, man named Gowen Evans, whom I had got to know well, upbraided me with my laziness, which as I told him was no business of his, and then pressed me to write a review for the paper of a novel by Marcus Clarke, which had just appeared. Marcus Clarke was then and for long afterwards the smartest *littérateur* in Melbourne, and it appeared that other writers of ability did not care to criticize his work. Evans persuaded me to undertake the task and I did it as well as I could.

So far as I can remember it was not a bad novel; but it described scenes in England which the writer had never looked upon, and dealt with the life he knew only by hearsay. While giving the author full credit for its merits, therefore, I did not hesitate to point out very clearly its defects. I never got greater fun out of anything I wrote. As I have said the Melbourne of that day rejoiced in anything that was lively in the way of journalism or letters, and it was amusing to hear the talk going on as to who had been so rash as to criticise thus adversely the writing of this promising and rather prickly young Australian. The secret was well kept, and when at last it leaked out Marcus Clarke and I had become excellent friends. At the end of the review I had said that I felt sure if the author would turn his attention to the life and character of his own native country he would make a great name for himself. I only mention this now because years later, Marcus Clarke, recalling this remark of mine, sent me a copy of his novel entitled *His Natural Life*.[31]

Hyndman appears to have thought that Clarke was born in Australia, despite their becoming 'excellent friends'. Clarke later remarked of Hyndman's review of *Long Odds*: 'the work, by the way, was properly damned by a genial critic spending twelve months in Australia in order to "know all about the infernal colonies"'.[32]

The Melbourne Club was very much a conservative, establishment, rich man's venue. Hamilton Mackinnon wrote in the *Memorial Volume* that 'Clarke was unfortunately induced, by the foolish advice of friends, who felt flattered by his company, to live at a rate far exceeding his income. In other words, he became a member of the Melbourne Club, and tempted by its glitter threw himself into its extravagant ways … and, naturally, got involved in debt' (35). When the biography was reprinted in the *Austral Edition* in 1890, the specific reference to the Melbourne Club was omitted.

The journalists, writers and theatre people in 1860s Melbourne tended to frequent the Café de Paris, attached to the Theatre Royal. Clarke soon became an habitué. He describes it in his account of 'A Day in Melbourne' that he sent to Hopkins (Chapter 8), and he wrote about it again years later as the Café Lutetia.

I was then in Fig Tree Court with my friend Savage, and we dined at the Café daily. We were not rich, for we had both dissipated our incomes in the exact manner recorded of the Prodigal Son. I wrote for the *Peacock*, and Savage for the *Screechowl*. We made some four pounds sterling a week – and we were really thankful (not being grocers or drapers) to earn so much. The morning was spent in scribbling, the afternoon in tobacco, the evening in dinner, theatre, and gaslight. I fear we did not lead virtuous lives. I am sure that we were often out of bed after the small hours. I know that Madame Gogo and Lisette de Jambejolie assisted in the spending of the *Peacock's* bounty. We were utterly useless beings, but then – well, we had good digestions and did not bother ourselves with high resolves and sentimental love-making.[33]

Charles Bright, then on the parliamentary staff of the *Argus*, wrote an account of meeting Clarke drinking absinthe with the actor Walter Montgomery in the Café de Paris at this time, which Hopkins quotes in Chapter 22. In the literary and journalistic world of 1860s Melbourne, the writers for the different publications readily came to know each other.

With the founding of the Yorick Club in May 1868, they provided themselves with a regular forum for meeting, late night drinking and planning further publications. The members included Clarke, Adam Lindsay Gordon, Henry Kendall, F. W. Haddon, J. J. Shillinglaw, G. A. Walstab, Alfred Telo, James Smith, James Edward Neild, R. P. Whitworth, Garnet Walch, George Gordon McCrae, Hamilton Mackinnon, Henry Gyles Turner and Patrick Moloney amongst others.

The club had its origins in the Saturday night gatherings arranged by F. W. Haddon at his lodgings in Spring Street. Frederick Haddon had come out from England in 1863, the same year as Clarke; he was appointed editor of the new, weekly *Australasian* in 1864, and in 1867 became editor of its parent daily, the *Argus*, a position in which he continued until 1898. When he moved into Dr Aubrey Bowen's rooms in Collins Street, there was no suitable large room for the Saturday night meetings. Clarke also seems to have moved into Aubrey Bowen's around this time. There is a photograph of Clarke, Haddon and Bowen together, generally assumed to have been taken to commemorate the formation of the Yorick Club.[34] Two years later, in January 1870, Haddon accompanied Clarke to Tasmania when Clarke researched the convict records for his 'Old Tales Retold' series in the *Australasian* – material which helped to generate, and fed into, his great novel, *His Natural Life*, which he began serialising in the *Australian Journal* in March the same year.

The Yorick Club rented a room for £1 a week in the *Punch* office, 74 Collins Street. The *Argus* office was next door. Mueller's tavern was below. 'In its early days Mueller catered for the club until two o'clock in the morning, after which it stayed open until four or five o'clock for members who were newspaper printers.'[35] Dr Patrick Moloney, a friend of Clarke's referred to by Hopkins, at this time an intern at Melbourne Hospital, gave Clarke a skull – 'or rather a sconce, for its articulation was incomplete' (Elliott (1958) 102). Clarke brought it to the first official meeting of the club, 1 May 1868, placed it on the mantelshelf with a pipe under its jaw and suggested the club should be called the 'Golgotha' because it was 'the place of skulls'. According to the official history of the Yorick Club,[36] Clarke 'hammered away at the idea all night' but the club ended up being called the Yorick. Clarke 'got very huffy, and, taking his skull with him, disappeared and did not return for some days' (Elliott (1958) 102). Nonetheless he took on the office of secretary for the first few months. He gave the skull to Walter Montgomery, who was playing Hamlet at the time and used it for his Yorick soliloquy. Marian Dunn, whom Clarke was to marry a year later, was Ophelia.

In his 'Peripatetic Philosopher' column in the *Australasian*, Clarke referred to the Yorick as the Golgotha, anyway.[37]

> Everybody wants to know the secrets of the prison-house, and as Timmins, one of our number, incautiously told his wife that we keep a skull on the mantelshelf, there is much suspicion and terror around. I may briefly mention, however, that the story of the newspaper lad being scraped to death with oyster shells at a late supper, and buried in the back kitchen, is not absolutely true in all its details; also I may, without breaking faith, refute the accusation made by a friend, that the members sit on tubs round the room, smoke green tea, and drink neat kerosene out of pewter pots. More I cannot reveal.

Clarke provided an account of what the Yorick Club members did *not* do. But what exactly did they do? On one occasion

> Alfred Telo, a leading light of the club, had purloined the brass knocker from Neild's door to add to a collection kept in rooms shared with Clarke. The victim fumed in the press and on the following day woke to find his home decorated with 'a fishing-rod and gilt fish, a pawnbroker's sign and an undertaker's board'. While no date is given for this escapade by the club's official history, it could well have had something to do with Neild's less than enthusiastic review of Telo's *Christine Johnson* in the *Australasian* of 28 November 1868.[38]

The club's history recalls of Adam Lindsay Gordon that 'at times he was wildly jovial, and one evening pitched Clarke up to very near the ceiling and caught him again coming down'. Clarke 'was always ready for mischief night and day', and 'Adam Lindsay Gordon was as much a ringleader as anybody else. When he played, he played hard.' The account continues, however, 'of course, the frivolities of 1868–9 were carried on by and known only to a limited coterie: the majority of Yorick members were staid and orderly men, who would not have sanctioned practical joking had they been aware that the club was made a centre for the hatching of little plots against the public peace' (Hutton 149). The club was a place for relaxation, for company, for networking. In origin its members were primarily literary and journalistic – editors, journalists, poets, novelists, reviewers, dramatists. Some were on staff, others freelance. The club was a place to trade information on who was publishing what and where, a way of arranging introductions to get work. In the end it became successful and began to change its nature, attracting businessmen, bankers, lawyers and such like professionals. Clarke and various of the 'literary bohemians' withdrew and set up the 'Cave of Adullam' 'in Flinders-lane, behind the *Argus* office'.[39]

An anecdote by the Melbourne solicitor James Moloney records a day spent with Clarke, Walter Montgomery and Adam Lindsay Gordon at this time, riding across what was then Elwood Swamp to the seaside suburb of Brighton, where Gordon was living:

> an unforgettable day by virtue of two facts: first, the romantic rhetoric which poured unceasingly from the lips of Marcus Clarke on all subjects in heaven and earth and the waters under the earth, broken at frequent intervals by the declamations of Montgomery of relevant or irrelevant passages from Shakespeare; and secondly, by the contribution of Gordon to the wild symposium. Mounted on a little pony, his legs almost touching the ground, Gordon raced it at every obstacle that could be construed into a jump, and then darted back to the other three, firing off long quotations from his favorite Latin authors, the jaunt thus begun not ending till the 'wee sma' 'oors' in the poet's house at Brighton.[40]

Gordon got to know Clarke when he sold up his livery stables in Ballarat and moved to Melbourne in October 1868. He wrote to his friend John Riddoch that month, 'I am going to send you the new *Colonial*, it is a very good magazine. Marcus Clarke the Editor is a very nice young fellow.'[41] Mackinnon reprints an undated letter from Adam Lindsay Gordon to Clarke: 'Yorick Club. Dear Clarke, Scott's Hotel, not later than 9.30 sharp. Moore will be there. Riddoch and Lyon, Baker and Powers, besides us; so if "the Old One" were to cast a net – eh? – Yours, A. Lindsay Gordon.'[42]

Another literary associate at this time, the poet Henry Kendall, was more ambivalent about Clarke. He had arrived from Sydney in April 1869, and he too became a member of the Yorick Club – Clarke seconded his application for membership on 29 July 1869.[43] Kendall later claimed 'In conjunction with Marcus Clarke I edited *Humbug*',[44] but it is not clear what this involved nor how closely they worked together. Kendall describes Clarke at this time – under the name of Perks – in 'A Colonial Literary Society', written two years later.[45]

> A casual observer of this young writer would very likely set him down as being merely a brilliant mime with a considerable stock of vanity, and a clever way of persuading everybody that he knew everything. Perks was not a genius, but he was something more than a brilliant mime. There was stuff in the man – good stuff too, only he himself did not appear to value it. Nothing seemed to satisfy him better than the borrowed and theatrical garb under which he contrived, too successfully sometimes, to hide his inherent gifts; in short, to affect the cynicism of a Coldstream, to carry that affectation into ordinary conversation, to make it the staple of his literary work, to look, talk, and write like a 'blasé' libertine, constituted the chiefest delight of my juvenile friend – my budding philosopher. Occasionally, however, in rare and happy moments, he would fling his cant aside, and speak or write out his own thought like a man, and it is to those brief spaces of time that we are indebted for all that is worthy of association with his name. Should any of my readers be curious to know more of the gentleman immortalized here under the nom-de-plume of Perks, they can hunt up the files of a great Melbourne weekly and glance over its gossip, with a perfect faith that they will find his portrait painted there in glowing colours by himself.

This is how the mercurial Clarke – upper middle-class English, Bohemian, man of the theatre, columnist, wit – could appear to the native-born, rather gloomy, wage-slave Kendall. It does not contradict the picture Cyril draws.

The freelance world was more precarious than Clarke revealed to Cyril. He had married the actress Marian Dunn, 22 July 1869. Throughout his life he was involved with the theatre, writing and adapting a score of plays, pantomimes and vaudevilles.[46] In 1870 he sought financial security by taking up a permanent position as clerk, later secretary, to the Trustees of the Melbourne Public Library. He gave up his regular 'Peripatetic Philosopher' column, 11 June 1870: 'I have sold my birthright of free speech for a mess of official pottage, and so to all intents and purposes my

"Peripatetic" is dead' (Elliott (1958) 169). But he continued to contribute stories, verse and articles to the press, and to write for the theatre, no less prolifically.

Clarke was appointed to the Melbourne Public Library on 10 June 1870 and was employed there for the rest of his working life, until his resignation consequent upon his second bankruptcy, on 2 August 1881. With the resources of this major institution on hand, Clarke had ready access to a huge range of books freely available on the shelves. He claimed in a letter to Hopkins that the holdings of the Melbourne Public Library numbered two hundred thousand volumes; he may have been exaggerating somewhat. Trollope estimated the figure at 60,000 in 1870, and Sir Archibald Michie suggested 'upward of 100,000' in 1879 (Elliott (1947) 172, 175). Whatever is the correct figure, it was a substantial collection.

Hugh McCrae recalled how his father, the poet George Gordon McCrae, 'often pointed out to me a green metal lion half-way up the steps leading to the Melbourne Public Library. It was into the mouth of this lion that Marcus used to commit his unfinished cigar, before being manacled to the desk at his office. The lion, smoking the cigar, became a signal to his friends that Marcus was within.'[47] He continues, 'Clarke coveted his freedom so much that he would rather scintillate outside than be earning his salary as sub-librarian locked up among books.'

Yet other evidence suggests that Clarke took his position at the Library seriously. The title page of his *Old Tales of a Young Country* (Mason, Firth & McCutcheon, Melbourne, 1871) proclaimed 'By Marcus Clarke, Secretary to the Trustees of the Public Library, Museums, &c., Melbourne', in the way academics used to, and sometimes still do, indicate their university affiliations in their publications. The following page announced: 'To the Trustees of the Public Library, Museums, & National Gallery of Victoria, this little work is inscribed, by their obedient servant, the author.' And in the preface, Clarke writes of the tales to follow: 'They were dug out by me at odd times during a period of three years, from the store of pamphlets, books, and records of old times, which is in the Public Library.' The preface is dated, 'The Public Library, Museums, &c., Melbourne, 30th November, 1871'.[48]

In announcing that his researches for the book came from the Library's own holdings, Clarke was clearly seeing his role as one of publicising and promoting the Library. In 1874 he edited a volume for the affiliated institution, the National Gallery, contributing prose commentaries to *Photographs of Pictures in the National Gallery, Melbourne* (F. F. Baillière, Melbourne, 1874), originally published in eighteen monthly parts from October 1873 to March 1875. The dedication of the book version of *His Natural Life* (George Robertson, Melbourne, 1874) to Sir Charles Gavan Duffy, a Trustee of the Library, was signed 'Marcus Clarke, The Public Library, Melbourne'. Unusually for a novel, it contained a four-page appendix of bibliographical documentation. And he contributed a dozen items to the scholarly, bibliographical and antiquarian English journal *Notes and Queries*.[49] The commentators[50] who have questioned Clarke's commitment to his Library job make no mention of these activities. But they are activities that assert a wider interpretation of a librarian's role. In his unsuccessful application for the position of Librarian, 28 October 1880, he wrote:

> For knowledge of bibliography I may claim special consideration. My personal tastes and public circumstances have alike led me to make that branch of information my peculiar study. Privately I have collected largely while it has been my good fortune to have been entrusted with the compilation of the *Bibliographical Catalogue of the Public Library* which – in my holograph – has been used in stocktaking since 1874, and I have also collated every book and pamphlet which has come into the library for the last 7 years.[51]

Nonetheless, there is undoubtedly a truth in the view expressed by a later Chief Librarian, Edmund La Touche Armstrong, and quoted by Cyril Hopkins: 'His literary work was his life's work, and to it his Library work was entirely subordinate.'[52] Certainly he continued to be immensely productive during these first years at the Library. In March 1870 he began editing the *Australian Journal*, continuing until September 1871. In the same month he began serialising his great novel, *His Natural Life*, in its pages, a project that ran for over two years. For much of this time he was also writing his series of stories of Australia in the early days, 'Old Tales Retold', a series of fourteen historical tales that appeared in the *Australasian* from 19 February 1870 until 24 June 1871 and were collected in *Old Tales of a Young Country* in 1871. In 1873 Clarke collected eight of his short stories into the volume *Holiday Peak and Other Tales* (George Robertson, Melbourne, 1873), dedicated to the American writer Oliver Wendell Holmes.[53]

The serialisation of *His Natural Life* was completed in June 1872. Clarke then set about revising it for book publication. He approached Charles Gavan Duffy, the Irish nationalist, editor and writer who lived in Australia from 1855 to 1880. As well as being a member of the Victorian legislature at that time, he was one of the Trustees of the Public Library. Duffy recalled the details in *My Life in Two Hemispheres*.[54]

Marcus Clarke spoke to me more than once of a story entitled "His Natural Life" which he was publishing in a Melbourne periodical. He invited me to look at it, which I promised to do whenever I had leisure, and finally, as it was drawing to a close, he sent me the portion published:

"My Dear Sir,

I take the liberty of sending some numbers of the *Australian Journal* containing all that is yet published of my new novel, 'His Natural Life.' 'His Natural Life' is an attempt to expose the infamies that attended the old transportation system, and the episodes are merely dramatized versions of the facts. I have taken much trouble to collect materials for the story, and to read up and collate the almost-forgotten records of early colonial prisons, &c. I want to show that in many instances the *law* makes the criminal.

"I should be very grateful for a criticism from you on the story – if you can find time to look over it – as I hope to publish it in England as soon as it is completed in monthly numbers. – I am, my dear Sir, very faithfully yours,

"MARCUS CLARKE."

I examined the story carefully and answered his inquiries with the frankness due to a man of judgment and discretion. The narrative was, in my opinion, a singularly powerful and original one, marred by serious faults. For example, it was intensely painful – a sentiment which would become tragic if it concerned persons whom we respected; but whom did he intend us to respect? The hero was an unhappy creature, suffering innocently a life-long martyrdom, without any adequate of almost any intelligible motive. Unless the motive justified such a sacrifice, the reader would not sympathise with him, and the story would necessarily want interest – a fatal want. The narrative was long and it was unduly protracted, as it seemed to me, by introducing the Ballarat riots under a leader caricatured as Peter Brawler; all this in my judgment ought to be mercilessly expunged. And the song in French *argot*, with a translation into English slang, would be taken for his own if it was not specifically disowned; but it could not possibly be his own, as I had read it in *Blackwood's Magazine* before he was born. The translation was probably by Dr Maginn. The novelist had precipitated a douche-bath of criticism on his head, but he bore it manfully. In his reply he took the objections in good part, and set to work forthwith to amend the original plot.

THE PUBLIC LIBRARY,

July 22, 1870[55]

"MY DEAR SIR,

I have to thank you very much for your kindly criticism. Such observations as those which you have made are exactly what I wanted. I confess that I feel a pang at your suggestions for vigorous cutting, but I am sure you are right. I will act upon your advice, and cut off the beginning and end of the book. As thus:

"Open on board the convict ship. Make Dawes a noble fellow who has sacrificed himself to spare a woman whom he loves and whose *lover* has committed the offence for which Dawes is condemned. (North might be this lover and thus heighten the effect of the story.) When North thinks of taking away Dora, Dawes says, 'I am the man who is suffering for your sin,' &c. North remains in the prison and Dawes escapes. In the meantime Rex, having claimed and enjoyed the money, is discovered. Dawes's conscience and identity simultaneously disclosed. The wreck; Dawes saves child Dora who dies, Maurice is murdered by prisoners, Dawes is saved, and departs like Monte Cristo. Thus the Ballarat Riots and that idiot Dorcas, who was worse to me than Mercutio was reported to have been to the divine William, excluded, and the compactness of the novel preserved. The great difficulty, however, is the motive. What motive would induce a *young* man to suffer himself to be transported for the life of another?

"You speak with praise of 'Long Odds' and 'King Billy's Breeches.'[56] King Billy is so-so, but 'Long Odds' appears to me now to be the greatest *trash*. Many thanks again for the trouble you have taken. When I have altered the book according to your suggestions I think it will be readable. I shall then ask your permission to dedicate it to the Hon. C. Gavan Duffy, as the only way in which I can express my thanks. Very faithfully yours,

"MARCUS CLARKE."

But he had not yet done his best; on further consideration he adopted the present plot, in which the protection of his mother's honour furnished a high and adequate motive for the tragedy of his hero's life and death.

His Natural Life was published in volume form by George Robertson in Melbourne in 1874; Robertson then used his agent F. F. Baillière to negotiate for English publication. It was published in London by Richard Bentley in September 1875. Gavan Duffy arranged for the proofs of the English edition to be read by Mrs

Cashel Hoey, wife of one of his associates, and a cousin of George Bernard Shaw. Her husband John Cashel Hoey had edited *Nation*, the Irish nationalist journal Duffy founded, while Duffy was a member of parliament in Westminster. Clarke wrote to Duffy, 30 November 1875:

> Very many thanks for all the trouble you have been at on my account. It is rare indeed to find anyone who will really "work" for a man who wants help. I hope that it may one day be my good fortune to aid *you* in something which you want done. I have received from London the *Natural Life* in three vols., and have written to thank Mrs. Hoey; I have told her that she is a "brick" – the only word in the English tongue which cannot be applied to any person having a hint of selfishness in them.[57]

In the meantime Clarke's *Long Odds* had been re-run in the *Australian Journal*, February to September 1873, and his historical novel *Chidiock Tichbourne* serialised there from September 1874 to March 1875. At the end of 1875 George Robertson published Clarke's novel '*Twixt Shadow and Shine: An Australian Story for Christmas*. Clarke took a quotation from Adam Lindsay Gordon for its title, and its characters from the Cave of Adullam, the gathering that Clarke and his fellow Bohemians created after the Yorick Club became too respectable and boring.

Then in 1876 he contributed the famous preface to the reissue of Gordon's *Sea Spray and Smoke Drift* (Clarson, Massina). It was reprinted in 1880 in the collected *Poems of the Late Adam Lindsay Gordon* and frequently reprinted thereafter. Ian McLaren assembled eighty-eight editions and variations of it for his collection of Gordon's works, now in the Baillieu Library, University of Melbourne (McLaren 92). Cyril significantly quotes from it, recognising it as one of Clarke's major texts.

The concluding two-fifths of the preface recycled material Clarke had written a couple of years earlier as text to a book of photographs of paintings in the National Gallery, Melbourne. The passages were originally attached to Louis Buvelot's *Waterpool near Coleraine* and Nicholas Chevalier's *The Buffalo Ranges*. However, the famous proclamation 'What is the dominant note of Australian scenery? That which is the dominant note of Edgar Allan Poe's poetry – Weird Melancholy' is original to the preface.[58] According to Elliott (1958), 'The utilization of the passages was not incongruous, since Clarke had Gordon's poetry in mind when he wrote them' (257).

Nonetheless this might seem a strange way to write a preface to a friend's book. We do not know Clarke's immediate circumstances at the time – how busy, how stressed, how pressed for time he was. After the sale of his library, 8 August 1874, he may no longer have had copies of Gordon's books to work from.[59] Perhaps he felt unable to assemble adequate biographical details; perhaps he found himself unable or unwilling to write literary criticism. Perhaps he felt the material he had written was too good to be lost to view, so used it again. In that he was correct. As Brian Elliott (1958) remarks, this seminal description was 'in its own time the revelation of a new poetic faith in the landscape of Australia … [expressing] the kind of sensibility which had developed in Australia' (61). Because of its evocation of Australian scenery, the preface has been endlessly reprinted and cited, not only in editions of Gordon's work, but in anthologies and studies of both Australian literary criticism and Australian landscape. Clarke achieved what he had set out to do years earlier: lay down the ground work for a future literature of Australia. A literature in which he and Adam Lindsay Gordon would be recognised and honoured as founding fathers of 'something very like the beginnings of a national school of Australian poetry'.[60]

A further collection of short stories, *Four Stories High* (A. H. Massina, Melbourne, 1877), was dedicated to the opera producer, William Saurin Lyster.[61] In that same year F. F. Baillière published Clarke's pamphlet *The Future Australian Race* and the *History of the Continent of Australia and the Island of Tasmania* that he edited, and in 1880 the controversy *Civilisation without Delusion*. Throughout these years Clarke continued to produce a prolific amount of uncollected journalism, stories, sketches, essays, poems and theatrical works. The novel *Felix and Felicitas* remained uncompleted at the time of his death, 2 August 1881.

Cyril Hopkins' biography is especially valuable for the details he gives us about Clarke's love of books. It provides a unique record of the books he was reading. Clarke was an immensely well-read writer. The catalogue of the auction sale of Clarke's library, 8 August 1874, put on the market after his first bankruptcy, provides valuable evidence of his voracious appetite for literature.[62] Library catalogues, however, need to be adduced as evidence with care. Not all the books a writer has read or been influenced by will necessarily be found in his library. Nor do we know whether certain volumes, authors or subjects were disposed of separately, earlier; nor, indeed, whether certain other volumes not belonging to Clarke might have been added into the sale by the auctioneer. And the fact that he possessed a book does not necessarily mean that he had read it: writers regularly receive books – complimentary copies from fellow writers, from publishers, review copies – and they buy books, often compulsively, with a view to future reading. Clarke writes to Cyril of buying a set of De Quincey, but did he read it in its entirety? Had he read the entire forty-volume French edition of Balzac he possessed? Writers' libraries consist in part of good intentions, gifts received and bargains acquired. It is useful to know that a writer owned a certain book, but he may have read it without owning it, or owned it without reading it.

Moreover Clarke may often have read something in a book borrowed from somebody else's library. He had certainly read in his father's library. Indeed, it may be that some of the books listed in Clarke's library catalogue had been inherited from his father. Cyril quotes from Clarke's story, 'In a Bark Hut': 'I had been a sickly brat in my infancy and having unfettered access to the library of a man who owned few prejudices for moral fig-leaves… read many strange books.'[63]

In his letters to Hopkins, Clarke makes a point of telling Hopkins what he has currently been reading. There may be exaggeration or censorship in the lists, of course. But at least we can assemble from Hopkins' account a list of books that Clarke reported he had been reading. It is important information: a part not just of the literary context of Clarke's own writing, but also evidence of the state of cultural development of mid-nineteenth-century Melbourne. One way or another books, and current books, were available. From the publication dates provided in the notes, it can be seen how Clarke made a point of keeping up with the contemporary, as well as consolidating his reading of the classics of the immediate past like Balzac, Dickens and Thackeray.

Of course, writers' letters need to be treated carefully as proffered evidence rather than as the certain truth. It all depends on the recipient and the writer's intentions in regard to the recipient – impressing, soliciting sympathy, requesting help, or showing independence. Cyril Hopkins, however, is an especially privileged source, from his acquaintance with Clarke at Highgate School, and from Clarke's letters to him from Australia. Clarke's letters to Hopkins are not obviously manipulative. He is not writing to a wealthy patron attempting to elicit cash. He is not applying for a job or begging to get published. He asks Hopkins to try to help him get published, which is something different. He is writing to a young contemporary who is not in vastly more privileged circumstances than Clarke himself. Clarke may be self-dramatising his arrival in Australia, of course. The tone of those early accounts of Melbourne sounds a note that the Hopkins brothers would recognise – the no-nonsense, un-deluded, veering on the risqué, the sophisticated, sardonic, cynical, ironic Englishman abroad – a note struck by Kinglake in his *Eothen* and Thackeray in his *Paris Notebook*. There is some literary self-dramatising, some posturing. But what writing is without that in some form or another?

Upper middle-class London values are shown as ridiculous in colonial Melbourne, but nonetheless it is important to be able to recognise and emulate them, with a witty detachment that pre-dates Wilde and Wodehouse. The mode was already current. Frances Donaldson in her life of P. G. Wodehouse (1982) noted the origin of his humour in nineteenth-century English theatre with its set types and expected roles. And Clarke, as his letters show, and his playwriting career confirms, was, like Wodehouse, an habitué of the theatre.

Hopkins is also a source of evidence on Clarke's literary ambitions, offering an invaluable record of Clarke's early attempts to achieve publication in England. Clarke asks him to try to place poems, articles and stories, no doubt hoping that he had access to his father Manley's literary connections. But Clarke had left England too young, before he had established a literary reputation, so his name was not known. Many English writers were to take themselves off into expatriation – Robert Louis Stevenson, D. H. Lawrence, Aldous Huxley, W. H. Auden and Christopher Isherwood. But they had already established their reputations before leaving. Writers could also arrive from the colonies or the United States and establish themselves in the metropolis, such as Mrs Campbell Praed, Rudyard Kipling and Henry James. But to do that they had to take up residence in Britain. Clarke, having left England at sixteen, and never returning, was in a different situation. He was one of the earliest of British expatriate writers, and suffered the fate of most pioneers: neglect. Cyril's attempts to get Clarke's work published came to nothing. Nor was Clarke more successful himself. Elliott records that he sent 'Human Repetends' to the *Cornhill Magazine*, but it was rejected.[64]

In 1872, however, Sefton Parry adapted Clarke's novel *Long Odds* for the London stage, and it ran for a month.[65] The adaptation was pirated and Clarke received no payment, as he pointed out in a letter to the *Australasian*, 6 April 1872:

> I am willing that the copyright law be altered, for Mr. Sefton Parry dramatized my novel *Long Odds*, and played it for nearly a month in London, without paying me for it. (434)

Only one story of Clarke's was published in England in his lifetime – 'An Australian Mining Township' in *All the Year Round, incorporating Household Words*, 22 February 1873, the magazine founded and edited by Charles Dickens. This was arranged not by Cyril Hopkins but by Mrs Cashel Hoey. Apart from that, there were the dozen items contributed to *Notes and Queries*. And then he was invited to contribute to the London

Daily Telegraph on Australian matters. This was an invitation of some significance. The *Telegraph* boasted 'the largest circulation in the world' of any newspaper. Clarke published six articles in its pages between 1877 and 1880.

His Natural Life appeared in London 1875, and an American edition was published by Harper and Brothers, New York, in April 1876. Clarke wrote to Duffy in June that year:

> The *Boston Review* speaks very favourably of the book, and Harper, who has republished it, sends me £15. Why this curious sum I don't know. I suppose it represents something in dollars – Harper's conscience perhaps!
>
> I hope that you will like the book better in its amended condition. I have I think followed your advice in all particulars.[66]

After his death, English publication was achieved for *'Twixt Shadow and Shine* (Swann Sonnenschein, London, 1893), *Chidiock Tichbourne* (Eden Remington, London, 1893), *Long Odds*, retitled *Heavy Odds* (Hutchinson, London; J. P. Lippincott, Philadelphia, 1896),[67] and *Stories of Australia in the Early Days* (Hutchinson, London, 1897);[68] while *His Natural Life*, retitled *For the Term of His Natural Life* in 1885, was reprinted and reissued by numerous English publishers, including Macmillan (who took over Richard Bentley in 1897), Ward Lock, Collins in their Collins Classics series, Oxford University Press in their World's Classics series, and Penguin, as well as being filmed numerous times.

Posthumous fame was something he shared with his friend Adam Lindsay Gordon, who shot himself at the age of thirty-seven, unable to pay the printing costs of his last book of poetry, and with the friend of his school days, Gerard Manley Hopkins. Hopkins is now firmly in the pantheon. And Gordon and Clarke retain a popular reputation. Gordon's 'The Swimmer' is still performed in Sir Edward Elgar's setting in *Sea Pictures* (opus 37, number 5, 1899), and lines from Gordon's 'Ye Wearie Wayfarer' were amongst Princess Diana's favorites:

> 'Life is mostly froth and bubble,
>   Two things stand like stone,
>   KINDNESS in another's trouble,
>   COURAGE in your own.'

His Natural Life continues to remain in print in Britain as well as Australia.

Clarke was not without recognition in his lifetime and in the years immediately following his death. And Cyril Hopkins is a major source of information here. With extraordinary comprehensiveness, possibly with the assistance of Clarke's widow, his biography cites almost every major nineteenth-century review and critical assessment of Clarke, whether in newspaper, journal or book.

Provenance of the manuscript

There is some extant evidence about the provenance of Cyril Hopkins's manuscript biography of Marcus Clarke: when he wrote it, what plans for publication he had in mind, his method of composition and what revisions were made. He wrote it, as he said in the preface, as a remembrance of his school friend, suddenly wrenched away from his life forever when they were both teenagers. Cyril had his swag of unique letters from Clarke as well as his first-hand school memories to spur him on.

Cyril had been British Vice-Consul for Hawaii from 1896 to 1900. He probably used his earlier years of retirement to write the life, possibly beginning about 1903 or 1904, stimulated by the fact that the only substantial biography was Hamilton Mackinnon's compiled some twenty years previously and based mainly on knowledge of Clarke's life in Australia.

In the Preface Cyril refers to Clarke's 'premature death a quarter of a century ago.' This was later changed to 'forty-three years ago.' Clarke died in 1881, so we can deduce that Cyril's manuscript was first written around the year 1906, and was revised in 1924. In Chapter 9 when Hopkins dates Clarke's 'A Day in Melbourne' as 1865, he refers to this as being 'forty five years ago', which would make Hopkins' time of writing as around 1910. This was later changed by handwritten addition to 'more than 50 years ago', suggesting he was revising the manuscript in 1915, or thereabouts. In 1912 A. H. Massina's copyright in Adam Lindsay Gordon's poems lapsed. As a consequence there were three editions of Gordon's poems published in Britain that year: Frank Maldon Robb's edition from Oxford University Press, Douglas Sladen's from Constable, and an edition from T. N. Foulis. The same year Constable published the substantial *Adam Lindsay Gordon and His Friends in England and Australia*, edited by Edith Humphris and Douglas Sladen, containing a lengthy biography by Sladen and extensive ancillary material. These four books received press coverage in Britain, which may have prompted Cyril to think that if the expatriate Gordon was now being celebrated, perhaps he should do something for Clarke. It may be that this provoked his returning to the manuscript around this time, and making some minor revisions.

Glimpses of the biography's history occur in some surviving correspondence with Clarke's daughters. In a letter to Rose Clarke, Marcus's elder daughter and third child, July 1905, (ML MS 55/2 CY Reel 717) Cyril writes about not being able to continue the 'copying' of the manuscript since the last December, while mentioning that 'most of it is copied, however.' In the same letter to Rose, Cyril asked for permission to quote an anecdote from James Moloney, brother of Dr Patrick Moloney about an occasion when Clarke may – or may not – have been contemplating suicide. This ultimately appeared in Chapter 23 (ii), and Dr Patrick Moloney's anecdote in the last chapter, Chapter 28.

> … will your mother object to the mention of the incident you tell me of your father's strange behaviour during that country walk? Because, of course, although his impulse to leap over the edge of the cliff may have really arisen from mixed motives, the ordinary reader will regard it as simply an attempt at suicide.
>
> As a boy he possessed a remarkably cool head for climbing …
>
> I have (temporarily) inserted the incident in the last chapter but followed it up by saying that his nature was far from morose and that he evidently enjoyed a joke as shown by Dr Patrick Moloney's anecdote … Your father's nature was delicate, affectionate and, at heart, romantic – as I always thought (– indeed *knew*) and as Walter Murdoch, in his article, implies or guesses. I could tell you something that he said to me the last time I ever saw him & within 24 hours (– at all events –) of his leaving England for ever that proves it, though he may never have told or repeated his confidence to me to another human being. That however does not change the essential fact that *without* such a nature as I mean he would never have said anything of the kind to anyone, as he then said to me … I am now going to study his plays as a short chapter about them ought to be published …

This chapter on the plays was apparently never written. Cyril suggested to Rose that the plays be sent to the Mermaid Society and asking whether Col. Sir George Sydenham Clarke, a member of the committee, was a 'cousin', presumably of Marcus Clarke's, adding 'but let us leave that until Mr. Macmillan has my MS. and I will consult him about them'. This is the only indication of Hopkins' publication plans for his biography. Apparently, if it were eventually offered, Macmillan declined publication and if Hopkins submitted it elsewhere he was unsuccessful.

On 30 May 1906, Hopkins wrote again to Rose Clarke, about the 'copying' of his manuscript: 'Ever since 31 December [1905] I have never had a chance to copy a line of my MS. (most of which is copied, however) for I have been immensely immersed in some very troublesome family business, but am just on the point of continuing it. The delay is most irksome to me *but I cannot help myself ...*' The letter breaks off here and a final page appears to be missing (ML MSS 55/2, 1-9).

Hopkins was writing in reply to Rose's 'kind letter of April 22nd [1906]'. He refers to Clarke's son, Rowley going into the army and following Clarke family tradition; to the death, announced in the London *Times*, of F. W. Haddon, editor of the *Argus*, with whom Clarke once shared rooms, and with whom he went to Tasmania to write up the convict records in 1870; to 'your account of the friends living at the Melbourne Club'; to Alfred Telo and to Lermontov, adding that he, Hopkins, only found out a few years ago (and so never had chance to 'tell your father') about 'an analogy between your father and the [latter] author'.

On July 30 1922 Cyril wrote to Rose that his health has 'completely broken down', and that consequently he stays continually inside his house and garden, where he has to use a stick to walk with, and is lame; it is all he can do to walk across the lawn. 'It is nearly entirely due to that and the crippled condition it has reduced me to, that I have never been able to complete my book on your father's life and works. ... I find myself left with no leisure time at all during the day except for reading some of the *Times* out to my wife whose eyesight ... has suddenly failed her.'

The letter goes on to remark that he knew and corresponded with Mrs. Cashel Hoey, and to discuss legal rights concerning the film of *His Natural Life*.

Nonetheless, the biography was virtually completed, except for the chapter on the plays, and moreover, as he had written earlier, most of it had been *copied*. The manuscript in the Mitchell Library, in copperplate handwriting, with a few revisionary additions or after-thoughts, has 'Finis' written at the end of the final Chapter (28). It is apparent, however, from some repetition in the later chapters that Hopkins had difficulty in completing the work, as he had no direct knowledge of Australia and of Clarke's final years after their correspondence ceased.

Hopkins had met Clarke's widow and some of the children in London. As he wrote to the younger daughter, Ethel Marian Clarke,[69] regarding possible publication of his biography in Australia by Angus and Robertson: 'I had the pleasure of making the acquaintance of your mother and sister Rose and brother Willie when they were in London. Afterwards we got to know – very much more intimately – Rowley[70] himself who came to England twice; and stayed with us on his second visit at St. Leonards-on-Sea' (19 December 1926, ML 55/2).

Accordingly Hopkins thought the dedication to the proposed book 'should be to the "late widow and family of Marcus Clarke", or to the "late Mrs. Marcus Clarke and family."' Indeed he supported publication in order to help the family: 'I am very glad that you care for, and are doing your best to help poor, dear Rowley's widow and need scarcely say how gratified I should be if Angus [and] Robertson of Sydney, or any other publisher could be persuaded to publish my little sketch of your father's life and works (it is scarcely a biography) and that it should bring her a little money.'

The manuscript was offered unsuccessfully to Angus and Robertson shortly after December 1926 when Cyril had given his permission. In 1928 it was sold to the Mitchell Library. A pencilled note in Library code refers to 'Miss M. [Marian] Clarke £170 May 1928'. (ML A 1971). The purchase is noted under Special Submissions in the minutes of the Library Committee meeting held 15 May 1928. These are the sole references traceable in Library records. But under Finance, payment is approved to Miss M. M. [Marian Marcus] Clarke for 'the original MS. of "Felix and Felicitas" with letters etc'. The only other reference in Library records to Clarke papers is a library letter of 28 November 1928 to Miss E. M. [Ethel Marian] Clarke saying that other papers offered were 'of a private and family nature and were not the class of material that the trustees purchase for a library'. (One might note in passing how times have changed: private, including personal and scandalous papers are now held in Libraries and are sought after by researchers.) The present editors' thanks are due to Arthur Easton of the Mitchell Library who traced this and other accession details.

Hopkins' use of Clarke letters

Hopkins' manuscript depends for its main value, apart from school days memories, on the quotations from Clarke letters. There is little or no documentation of these letters in the manuscript by the provision of dates or other details. Indeed the use of the letters often appears unmethodical, even at times haphazard. Hopkins was not of course writing as an experienced, let alone a scholarly, biographer. But he was nevertheless taking considerable time and care.

The problem of documentation is compounded by the fact that none of these letters is extant. Perhaps Hopkins destroyed them thinking they contained material that reflected badly on Clarke. Such misgivings may account for many gaps, perhaps not all signalled, in Hopkins' transcriptions.

The 1958 biography by Brian Elliott, while carefully, even scrupulously researched for its time, is not well documented as to its sources. Elliott was, however, much more informed than Hopkins about the Australian background and undertook extensive research in trying to establish facts from 'outside' the letters (though perhaps he was over-careful in minimising speculation). Elliott comments only *inter alia* on the problems of Hopkins' transcription of the letters, as in a note in which he questions a place name:

> Cyril Hopkins … mostly preserves Clarke's letters fragmentarily and without date references. A certain boldness is therefore necessary in assigning them to periods or even deciding upon sequence, particularly as there often seems to be some confusion in his arrangement. These hazards may not have been always overcome successfully… (257)

Elliott is in a position to question Hopkins only sporadically (rather than exercising 'boldness') through his external controls of establishing dates or using contextual information. Apropos of Clarke's reported comment, 'he never saw his mother', which cannot be true (she died when he was four), Elliott says that this is 'characteristic of Clarke's occasional carelessness in expression. Often in an emotional context he failed to stop and consider the literal sense of a striking phrase' (254). Perhaps Clarke meant that he did not remember having seen his mother. Again Elliott comments on the 'curious' inaccuracies (Clarke overstates both the holdings of the Melbourne Public Library and his salary as librarian there) in one of Clarke's letters: 'Perhaps they may be set down merely to a slap-dash style; perhaps they are due to petty vanity' (175). Elliott comments at one point on a 'remarkable passage', that 'one cannot be sure of its date' (69), and speculates that Clarke wrote a letter but neglected to send it for some time 'adding a postscript and sending it off only when he had something to say which gave him pleasure' (73). In addition to gaps in the correspondence, the mails could be irregular, for Hopkins once received a bundle of five letters together (72). Elsewhere Elliott comments on an uncertain dating suggesting that 'two or three letters seem to have been inadvertently telescoped' and probably patched together (171, see also 181). This silent sewing together of different letters, involving omissions, is seldom commented upon by Elliott and, being hard to spot, may have happened more often than he noticed. It is clear, for instance in Chapter 9 and elsewhere, that Hopkins drew on only a selection of letters. One is quoted as ending with characteristic abruptness, suggesting that Clarke may have written his letters piecemeal, as with the writing of a diary. It appears that Hopkins sometimes relied on memory instead of working methodically from texts at first hand (see notes to Chapter 11). To make things even less clear, Hopkins rarely quotes Clarke's signings-off (see note to Chapter 13).

While the letters can be difficult to date reliably, the accuracy of transcriptions must also remain in some doubt. Original readings are beyond recuperation, in the absence of the original documents, so it is impossible to tell whether misspellings are Clarke's or Hopkins'. Emendations to MS readings are recorded in the notes.

Cyril not only had Clarke's letters from Australia to draw on, but also materials that Clarke had sent in manuscript, sometimes with requests to try to arrange publication. Some were never published – like 'A Day in Melbourne' of Chapter 8. In other cases, the texts Cyril quotes from Clarke's poems 'The Lady of Lynn' and the translation from Horace, 'Ad Barine', and from the story 'Human Repetends', all differ from the published versions. Where Cyril is evidently quoting from a distinct manuscript version of a Clarke text, Cyril's version has been followed, and this is indicated in the notes. Otherwise, where possible, the material he quotes from Clarke and other sources has been checked with the published versions, and corrected accordingly. Chapters 19 and 21 both exist in two versions each. The variants are slight and are recorded in the notes. Cyril affixed footnotes to his text, unnumbered, marked with an asterisk, sometimes prefacing them with 'Note', sometimes signing them 'C. H.' The notes, minus prefixes and suffixes, have been preserved, and numbered consecutively. Editorial notes follow the end of the text.

Acknowledgements

The manuscript of Cyril Hopkins' 'Biographical Notice of the Life & Work of Marcus Clarke' is held in the Mitchell Library, State Library of New South Wales; it is not to be further reproduced without the permission of the Library Council of New South Wales. Every effort has been made to trace a copyright holder. The photographs of Gerard Manley Hopkins and Cyril Hopkins are published with permission of Harry Ransom Humanities Research Center, the University of Texas at Austin. The other photographs are reproduced with permission from the State Library of Victoria.

The editors gratefully acknowledge the assistance on specific points from Bill Beach, Fryer Librarian, University of Queensland, and the staff of the Fryer Library, Christopher Bentley, Jennifer Broomhead (Intellectual Property and Copyright Librarian, Mitchell Library, State Library of New South Wales), David Carter, Thomas

N. Corns, Peter Corris, Richard Crabtree, Victor Crittenden, Robert Cummings, H. Neville Davies, Robert Dixon, Arthur Easton, Peter Edwards, Marianne Ehrhardt, Karen P. Entwistle, Michael Fagg (Reference Librarian, University of Queensland Library), Mark Finnane, Richard Fotheringham, Sue Gore, Bill Garner, Don Graham, Robert Grant, Margaret Harris, Carol Hetherington (content manager, Austlit data base), Veronica Kelly, Brian Kiernan, Stephen Knight, Dorothy McMillan, Peter Morton, David Myers, Peter Pierce, Nicholas Pounder, David Skilton, Vivian Smith, Barry Spurr, Graham Tulloch and Robert Yeo, and to Project Gutenberg, Fisher Library (University of Sydney), and the Mitchell Library (State Library of New South Wales). Special thanks are due to the Fryer Library and Australian Studies Centre (University of Queensland); for granting Laurie Hergenhan an Honorary Fryer fellowship, to the School of English, Media Studies and Art History, University of Queensland; to the School of Letters, Art and Media, University of Sydney; to the School of Humanities, University of Western Sydney; and to the Australian Research Council for support for Ken Stewart's project on Colonial Victorian Literary Culture. This work was published with the assistance of a grant from the Australian Academy of the Humanities.

---

1   He seems to have completed it c. 1905; however, he returned to it and made minor changes in the succeeding years.

2   *The Marcus Clarke Memorial Volume*, ed., Hamilton Mackinnon (1884). The text of the biography was revised for *The Austral Edition of the Selected Works of Marcus Clarke*, ed., Hamilton Mackinnon (1890).

3   Gerard's description is echoed in Hugh McCrae's account of the characterisation of Marcus by his father, George Gordon McCrae: 'careless of all cares – into the world and out again – quivered for a new minute, like Jack o'Lantern, against our parlour wall'. Hugh McCrae, *My Father and My Father's Friends* (1935) 14.

4   John McDermott, *A Hopkins Chronology* (1997) 1.

5   Norman White, 'Gerard Manley Hopkins', *Oxford Dictionary of National Biography* (Oxford University Press, Oxford, 2004) vol. 28, 54.

6   R. B. Martin, *Gerard Manley Hopkins: A Very Private Life* (1991) 9.

7   Claude Colleer Abbott, ed., *Further Letters of Gerard Manley Hopkins including his correspondence with Coventry Patmore* (1956) 8. Ernest Hartley Coleridge (1846–1920) was at Highgate School 1858–60. Cyril was in Germany in May 1862, when Gerard wrote to C. N. Luxmoore, *ibid.* 4.

8   Norman White, *Hopkins: A Literary Biography* (1992) 34.

9   Martin 12.

10   White (2004) 54.

11   Martin, *Gerard Manley Hopkins*, 9–10, 77, 172; W. H. Gardner, *Gerard Manley Hopkins (1844–1889)* (1944–49) 1, 3n.

12   13 June 1890, in Abbott, ed., *Further Letters of Gerard Manley Hopkins*, 395.

13   Abbott, ed., *Further Letters of Gerard Manley Hopkins*, 14.

14   'The Lady of Lynn' was published in the first issue of the *Colonial Monthly* that Clarke edited, March 1868, 15–17, reprinted in the *Memorial Volume*.

15   Brian Elliott, *Marcus Clarke* (1958) 25–6.

16   Abbott, ed., 2–3. Charles Noble Luxmoore (1844–1936) was at Highgate School from January 1858 to July 1861.

17   Martin 12, 14–17.

18   Abbott, ed., 396.

19   Clarke's acquaintance Charles Gavan Duffy describes his own outraged response to being flogged at school in *My Life in Two Hemispheres* (1898) vol. 1, 12.

20   Abbott, ed., *Further Letters of Gerard Manley Hopkins*, 3–4.

21   White (2004) 54–8.

22   White (1992) 30.

23   'Holiday Peak', *Australasian*, 18 January 1873, 72; 25 January, 104, collected in *Holiday Peak and Other Tales* (1873).

24   Abbott, ed., *Further Letters of Gerard Manley Hopkins*, 231. See further R. K. R. Thornton, ed., *All My Eyes See: The Visual World of Gerard Manley Hopkins* (Sunderland, 1975).

25   See below, Chapter 19; and Brian Elliott, 'Gerard Hopkins and Marcus Clarke', *Southerly*, 8 (1947) 218–27.

26   Quoted at the end of Chapter 27.

27   Humphrey House, ed., *The Note-Books and Papers of Gerard Manley Hopkins* (1937).

28   Elliott (1958) 49.

29   See Eugene R. August, 'A Checklist of Materials Relating to the Hopkins Family in the State Archives of Hawaii', *Hopkins Quarterly*, 6, 2, 1979, 61–83.

30   'Alfred Telo: A Reminiscence', *Leader*, 11 October 1879.

31   H. M. Hyndman, *The Record of an Adventurous Life* (1911) 97. Cyril quotes from Hyndman's response to *His Natural Life* in Chapter 22 (ii).

32   'Alfred Telo: A Reminiscence' 18–19.

33   'The Café Lutetia', *Weekly Times*, 28 February 1874, 9. Savage was Alfred Telo, the *Peacock* was the *Argus* and the *Screechowl* was the *Age*.

34   Moir Collection, SLV: McL 3013.

35   Geoffrey Hutton, *Adam Lindsay Gordon: The Man and the Myth* (1978; 1996) 148.

36   *The Yorick Club: Its Origin and Development, May 1868, to December 1910* (1911) [attributed to F. T. D. Carrington and D. Watterson].

37   *Australasian*, 9 May 1868, 593, collected in *The Peripatetic Philosopher by 'Q'* (1869) 48. Henry Kendall calls it the Golgotha in 'A Colonial Literary Club', *Town and Country Journal*, 18 February 1871.

38   Harold Love, *James Edward Neild: Victorian Virtuoso* (1989) 199, citing *The Yorick Club: Its Origin and Development*, 13–15. 'The story goes that when he missed his knocker the doctor rushed into print (as he was prone to do) with a letter to the *Argus* denouncing "the idiots who could find nothing better to do than to wrench off citizens' knockers"' (Elliott (1958) 104). Neild, a doctor as well as the *Australasian*'s drama critic and a founder member of the club, at this time lived at 166 Collins Street East, in a house called 'New Place' after Shakespeare's house in Stratford-upon-Avon (Love 139).

39   Mackinnon, ed. (1884) 49 and Mackinnon, ed. (1890).

40   Frank Maldon Robb, ed., *The Poems of Adam Lindsay Gordon* (1912) xxi–xxii.

41   Hugh Anderson, ed., *The Last Letters, 1868–1870: Adam Lindsay Gordon to John Riddoch* (1970) 30.

42   Mackinnon, ed. (1884) 33, and Mackinnon, ed. (1890).

43   Ian F. McLaren, *Marcus Clarke: An Annotated Bibliography* (1982) 3072c.

44   Letter to J. S. Moore, 5 August 1876, quoted in Ken Stewart, '"A Careworn Writer for the Press:" Henry Kendall in Melbourne', in R. McDougall, ed., *Henry Kendall, The Muse of Australia* (1991), reprinted in Ken Stewart, *Investigations in Australian Literature* (2000) 58.

45   *Town and Country Journal*, 18 February 1871. Kendall wrote an obituary of Clarke in the *Sydney Mail*, 13 August 1881, 277. His elegy 'In Memoriam – Marcus Clarke', *Bulletin*, 3 September 1881, 1, is reprinted by Mackinnon, ed. (1884) and Mackinnon, ed. (1890). On Kendall's often fraught relationship with Clarke, see Stewart (2000) 47–88.

46   McLaren 120–7. Mitchell Library holds 21 items, purchased from Marian Marcus Clarke in 1933 (McLaren 255–6). Though performed, most are unpublished, or published in synopsis or fragmentary form.

47   McCrae 47.

48   Three years would take the beginnings of Clarke's researches back to November 1868, eighteen months before he joined the Library staff in June 1870. The first of the tales published, 'The Settlement of Sydney', appeared in the *Australasian*, 19 February 1870 (as 'The Settlement of Port Jackson').

49   See Joan E. Poole and Michael Wilding, 'Marcus Clarke's Contributions to *Notes & Queries*', *Australian Literary Studies*, 6, 1973, 186–9.

50   See Elliott (1958) 171.

51   Elliott (1958) 266.

52   Quoted by Cyril Hopkins in Chapter 22 (i), from Edmund La Touche Armstrong, *The Book of the Public Library, Museums, and National Gallery of Victoria, 1856–1906* (Ford & Son, Melbourne, 1906) 118–20.

53   There are five MS letters from Holmes to Clarke in the Mitchell Library, Sydney (McLaren 3137–41); one about 'Pretty Dick' is printed and another about *His Natural Life* excerpted in Mackinnon, ed. (1884) 44, 40–1, and Mackinnon, ed. (1890).

54   Duffy (1898) vol. 2, 312–14.

55   Elliott (1958) writes: 'I have assumed that the 0 is miscopied for 2, which would be an easy mistake given Clarke's handwriting. 1870 is impossible, but 1872 would be very probable' (161n).

56   'King Billy's Breeches', *Australasian*, 12 August 1871, 197, collected in *Four Stories High*.

57   Duffy (1898) vol. 2, 367.

58   The recycling begins two sentences later with 'The Australian mountain forests are funereal, secret, stern' from the Chevalier text, and runs for a paragraph. It is followed with two paragraphs from the Buvelot text, which conclude the preface. Shorn of the specific references to Gordon, Mackinnon reprinted the preface as 'Australian Scenery' in both his volumes. See S. R. Simmons, *A Problem and a Solution: Marcus Clarke and the Writing of* Long Odds (1946) and L. T. Hergenhan, 'Marcus Clarke and the Colonial Landscape' (1969) 31–51.

59   Among the volumes listed for sale in the catalogue were Gordon's *Ashtaroth*, marked 'scarce' and 'now out of print', *Bush Ballads and Galloping Rhymes*, and *Seaspray and Smoke Drift*, in a 'special edition, on toned paper' (McLaren 344, 346, 350. Ashtaroth misspelled as Astaraoth).

60   Preface, in *Marcus Clarke*, ed., Wilding, 645.

61   On Lyster see Harold Love, *The Golden Age of Australian Opera: W. S. Lyster and his Companies 1861–1880* (Currency Press, Sydney, 1981).

62   *The Well-Selected Library of Mr Marcus Clarke* (May & Company, Melbourne, [1874]). It is reproduced in facsimile in McLaren. See A-M. Jordens, 'Marcus Clarke's Library', *Australian Literary Studies*, 7 (1976) 366–412.

63   'In A Bark Hut', *Australasian*, 17 May 1873, 616. The young Jorge Luis Borges had a similar literary childhood and adolescence: 'Dr Borges accorded his son the privilege of unrestricted access to his personal library of over a thousand volumes. This collection of mostly English and French books was arranged on glass-fronted shelves and kept in a room of its own, and here George would become a voracious reader, reveling in the freedom books afforded him to venture in strange, faraway lands ...' Edwin Williamson, *Borges: A Life* (Viking, New York and London, 2004) 41. Clarke's story 'Human Repetends', *Australasian*, 14 September 1872, 326, collected in Marcus Clarke, *The Mystery of Major Molineux and Human Repetends* (1881), is a Borgesian prefiguring of Borges' fictions.

64   Elliott (1958) 185. Clarke published it in the *Australasian*, 14 September 1872, 326.

65   Allardyce Nicoll, *A History of English Drama 1660–1900* (Cambridge University Press, Cambridge, 1959) vol. 5, 515.

66   Duffy (1898) vol. 2, 367.

67 Simmons (1946) quotes some of the favorable reviews of *Heavy Odds*, 35.
68 This was reissued from Mackinnon, ed. (1890) and comprised *Old Tales of a Young Country* together with five additional pieces.
69 Named Marian after her actress mother; she was to play Lady Devine in Raymond Longford's 1927 film version of *His Natural Life*.
70 Clarke's third son, Ernest Hislop Clarke.

Marcus Clarke

Biographical Notice of the Life & Work of Marcus Clarke

Author's Preface

For many years past it has been evident to me from the recurrent allusions to his personal characteristics and genius in the literary columns of the Australian press as well as from verbal communications and letters from friends that great interest still attaches in literary circles in Australia and perhaps elsewhere to the name of Marcus Clarke. No complete biography has yet been published of him; and I think I may claim to have read every memoir and obituary notice that has appeared since his premature death forty-three years ago. All such have this defect that they omit to a great extent the circumstances of his early life and the latter were unusual and of a nature to exercise a powerful influence upon one of his temperament and character.

A well known Melbourne journalist referred to this lack of information in these words:

At present we have to depend for our knowledge of Clarke's history mainly on the monograph of Mr Henry Gyles Turner; but, kindly and sane and trustworthy as that monograph is, it was assuredly intended only to stop the gap till a full and authoritative biography should appear.

This is to ignore the biography composed by Marcus Clarke's friend and fellow-journalist, the late Mr Hamilton Mackinnon, and published at Melbourne in 1884. It was the opening sentence of this work, however, that first inspired me with the idea of endeavouring to fill the gap referred to, for the author remarks, 'Owing to the almost morbid reticence of the late Marcus Clarke about his early childhood and later boyhood, it is by no means an easy task to give anything like a full record of him in those days, when his highly impressionable nature was first subjected to the influences around it; influences which, doubtless, affected his after career in no small degree, and which may be held chiefly accountable for the comparative failure in results of an intellect so gifted as was his.'

But to do this was not my only object. For I seemed to hear the chilling enquiry of some modern critic demanding to be informed of what interest these further particulars can be to the reading public of today? In reply to some such question, I would say that having regard to all that Australia has hitherto produced in the literary domain, it may well be that the world will be interested in the lifestory of a writer whom an eminent public man characterised in an obituary notice as one of the 'most notable pioneers of Australian literature.' A pioneer-writer, who had depicted the life of the then newly-settled districts of Victoria much as Bret Harte had done that of California of the Fifties, and one whose name would in all probability have become as familiar to the English speaking world, had he but lived, as that of others of the same calibre such as Robert Louis Stevenson or Rudyard Kipling with both of whom he had, perhaps, something in common.

Even as it was, he had compelled the attention of the reading public by his extraordinarily powerful novel, *For the Term of his Natural Life*, pronounced by Lord Lytton and other good judges to have been, in their opinion, one of the most remarkable of those produced during the whole of the late nineteenth century. In his work on Australian literature, Mr Desmond Byrne thus alludes to him: 'In the peculiarity of his fitful talents and in the character of his best work in fiction … Marcus Clarke is still alone in Australian literature,' adding that had his life been prolonged, 'he might almost have done for Australian city life what Thackeray did for the London of seventy years ago.'

It was therefore not only with the view of relating the material facts of Marcus Clarke's life but also of giving a general idea of his varied work, his essays, short stories, novels and plays that I took up my pen, dominated by the keen desire of putting on paper (however unfit I might be for the task) my own personal reminiscences of him, and of turning to account some of the graphic and picturesque letters he wrote me during the earlier period of his career. These show something of his first impressions of a country whose characteristics would, he contended, eventually so influence the temperament of its inhabitants that they would materially differ from the Anglo-Saxon type from which they originally sprung. He describes the Australian national character that would, in his opinion, be evolved by the agency of climate and environment in that quaint but brilliant prophecy, *The Future Australian Race*, and also seems to foretell the federation of the various states into one Commonwealth in those lines of his:

> But never let our sons forget,
>   Till mem'ry's self be dead,
> If Britain gave us birth, my lads,
>   Australia gave us bread!
> Then cheer for young Australia,
>   The Empire of the Free,
> Where yet a Greater Britain
>   The Southern Cross shall see!

Nevertheless, although at one time his name was as well known to the Australian reading public as that of A. L. Gordon the poet (whose own popularity owed something at least to Clarke's appreciation and notice of his work), I observe with regret that an Australian writer of today, who deals with the very same material as that of Clarke's early Bush tales, appears to ignore it. For in a story entitled *My Brilliant Career* (to which Mr Lawson contributed a preface attesting its fidelity to life) occurs the following passage, 'Copies of Gordon, Kendall, and Lawson were on my lap … my sworn friends and companions.' But no mention of Marcus Clarke, an omission which seems to point to the conclusion that his Bush stories were unknown to the writer in question.

That such is not the case with his grim narrative of the convict days, however, convincing proof was recently forthcoming. For in a selection of the twelve best novels instituted by the Melbourne *Argus*, the only Australian work that figured in the final analysis of close on twelve hundred lists sent in was Clarke's *For the Term of his Natural Life*, the remaining eleven consisting of selections from Thackeray, Scott, Dickens,

George Eliot, Blackmore, Charles Kingsley, Dumas, Charlotte Bronte and Mrs Craik. Far down amongst the rejected was that description of early Australian pastoral life, *Geoffry Hamlyn* by Henry Kingsley, so much admired by many competent judges amongst whom was Marcus himself.

Whilst on the subject of novels I may here mention that in the following pages will be found the full text of *Felix and Felicitas*, the fragment of one he left behind when death overtook him. It was to have been essentially a psychological study and the few completed chapters now submitted to the reader will enable him or her to judge how far the author's purpose was likely to have been successfully achieved.

At least I know that they created a most favourable impression on the minds of the London publishers to whom they were shown.

But it is time for me to explain the nature of my connection with the brilliant subject of this memoir and to describe the manner in which I made the acquaintance of Marcus Clarke.

There are, I should surmise, few small seaside resorts in the south of England that have changed less during the last half century than that hamlet lying just outside Ryde known as Seaview. During a visit to that pleasant corner of the Isle of Wight some few years ago, the wooded slopes and the sands below them appeared (to me, at least) the same as on a certain summer afternoon in the Fifties, when a brother [Gerard Manley Hopkins] and myself were busy making sandcastles, or engaged in paddling in the pools surrounding the rocks, and watching the yachts passing up the Solent and the larger vessels coming out of or approaching Portsmouth Harbour and Spithead. Whilst looking about us, he noticed a young boy of our own age who, propped against a convenient rock with a cushion at his back, sat regarding us. He had fine, grey, searching eyes and a most winning smile, and on our approaching and speaking to him cordially responded to our timid advances. He explained that he was not allowed to run about or play like other boys because of his weak shoulder, and, soon reaching the confidential stage, informed us that he had lost his mother and that his name was Marcus Andrew Hislop Clarke.

This bodily weakness, which has given rise to much misconception amongst those who have written about him, is thus referred to by the late Dr. Patrick Moloney who attended the Clarke family in Melbourne and who was called in during Marcus's last illness and had known him for years: 'as a child he had a disease of the left humerus and a deep cicatrice nearly its whole length marked the operation of the removal of the dead bone.' It was not long before his father, a widower, attired in deep mourning, made his appearance and after a brief warning to us never to persuade Marcus to join us in digging or active play, expressed, with this limitation, his approval of the acquaintance between us and sealed it by giving us all some fine hot-house grapes from a basket he had brought with him. There ensued a friendship that, aided by the intimacy of close companionship at school, survived the ordeal of time and distance and was maintained by correspondence until within a year or so of Marcus's death.

Now although much interest, I gather, still lingers about the personality of Marcus Clarke in Australia, owing to the lack of knowledge of his early life already mentioned, no adequate account of him has ever been published; and induced by the desire of in some measure filling up the gap, I have attempted to supply the reading public there and at home with an account of it – the attempt of a tyro and inexperienced writer, to whom, on that account, I hope, leniency may be shown. Said a recent reviewer in the *Times*, 'We are all of us ready enough to read what a man, who has seen and known them, has to tell us about the personalities of men who have amused, instructed or otherwise attracted us in books or on the stage, but the age is a hasty one and impatient of prosing or commonplace.' It is difficult to avoid these faults, I fear, when endeavouring to draw the portrait of a very gifted man in the early stages of his life.

But strong in the conviction that the personality of Marcus Clarke, at all events in youth, was one of unusual attractiveness, and his literary talent equal to or even superior to that of other authors who, more fortunate in time and circumstance, have acquired a larger share of fame and notice, I venture to submit the following pages, inspired as they have been by the *dictum* of Clarke's favourite novelist, Honoré de Balzac, as expressed in his well known story, *La peau de chagrin*, 'Pour juger un homme, au moins faut-il être dans le secret de sa pensée, de ses malheurs, de ses émotions, ne vouloir connaître de sa vie que les événements materiels, c'est faire de la chronologie, l'histoire des sots!'

Few could in my opinion claim to possess this kind of knowledge who first made the acquaintance of Marcus Clarke in Australia, for the events that drew him thither made an impression that seems to have had the effect of sealing up altogether the confidences of one by nature proud and reserved. Indeed he seems at times to have deliberately endeavoured to give a false impression of his motives and real character.

His life however, like that of other masters of fiction, is to some extent told in his stories and the intention with which I took up my pen was partly to endeavour to interpret them, having, as I fancy, a key to the psychological problem implied; that supplied by the intimacy of early life and my recollections of the boyish confidences of the famous Australian author.

Cyril Hopkins

Chapter 1

Birthplace and parentage. – Family history. – His father's character. – Early death of the latter's wife (Marcus's mother). – Unfortunate effect of his bereavement on the character of William Hislop Clarke (Marcus's father). – His injudicious parental indulgence and laisser-aller *methods of bringing up his son. – Resentment of the latter in after life of his father's absence of supervision of him during youth. – William Hislop Clarke's sole aim and ambition in life with regard to his son.*

Marcus Andrew Hislop Clarke was born at No. 11, Leonard Place, Kensington. The house forms one of a row probably built early last century when Kensington was an aristocratic and almost rural suburban neighbourhood. Its front faces the busy High Street and from the first floor windows commands a view of the fine trees and lawns of Holland House across the road, whilst from those at the back one looks down upon the modest little garden at the rear of the house itself. For a London middle-class residence the situation is a choice one, the noise of the traffic in Kensington High Street being diminished by the strip of garden in front.[1]

---

1 By the courtesy of the tenant Dr. Ronald Carter, the author's widow and daughter together with the present writer, were allowed to inspect the house and examine the rooms that had once been Marcus's nursery and bedroom. The late Mrs. Marcus Clarke took away with her a small root of the ivy growing in the front court of No. 11, Leonard Place, which, on her return, she planted on her husband's grave in Melbourne [General] Cemetery.

The subject of this memoir came of a good North of Ireland family. From papers in his late widow's possession one can trace his pedigree back (in some degree) to the seventeenth century, for they show that in the year 1612 a certain William Clarke was made a burgess of Mountjoy, County Tyrone, and that in 1658, Thurloe wrote to Cromwell, desiring him to give Colonel Clarke land in Ireland for pay. Marcus once told me that he believed a former relative of his had attained high rank in the French service, a belief that seems to be confirmed by the notes in question, for they mention a certain Henri Jacques Clarke (born 1765) known in France as the Duc de Feltre.[2]

However all this may be, it is better to adopt the account given in the life of Lieutenant-General Sir Andrew Clarke, where the immediate family history is set forth in a clear and reliable manner. From this it appears that their great-great-grandfather was John Clarke of Grange, County Tyrone, whose Scottish ancestors settled in the North of Ireland in the seventeenth-century. John Clarke's eldest son, Andrew, about 1760, married Miss Flora Lindsay, by whom he had a large family. Of this family, the eldest son, John, became an Army Surgeon and served in the West Indies where he and the second son, Andrew, married sisters. This latter (Andrew Clarke) was the grandfather of both the late Lieutenant-General Sir Andrew and of Marcus Clarke of whom I am writing, for they were first cousins.

Born in 1764, Andrew Clarke entered the medical profession and in 1782 served on board *HMS Dublin*. Later he went to the West Indies where his elder brother, John, was serving, and was attached to a regiment of Foot. He married at St. Kitts, in 1790, Louise Downing, daughter of Anthony Johnston of Annandale and remained in that island for some years after his marriage. When Trinidad was captured by

---

2   The following reference to the Duc de Feltre appeared in *T. P's Weekly* for January 22nd 1909 from the pen of Mr. Arthur Machen: Mademoiselle Kien who has just died at Neuwiller, Alsace, was the last surviving descendant of Marshal Clarke, Duc de Feltre, Minister of War to Napoleon I, during the gigantic, armed struggle of 1807–1814. Clarke (like his uncle Shee, who brought him up and started him in his military career) came of one of the Irish Jacobite families which followed the fallen Stuarts to France. An accomplished linguist, he was sent by Louis XVIII as ambassador to the Prince Regent (afterwards George IV) during the 'Hundred Days.' A clever strategist (he was Chief of the topographical Cabinet to Carnot, the 'Organiser of Victories'), a brave soldier (he took a stand of colours and many cannon at Ulm), humane and of high integrity (the Czar gave him a diamond-hilted sword for his generous treatment of Napoleon's Russian prisoners-of-war), he was also one of the least greedy of the French Marshals of the First Empire. His special weakness was his taste for genealogy. He traced his descent from (and connection with) so many illustrious families that Napoleon once rallied him before a numerous gathering of courtiers by inquiring how it was he had never made any claim to be the rightful heir to the throne of Great Britain itself. He gained his title of Duc de Feltre by his discomfiture of the English plans on Walcheren.

Abercromby in 1797, Dr. Clarke moved thither and became a planter and the owner of a considerable estate. He was a keen and active officer of the local Militia, and, in course of time, succeeded to the command of the battalion to which he belonged.

With Brigadier-General Sir Thomas Picton, who was Governor and Commander-in-Chief of Trinidad when Dr. Clarke arrived, he established a particular friendship. He was also on intimate terms with Sir Thomas Picton's successors in the Government – Sir Thomas Hislop and Colonel William Monro. The former stood godfather to his third son, William Hislop Clarke, and the latter showed his appreciation of the Doctor's services in command of his Militia battalion by selecting him for the command of the 1st Militia Division with the rank of Brigadier-General.

Dr. Clarke's family were all born in the West Indies, three boys and a girl surviving childhood …

The eldest son, Andrew (father of Lieutenant-General Sir Andrew Clarke) was born in 1793, the second, James Langton in 1800, and the third, William Hislop (father of Marcus) in 1806. Marcus told me that his grandmother had (he believed) inherited from her father (Anthony Johnston) who was a prosperous sugar-planter, his West Indian estates but that the latter had been eventually sold – I presume about the year 1818 when (according to the authority above-quoted) Dr. Clarke quitted Trinidad for good and returned to Ireland, settling first at Strabane, County Tyrone and afterwards at Belmont, a house built for himself on a property previously purchased near Lifford, County Donegal, where he died in the year 1836.

These West Indian Estates had probably been sold prior to the Emancipation Act of 1834, for, according to Marcus, his father was in the habit of referring to this measure which, whilst finally abolishing slavery in the British dominions, had a disastrous effect both in our South African [colonies] and on the prosperity of the West Indian islands, just as thirty years later a similar result was produced in the cotton-growing states of the American Union by the Civil War in that country.

The father of Marcus (as previously mentioned) was William Hislop Clarke, who, born in 1806, was, according to the biographer of Sir Andrew, educated, as were his two elder brothers, for the army, but on growing up, abandoned his intention of joining that profession for the same reason as his brother, James Langton, namely the stagnation in promotion that had followed the close of the Napoleonic wars after the battle of Waterloo, both younger brothers eventually joining the bar.

William Hislop Clarke started in life (Marcus informed me) as a clerk in the bankruptcy division of the Law Courts in Dublin under Sir Anthony Hart, but relinquishing his position in that department, came to London and was called to the Middle Temple, June 25 1830. He had taken high honours at Trinity College, Dublin, and was an ambitious man. It is worth noting that his father refers to him in a letter quoted in the life of Sir Andrew, when he (William Hislop) was a boy, as 'a first rate scholar for his age.' It was from his lips Marcus heard the story introduced into the pages of 'The Peripatetic Philosopher' as a 'West Indian anecdote.' It turns on the extraordinary behaviour of the officers of a certain West Indian regiment, as related by a guest at their Mess, who, in despair at their many eccentricities, had appealed to the Colonel for an explanation. The only one vouchsafed, however, was, 'My dear Sir, ... it is impossible for me to hear you when my aunt's butler is up the chimney playing the dulcimer.' Everyone had *delirium tremens*!

In a letter accepting the dedication of *The Marcus Clarke Memorial Volume* (published at Melbourne in 1884) Lord Rosebery compares the genius of Marcus Clarke with that of Emily Bronte and it has struck me as curious that the parentage of both was somewhat similar (see also next chapter). Patrick Bronte, father of the celebrated sisters, came from the North of Ireland (although his family had originally migrated from the south) and although in humble circumstances, was of good extraction. Being a man of great ambition and intelligence, he determined to try his fortune in England.

William Hislop Clarke, too, left his father's house in Donegal for Dublin and then for the great metropolis where he eventually married Amelia Elizabeth Matthews who (and here perhaps the comparison may be thought to fail) may possibly also have been of Irish origin, for her parents were Roman Catholics. He acquired a good practice at the Chancery Bar and was engaged in at least one *cause célèbre*, an action for breach of contract brought by the lessee of the Royal Italian Opera House, Lumley, against a certain German *prima donna*, Wagner by name, in which he was successful in gaining a verdict for his client. At this period he occupied rooms in Vere Street, Oxford Street, his professional chambers being at No. 1, New Square, Lincoln's Inn Fields. He remained until somewhat past middle life unmarried, and, as much misapprehension evidently exists in Australia on the subject of Marcus Clarke's mother, I will proceed to state what I know about her.

The drawing-room floor of the house in Vere Street was rented by W. Hislop Clarke from a couple named Matthews, the husband a musician employed at the Opera House, where my informant thought that his wife may also at one time have been engaged in some capacity but not, he believed, as a regular member of the dramatic profession. Their only daughter, very young when Mr. Clarke first went to live there, grew up under his eyes, so to speak, and from an engaging child developed into a beautiful girl, gifted with unusual intelligence and great sweetness of disposition. Becoming intensely interested in her, he took upon himself the cost of her education and had her sent to a then very fashionable school at Kensington, kept by a Mrs. Teed (Campden House) where the best masters were provided and the accomplishments deemed necessary for the daughters of the upper-middle class instilled. Marcus himself was under the impression that his mother had been educated in a convent school in France or Belgium, but if so this could only have been (I was told by the same authority)[3] for a short period after leaving the school at Campden Hill, if at all. Be this as it may, she was a well educated and an accomplished girl at the time of her marriage to his father, who took her to the home he had provided in Leonard Place, Kensington, already described. Marcus himself had not the faintest recollection of his mother. In reply to an allusion of mine on the subject he wrote me, on one occasion, as follows:

> I never saw my mother, nor a portrait of her; knew none of her relations, did not even know her maiden name. I knew that her Christian name was Amelia Elizabeth. She was only seventeen, I believe, when my Father married her.
>
> She was a Catholic and was sent by my father to a convent school abroad to be educated before he married her. She died when I was three years old.
>
> I remember, when I was about eight, Lumley, the manager of the opera coming to dine at our house with some friends. I was down at dessert, and (my Father being out of the room for a short time) Lumley turned to one of the company and said, 'His mother was the loveliest girl I ever saw.' … I do not wish to pursue the chain of thought further but I know that the whole thing (i.e. his father's attachment and marriage) was somewhat romantic. Indeed I used to wonder at lady friends of the family petting me when a boy and asking me if I remembered my mother? And the whisperings and noddings that used to take place between them!

These notions concerning his mother were not, as we see, altogether accurate, but it must be understood that his father was reserved and taciturn upon the subject and Marcus could elicit little or no information from him in connection

---

3   The late Lieutenant-General Sir Andrew Clarke.

with it. The fact was that the early loss of his wife, for whom he had cherished so romantic an attachment, produced an unfortunate effect upon the character of William Hislop Clarke. He became extremely unsociable, seldom entertaining or going into society but continuing assiduously to practise his profession, 'seeming to think,' as Marcus put it, 'only of making money for me.'

But although, as that expression proves, undoubtedly devoted in his way to his son, who invariably accompanied him to the theatre or opera during his Christmas holidays and was his father's companion on his summer visits to his family in Ireland, or, as on one occasion that I remember, to the Scottish Highlands, nevertheless he undoubtedly failed in his duty towards him. He never stinted Marcus in pocket-money and the boy had more than his share of amusement but, on the other hand, he omitted to exercise such care and supervision as might at least have been expected from the widowed father of an only son, a neglect of duty of which that son in after life was but too painfully well aware. This is evident in more than one passage of his writings.

For instance in a beautiful, fantastic story of his entitled 'Holiday Peak or Mount Might ha' been,' he makes one of the characters say in reference to Marcus's literary success on meeting him at the enchanted mansion:

> 'Ah! lucky fellow! … How different things *might have been* if you hadn't taken your uncle's advice.'
>
> 'You are right,' said I, 'but help yourself to wine, and let us walk somewhere. To tell you the truth, my head feels a little queer this morning.'
>
> 'That is often the case,' returned Gerard, 'when one first comes to Holiday Peak, but you will soon get used to our mountain air. Order your horses, and we will go and call on Mostyn. He didn't marry the widow after all, and is still the same jolly fellow as of old.'
>
> 'Ay, I remember how he used to take me up from Aldershot in the baggage-train and introduce to my schoolboy eyesight the wonders of London at midnight. Pray, are the Armida-gardens still existent?'
>
> 'I don't know what you mean. Mostyn never took you to London with him. You were never in the Armida-gardens in all your life.'
>
> 'Thank goodness, Gerard! Are you sure?'
>
> 'Quite certain. You *might have* wasted your youth in such places, and got into no end of mischief, had not your father kept such a strict and kindly eye upon you.'
>
> 'Ah!' said I, 'you are right. Let us, then, remain at home to-day. Mostyn can wait.'

'As you please,' said Gerard. 'Here is the end of *Denis Duval*. Have you read it?'

'The end of *Denis Duval*! Why, poor Thackeray died before he finished it.'

'Nonsense! He is as hearty as you or I!' …

'Gerard, my dear fellow,' said I, rising, 'I – I feel a little confused; leave me for a while. We will meet at dinner.'

The second allusion to his early life is the passage in his story, 'Human Repetends,' quoted by Hamilton Mackinnon and others[4] as being undoubtedly intended to unveil what the training in his father's house had been and as a description of the kind of people who frequented it.

My first initiation into the business of 'living' took place under these auspices. The only son of a rich widower, who lived, under sorrow, but for the gratification of a literary and political ambition, I was thrown while still a boy into the society of men twice my age, and was tolerated as a clever impertinent in all those witty and wicked circles in which virtuous women are conspicuous by their absence … I was suffered at sixteen to ape the vices of sixty … You can guess the result of such a training.

Again in another passage referring to this period of his life, he writes,

Let us take an instant to explain how it came about that a pupil of the Revrd. Gammon's, up in town for his holidays, should have owned such an acquaintance. My holidays, passed in my father's widowed house, were enlivened by the coming and going of cousin Tom from Woolwich, of cousin Dick from Sandhurst, of cousin Harry from Aldershot. With Tom, Dick and Harry came a host of friends – for, as long as he was not disturbed, the Head of the House rather liked to see his rooms occupied by relatives of people with whom he was intimate and a succession of young men of the Cinqbars, Ringwood and Algernon Deucedere sort, made my home a temporary roosting-place. I cannot explain how such a curious *ménage* came to be instituted, but such was the fact, and 'Little Master' instead of being trained in the way he should morally go, became the impertinent companion of some very wild bloods indeed. 'I took Horace to the opera last night, Sir,' or 'I am going to show Horatius Cocles the wonders of Cremorne this evening,' would be all that Tom, or Dick or Harry would deign to observe and

---

4   See *Australian Writers* by Desmond Byrne, *inter alia*.

my Father would but lift his eyebrows in indifferent deprecation. So, a wild-eyed and eager schoolboy, I strayed into Bohemia, and acquired in that strange land an assurance and experience ill-suited to my age and temperament. Remembering the wicked, good-hearted inhabitants of that country, I have often wondered since 'what they thought of it,' and have interpreted, perhaps not unjustly, many of the homely tendernesses which seemed then so strangely out of place and time.

Readers of novels may find a somewhat analogous passage to this in one of James Payn's earlier stories. They will note on reference to the *Family Scapegrace*, that that individual, taken early away from school and sent up to London to serve in his uncle's warehouse, has very similar experiences. He is taken to places of amusement by a friend of his landlady's (in reality her son) a certain Mr. Jones for whom he cherishes a boyish admiration, who 'introduced him to Cremorne, where Mr. Jones seemed to have a large circle of acquaintances and to be especially a favourite among the ladies, though we are bound to say that the evening in question was not that famous one upon which no female was admitted beneath the rank of a baronet's wife.'

In short, W. Hislop Clarke, in the words of an Australian writer and friend of Marcus[5] 'gave his son an excellent education, but took no personal charge of him, and only smiled grimly when men of the world, his friends, attracted by the youth's ebullitions of wit and precocious cleverness, took him away on excursions and showed him off in scenes and among associates not of the highest moral character.' With regard, however, to Marcus Clarke's allusions to his own early life in his stories and essays, Mr. Hamilton Mackinnon has done well in addressing a word of warning to his readers that they must make allowance 'for the play of an imagination which was of so brilliant a nature as to cast a glamour over the most common-place objects.' Moreover to the best of my belief (although the point is not perhaps of much importance) his father never concerned himself with either politics or literature except as a relaxation, for he had literary tastes and possessed an excellent library. In fact he confined his ambition to amassing a competence or a fortune for the benefit of his son, an ambition that would probably have been realised but for the fatal breakdown of health and collapse of will-power and judgement that overtook him just as his purpose seemed in the fair way of accomplishment.

---

5   Charles Bright, *Cosmos* magazine, April 1895.

Chapter 2

Early education. – A lesson in elocution. – Removal to Highgate Grammar School. – His first appearance at Elgin House (his boarding house at Highgate). – Boyish acuteness, agility and recklessness. – Dislike of mathematics. – Admiration for Horace and the classics. – Gift of narration and repartee. – His first essay in fiction. – Nature of the story. – Description of the frontispiece supplied by my brother. – Familiarity with The Ingoldsby Legends. *– Lord Rosebery's comparison of the genius of Marcus Clarke with that of Emily Bronte.*

Marcus being, as previously mentioned in my introductory chapter, a delicate and physically rather backward child, at first attended a day school in Kensington kept by a lady not far from his own home. Whether the person in question had once been connected with the dramatic profession I do not know, but the following anecdote concerning her methods may perhaps point to that conclusion. For when still very young, Marcus related to me (in the graphic manner characteristic of all clever and observant children, particularly when their feelings have been excited) how one day when directed to learn by heart and repeat aloud Cowper's verses commencing

> The rose had been washed, just washed in a shower,
> Which Mary to Anna conveyed,

he had hurried through his uncongenial task in the monotonous sing-song beloved of childhood, but his governess who doubtless piqued herself on her histrionic abilities, had determined that the recitation should not be slurred over in that manner. He was therefore ordered to repeat the verses after her in the correct style of delivery and had of course no choice but to obey. But when the lines were reached

> And swinging it rudely, too rudely alas!
> I snapped it: it fell to the ground,

she became to his thinking so intolerably affected that he followed with such an exaggerated imitation of her voice and manner as could not fail to attract her attention, the result being that he incurred her severe displeasure and received a smart box on the ears.

A year or two later he was removed from this preparatory school to the grammar school at Highgate and placed in one of the assistant-masters' houses, known as Elgin House on Highgate Hill, with the suburbs of Holloway and Kentish Town at its base. Not far off was Cromwell House, a fine specimen of Elizabethan architecture, also used as a school, but whether for boys or girls I cannot remember.

In Du Maurier's last story *The Martian*, there is a certain illustration, 'The New Boy.' I was reminded by it of the first appearance at Elgin House of Marcus Clarke and his father; their two figures being by no means unlike those in the picture in question, the senior Clarke a brisk, well set-up man of medium height, rather thick-set, and Marcus a slim, fair-haired boy with a refined face and bright, engaging manner. On the evening of the day of his arrival he was subjected by his new companions to certain interrogatories such as fall to the lot of most 'New Chums' (to adopt the colonial expression), one of the first being, 'Can you write like a duck?'

Albert Smith, in those entertainments of his that were the delight of London in the days of my boyhood, used to describe how a young English lady with whom he fell into conversation on board of a Rhine steamer, exclaimed enthusiastically on his mentioning the name of Alfred Tennyson 'Oh! He writes like a duck!' But it was not in this sense that the phrase was understood at Elgin House. To 'write like a duck', it is perhaps superfluous to explain, was to be forced to hold a pen with one's teeth instead of one's fingers, and then, whilst endeavouring to form some legible signs with it in this position, to feel it suddenly wrenched sideways from one's mouth, the victim being left to splutter out the ink at his leisure. But Marcus (who had seen through the intended manoeuvre at once) after allowing the pen to be placed in his mouth, with admirably assumed unconsciousness of what was going to follow, gripped it tightly with his teeth, made one or two strokes very rapidly on the paper and then before his would-be persecutors were quite aware of his intentions, dropped it suddenly on the floor, whence picking it up, he politely handed it to the boy who had thought to trick him, saying with a bright smile and a meaning glance from the fine, grey eyes, 'There is your p-p-pen! I've managed to write like a d-d-duck but I'm afraid I've s-s-spoiled your fun!' It was all done with so much tact and *bonhomie* that few further attempts at playing off practical jokes upon him were made, and he very soon acquired that desirable reputation for a schoolboy, namely a reputation for *savoir faire*.

But over and above this there was an indefinable charm about him that would have made him universally popular with his schoolfellows had he cared to cultivate popularity. He was quite indifferent to it in those days however, and apparently a mere creature of impulse, a human butterfly; at least, judging him as they did by certain of his words and actions, all but his most intimate friends so regarded him, during his early years at school. To the latter he occasionally revealed glimpses of a different nature, showing that he could on occasion be more than the wayward, devil-may-care, laughter-loving imp his tutors and the majority of his schoolfellows considered him.

Needless to add that at first he was far from studious, in fact rather abnormally idle, but so quick and intelligent that he easily managed his class-work, with the exception of mathematics, a subject to which in those days but scant attention was paid at Highgate Grammar School, and which Marcus for his part cordially detested.

I was reminded of this by a passage in a novel I once read entitled *Ripple and Flood* cast in the form of autobiography, the hero of which, referring to his school days, says,

> I was but slackly interested in arithmetic. The most pleasure I could get from an arithmetical exercise was in forgetting it as soon as I had solved it, while the bald statement that Drake sailed 'round the world in three years,' or even a mere geographical enumeration, 'Rice, millet, sorghum, coffee, dates, the banyan, the plantain and melon,' would raise bright-hued images in my mind of unmeasured oceans and lands where the sun shone and made no shadow.

I have a letter from Marcus written soon after his arrival in Australia, in which he refers to his own very similar experiences in the following terms:

> Do you remember the arithmetic? and the refreshments thereat? and how you did all the examples and I cribbed them? Dase of me boyhood, I'm dreamin' on ye now! ...

But if he detested mathematics, he delighted in Horace and the classics. Even as a boy he was fond of trying his hand at turning the odes of Horace into English verse and that clever travesty 'Horace in the Bush' will well repay perusal.

Although when he first came to Highgate Grammar School he had not quite outgrown his constitutional delicacy and despite the slight stiffness of his left arm caused by the contraction of the muscles, he possessed much bodily agility, and true to his Irish blood was utterly careless of risk or danger. Indeed he met with an accident during a game of hockey that nearly disfigured him for life, and owing to the numerous cuts, sprains and bruises he sustained, the Matron of our boarding house used to lament that 'young Clarke' (as for some inscrutable reason, he was invariably designated) 'was always in the wars.' And this was decidedly an instance of the triumph of spirit over matter, for his frame was slight and, as Dr. Patrick Moloney, his medical attendant in Melbourne (to whom I have referred in my preface), states, 'Marcus Clarke's left shoulder-joint was anchylosed and his left arm at least two inches shorter than his right.'

But perhaps his most distinguishing trait was his gift of story-telling; the narratives chosen being sometimes avowedly his own compositions, and sometimes repetitions from memory of those he had met with in the course of his promiscuous reading. Sir A. Conan Doyle mentions the practice he acquired in early life by inventing tales for the entertainment of his schoolfellows. Marcus Clarke did the same thing, prompted probably by a natural and uncontrollable desire of airing the restless young wings of his brilliant imagination.

Two of his stories I remember well. The first was the history of an adventure that was supposed to have befallen the wife of an Austrian officer obliged to put up at a lonely inn on the outskirts of a vast and dreary plain (the Steppes or Pusztas, I presume) in Hungary. Mr. Crockett in his story *The Raiders* gives a variant of this legend under the heading 'The Wolf's Flock;' in this he describes the escape from a violent death of a traveller who has taken refuge from a storm in a lonely hut in the Galloway Mountains, the occupants of which live by murder and robbery. The hero in the *Raiders* escapes; his suspicions having been aroused from the first and confirmed by the discovery of the ghastly nature of the contents of a sea-chest in the bedroom assigned to him. The hut, situated near a gloomy mountain town, is, it appears, notorious in the district as 'The Murder Hole.' In Marcus Clarke's version the scene was laid (as already stated) in a lonely inn on the verge of one of the great Hungarian plains, and the rescue of the intended victim was effected in the nick of time by the unexpected arrival of her husband at the head of a squadron of hussars of his regiment.

The second was, he assured us, the description of an incident actually witnessed by his father or some other relative; namely a blood-curdling 'fight to the finish' between two men in the bedroom of a house overlooked by that of the involuntary and horror-stricken spectator. The gruesome details (some of which I can perfectly remember) seemed to bear the stamp of truth. But he had many other narratives; some of a totally different character. And, as will be seen later on, this gift of impromptu narration did not desert him in after-life, but stood him in good stead when he was living on certain occasions in a bark hut with one or two companions on a large sheep and cattle-station in a remote part (then popularly known as the 'back blocks') of the colony of Victoria which will be treated of anon. Mr. Charles Bright, referring to this period, writes:

> I want to give one more extract from this same sketch of Clarke's, in proof that though the 'Colonial Experiences' on which he dilates may not have been those most appropriate to an embryo squatter, they were calculated to be extremely useful to the budding novelist. One of his companions of the hut whom he names McAlister[6], was, like most of his countrymen, great at arguing, and discussions on all sorts of subjects, physical, metaphysical, and psychical were carried on by the evening grease lamp. Then came Clarke's turn for a special innings:
>
> 'The arguments not unfrequently merged into story-telling, and in that department my memory served me in good stead. I had been a sickly brat in my infancy, and having unfettered access to the library of a man who owned few prejudices for moral fig-leaves, had, with the avidity for recondite knowledge which sickly brats always evince, read many strange books. I boiled down my recollections for McAlister, and constituted myself a sort of Scherezade for his peculiar benefit. He would smoke, and I would fix my eyes on a strip of bark which hung serpentwise from the ridge pole, and relate. I think if that strip of bark had been removed my power of narration would have been removed with it. In this fashion we got through a good deal of Brantome, several of the plays – or rather plots of the plays – of Wycherley, Massinger, and Farquahar, and most of Byron. We rambled over the continent with Gil Blas, discussed the alchemists, strolled up and down Rome with Horace, and investigated the miracles of the early Saxon churchmen, in company of a lot of queer fellows who lived somewhere about the time of the venerable Bede. We talked *Candide*, and Dr.

---

6   The late Hon. John Mackenzie, afterwards well-known in political circles in New Zealand.

Lardner's *Encyclopaedia*, we saw Hogarth with Ireland's descriptions; we quarrelled bitterly over Tom Paine's *Age of Reason*, and made friends again over the pathetic adventures of one Moll Flanders, a friend of Daniel Defoe.'

Marcus also possessed a ready wit and was quick and apt at repartee. The effect of the latter was rather heightened by the slight stammer which, although an impediment of speech, was, in his case, rather attractive than otherwise and seemed, as was well said by a contemporary in Australia, to 'add point to an even commonplace remark.' I recall a couple of instances but they were of course a constant occurrence.

One morning soon after Marcus's arrival at Highgate, he, my brother and myself (all three junior boys) were on our way from Elgin House (our boarding house) to morning school, when we met the members of a ladies' school out for their daily airing with a rear guard of elder pupils and assistant governesses walking two and two together. Marcus, turning to us with a bright smile and wave of the hand, exclaimed, 'The f-f-feudal system exemplified!'

The second one occurred at a later date when he was older. He had, accidentally in passing, disturbed a schoolfellow engaged in some temporarily absorbing occupation (such as changing the leaves in a box of silkworms) and the latter had angrily exclaimed, 'Oh! blow you, young Clarke!' when Marcus, thus apostrophized, replied in an artificial and dramatic manner,

> Blow! Blow! Thou winter wind,
>> Thou art not so unkind as man's ingratitude!

to the intense astonishment of the worthy youth, who, ignorant of Shakespeare, but with a vague suspicion that the words were a quotation from some unknown author, retorted, with an expression of bewilderment on his face as at some human phenomenon, 'Why, you must be *cracked*, young Clarke!', words commonplace enough in themselves, but uttered with somewhat of the awestruck emotion that we associate with the scriptural outburst, 'Paul, Paul, thou art beside thyself! Much learning doth make thee mad! ...'

Needless almost to add that any conspicuous instance of a want of the sense of humour in his companions, especially when allied to an affectation of manner, called forth his amused contempt and powers of raillery. Here is a case in point. It was customary in those days at the end of the term to have a so-called 'Breaking-up

supper' at each assistant master's house at which all who could sing were expected
to do so. At such functions Marcus himself would give his own rendering of 'Bryan
O'Lynn' or 'Having tea in the arbour,' comic ditties much favoured in those days.
One of our schoolfellows who, though very bright and intelligent, was utterly
lacking in humour and at times more than a little affected, contributed as his share
of the entertainment a ballad enumerating the virtues of the British yeoman, each
verse ending with the line, 'And I manage to exist and be content, John Brown!'
The line preceding this refrain in the last verse ran somewhat as follows:

> I've one hundred pounds a year,
> And I manage to exist and be content, John Brown!

The intention of the words was, of course, merely to emphasize the impression
that, although not overburdened with money, the yeoman nevertheless being of an
unselfish and cheery disposition, was happy and contented, but the singer utterly
misapprehending the lesson the verses sought to convey, thundered out in a solemn
and excited manner (he had a sweet boy's voice)

> I've one hundr-r-red pounds a year,
> And I manage to exist and be content, John Brown,

as if the income in question had been one hundred thousand a year and the
possession of such ample means the sole cause of the yeoman's cheeriness. Marcus,
on my drawing his attention to this singular error in interpreting the lines on the
part of our friend, burst into that silvery laugh of his, that seemed to run up and
down the vocal scale, and on the first opportunity subjected him to a fire of good
humoured *badinage*.

The late Andrew Lang said with regard to born novelists, 'Nature has supplied a certain
percentage (a small one) of the human race with the inexplicable power of interesting
the world by narration' and Marcus Clarke at, say, thirteen had been tacitly recognized
by his schoolfellows as one of the favoured few; they were therefore not surprised that
in after-life he should have made his mark as one of that still smaller minority who, to
adopt Mr. Lang's words, can 'narrate with pen and ink.' For somewhere about this age
he composed his first story, 'Prometheus.' I was reminded of this first attempt of his in
the domain of fiction by an account in *The Sketch*, July 1905 of Mr Stephen Phillip's

play, *Aylmer's Secret*, which the writer described as a modernisation of *Frankenstein*. And, although except in the central idea there is but little resemblance between that play and Marcus's story, nevertheless *Frankenstein* was doubtless also the source whence his boyish mind derived its inspiration. Be it remembered, in passing, that this story of 'Prometheus' was written when he was but 13 or 14 years old. The author of an article in the *Melbourne Review*, published some six months after Marcus Clarke's death, stated that a story entitled 'The Apothecary of Mantua' was his first attempt at fiction. This is an error, as in addition to the story of 'Prometheus,' he was the author of various experiments in prose and verse before as well as immediately after leaving school, the most notable being the weird and powerful verses, 'The Lady of Lynn,' described in a subsequent chapter.

Nevertheless the words of the writer in the *Melbourne Review* are worth quoting, although he is in error on this point, for he remarks with regard to the last short story Marcus ever composed, *The Mystery of Major Molineux*, 'It revels in an unwholesome field, but in its amplitude of physiological details, its notebook-like record of sequence, and its absence of sentiment, it forcibly recalls some of the more ghastly stories of Edgar Allan Poe. It was the last completed effort of his imagination, and while, in its familiar references to the literature of mental disease and the bold attempt to place a finger on the exact physical irregularity that caused it, there is a widespread advance displayed in the writer's reading and knowledge, yet it is singularly like the weird, uncanny style of his first juvenile effort at fiction which he called the "Apothecary of Mantua."' Something of this 'weird, uncanny style,' then, is observable in 'Prometheus,' the outline of which I will now endeavour to sketch.

After reading the first few lines, one recognizes that the boyish author has set himself to compose a tale of mystery; having previously imbued himself with the spirit of what is now known as the 'cult of the occult.' He is evidently working up to a climax the exact nature of which he endeavours to conceal from his readers until (as he conceives) the psychological moment for its revelation has arrived. Yet the mystery is easy to penetrate. A boy of studious bent surreptitiously frequents his father's library wherein he discovers an old treatise on anatomy, containing 'for the most part, mistaken ideas of the power of various substances in the case of diseases, mixed up with wild flights of the imagination as the author endeavoured to prove that the soul was a tangible thing and not only a spirit.' He also discovers an old Dutch Bible, enclosed within which is a musty pamphlet in the German language (of which he is ignorant) but the contents of which he can partly guess at from some marginal notes in English and from the nature of an engraving inserted as an illustration. His investigations, however, are cut short by the advent of his father who forbids him the further use of the library and it is only after a considerable lapse of time that he is occasionally allowed access to it. In the interval both Bible and pamphlet have disappeared. The boy grows up, and, as he approaches manhood, is sent to a German university where he studies medical science. After a year or two's residence in Germany he is summoned home on account of the illness of his father who expires soon after his arrival. While making an inventory of the contents of the library in winding up his father's estate, he discovers the Bible and pamphlet which he can now read, having by this time of course become familiar with the German language. Elated with the knowledge thus gained, he proceeds to London, taking with him as servant a half-witted boy whom his father had employed out of charity. Arrived in London he secures a lodging in an old and dilapidated house built before the great fire and pursues his medical studies at various hospitals. It would be interesting to know, *en passant*, at what period even a junior schoolboy (such as Marcus Clarke then was) could have supposed such a house to have existed in London, and even if it existed, to have been so deserted (although conveniently near the hospitals) as to count for its only tenants one medical student and his servant! And he fixes the period of the story, as will be shortly be seen, as that of the Gordon riots!

However there is a sense of pleasant vagueness about the narrative throughout. The student, in addition to securing these conveniently lonely lodgings, avoids as far as possible all intimacy with his classmates and lives a solitary life, having but one friend, a fellow-student, who, by a refinement of cruelty is carried off by a fever contracted at the hospital. Whether from dejection at his loss or from becoming so gradually absorbed in his self-imposed task he even ceases to attend the lectures at the hospital, until, aroused by the discovery that some pages of the previous pamphlet are missing, he resolves to endeavour to find them, and at this point exclaims (not without reason one would think), 'But where? Where through this vast globe was I to search for a few pages of German black letter?' Recovering his equanimity, however, with enviable facility, he continues in a reassuring strain, 'Courage! I whispered to myself, Courage! I will find the thing I want even should I have to travel to the end of the world!'

This resolve to prosecute what, on the face of it, does certainly appear a hopeless enterprise, is conveniently rewarded by the discovery of the object of his search in a book belonging to his recently deceased friend exposed for sale on a bookstall in the neighbourhood. But at this point of the story there is a considerable *hiatus* in the MS dotted with asterisks. We gather from the next paragraph that the narrative had been interrupted but is resumed at the point where broken off. For, without explanation of this *hiatus*, the story proceeds,

> It was a gloomy evening in September! The rain was falling fast and the few foot-passengers were hastening to their homes or to shelter, struggling against the force of the cold wind that swept round the corners of the streets and houses. No one would choose to stay out such a night as this!

But again the narrative breaks off abruptly, and again a blank space intervenes, followed by a fresh paragraph this time purporting to be from the pen of the Chaplain of Newgate Gaol and to the effect that a prisoner awaiting his trial for murder was found writing the foregoing history when the prison was set on fire by the mob during the Gordon riots. This interpolated note is succeeded by another blank space; after which the story is once more resumed and we learn that on re-entering his study that fatal September evening Edward Moreton (for that is the student's name) had discovered his half-witted servant engaged in 'dashing on the floor with awful screams the body of a man.'

At the same time he perceives that a dagger protrudes from the chest of the latter and that the previous pamphlet from which he had gathered his occult knowledge is nearly consumed by the flames into the midst of which it had been thrown. Roused to fury at seeing the labour of years destroyed and all hope of achieving his purpose frustrated (which, we gather, was to impart to a lifeless human body the vital principle) Moreton, snatching the dagger from the body, stabbed his unfortunate servant to death and then rushing from the house either gave himself up or was arrested and imprisoned in the Old Bailey. Then follows the comment of our friend the chaplain on the prisoner's confession:

> This extraordinary manuscript was found tightly clasped in the hands of Edward Moreton, condemned to death on a charge of murder but reprieved as a confirmed maniac. The unfortunate man would not leave his cell during the burning of Newgate by the Gordon rioters and although saved from the flames before life was extinct, died a few hours afterwards. Struck by the singular nature of the contents of the manuscript, I was induced to publish it, hoping that it might afford a few hours reflection and instruction to some of those who come after me.
>
> November 3rd 1778. Chaplain of Newgate Gaol

The frontispiece, supplied by my brother Gerard,[7] represents the interior of an attic lighted by an oblong window with crescent-shaped apex. The moonlight, streaming through, reveals the chimney pots and roofs of the adjacent houses, whilst a mass of cloud is visible in the background, indicating the stormy, unsettled character of the night. A large, open chest occupies the centre of the apartment and over it a dwarfed, misshapen man, dressed in jacket and knee-breeches is leaning, apparently absorbed in contemplation of a human body just thrust inside and from the breast of which the handle of a dagger is seen protruding. In the foreground the eye is caught by an overturned chair and brazier whilst various articles such as a pestle and mortar, books, a skull, surgical instruments, a phrenologist's bust, stove and tripod, are distributed about, the walls of the chamber being hung with anatomical engravings and a few surgical models placed on brackets, whilst playing-cards, old letters and other objects litter the floor. Moreton is represented in the act of entering the room with outstretched arms and horror-struck countenance.

The allusions to the Gordon riots and the burning of the Old Bailey were doubtless suggested by the descriptions of those events in *Barnaby Rudge*, a story that Marcus admired when at school and which, it appears, in after-life he preferred to any other of Dickens' novels. But the reference is of the briefest and merely introduced to explain the manner of Moreton's death and of the Chaplain's obtaining his confession.

The idea of the story may also possibly have been suggested by one to be found in the *Ingoldsby Legends* which Marcus was fond of discussing with me. It is a prose tale, inserted between the ballad of 'The Witch's Frolic' and that of the 'Jackdaw of Rheims,' entitled, 'Singular passage in the life of the late Henry Harris, Doctor in Divinity.' Readers who have forgotten their *Ingoldsby* or who do not care for the trouble of referring to it, may be here reminded that it is concerned with a certain confidential communication made by a sick girl to a clergyman concerning an extraordinary and painful experience of hers in connection with her lover, absent from England, and studying at the University of Leyden. She believes that by the exercise of some kind of occult and unholy science he has acquired the power of forcing her spirit to quit her body and come to his rooms where she undergoes unspeakable torture and humiliation. Although when she recovers her senses she perceives that

---

7   Father Gerard M. Hopkins, S.J. died 1889.

she is in her own bedroom at her mother's house and has apparently never quitted it, nevertheless as she is conscious of having passed through a transition-stage of acute bodily agony during the interval, she acquires the conviction that her experiences have been real and tangible and not the delusions of a bad dream. All arguments to the contrary fail to move her, and after a second experience of the same kind, she expires under the influence of the impression.

Marcus's story 'Prometheus,' whether suggested by this or other analogous theme, is of interest as indicating the bent of his mind which, in contradistinction to his boyish high spirits and genial manners, was always of a morbidly imaginative character. Undoubtedly Lord Rosebery's comparison of his (Marcus Clarke's) genius with that of Emily Bronte was apt and striking, but he might perhaps have included other names beside that of the gifted author of *Wuthering Heights*. He was probably thinking of the similarity of circumstance by which both became known to the world at large, viz., as the author of a novel of extraordinary power, or, to adopt the phrase of a reviewer of Mr. Clement Shorter's book on the Brontes, 'one sombre and volcanic novel.'

Chapter 3

Marcus Clarke an indefatigable reader. – Boyish admiration for the writings of George Augustus Sala and for the stories and verses of Edgar Allan Poe. – Our boarding house library and Sunday afternoon readings therefrom. – Modern languages at Highgate Grammar School in the sixties. – Penchant for Molière; his (Marcus's) adaptation of Le Bourgeois Gentilhomme *played in Australia. – The German professor at Highgate Grammar School. – Marcus Clarke's album and epitaph on himself therein. – Comparison with a similar one composed by R. L. Stevenson. – The street singers on Highgate Hill and Marcus's strange comments and reflections on human physiognomy. – His relations with the school authorities. – His love of art and comments on the work of the Australian landscape painter, Chevalier.*

It will probably surprise no one to learn that as a boy Marcus Clarke was an indefatigable reader. Familiar with Bulwer Lytton's, Lever's, Reade's, Marryat's, Fenimore Cooper's, Harrison Ainsworth's and James Grant's novels, but especially with the two first named, he was a student of Dickens, Thackeray and Sala, but never cared for either George Eliot or Sir Walter Scott.

For George Augustus Sala he cherished a sort of childish affection. On the report that that gentleman was coming to Sydney he sent the following to the *Sydney Morning Herald*:

The mail shortly expected in Sydney will bring to these shores my earliest literary friend, Mr George Augustus Sala. Mr Sala will probably be surprised to see this statement in print, inasmuch as he never saw me in all his life and I never saw him. My acquaintance with Mr Sala, however, was made very agreeably when I was about eight or nine years of age. It occurred in a railway carriage on the road between London and Brighton and was made through the medium of a 'Bottle of Hay.' If you will turn up the early numbers of *Household Words* (I have not got the books or I could find the paper in a twinkling) you will see a description of a public house in what was then the outskirts of London. I always imagined that my own birthplace of Kensington was meant … There is nothing very wonderful in this you will perhaps say.

True, but the story of the 'Bottle of Hay' was told in a new style. Anybody can do you a Dickens-esque interior now-a-days in the same way that anybody can write verses like the 'Lady of Pain' – Mr. Swinburne having shown them how to do it. But in the time of which I write, Sala was unique. His *Twice Round the Clock* is as fine a piece of literary workmanship in its own way as is Ruskin's *Lamps of Architecture* in *its* way,

and there followed a brief but brilliant review of Sala's principal works. Mr. Sala's visit to Australia however did not take place at the date anticipated but was deferred until March 1885 (more than three years after the death of Marcus Clarke) when the above article in reference to him (Sala) was published. In a note addressed to Hamilton Mackinnon he (Mr. Sala) expressed his admiration for Marcus's novel, *For the Term of his Natural Life*.

But to return to the subject of this memoir. He had English translations of some of Alexandre Dumas's best known romances and one of the younger Dumas's *Lady with the Camellias* in a shining, yellow millboard cover surmounted by a woodcut of the consumptive heroine, the sort of volume that one was accustomed to associate with Railway Station bookstalls in former days. Before he left school he had acquired, I am afraid, a far more accurate notion of the Marguerite Gautiers of London than was at all good for him but this arose from no vicious tendency in himself (far from it) but from the promiscuous society into which he was sometimes taken owing to the unaccountable parental laxity. In addition to the authors above-mentioned, I also remember how he, my brother and I laughed over *Valentine Vox*, and *Little Pedlington* by John Poole, and how he enjoyed and quoted *Don Quixote*, which many lads of his age (if they ever read it at all) think insufferably dull; while for the stories and verses of Edgar Allan Poe, he had the keenest admiration. I have still in my possession the copy of Poe's works given by him to my brother Gerard as a parting gift and memento.

Elgin House contained a meagre library, to which the boys occasionally had recourse on Sunday afternoons and wet half-holidays *faute de mieux*. They were perhaps not able to extract much mental entertainment from the majority of the books for these were mainly of the type of *Nicholl's Help to Reading the Bible*; in other words neither of a very stimulating nor refreshing character, even for a drizzling half-holiday or for a sleepy Sunday afternoon's diversion. But there were a few exceptions; amongst the latter a history of the adventures of two Englishmen in that part of the South American continent familiar to the present generation as 'Argentina,' but formerly designated 'The River Plate.' The name of this book I have long since forgotten but was recently reminded of it by a charmingly written account of life in Uruguay in the sixties and early seventies entitled *The Purple Land* by the late W. H. Hudson, treating of very much the same subjects and people although of course at a much later date. The book Marcus and I read together contained descriptions of the manners and customs of the *gauchos* and the pictures drawn of those dashing horsemen had for us a pleasant fascination; poor Marcus not foreseeing that in a few years from that date he would have ample opportunity of testing the delights of 'rounding up' and branding cattle so much vaunted in this book under the heading of 'Rodeos' though the scene would be laid elsewhere than on the ranch of an Argentine *estanciero*.

At the period of which I am writing, modern languages were but indifferently taught at most English public schools, Sir Roger Cholmeley's at Highgate being no exception to the rule, nor were they regarded by the School authorities with much favour, so that if a boy's friends wished him to study German he was debarred from learning French, and *vice-versa*. I was in the German, Marcus in the French class.

He was much given to poring over the reading-book in use, Delille's *Répertoire des prosateurs français*, and to discussing certain passages therein. One was an extract from Balzac's story of the money-lender, *Gobseck*, commencing with the words, 'Saisiriez-vous bien sa figure pâle et blafarde à laquelle je voudrais que l'Académie me permit de donner le nom de face lunaire, et qui ressemblait à du vermeil dédoré?'

Whether the short extract from this story or the other example of the author given in the work in question were the germs from which sprang the desire for that minute study of Balzac undertaken by Marcus in later life I do not know, but think it not unlikely.

Another favourite passage was an extract from De Jouy's '*L'ermite de la Chaussée d'Antin*' headed, 'Le Tartufe de franchise,' commencing 'Parmi les nombreuses variétés de Tartufe, l'espèce la plus dangereuse est celle de ces faux bonshommes dont Merange est le modèle le plus achevé … Sur quelque chose que vous l'interrogiez, sa réponse commence toujours par ces mots: "A vous parler franchement."' Marcus borrowed this formula in his first novel, *Long Odds* (republished as *Heavy Odds* to avoid confusion with one of similar title by another author) for one of the characters, Randon by name, by profession a *flâneur*, who 'had an impediment in his speech, and was the most impudent man in London. His weakness was a desperate assertion of frankness. He wore his heart upon his sleeve and was constantly inviting daws to peck at it.' If the reader refers to the story he will find that Randon's remarks generally commence with the words, 'I own – I f-fwankly own' and so on. Marcus at one period of his school days was wont to preface a chaffy remark by this quotation, '*A vous parler franchement*,' which he never succeeded in doing, however, without a momentary pause before the 'p' in *parler* owing to the slight impediment of speech previously mentioned and with which he took care to endow his character, 'Randon.' From the time he could read French with tolerable ease he was a great admirer of Molière whose *Bourgeois Gentilhomme* he afterwards adapted to the stage in an English version and which was produced at Melbourne under the title of *Peacock's Feathers*, the piece achieving a considerable success.

The German professor at Highgate Grammar School in our time was a tall, round-shouldered but rather fine-looking man past middle life, who wore gold-rimmed spectacles and was consumed with self-importance. He professed to have travelled extensively and *informed* his pupils that if they should ever visit Egypt they would find *his* name inscribed on the Pyramids, but whether scrawled in chalk, or notched with a pocket knife after the fashion of 'Arry on Bank holidays in the rural haunts he honours with a visit, was never explained. My reports of the remarks let fall by this gentleman during the German lessons amused Marcus immensely, especially the reiterated assertion that the use of the personal pronoun 'I', written with a capital, was a striking proof of the intense egotism of the British nation, an assertion going far to prove that there is nothing new under the sun: for the late M. Zola when he astonished Mr. Vizetelly with the same remark during the former's exile at Norwood (from the Dreyfus prosecution) did but unconsciously repeat a well worn criticism made doubtless by many previous foreign students of our language. At all events it was a favourite indictment of our friend Dr. Munck, to whom Marcus alluded in one of the last letters I ever received from him as 'a worthy disciple of Baron Münchausen,' (which indeed he was) and concluded with the words underlined 'On de Pyramids you will find de name of Napoleon ('Na-po-lé-on' he wrote it, to remind me of the German Professor's monosyllabic, 'staccato' manner of speech) and you will also find the name of Munck!'

Whilst at school Marcus kept an album in which my brother inserted a paragraph describing a certain Marcus Scrivener (his nickname for Clarke adopted by the latter as a *nom de plume*) as a 'Kaleidoscopic, Parti-colored, Harlequinesque, Thaumatropic' being, and in which Marcus composed two epitaphs in doggerel Latin, one on himself, one on the present writer. The former (quoted in his memoir by Hamilton Mackinnon) runs as follows:

Hic Jacet

MARCUS CLERICUS

Qui non malus, 'Coonius

Consideratus fuit

Sed amor bibendi

Combinatus cum pecuniæ deficione

Mentem eius oppugnabat –

Mortuus est!

Et nihil ad vitam restorare

Posset.

One may pause to compare this boyish effusion with the equally playful epitaph on himself by R. L. Stevenson in a letter to his friend, Sidney Colvin, but composed at a much later period of his life:

Here lies

The carcase

of

Robert Louis Stevenson,

An active, austere, and not inelegant

writer,

who,

at the termination of a long career,

wealthy, wise, benevolent, and honoured by

the attention of two hemispheres,

yet owned it to have been his crowning favour

TO INHABIT

LA SOLITUDE

(With the consent of the intelligent edility of Hyères, he has been interred

below this frugal stone, in the garden which he honoured for so long with

his poetic presence.)

And one may perhaps discern a certain similarity of thought in each of the charming but eccentric personalities of the two authors.

Perhaps it was the natural tendency to Bohemianism inherent in him, perhaps it was only the curiosity of a schoolboy eager to study life: whatever the predisposing cause, Marcus Clarke's interest was always keenly roused by the occasional appearance in the streets of Highgate of a group of strolling acrobats, a Punch and Judy show, or an old man with a perambulating menagerie of small animals, possessed of antagonistic natures, such as cats, mice and birds huddled together in a cage and designated by a dirty label as 'The Happy Family.' One evening towards the end of May, he and I on our way home from school came upon a trio of musicians (two men and a woman) differing from the ordinary type of London ballad-singer (one of the most abject of street-types) and more akin to those met with at a fashionable watering place during the season. They had taken up a position on the slope of the hill where on either side of the road stand, or stood in those days, some pleasant, old-fashioned houses with their front gardens screened by a row of fine elms giving welcome shade from the westering sun. Here, then, to the accompaniment of a harp and violin, the woman, who had a pleasant and rather modest face, sang a ballad then very popular commencing with the words,

Who shall be fairest,
Who shall be rarest,
Who shall be first,
In the songs that we sing?

At the conclusion of the song we gave them a trifle and after a few minutes silence, Marcus said, 'I bet you anything that those people have had bad luck at the Derby and are trying to make it up.' Then he went on to sketch the probable chain of events that had led to the woman (who was above her surroundings) having at last come down to singing in the streets.

This little scene was vividly recalled to my memory by a remark in the Sydney *Bulletin* to the effect that Marcus Clarke occasionally made expeditions into out-of-the-way quarters of Melbourne in search of 'faces', during which 'the deceased author's strangest fancies were exhibited. For instance he would pretend to recognise in living members of the lower orders startling portraits of dead-and-gone celebrities who, he insisted, lived again in these persons. Thus a Collingwood bus driver was Julius Caesar and a barmaid in a Bourke Street Hotel "the positive presentment of Cleopatra." In a like manner he would discover extraordinary beauty in various types of both sexes where none to the ordinary observer existed.' Without meaning to assert that in his school days Marcus had actually developed any such theories, his rapid inductions from the woman's manner and actions in the instance given above (he had drawn his conclusions from the fact of her glancing round and blushing before she began her song) seem to indicate that the germs of them had already taken root in his mind.

Mr. Hamilton Mackinnon states in his short biography that he was unable to discover what Clarke's relations with the School authorities had been, but presumed from the fanciful dedication of an unpublished novel ('Chatteris') that the Headmaster (Dr. Dyne) 'had not failed to recognise the talents of his gifted pupil, nor yet be blind to his amiable weaknesses;' but I fear that the dedication in question was simply intended for satire. At least, I know that when Marcus won the prize for English verse (the subject being 'Julian the Apostate') the Headmaster disqualified him from receiving it on the ground that he had neglected his other studies. One can easily understand Marcus regarded this decision as an act of injustice not easily to be either forgotten or forgiven.

A certain passage in the biography of Anna Kingsford might with almost equal truth have been penned of the school-life of Marcus Clarke:

> independent of judgement, bent on the meanings of things as against their appearances, heedless of persons ... and keenly resenting injustice and oppression, Annie Bonus was scarcely likely to be a *persona grata* with the authorities ... they naturally confounded the cravings of a large and highly vitalised nature for expansion and unfoldment with the wilfulness of a rebel against all the proprieties, and accordingly regarded her as one whose example could not fail to be detrimental to others. Hence it came that, while her talents were recognised, her character was

mistaken, with the result of enhancing and confirming that disposition to revolt against conventional limitations with which she seemed herself to have been born.

However, if no great favourite with the other tutors, Marcus was always on excellent terms with the drawing master. One of his boyish ambitions (at least for a time) had been to distinguish himself as an artist, and although I do not think he ever attained to much skill in technical execution, the strong love of art remained with him for life, as can be gathered from his essays, more particularly from those on Gustave Doré and on the pictures in the National Gallery at Melbourne. I remember how much he admired a certain watercolour-painting possessed by my father – a copy of Leslie's 'Little Brigand' in the National Gallery (London) – and how he alluded to it in one of his letters in after years. Soon after his arrival in Melbourne he referred to Chevalier, the artist who accompanied His Majesty King Edward (when Prince of Wales) to India and who in his earlier years devoted much time to the study of Australian scenery, in the following terms, 'We have a real live artist here. I mean an artist in the true sense of the word; a Monsieur Chevalier. His pictures are very clever – perhaps too microscopic; remind one of Birket Foster and Olssen mixed together.'

An Australian writer, George Sutherland, remarks of the landscape-painters of Victoria:

> No one who has not seen the peculiar and almost mysterious effect of sunlight in the Australian forests could adequately appreciate the painting of some of the best Australian landscape-painters. The vertical foliage of the trees – casting shadows – and yet admitting the light – the floating mists of the hills – the mellow browns and olive greens of the bushes – and, above all, the clear brightness of the sky overhead, produce effects which must be seen to be understood.

But Marcus was on the spot, and although when he expressed his admiration for Chevalier, he had been but a short time in Victoria and was not so well acquainted as he afterwards became with the peculiarities of the bush scenery, he had probably, nevertheless, seen sufficient to enable him to recognise and appreciate the merits of the painter in question.

Chapter 4

Slight attack of smallpox. – Early convalescence. – Our manner of spending a half-holiday during the summer term at Highgate grammar school. – Marcus's inability to enter the army and his intention to qualify for the Army Medical Service. – Reasons for abandoning this intention and substituting the Foreign Office. – Swimming and riding lessons. – The unfortunate influences of his home life. – His ideas on the popular fallacy of the happiness of one's school days. – The nature of the events that brought them prematurely to a close. – The origin probably of those ideas.

One summer evening not long after the episode of the street-singers, Marcus complained of a bad headache. It was worse the following morning and proved to be the precursor of a mild attack of smallpox (of which there had been one or two cases that term) so that he was at once removed to lodgings in a quiet part of the town and a sick nurse engaged to attend him. When he reappeared at school after the midsummer holidays perfectly restored to health, there was scarcely any trace of the disease on his fresh, young face and he had brought back with him some amusing anecdotes of the sayings and doings of his sick nurse (one partaking more of the nature of Mrs. Gamp than of the modern variety) probably evoked by his characteristic methods of drawing her out during his period of convalescence.

After his recovery he grew rapidly and his mind developed still more rapidly even than his body, rendering a most fascinating companion. It was his conversation that was so delightful. On the school half-holidays he and I would frequently slip away unobserved from the cricket field and ramble about the adjoining Ken Wood, as I have seen it written, well known to the inhabitants of the northern suburbs of the great metropolis. Strolling in its shady glades during the spring and summer season or under the fir trees on Hampstead Heath near the Spaniards Inn (the spot mentioned in the prologue to his novel *For the Term of his Natural Life* as the scene of the murder of Lord Bellasis) we passed away the time in confidential chat and discussion of the chances life offered as viewed through those rose-coloured glasses, said to be the natural lenses of youth but, not unfrequently, instead of discussion my part would consist in listening as Marcus gave expression to the ideas with which his brain was teeming, for he sometimes on these occasions put into words his vivid and beautiful daydreams, either the spontaneous creations of his fancy or suggested by some line in Virgil or Horace (part of that morning's classwork) or perhaps by some phrase in the novel he had been surreptitiously reading at odd moments during the preceding week. Such a passage as the following will best illustrate my meaning:

At length, above a door of ivory, half-hidden by a purple curtain, I saw perched upon the bust of Pallas the mocking figure of a raven. The door yielded, and I entered. I was in a long apartment giving on a balcony open to the night, and as I entered, a lady clad in white came towards me. I knew her at once. It was the Lady Lenore!

Lenore! The lost Lenore! She who for ever waits and for ever eludes our passionate arms! Dante called her Beatrice, Petrarch Laura, Burns knew her as Mary, Byron as – but why multiply names? She is for all of us, this impossible woman …

Lenore!

She gave me two cool hands, and kissed me.

At last, then! At last, Lenore! The Raven prophesied falsely. Our pain and sorrow, our 'strange, unsatisfied longing', (note the quotation from his friend A. L. Gordon's verses) are over, and at last – oh other half of my soul – I have and hold thee!

She did not speak, but her clear eyes said more than words, and her slight figure trembled in my arms.

I drew her to the window, and with brain and blood on fire, pointed to the vessels at anchor at the quay …

She raised her head from my shoulder and looked around. In the far east, where the waves tumbled white upon the shore, trembled the dawn. The moon was fading, the city, the river, and the enchanted gardens lay lapped in a mysterious light – alas!

> The light that never was on sea or land,
> The consecration and the poet's dream.

'Come', I repeated; 'stern Heaven is kind at last, and we have met, why should we part again?'

But even as I pleaded in tones that had perhaps too much of earth in them for that fair spirit, she seemed to withdraw from me. One glance, sad and tender, pitying and hopeful, thrilled me, a farewell kiss, pure as fire, light as a falling roseleaf, brushed my lips, and – I was alone!

I do not mean to assert that quite such finished word-pictures as the above were drawn for my benefit on these occasions, but when the fancy swayed him, his thoughts would take shape in language sufficiently akin to warrant my quoting this passage as a fair sample of the brilliant, metaphysical soap bubbles thrown off by his powerful imagination. Let it not however be for a moment supposed that as a boy Marcus Clarke was a mere dreamer, absorbed in his own wayward fancies and but half alive to the realities of his surroundings. Nothing would be further from the truth. His proud, reserved nature seldom revealed itself even to his intimates, and to the majority of his school fellows he appeared to be merely a laughter-loving and original sort of boy, 'ready', as the phrase runs, 'for any mischief,' although the more observant may perhaps have noticed that he was a youth of moods who, when slighted or offended, could easily hold his own. But he was possessed of abundant tact and it was more natural to him to be sunny and pleasant-mannered than disagreeable and morose. And above all he had the gracious gift of laughter and high spirits, although perhaps not of a quality to survive the cares and anxieties that misfortune or rather his own fatally thriftless, happy-go-lucky disposition brought in its train in after-life.

Some two years before he left school in circumstances which I shall presently explain, it had been settled that he should study with a view to qualifying for an army-surgeon, since unfortunately the weakness in his left arm was held to disbar him from entering the active branch of the service as a profession. Be it well understood, however, lest a wrong impression should be conveyed by the foregoing and previous references to this bodily defect, that up to the time of his leaving England at all events, the fact of his left arm being shorter than his right was quite imperceptible to the ordinary observer, and as the events of his after-life prove, never incapacitated him from taking the most active forms of bodily exercise, although it may be that it was for this reason, as Dr. Moloney says, that 'he wore a sac coat with his left hand pocketed.' He wrote to me, however, with reference to this entering the Army Medical Service, 'I am afraid that the chance of my smoking my cigar and swearing "I'm on duty" will be small (quoting an old song concerning military life entitled "Cigars and Cognac") as my arm, you must know, prevents me altogether from entering the army.' He had with boyish eagerness and determination made a personal appeal to the Commander-in-Chief (the Duke of Cambridge) and had received a kindly-worded reply but it was to the effect that it was unhappily impossible to grant the favour demanded. The result was that the Foreign Office was substituted by his father for the Army Medical Service.

Nevertheless he had gradually become more robust and used to take riding lessons during the holidays, while at school he took to cricket and practised swimming and diving under the instruction of Beckwith, the then champion swimmer of the Thames, at a pond in Lord Mansfield's beautifully wooded meadow where the grammar school boys were allowed to bathe. There was a rough plank, secured to a beam, serving as a diving-board, some six or seven feet above the surface of the pond in question, which was of considerable depth, and from this board Marcus would take a header fearlessly enough, sometimes diving right down to the bottom, bringing up in his hands some weeds and gravel as a proof that he had touched it. He was still, be it remembered, but a slip of a boy at the time, although no novice in the art of swimming, having had some previous practice during the midsummer holidays passed at Deal and Folkestone; a friend of his father's being Rector of Great Mongeham near Deal.

I have alluded to his singing but he had not much voice, although extremely fond of music, and was familiar with the many popular airs from *Dinorah*, *L'Elisir d'Amore*, *Il Trovatore* and *La Traviata*, all of them operas then so frequently given and which he had heard with his father or in the company of the gay sightseers from Aldershot and Woolwich of whom he gossiped afterwards to his readers. 'Life is vanity we know' – so runs his essay on the pursuit of pleasure – 'but still we go on living and loving and making fools of ourselves until one day the skeleton taps us on the shoulder and we vanish from among the dancers –

> Life is but an idle dream,
> Be happy while we may

as the lady in the naughty opera sings in the words of Herrick.' The liberty accorded at home – liberty to go astray unchecked – came to be regarded by him in after years with disgust and filled his soul with bitterness leading him to describe the associates with whom he had been thrown by parental indifference or obtuseness as 'middle-aged Mephistopheles … cynical, well-bred, worshippers of Self who realise in the nineteenth century that notion of the devil which was invented by early Christians.' The extent of liberty accorded him when home for the holidays may be judged of by an extract from a letter written during the last year he spent at school, and dated from his father's house: 'I must tell you of a little escapade of mine which does not show much practice in my preaching. I went to spend a few days with a fellow I know whose 'governor' has a villa on Lake Como and knows mine … I stayed two days with him on one of which we dined with two opera girls (chorus-girls), the opera being closed …'; or by the blasé tone (for a schoolboy of those days) of the following:

> I went home yesterday and saw Lord Dundreary (*Our American Cousin*) for the second time but it was very stale. The play is a take-off of the English aristocrats and has amused London for the last two months.
>
> I left after the first two acts … I suppose you have not heard of the Randolph Stewart affair. It is about two officers of the Guards betting on the spelling of the word 'reindeer' and it is asserted that they had looked out the word previously in Johnson (who spells it 'raindeer') and thus cheated the other man (a Mr. Jen Bröck). The Jockey Club met to discuss the case and column after column of the *Times* has been filled with letters on the subject. I dined at Woolwich yesterday with my cousin and met a fellow who knows Randolph Stewart (one of the guardsmen referred to) intimately and he says that his character is most honourable. The dispute is still in abeyance but if it is decided against them, both will be cashiered. I saw M. yesterday (of whom I told you) in Brook Street....'

Thus the allusions in his own stories and essays to the curious experiences of this period of his life had at least some foundation in fact. He never professed to be very happy at school nor to have any particular affection for the majority of his schoolfellows and yet his nature was an affectionate and responsive one. He may have felt that, although enjoying a surface popularity as an amusing boy, he was not really understood or appreciated. In an essay entitled 'Speech days and school days' he concludes with the following apostrophe, which, I am sure, came from his heart,

It is a popular notion that school days are the happiest days of one's life. Are they? I ask it boldly of Tomkins who has been 'kept in' to learn one hundred lines of the sixth book of the *Æneid*; of Snivellor Quintus, who has been torn from the perusal of the 'scalp-hunters' to fag out in the cricket field; of Bloggs Secundus whose rich and rare plum cake has been incontinently devoured by a large creature with red whiskers, a ring, and a reputation for smoking and intrigue who calls himself 'Cock of the school'; of you, luckless Tommy Tug, whose head has been broken by a fierce Oppidan in a Lilliputian town and gown riot; of you, Hon. Claude Tufton, who, despite your quarterings, have been caught returning from Christopher's and will be democratically switched tomorrow? What say the skeleton-drawing Thomas Traddles, the luckless David Copperfield, the unhappy Paul Dombey? The happiest days of one's school days? A thousand times, 'No'!

But long before this passage appeared in print, in one of his earlier letters to me, he had soliloquised on his school days in somewhat the same vein: 'When one looks back upon those times, one wonders how it was one hated them so. It seems a wise dispensation that one only remembers the sweets and forgets the bitters … For oh! the heart-burnings, the miseries, the vexations, the birchings, the humiliations!' Perhaps it was the painful nature of the events that suddenly brought his school days to a close and the mental shock he then sustained rather than any of the minor troubles of a schoolboy's life that prompted him to write in this strain, for he had been a lad of too buoyant and high-spirited a character to be daunted by petty trials and annoyances.

But these events were such as to impress him painfully and formed a sort of moral Rubicon, a sharp line of division between his boyish years of careless ease, mirth and prosperity and his maturer youth and early manhood of disillusion, struggle and endeavour; between pleasant, luxurious surroundings and new unfamiliar, uncongenial ones; between a season of abundant pocket money and one when want of means brought many carking cares and many difficulties with which he, from want of training, and owing to his naturally careless and generous disposition, was ill fitted to cope. For before he had quite attained his seventeenth birthday, fate dealt him a sudden blow, not very dissimilar to that sustained by another young man of genius some years previously (Coventry Patmore) the details of which must form the subject of another chapter.

Chapter 5

Illness and death of W. Hislop Clarke. – The confusion in his affairs. – Result of the investigations of his executors. – Change in Marcus's circumstances and prospects. – His cousin's liberality. – Resolve to emigrate to Australia. – Interval before leaving England. – How filled up. – Composition of the verses 'The Lady of Lynn.' – Preamble to the original MS. – Nature of the poem. – Farewell visit to us at Oak Hill, Hampstead. – Marcus's personal appearance at the time of his leaving England. – His character as exhibited in youth.

A passage in Marcus Clarke's story 'Human Repetends' (already referred to in my first chapter) is cited by Hamilton Mackinnon in his *Memorial Volume* as being to his knowledge autobiographical:

> My father died suddenly in London, and to the astonishment of the world left me nothing. His expenditure had been large, but as he left no debts, his income must have been proportionate to his expenditure. The source of this income, however, it was impossible to discover. An examination of his banker's book showed only that large sums (always in notes or gold) had been lodged and drawn out, but no record of speculations or investments could be found among his papers. My relatives stared, shook their heads, and insulted me with their pity. The sale of furniture, books, plate, and horses, brought enough to pay the necessary funeral expenses and leave me heir to some eight hundred pounds. My friends of the smoking-room and of the supper-table philosophised on Monday, cashed my I. O. U.s on Tuesday, were satirical on

Wednesday, and cut me on Thursday. My relatives said 'Something must be done,' and invited me to stay at their houses until that vague substantiality should be realised and offers of employment were generously made, but to all proposals I replied with sudden disdain, and, desirous only of avoiding those who had known me in my prosperity, I avowed my resolution of going to Australia.

The real facts were the following. During the autumn of 1862, W. Hislop Clarke was taken ill and died, after some weeks of suffering, on December 1st in a nursing home at Stoke Newington. Some time before death ensued, his intellect had become disordered and Marcus always referred to his illness as having been of a very painful character. By his will, dated a few years previously, he had left his property in trust for his son until the latter should have attained the age of twenty-five. The idea prevalent among his relatives and friends had always been that W. Hislop Clarke was a man of substantial means, if not wealth, and their astonishment was great when it transpired that he had left but very little indeed for his son to inherit.

The small property called 'Belmont,' near Lifford, County Donegal, originally I believe bequeathed to him, had passed, it appeared, into the possession of another member of the family and the only documents of value found in his box at his banker's were the title deeds of three houses in St. Martin's Lane which, with a certain balance in cash, and the pictures, books and furniture of the house in Leonard Place, Kensington, constituted the whole of his possessions. Even on the houses in St. Martin's Lane there was mortgage of nearly fifteen hundred pounds (£1500) ... Perhaps the facts are more forcibly summed up in a letter written soon after Marcus's arrival in Australia than in any words of mine, or even of his own, when disguised in the half-truths of fiction:

> I remember, when my father was first taken ill, his telling me that I should be well provided for. He worked too hard and too long; which produced his final and fatal attack of paralysis ... My cousins thought that he was worth at least seventy thousand pounds (£70,000). Judge then of our consternation at finding affairs in the greatest confusion, the house in Ireland (left him by his elder brother) sold, and only a certain sum at his banker's. Records of nothing! His cheque books showing large sums of money drawn out of his banking account with no trace of where they went to ... I will not detail the sad events which took place on his illness. Suffice it to say that no one could touch the money in the bank and there was no money for me! But this money I shall get when I am twenty-five.

Such then were the circumstances when, with the assistance of his cousins, principally that particular cousin, Captain (afterwards Lieutenant-General Sir Andrew) Clarke, R. E. who had always been on terms of close friendship with him, and had received many kindnesses from W. Hislop Clarke (his paternal uncle), Marcus was enabled to sail for Melbourne with approximately the sum mentioned in 'Human Repetends.' That is to say, with a sum which, had his talents been at all of the commercial order, was possibly sufficient wherewith to have laid the foundations of a fortune in those days of enterprise and expansion in the colony of Victoria. But although staggered by the financial reverse that had befallen him, Marcus was by temperament and training too careless about money and too generous and free-handed with it, to be moved to the study of that severe and systematic economy which is the indispensable stepping-stone to an improvement of one's circumstances and to regaining some degree of financial independence. Nothing would probably have induced him to adopt the course of conduct which is supposed to lead from the possession of the proverbial half-crown to that of a large fortune.

He paid us a brief farewell visit at Oak Hill, Hampstead, coming over for a couple of days from Charlton, near Woolwich, where he had been staying with his cousins. Although the first shock of his bereavement was over, and his manner still eager and affectionate, he was – naturally enough – subdued and reserved, and reticent about his future plans and recent reverses. He did however mention that, shortly before he was taken ill, his father had promised him an allowance of three hundred a year until he was twenty-five if he were able to gain admittance to the Foreign Office. In another letter he dwells on his bewilderment of mind at this period. 'Imagine – if you can – my position before I left England. I was nominated to the Foreign Office and was about to go to France for three years when suddenly the whole prospect faded away! ... My cousins told me that they thought they could get me a commission in the Line' – probably knowing nothing of his physical defect and the refusal of the Army medical authorities to pass him even for that branch of the service. 'I could not take it and in a sort of hope of getting rid of things or desire of leaving England and escaping the pity of friends, decided to come to Australia.'

The interval between his adoption of this resolve and of carrying it out was filled up by visits to the houses of friends or relatives and utilized to some extent by a hasty attempt to qualify himself at the eleventh hour for a commercial career, as the following passage from a letter of his written from Charlton (Woolwich) shows:

I fag at arithmetic, accounts and book-keeping all day and read in the evenings. The
books I have been reading are Mrs. Gaskell's *North and South* and two historical works,
Dr. Russell's letters from the seat of war in America (republished from the *Times*) and
the first two volumes of Kinglake's *Invasion of the Crimea*. I was disappointed with the
first and overwhelmed by the second.

He enclosed some photographs of himself just taken and a copy of verses, 'The Lady of
Lynn', for which he requested my brother, Gerard, to draw him an illustration.[8] This was
accordingly supplied and some slight alterations in the wording of one or two lines
suggested at the same time. The latter were adopted and two more verses added.

Soon after his arrival in Melbourne, Marcus posted a copy of the poem to me
with a view to its insertion in *Once a Week*, a periodical then at the zenith of its
popularity. Some of the best novels of the day had first seen the light in its pages,
as for instance George Meredith's *Evan Harrington*, *The Silver Chord* by Shirley
Brookes, *Ready-money Mortiboy* and others, whilst verses by Tennyson, Swinburne,
Rossetti, Meredith, F. L. Lampson, Austin Dobson and other distinguished authors
occasionally appeared on it with woodcuts by Millais, F. Walker, John Leech,
Hablot K. Browne, Green, Du Maurier, rising or successful artists of the early
sixties. We three had jointly taken it in at school, (the editor, Edward Walford
was a family friend of ours) and Marcus was thus justified in hoping that, as he
expressed it, 'With an engraving by Walker or Green of the Fiend in the pulpit
with the flickering taper throwing his shadow along the wall, it would be accepted.'
Unhappily such was not the case; although on what grounds such striking and
uncommon verses were rejected, I am at a loss to this day to understand.

I returned the MS to Marcus and never saw the lines again until I re-read them
in *The Marcus Clarke Memorial Volume*. What impression they would have made on
a professional critic I do not know, but probably even he would have been struck by
the weird and ghastly imagery and the riotous fancy displayed in them; the original
and spontaneous creation of a boy of sixteen. The spirit that breathes in this strange
ballad is akin to that of Edgar Poe's 'Raven' or 'Ulalume' or of his more morbid
prose tales such as 'The Fall of the House of Usher' and others of that description.
It might aptly be described as a 'chimera in rhyme' (to adopt the appellation of
the author of *Richard Savage* for his weird poem, 'Ippolito'). I took a copy of the

---

8   Father Gerard S.J. died 1889.

original MS of Marcus's verses which contained the following preamble, omitted in the published version of them in the *Memorial Volume*:

> In some part of England, there is a superstition that any person visiting a church at midnight on St. John's Eve will behold the spirits of all those who are to be married within the year. A legend of the town of Lynn (of which the following is an amplification) relates that on a certain stormy St. John's Eve in the reign of Queen Elizabeth, the Lady of the Manor, known by the title of the 'Lady of Lynn,' visited the parish church for this purpose and was never seen again. As her cloak, much torn and discoloured, was found in the porch, it was currently reported among the peasantry that the unfortunate woman, who was noted for her daring impiety and wickedness, had been carried off by demons and become the bride of the Fiend himself.

I will take the liberty of quoting two verses, the first and the eleventh, as especially interesting both from a literary and biographical point of view:

> The moonbeam bright
> With its silver light
> The topmost foliage laces,
> But under the wall
> In shadow, lies all
> Where the wind and the leaves run races,
> And the tombstones white
> Through the murky night
> Gleam out like dead men's faces.

The picturesque force of these lines is only surpassed by the ghastly imagery and rollicking swing of the eleventh verse,

> He pressed her brow with his fleshless jaw,
> He patted her cheek with his horny paw,
> She lost her sight, she lost her hearing
> Into her brain the kiss was searing
> Flesh from bone his touch was tearing
> Ho! Kiss me, Dearest! 'Tis a Sin
> To faint at thy bridal, My Lady of Lynn!

But for a certain grotesqueness that perhaps rather mars them, due probably to the author's youth, these verses might almost compare with Hood's 'Haunted House', or even with Coleridge's 'Cristabel.'

There is another passage in 'Human Repetends' of an autobiographical character. Hugh Pontifex, when reduced from affluent circumstances to comparative poverty by the sudden death of his father, and staggered by the discovery of the slenderness of his own inheritance, resolves to retain an engraving which he has always treasured. It is the portrait of a woman whose identity could never be discovered and he takes it with him to Australia. Marcus himself reserved from the sale of his father's effects a fine engraving of Millais's well known picture, 'The Huguenots'. It was hung in the study of his house at Brighton (near Melbourne) and he cherished to the last an extraordinary affection for it. The picture in question is still in the possession of the author's family. So that two incidents in this story were those of his own early life and the shadowy personality of Hugh Pontifex was but a sufficiently transparent disguise for the very human and sensitive one of Marcus Clarke.

The photograph we selected (from those sent) is that of a slightly built, gentlemanly looking youth with a well-shaped head, oval face and fairly regular features. He is standing in an easy, unconstrained position with an expression of face that seems indicative of his mental attitude towards the world: the outcome of mixed feelings; half amusement, half contempt. The portraits of him in later life show that his face had become more thoughtful and acquired a careworn, anxious expression, as might have been expected; but the fine, wistful eyes have not changed and must have been compelling to the last.

During his brief farewell visit we went to see the preparations being made in the London streets for the wedding of the Prince of Wales afterwards His Majesty, King Edward for which event Marcus would have liked to remain, but his ship, the *Wellesley*, was timed to leave Plymouth before the date in question.[9] His two days visit drew to a close. We exchanged farewells and mutual promises to correspond. Finally with some specially kind words at parting which (in view of his reserved disposition) made a deep and lasting impression on me, he left us towards the close of the second day, returning that night to Charlton and quitting London for ever the following morning to join the *Wellesley* at Plymouth.

---

9   March 10th 1863.

This seems then an opportune point at which to pause and try to summarise the leading features of his character, as they appeared to us, at this critical junction of his life. His naturally sunny and sweet-tempered disposition occasionally was marred by fits of caprice and irritability – defects of the literary and artistic temperament (very often met with in those possessed of it). Keenly alive to the Beautiful in nature or art, he seemed to have, nevertheless, a decided bias in favour of whatever was strange, mournful or grotesque. Although, however, *au fond*, his temperament inclined towards that 'weird melancholy' which he himself characterized as the keynote of Edgar Allan Poe's poetry, he knew how to suppress this side of his character from the observation of his schoolfellows, most of whom supposed him to be given up entirely to the coining of jokes and the composition of clever nonsense, incapable of serious thought. They were of course mistaken but although he was so much averse to 'wearing his heart upon his sleeve for daws to peck at' as to partly mislead his companions, they were possibly not so much mistaken in their estimate of his character as those who only knew him in after-life might have supposed. For the change wrought in him by the tragedy of his father's death and the collapse of his prospects in so sudden and unexpected a manner was obvious enough to my brother and myself during that farewell visit to us. He was no longer the flippant, amusing schoolboy we had hitherto known but a youth who had tasted of 'the tree of knowledge and of the cup of sorrow'. One could, however, aptly apply to him the very words of Hannay in his memoir of Poe:

> Always he signalised himself by early intellect, quickly learning all that came in his way, brilliant, vivacious, passionate … this youth, –
>
> To whom was given
> So much of earth, so much of heaven
> And such impetuous blood….

Chapter 6

His first letter after leaving England. – Incidents and impressions of the voyage. – Narrow escape of a boy belonging to the crew. – Ceremonies on crossing the line. – Portrait of the only pretty girl on board. – Description of a sunset at sea. – The resemblance of his ideas on the sunset to those of R. L. Stevenson's at Vailima. – Seabirds. – Catching an albatross. – Sighting the Australian coast. – Arrival at Melbourne.

The first letter I received from Marcus, written at intervals during the voyage, contains a passage bearing a striking resemblance to one of R. L. Stevenson's letters from Vailima, but of this anon. The whole letter is so interesting that I will quote the greater part, as it is rather in the nature of a diary:

> After undergoing the most fearful sufferings I fulfil my promise of writing. We left Plymouth – it seems to me years back – and after being sick to the utmost 'tenison of nature' in the 'Bay of Biscay Oh!' we are now becalmed off the Line. The thermometer is 98 in the shade. In the sun on the quarterdeck it is over 160! You may form some idea of the heat when I tell you that the pitch in the deck-seams is melting and sticks to one's boots … The nights in the tropics are most heavenly, deliciously cool, with a large moon, and the ocean, as far as one can see in the ship's wake, one mass of flame. About 11 p.m. the ladies retire and the men chat with the officers on watch, drink cold coffee and smoke the light cigar. You cannot think how cooling and soothing in

this hot weather is the fragrant weed. All the same, this floating in the middle of the ocean is rather slow and I wish we were at Melbourne.

He proceeds to narrate an incident that was near having a tragic termination:

Some of the crew had been sent into the hold for fresh water and one of the party, a boy, managed to get left behind, was not missed for a time and was in fact forgotten. While the hatch was being battened down again faint cries and knocking sounds were heard but the men at work appear to have attributed these sounds to some comrade who was having a little practical joke at their expense and wished to startle them. Consequently they paid no attention. But about an hour afterwards one of the boys in the Officer's Watch was missing. Search was made for him unsuccessfully and it was suggested that he was in the hold. The carpenter tore up the hatch and there stretched underneath, lying on a bale of goods, the little fellow was discovered, half-suffocated and panic-stricken. When at length he recovered, he said that thinking he had been left behind by way of a practical joke, he had knocked, but obtaining no answer realized what had occurred and concluded he was buried alive; for this it would have been to all intents and purposes, as the hatch would not have been opened again for a considerable time and the space where he was found lying was not more than two or three yards square.

The mock ceremonies attendant on crossing the line are then briefly touched upon. Although I believe practically a thing of the past (an exception was made during the Prince and Princess of Wales' voyage to Australia but the ceremonies were only revived in a very modified form I gathered from the published accounts) they were usual at the date I am writing of and Marcus remembered that they had figured largely in the nautical stories we had both of us read in our school days. 'We, the passengers (he explains), got off by payment of a tip to the old buffer who personated Neptune but the midshipmen and men before the mast were operated upon with much success. This has been so often described that I shall not attempt it. Suffice it to say that the operation of shaving is the most loathsome one that can be conceived.' Readers of Mark Twain will find that that amusing writer's views on the subject coincide with those of Marcus Clarke. He says in *More Tramps Abroad*:

Afternoon; crossed the Equator … We had no fool ceremonies, no fantasies, no horseplay. All that sort of thing has gone out. In old times a sailor, dressed as Neptune, used to come in over the bows with his suite and lather up and shave everybody who was crossing the equator for the first time, and then cleanse these unfortunates by swinging them from the yard-arm and ducking them three times in the sea. This was considered funny. Nobody knows why.

But continuing to moralise in his droll way on the subject, Mark Twain comes to the conclusion that the ceremonies originated in a natural longing to relieve the monotony of the long voyages of former days. Probably he is right and in any case his opinion must be recorded with respect, not only on account of his own reputation but *also* because he has both spoken and written in terms of warm commendation of the literary work of Marcus Clarke, expressing surprise (at the time of his visit to Australia) that more appreciation was not accorded the former in the land of his adoption.

Marcus next presents me with a portrait of the 'only pretty girl on board' not unlike, be it observed, the picture he has drawn of Sylvia Vickers in *For the Term of his Natural Life*.

> Very 'petite', with exquisitely small hands and feet; hands indeed so small that one can see every little vein and muscle, and rosy in the palms like a pink sea-shell. Hair brown with a ray, so to speak, through it, which gives it the appearance of burnished copper, the said hair curling like flame and blown back from off her forehead and sometimes playing about her eyes like floss silk. Eyes dark, liquid brown, with somewhat of a Spanish glance and at times brilliant and flashing, then, when you interest her, melting and swimming with a luxurious tenderness. Her face is, if anything, of a classical cut, the nose small with a sort of swelling and curving in the nostril that reminds me of a thoroughbred horse. Her forehead is wide and rather low and tinted with blue in the temples. The mouth is small with a curve in the upper lip that shows the white, pearly front teeth below.

From this very telling and life-like word-picture of a woman I pass on to that of a sunset that much impressed him, following it up with the passage from R. L. Stevenson's letter with which I have compared it:

> Last night there was an exquisite sunset, the whole sky one large fleecy cloud, save in the extreme East where it suddenly stopped like a curtain, leaving the rest of the Heavens a pure apple green. As the sun sank, the fleece became pink, rosy-red, and

finally like blood-red wool, torn with a reaping-hook in pillows or haycocks; while the apple green became violet and then saffron.

The sun slowly dipped, a bloody disk, into the creaming waves and, as he did so, one long, milky cloud like a milky, opaque opal shadowed out (for I can use no other term) from the mass of delicate, crimson foam and completely obscured it so that the horizon and a small space above it was in this form:

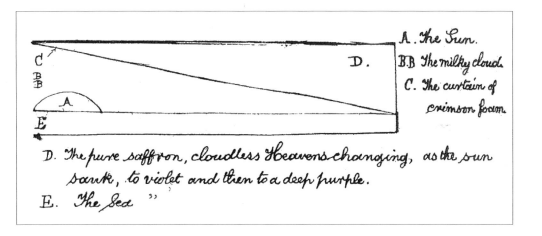

A. The Sun.
B.B The milky cloud.
C. The curtain of crimson foam.

D. The pure saffron, cloudless Heavens changing, as the sun sank, to violet and then to a deep purple.
E. The Sea ”

Now for the passage in Stevenson's letter to which the above bears a resemblance:

As I rode down last night about 6, I saw a sight I must try to tell you of. In front of me, right over the top of the forest into which I was descending, was a vast cloud. The front of it accurately represented the somewhat rugged, long-nosed and beetle-browed profile of a man, crowned by a huge Kalmuck cap; the flesh part of was of a heavenly pink, the cap, the moustache, the eyebrows were of a bluish gray; to see this with its childish exactitude of design and colour, and hugeness of scale – it covered at least 25 degrees – held me spellbound. As I continued to gaze, the expression began to change; he had the exact air of closing one eye, dropping his jaw, and drawing down his nose; had the thing not been so imposing, I could have smiled; and then almost in a moment, a shoulder of leaden-coloured bank drove in front and blotted it.

My attention spread to the rest of the cloud and it was a thing to worship.

It rose from the horizon, and its top was within thirty degrees of the zenith; the lower parts were like a glacier in shadow, varying from dark indigo to a clouded white in exquisite gradations. The sky behind, so far as I could see, was all of a blue already enriched and darkened by the night, for the hill had what lingered of the sunset. But the top of my Titanic cloud flamed in broad sunlight, with the most excellent softness and brightness of fire and jewels, enlightening all the world. It must have been far higher than Mount Everest, and its glory, as I gazed up at it out of the night, was beyond wonder …

I could not resist trying to reproduce this in words as a specimen of these incredibly beautiful and imposing meteors of the tropic sky that make so much of my pleasure here; though a ship's deck is the place to enjoy them.

O what AWFUL scenery from a ship's deck, in the tropics! People talk about the Alps, but the clouds of the trade wind are alone for sublimity.

It is particularly these last few lines as well as some similarity in both writers' description of natural phenomena that led me to quote the above passage from the letter of R. L. Stevenson. With regard to Marcus Clarke's account of the sunset, occasionally, no doubt, one comes across an equally good piece of word-painting, but not often; especially in the letters of a youth of seventeen writing on board ship to an old school-chum in careless intimacy. While perhaps to his fellow-passengers (to borrow the language of a novelist of the day) the miracles of sunrise and sunset were only the familiar indications of a celestial timepiece … there was here an eye keen to note the play of light and shadow and colour, the glint of wave and the spume of tossing seas, the gracious fairness of cloud and bird and blossom, the magic of sunlight sails in the offing … a soul haply absorbing nature to give it back one day as art.

After experiencing some rather rough weather in those seas where, according to De Beauvoir, 'more than a thousand meters separate the summits of two succeeding waves', there being 'at this distance from the Cape of Good Hope and Cape Horn, no land to break the force of the armies of waves' and where after a storm many varieties of seabirds, including the albatross, hover round the ship, Marcus's letter continues:

We have got from hot to cold weather now and great coats and cloaks are the order of the day. There are lots of enormous birds about. I caught one (a kind of albatross, white, with black wings) by means of a line and a hook baited with pork. The doctor and I have skinned it. It measures seven and a half feet from wing to wing. I will send home the skin to my friends when I reach Melbourne, and if I get another, you shall have it.

Not very long after this the Australian coast was sighted. Reflecting on these experiences of the voyage (probably akin to those of the great majority of voyagers to Australasia in those days) one can understand how he came to write in one of his chatty essays:

> To many thousands of colonists the names of the 'Eagle Line' the 'Black Ball', the 'White Star' and the 'Wigram and Green's'[10] lines of packets will be connected with their first view of the shores of Australia.

The *Wellesley* (in which he was a passenger) was one of Wigram and Green's line, and her voyage to Melbourne on this occasion terminated June 26th, 1863. Marcus landed with a feeling of intense relief that its tedious duration was over for it had lasted nearly one hundred days. Some twenty years earlier a voyage to New Zealand in a fast clipper had occupied one hundred and thirty eight days[11] whilst in the early decades of the nineteenth century a voyage to Australia was a matter of six or seven months.

The following passage from the diary of a voyager to Sydney of those days is significant too in its reference to the drawbacks of such a long spell on board ship:

> As we neared the end of our voyage it became very monotonous to some, as we were growing tired of one another; and to those who were going to an unknown country and who had heard a great deal more about that country than they had known prior to leaving, there was a dread of what the future might have in store for us.

No wonder that Marcus, always quickly tiring of any experience of which the novelty had worn off, wrote: 'At last arrived in Melbourne! Free from the ship and all its miseries!' Doubtless the latter were but minor discomforts for the letter concluded in a pleasant, bantering vein with some amusing anecdotes concerning the peculiarities of certain of his fellow-passengers.

He landed at Melbourne some five months after the imposing public funeral of the explorers, Burke and Wills, whose remains, brought in by Howitt and others

---

10   Now the 'Orient' Steam Navigation Company.
11   'The voyage took from August 26, 1843 to January 10, 1844, 138 days (four and a half months), more than thrice the length of a voyage to New Zealand today. And yet the ship was a veritable greyhound; she ran down every other boat, save one, leaving them far behind.' See 'A Pioneer Colonist's Story.' *National Review*, August 1909.

from the desert of the Interior, had been interred in the Melbourne Cemetery and the shadow of that calamity had not wholly passed away. Thus the step he had decided upon taking immediately after his father's death, when he learned of the change in his fortunes, was consummated; and in the words of Mr. Hamilton Mackinnon, 'the youth of bright fancies and disappointed hopes set foot in Melbourne.'

Chapter 7

Marcus's first ideas of how to start in life on his arrival at Melbourne. – His uncle, the judge, soon dissipates those notions. – A man about town. – His own social experiences and those of the ordinary newcomer to the Colony treated of in his essay on 'New Chums' and described in an unpublished article entitled 'A Day in Melbourne.' – Some preliminary observations upon this composition.

Influenced by the conversations he had heard on board the *Wellesley*, Marcus had arrived in Melbourne with a vague impression that it would not be very difficult to retrieve his pecuniary misfortunes by going into sheep farming, a pursuit the chitchat of the voyage had represented as very lucrative and promising. But he was quickly undeceived by his uncle (the county court judge previously alluded to) James Langton Clarke – who explained how chimerical were such ideas for a young man with only the very small amount of capital at his command that Marcus possessed. The judge promised however to use his influence with the directors of the Bank of Australasia to obtain a clerkship for him in that establishment as soon as there should be a vacancy.

Referring to the manner in which the leisure time at Marcus's disposal during the interval of waiting was filled up, Hamilton Mackinnon observes that after the manner of most 'New Chums' (with some cash at command and no direct restraining power at hand) Marcus 'set himself readily to work, fathoming the social and other depths of his new home.' The result of these studies from the life was partly embodied in a long letter to me so worded that with some slight omissions it could be published as a magazine article under the heading of 'A Day in Melbourne.' As, I think, will be freely admitted after perusal, it is by no means wanting in a certain vein of boyish, rollicking, Leveresque humour and vivacity – and there are in it some telling and graphic passages; but whether it conveyed a true reflexion of his first impressions of the city I have my doubts. Rather to my thinking it was inspired by Sala's *Gaslight and Daylight* (then very popular) and, with a view to catch on and amuse, a tone of grotesque exaggeration is adopted such as appears to commend itself to some readers as the essence of wit. Perhaps if the intention had only been to describe the outward characteristics of the city such a passage as the following from an ordinary handbook to Australia would have conveyed a clearer idea in a very few words:

> Melbourne is a chessboard city built on strict mathematical lines, its streets intersecting at right angles, the principal thoroughfares being of considerably greater width than is necessary or desirable in such a warm climate

whilst Tasma in one of her stories, *In Her Earliest Youth*, describes a day spent by two lovers, partly in the picture gallery of the Public Library (about which Marcus himself discoursed so pleasantly as will be seen anon) and partly under the shade of the sombre, native trees of the park, with happier effect.

Francis Adams remarks in a review of Clarke's and Gordon's work (contributed to the *Fortnightly*) that Melbourne appeared to him to be made up of curious elements:

> There is something of London in her, something of Paris, something of New York, and something of her own ... Melbourne has, what might be called, the *metropolitan tone*. The look on the faces of her inhabitants is the *metropolitan* look. These people live quickly; such as life presents itself to them, they know it: as far as they can see, they have no prejudices. 'I was born in Melbourne,' said the wife of a small bootmaker to me once, 'I was born in Melbourne, and I went to Tasmania for a bit, but I soon came back again. *I like to be in a place where they go ahead* ...' And she is a type of her city. 'Melbourne likes to go ahead.'

That this has always been one of her principal characteristics is proved by an interesting article Marcus Clarke himself contributed to the London *Daily Telegraph* in October 1880 on the occasion of the opening of the Melbourne Exhibition of that year. In his happy, graphic manner he therein sketched the history of the city from its earliest beginnings down to the date at which he was then writing. (The article in question appeared in the *Daily Telegraph* of November 16, 1880.)

There are one or two allusions in the letter or article 'A Day in Melbourne,' that at this distance of time would seem to require explanation. For instance, the allusion to the indignation of 'Seven Belgravian Mothers' had reference to some correspondence in the *Times* concerning the influence of the *demi-monde* on young men of fashion. Such topics were at that time a novelty for the press to handle and aroused some sensation. Then as to the behaviour of the imaginary 'New Chum' himself. The eccentricities of the numerous young men sent out to the colonies for a fresh start in life, (sometimes really with a view to getting rid of them) formed later on the subject of an article by Marcus in the *Australasian*, one of a series which almost immediately captured the public fancy and increased the circulation of the paper. Referring in this article to Dickens's enquiry as to what became of post-boys and donkeys, Marcus asks what becomes of these New Chums? For, he dryly remarks,

> If these young men are, and I suppose they must be, leaders of *ton*, and glasses of English fashion, it is to be regretted that they disappear so rapidly. As soon as one comes to know them by sight, they vanish from view altogether ... I find that they begin life at the Port Phillip or Scott's; that they play billiards frequently, and abuse the colony with immense gusto ... They are usually, so they say, connected with the aristocracy, and complain bitterly that 'there is no "society" in Victoria.' Yet with all this they seldom have introductions to anyone worth knowing, and are forced to consort with Jews, Turks, infidels, and heretics. In about a month the £100 scraped together by their widowed mothers, or saved from the wreck of their college allowance and unpaid college debts, is spent – and then?

Sometimes, it appears, a family friend – a squatter up-country – comes to the rescue and

> young Hopeful goes, and is put upon a rough bush horse, and made to ride in stock; or is sent to look after some fencing some ten miles from the home station; or is set to work foot-rotting, and soon finds out that life is not 'all beer and skittles'

but that more frequently no such *deus ex machina* makes his appearance.
Sometimes, continues the Peripatetic Philosopher (as Marcus signed himself at the
foot of these articles)

> the gorgeous butterfly of Collins Street comes to unutterable grief. His cheap finery
> wears out. Messrs. Moses'[12] garments wax rusty, and the gilt wears off his Brummagem
> jewellery. He falls, and great is his fall. One fine day he disappears, and men shake
> their heads for a day or two … The haunters of the Cafés and Varieties miss a familiar
> face, and one asks, 'What has become of young New Chum; I haven't seen him lately?'
> But the question is never satisfactorily answered, and I ask in vain – What becomes
> of all these young men?

Other Australian writers, however, solve the conundrum or hint at the sequel.

Readers of the novel by Tasma referred to above may remember the squatter
who coming across his father-in-law flying from justice and making his way across
the plains to the banks of the Murray, exclaims:

> I spotted the fellow first, you know … I took his measure at once you see. I've seen
> such a lot of these 'New Chums' one way or another. They knock down all their
> money at the first go off; and then there's nothing for them to do but to go and
> jackaroo up in Queensland.

Whilst George Sutherland, in his brightly written *Australia or England in the South*,
(explaining the phrase 'Colonial Experience') remarks much in the same vein:

> The youth who arrives in Australia from the old country for the purpose of being
> broken into the life of the Bush is a standing joke among 'Old Hands'. When he lands
> at Melbourne or Sydney he is clad in the usual *habiliments* of a Bond Street swell; he
> goes round to all the theatres and cafés; he picks up a few fast friends who help him to
> get rid of his loose cash and enjoy the fun of making him drunk occasionally, and finally
> if he escapes from their society with enough money to pay his travelling expenses up to
> some station, he is considered lucky. Then the breaking-in process commences.

---

12   Messrs. Moses were a well-known firm of cheap, advertising, London tailors in the sixties.

And the discomforts of the journey up-country having been detailed, the writer proceeds,

> If our 'Colonial Experience' youth has not had the good sense to abandon his swell clothes he will be throughout his journey, if not merry himself, yet 'the cause of mirth in others'. Going through among the clumps of small trees, he will hear on all sides, 'Now then, look out for that bell-topper (etc) …'

A writer on life at Johannesburg in the earlier years of the Rand says of the 'gentleman who has never been taught anything save a high regard for his family traditions,' that

> he finds himself laughed at and regarded as perfectly useless. Still, if he be plucky, he may find something to do. He can learn to be a waiter at cheap restaurant, and as he takes the orders of rough miners seated at rougher tables, he may sigh for the time when obsequious men in faultless attire waited on him. The old delights of London life, expensive luxury though it often prove, are gone for ever; and if amid the dust and sunshine he sees some companions of the saloon on the voyage out, he hurries down a bye-street,

whilst the experiences of a young friend of the writer's in Argentina were at first of a quite similar character.

Thus Marcus Clarke was true to life in his sketch of the manner in which a certain type of immigrant frequently inaugurated his sojourn in his new home. With these perhaps too discursive, introductory remarks, I submit the original to the reader's judgement and finally merely venture to hazard the opinion that at this distance of time from the date of its composition – apart from any question of style or of literary merit – the article has a value and an interest of its own from the sidelights it throws on the street and tavern life of the Melbourne of the sixties.

Chapter 8

'A Day in Melbourne'

An article written in the form of a letter from Marcus Clarke to the writer dated January 1865.

Most Englishmen have been everywhere and done nearly everything now-a-days. But although in France, Belgium, Italy, Turkey and Russia, India and America, the travelling Briton has come, seen and conquered, he is a being quite unknown at the Antipodes. Despite their close connection with England in trade, manners and religion, it is surprising how little very many Englishmen know about the Australian colonies. The writings of 'Go Ahead' Yankees[13] or the stories of some returned gold-diggers have been accepted in England as the faithful portraiture of life in Victoria at the present day. The colony is regarded by the majority of men at home as the

---

13   Possibly Dana is intended.

abode of 'diggers,' drunken and extravagant, and the paradise of squatters who farm a fabulous amount of acres and rear a fabulous number of sheep. The descriptions of *It is Never too Late to Mend* and *Geoffry Hamlyn*[14] (correct delineations of Australian life at the time they were written) together with some two-shilling Railway-bookstall 'sensations' of blood, murder, convicts, gold-digging and bullock-driving are taken by most people as accurate accounts of the everyday life of a resident in Melbourne in 1865.

Within the last twenty years, then, the changes which have taken place in the system of society and manner of life in the Australian colonies are hardly credible.

From a nest of wooden sheds built upon an unhealthy swamp, Melbourne has become a city already of some wealth and importance and the troops of drunken, blaspheming diggers who, maddened by the temporary possession of a few hundred pounds, ran riot in the streets, have given place to merchants, bankers and civilians, many rich beyond the average of their class, nearly all respectable and prosperous. The vast tracts of gum and wattle-trees which formerly surrounded the town have fallen beneath the axe of the settler, and already railways, running through miles of bush country, link together the principal towns. It is true that in the unsettled districts the natives are yet defending their hunting grounds as in the old days fifty years ago and that in New South Wales the daily journals teem with accounts of robberies and murders, but the resident in Victoria is as far removed from injury by these outbreaks as is the well-fed Kentish farmer in England from annoyance by the 'Derry Boys' or starving colliery rioters.

It is a common mistake for Englishmen in the Old Country to class all the settlements in the great Australian continent as one colony and to fancy that Dick going to Melbourne in '63 must of necessity meet Tom who sailed for Sydney in '42. The rough and tumble manner of living which was the characteristic of the place has now completely disappeared.

Melbourne is now as quiet and civilized a town as any in England or in the United States. Indeed, in its internal economy, it more resembles an American town than an English one; while the long streets which run in parallel lines, again crossed by others, thus dividing the buildings into huge squares or 'blocks', and the white-painted iron canopies which shade the pavement in front of nearly every shop,

---

14   Novels by Charles Reade and Henry Kingsley respectively.

together with the Yankee cars rattling up and down the thoroughfares, suggest to the stranger the idea that he is walking in Brownsville or Bunkum City.[15]

Though this is the appearance of the city, and the low life of it partakes of the same nature to some extent, the society is strictly English. Australians have already acquired a name for hospitality owing to the gentle blood which the torrent of younger sons, brief-less barristers and gentlemanly *émigrés* of all sorts from the upper and middle ranks of English society has infused into the old stock. In many cases the hospitality is of a nature that can be accepted with pleasure and gratification by the most fastidious. The 'good old times' are happily gone. One no longer sees the drunken diggers before mentioned rolling from tap to tap and flinging money like dust about them on all sides, and the carriages of these gentry no longer parade the streets filled with females dressed in rich silks and bedizened with gold and jewels. There are strange stories of these 'good old times', stories of diggers coming down from Bendigo or Ballarat for the getting rid of their earnings, dressing their wives in silks and velvet and being told by the smirking shopmen that the price of the stuff was only thirty guineas a yard and that it was the dearest in the shop, straightway paying fifty for it in order that Betsy or Polly might be more expensively dressed than her neighbours! Stories of lucky prospectors placing one pound notes sandwich-wise between two pieces of bread and eating them incontinently forthwith! Of men watering their horses with champagne and washing their brawny arms in the vintages of Burgundy and the Rhine – of ruffians with a taste for jewellery ordering barbarous *bijoux* of fine gold to be made for them by a certain day, paying for the same in advance and then disappearing for ever, being knifed in some drunken frolic!

Every old colonist has yards of this stuff at his fingers' ends and will horrify his listeners by the hour with hair-breadth 'scapes, extravagancies, chances, 'lucky finds' and the like – but Melbourne is a very different place now. The stranger or 'New Chum' landing at Sandridge[16] some four miles from the city has but to walk twenty yards and he is whisked up to Melbourne in a comfortable railway-carriage that would not disgrace the Great Western Railway at home.

On arrival where is he to go? Plenty of places, my friend. Look about you!

---

15   See note 19 with regard to Melbourne as in appearance an American city and to the limited amount of truth there is in this description.

16   The name of Sandridge has long been replaced by that of Port Melbourne.

Here is the Port Phillip Club Hotel, patronised by 'New Chums', being opposite the Railway Station or the Criterion in Collins Street beloved of merchants and rich men of trade; Scott's, the great resting place of squatters; or the Albion in Bourke Street, haunt of horsey men and 'sporting cards.' Be not bewildered by the plate-glass windows – gorgeous with many colours these last – or by the crowd at the doorway! If thou goest there, Oh blithe newcomer, take good heed not to play cards or billiards, neither bet, there be sharp men there and downy, and they will do thee utterly brown, Oh unsuspecting New Chum! What sayest thou to Port Phillip? Come! it is quiet and well-ordered.

Does the New Chum play billiards? He does a little. There is a capital billiard-room at the Port Phillip – a separable building away from the house – with an excellent table. See those two men playing now! One is Captain L'Encrier, the Chief Commissioner of Police, and the other is a rich squatter from the Western District.

The Captain can beat him easily; see how he plays with him! The little grey-headed marker laughs silently as he scores another 'five to spot.' That little marker has been twenty years in the colony and has never been twenty yards out of Melbourne. Passing the smoking room on our way out, New Chum is horrified at seeing two men drinking nobblers and another – already drunk – on the sofa. These, smelling a greenhorn, call to him to 'shout,' which means ringing the bell and calling for liquor.

In ancient days when men were many and drinks were few, one had to shout in order to attract the attention of the waiter in the general uproar. Hence the term!

New Chum feels half inclined to refuse the invitation, but as he has gumption enough to see that this would mortally offend the trio, he wisely accepts.

At the clink of glasses the ebriate one raises himself and after ordering another 'dark' for himself, requests to be informed if the New Chum is going to the Botanical Gardens? New Chum says he is quite a stranger and doesn't know where to go. 'Cos if you'll just knock up the 'coon at the door and just give him my card – or jes' mention my name to him – he'll be d'lighted to see you,' remarks Ebrius with many hiccoughs. New Chum is about to express his delight at the proposal and gratitude for the offer when a loud snore informs him that Ebrius is gone to sleep again and, as he forgot to mention his name, New Chum feels that his thanks are somewhat premature.

'Come away, New Chum, let us see the town!' The streets of Melbourne are built crosswise; that is to say, every principal street has another principal street crossing it at right angles. This, though bewildering at first, makes the topography of the place very simple; one has only to walk straight on to come into a street one knows. Would New Chum like to see the Post Office? New Chum will go anywhere and see anything. Come then, we will go down Flinders Street, up Elizabeth Street, and turning to our right, pass into Bourke Street to have a look at it. Afterwards we can return by way of Swanston Street to Collins Street.

New Chum, astounded by this torrent of names, feebly assents. '*Allons donc!*' 'Here Sir,' remarks the imaginary familiar of the New Chum, 'here is the Post Office,' or rather 'here will be the Post Office.' It is at present in process of building and will be, when completed, about five times larger than the one at St. Martins-le-Grand. The hoarding of tall boards all round it covered with gaudy placards of 'Barry Sullivan as Hamlet,' in letters a yard long or 'Jefferson!' 'Jefferson!' 'Jefferson!'[17]

'Lady Don in the burlesque tonight!' 'The Ridgeway Troupe again!' '*L'échelle perilleuse, or The Ladder in the Air,*' conceal the mass of scaffolding and brickwork from our view. Seeing the post office under these circumstances reminds one of Albert Smith's 'London in a Fog.' London was there – behind the fog. The Post Office is here – behind the hoarding.

Incline your head a little to the left, my friend, what do you see? A crowd at a doorway and some four or five boys in breeches and boots rushing half-broken horses in and out with great yellings and whip-crackings. That is Kirk's Horse Bazaar. Come out of our way a little and let us look at it. Here we are in a big, iron-roofed, tan-carpeted building open at both ends. On each side are stalls filled with the horses of the men who are standing around. Fronting us is the auctioneer's pulpit and behind us a small room, not unlike a porter's lodge; this is the betting-room, the 'Corner' of Melbourne. Let us hear what is doing! Poole, the auctioneer, is endeavouring to get rid of a 'little bay mare' – quiet to ride or drive – single or double harness. Whoop! Down the yard comes the little bay mare, the tan flying in showers behind her. Dick the riding boy flings her on her haunches before the stand. A pretty little mare enough, but the bucketing way in which she flings herself along speaks but ill for the

---

17   Mr Joseph Jefferson died in the spring of 1905. In an obituary notice of him published in *T. P.'s Weekly*, May 1905, the following reference is made to his visit to Australia (at the date the above was written by Clarke): 'Mr Jefferson acted in nearly every part of the English speaking world, including Van Diemen's Land. There was great excitement in Hobart Town the first time that he appeared in *The Ticket-of-Leave Man*, and at least a hundred of ticket-of-leave experts were in the pit to see that he did the part justice.'

trainer. 'Now then, how much for this bay mare quiet to ride and drive, single or double harness? Five pounds? Guineas? Six pounds! Six ten! Seven pounds! Going at seven pounds! This little mare, quiet to ride and drive single or double harness, going at seven pounds! Eight pounds! Thank you Sir! Eight pounds offered! Eight ten! Nine pounds! Trot her down, me Lad! Trot her down!'

And down the yard goes the little bay mare, Old Sam, the manager, giving her a delicate cut with his long whip over the quarters as she passes him. 'Nine pounds offered! This little bay mare quiet in harness and broken to saddle, going at nine pounds! Nine pounds! Nine ten! Nine pounds, ten shillings only! Nine ten! Going at nine ten! Nine pounds ten! Going! Going! Going! Gone!'

Rap! And the little bay mare is the property of yon tall stockman, who has lounged into the yard for a quiet smoke, but who having an eye for a horse, buys the beast. As he steps up to Dick to ask him some question and to hold her reins, another boy on another horse rushes past him at full gallop; New Chum thinks he has had enough of it, so we go out.

There are little knots of men about the doorway, some betting, some chatting, all smoking. Captain Sprott is there, late Secretary of the Victorian Club. He won and lost much money, did Sprott, in the old country, but horses have their charms for him yet. He is milder now, however, in his betting and, having made a lucky hit in mining speculations, keeps a drag and pair. The little, short, whiskered man on his left who looks like a butcher-boy out of work, is a member of a well-known firm of stock and station agents. Old H. is there too, the rich wool-broker. With his ruddy face, broad-brimmed hat and pendant seals he seems to have just stepped out of a cartoon of Tenniel's as John Bull.

We turn to the left past Morton's Hotel and down Bourke Street, named after Governor Bourke of glorious and immortal memory. Eating houses seem to abound here. We learn that 'Here is the place for a feed!' 'Only a shilling!' and see the *cartes* of the courses wafered to the greasy window panes. New Chum with his Bond Street air still upon him hurries past. What is to be done? Shall we see the University? No! New Chum doesn't care about the University. Or the hospital? He detests hospitals. What then? Oh! of course, the Public Library! As we progress to that bourn up Swanston Street we pass the *Herald* office lurking up an alley while its brother-in-arms, the *Argus* has a gorgeous palace like a *Telegraph* office[18] all to itself in Collins Street. Past the Scotch pie-house which blooms in all the bravery of jellies, pies, buns and 'collies'; steering clear of this danger and deaf to the (figurative) music of the siren shop-girls within, we reach the cab-stand at Bignells.

'Queer things, Melbourne cabs!' remarks New Chum. True my friend, they are queer things! None of your delightful shilling hansom rides here. Our hansoms charge half a crown to take you up the street. Our cabs are our pride. The domestic jingle or 'car' of commerce is of American origin and workmanship. In shape they are not unlike a butter-boat with a canopy overhead and wheels on each side. They are delicious things to ride in, only one must pay attention to the 'balancing' as, owing to the peculiar beauty of their construction, a fat man getting suddenly out of the back will cause the front passenger to fall upon the neck of the horse with some velocity! Figure to yourself an Irish jaunting car with shafts at the feet of the sitter and two enormous wheels where the backs of the passengers touch with a four-post bed tester hung atop and you will have a Melbourne cab! Disdaining the offers of the drivers of these vehicles, deaf to the cries of 'Emer'ld 'ill!' 'St. Kilda! St. Kilda!' 'Going right up, Sir!' 'Take yer for a couple of bob, Sir!' 'Collin'ood!' ''ood!' that assail us on all sides, we turn sharply off at the corner through a little door on the right, up a flight of steps, and the full glory of the Public Library bursts upon us.

The approach to the building is good. After passing up the flight of steps aforesaid and traversing some twenty yards of pavement, more steps are ascended and we stand in the porch of the building. It has evidently been built after the fashion and in imitation of the British Museum with a façade and heavy pillars running its whole length. Like most Melbourne public buildings, however, including the Parliament and Custom-houses, the original design has not been carried out in its entirety through lack of funds, and the present aspect of the library is but a poor one, the pillars only running halfway along its front and the bare bricks of the wings not yet covered with plaster.[19]

On entering, however, New Chum is struck by the resemblance to the British abortion. In the entrance-hall casts of the usual groups abound, while in the now nearly completed right wing objects of art, pictures, statuary, models, bas-reliefs and bronzes surround him on all sides. We pass up the stairs to the library. A

---

18   The allusion here is to the London *Daily Telegraph* then just beginning to acquire influence and popularity at home. It is curious that in after years Marcus Clarke should have been appointed to the post of its Melbourne correspondent.

19   This was in 1865. At a later period [emended by CH from 'at the present time'] Mr Archibald Marshall writing of Melbourne says:

'It is the custom to refer to Melbourne as an American city. It is so only as regards the plan. Wide streets alternating with narrower ones – but named, not numbered – have been laid out at right angles to one another on ground not near the sea, not on the banks of a great river, nor within sight of any high ground.

fine collection of books it is too. New Chum is astonished for classics, history, travels, scientific works and works of fiction gleam from the walls in all the glories of morocco and gilding. New Chum attempts to take down a volume but in doing so, stumbles over a drunken mechanic who is snoring with his head pillowed on a copy of *Eothen* at one of the tables. As the admission is free, the library has become a fashionable lounge for the idle, drunken and dirty loafers who infest the town.

Here is one gentleman in a ragged, red 'jumper' leaning drowsily over the *Saturday Review*; here another blackening with his filthy and beer-stained fingers a volume of Burnett for whom he cares as much as ordinary readers for the Grand Cyrus. A third, comfortably sunk in slumber, snores away an hour or two until the sun shall have set and he can resume with ease his avocations of loafing, drinking, sponging and perhaps thieving. In the midst of the general silence the sound of a quick footstep is heard and a portly, rubicund old gentleman walks sharply down the hall. This is Sir Harry Bedmont,[20] judge of Supreme Court, the patron of the library and its most liberal donor. He is a thorough gentleman of the old school and though somewhat pompous, a benevolent, hospitable man and excellent judge. Let us leave him to chat with Buffins the Librarian. See how he bows to him! Buffins is a little man who dabbles in literature, has written a burlesque for the *Royal* and pens weekly criticisms for *Bell's Life in Melbourne* under the *nom de plume* of Oliver Oldworthy. New Chum here wonders if beer can be obtained anywhere? Beer? Bless you, yes! Allsop or Bass? Perkins or Barclay? Meux or Guiness? New Chum says he doesn't care which! Be warned, Oh New Chum, against asking for 'beer in its general sense.' A Melbourne waiter will be sure to bring you stout. Will New Chum try a 'John Collins?' What is a 'John Collins?' A drink, Oh New Chum, peculiar to this Colony. It may be known perhaps in Yankee land, that paradise of the toper, but by a different name. Compounded of lemonade, gin, lemon, curaçoa and Heaven knows what beside, the 'John Collins' is a drink that will hand down to posterity the name of the lucky man who originated it.

But why waste words? Here stand the two tumblers gleaming with lemon and sparkling with ice – try it! 'Glorious, by Jove!' says New Chum, drawing a long breath as we come out of Bignell's[21] where the nectar was concocted. Being refreshed by the draught our stranger looks about him, and after proceeding some yards up the pavement, comes to the conclusion that it's 'devilish hot.' True, Oh

---

20   Pseudonym for Sir Redmond Barry, the well known Victorian judge.

New Chum, you are not yet used to our glorious Australian climate! Floods in winter which compel merchants to withdraw to their upper storeys and brokers, bank clerks and postmen to follow their business in boats up and down the streets; and in summer glorious days with a blazing sun above and hot winds blowing 'from morn till dewy eve.' Unless I am much mistaken we shall have a scorcher now! I thought so! The air grows hotter and hotter and plays upon New Chum's face like a furnace-blast while the trees bend and crack and unlatched doors fly back with loud bangings and the dust, blinding and suffocating, is borne down on us in clouds.

At a short distance from us are three men 'turning on the Yan Yean' – which means (in ordinary Saxon) watering the streets. New Chum lingers awhile by the jet to enjoy its coolness and to admire the process of turning on. No tedious business of water-carts here! An enormous hose is fixed to the fire-plug and a stream is immediately procured which, if allowed to come forth with full power, would rise sixty or seventy feet into the air and almost demolish a brick wall if turned against it.

Instances have been known of dogs being killed by accidentally crossing the path of the jet whilst playing with full vigour. Thanks to the reservoir of the Yan Yean Melbourne is now amply supplied with water and this necessary, instead of being sold by the bucket, as formerly, is now brought by means of piping from the reservoir within easy reach of the poorest.[22]

The hot wind grows fiercer and fiercer and the dust clouds sharper and more blinding. Heat-suffocated Australians pass us with their turban-bound hats reversed so that the pugree (a white silk or cotton turban) may hang with its floating ends in front to protect their eyes from the dust. New Chum, approving of the arrangement, goes forthwith into the nearest hat-shop and purchases the same – hat and all. You may leave your bell-topper, beloved of Bond Street, behind you, my friend! Few men wear them here in the summer.[23]

We turn down Collins Street now. Being the fashionable street, up to 5 p.m. Collins Street is crowded and as New Chum looks up the hill and sees carriages, horses, carts, cars and buggies, he begins to feel more at his ease. The white iron canopies that most shops have from their windows to the kerb-stone make a

---

21   A fashionable Melbourne hotel of that period and, I believe, still existing.

22   According to the published statistics the Melbourne water supply had cost the city by the end of 1876, or some 11 years after the above was written, £1,500,000.

23   It must be remembered that at this period (1865) the use of the tall, silk hat was universal in London.

pleasant arcade to walk under. The pavement is crowded with people all lounging slowly up and down; Melbourne in December is far too hot to hurry in. Here comes L'Encrier again, having finished his billiards, arm in arm with Manderson, the Commandant of Volunteers. A jovial looking fellow is Manderson and he nods cheerily to a couple of friends who pass him, Quarantpole the rich squatter and Shute Fairlie, the High Sheriff. Here too comes Sprott again in his dray with his black-ribboned straw hat set jauntily on one side of his head as he drives slowly up to the Club. On the pavement-edge we see two more worthies, John Brown Esquire, late Mayor of Melbourne, whose fancy-dress ball astonished the colonials and made the hearts of tailors to leap for joy, and Robinson, Manager of the Bank of Australia.[24] Robinson prides himself on looking like Napoleon and,

> Assumes the god,
> Affects to nod,
> And seems to shake the spheres.

A. Spendall, the editor of Punch, says that Robinson's face as he receives customers in his bank parlour is worth two hundred a year extra to the Bank. He certainly is a decided looking little man.

New Chum here stares aghast as a lady richly and elegantly attired in blue silk with a black silk tail-coat, the latest Parisian mode, sweeps past him. With his remembrances of the 'sunny side of Regent Street' strong upon him, he whispers, 'who on earth is that?' 'That, my friend, is Mrs. Fogge Hanton, the wife of a respectable merchant of that ilk. She has been but lately married poor thing! so Foggy permits her to overdress herself a little at first.'

Arm in arm behind this Antipodean Cleopatra come two Jews and close on their heels, looking uneasily from side to side, a little, cunning-looking man in a straw hat. The Jews are Messrs Moses Marks and Louis Hieschel. The first is a money-lender and bill-discounter, well known to Government clerks and would be fast young men about town; the second, the manager of the Australasian Advance and Loan Office. They pass conversing unctuously; observe well the third. He is a wonderful instance of Self-Help. Had Dr. Smiles ever visited Melbourne he would unquestionably have cited Mr. Alfred Medlicot of Eldon Court as an example of a

---

24 Henry Gyles Turner, manager of the Bank of Australasia.

self made man. Originally a porter in the London and Holloway Bank (in London) he came out here under a favourable star and from small beginnings, lending five or six pounds at ninety per cent, rose to be what he is, the friend of the unfortunate and needy. He lends to those impecunious ones in the goodness of his heart fifty or sixty pounds at heavy interest with good security on their bill at three months. From being the *Custos* of Eldon Court he has risen to occupy chambers there and rides, with toes much turned out and uneasy seat, a cock-tailed, little black cob about the city. All honour to him! Long may he flourish and may his shadow never grow less! Fattening on the spoil of the Philistine and bloated with usury, he put up for the House of Assembly the other day; but to the shame of the men he had befriended and the disgrace of the ungrateful victims who had paid him cent per cent, he was so ill supported that he withdrew before the polling day.

Yonder at the corner stands Thomas Moulinet, familiarly called Money Moulinet. He is a rich man and his hand is ever open to the unfortunate and, although uncharitable people call him miserly and grasping, I daresay that Money Moulinet could tell – perhaps does tell – many stories of the sums he has bestowed upon local charities and of the starving wretches who have partaken of his bounty. Doubtless modesty is his besetting sin!

Does New Chum see the stout man 'tilupping' up the street on a big, brown horse? That is the Hon. Thomas Blowhard Bellows, barrister with a large practice; his wife leads the fashion and is considered quite the *ton* in Melbourne. On the other side of the way, swinging a white umbrella, may be observed Edward Gibson, newspaper-proprietor and small *littérateur* generally. He used to be a popular man until he made himself ridiculous by a scheme to send back the expiree convicts to England.

Carriages line the kerb opposite the great millinery establishment of Malstone and Pounds. New Chum can find no fault with the carriages but it seems that the horses are not to his liking. 'If a coachman conducted himself like that at home, too!' suddenly exclaimed the newcomer, 'he would be sacked on the spot!' Well, it certainly is not the most reverend posture for a coachman! Some Jehu in charge of a carriage and pair is lolling on the box and, with one booted leg cocked carelessly over the hammer-cloth and his left arm pillowed comfortably on the cushions, is surveying the streets at his ease! His mistress is coming out of the shop but no alert John in all the splendour of calves and plush springs down to open the door. She has to unscrew the door-handle herself and with some difficulty gets in. The driver then condescends to sit upright and the horses, one cantering, the other trotting, drag the ill-matched carriage homewards.

Having come to the top of the street New Chum suggests Port Phillip and dinner. 'Dine there my good friend? Nonsense! on your first visit to Melbourne you must dine at the Café Royal of course.' New Chum turns and we descend the hill again. The crowd is less dense now and people are strolling homewards. Bankers' clerks, released from durance, trot amiably down to their respective railway stations (nearly everyone who can, lives in the suburbs) and solicitors, barristers and merchants, all homeward-bound, take the place of the crowd of idlers we met half an hour since. As we come to the corner of Swanston Street we catch a glimpse of the flag flying at the Treasury flagstaff, sign of gubernatorial presence. It is lowered however immediately and from over the crest of the hill comes the Governor's carriage with His Excellency smiling affably within. New Chum, remembering park meetings with royalty, raises his hat and gets a courteous bow in return.

As we proceed café-wards we are stared at all the way up the street by the *habitués* of the place. Victorians never notice the Governor, why I can't think. Perhaps, half of them regard him as a lay figure to be bowed to at *levées*, or a name to head a subscription list, while the other half think him a bright, ethereal being too brilliant for plebeian eyes to gaze upon. The sun has nearly set now and it verges fast upon the hour of six as we turn up the cocoa-nut fibre matted stairs of the café!

The dining-room is a large, cheerful apartment with little recesses or rather divisions on each side, somewhat after the fashion of London eating-houses; a bright fire at one end of the room glowing through a grating of sloping bars upon which hiss and crackle several steaks. A white-coated and linen-capped cook carefully tends them with a pair of polished tongs. On the opposite side is the billiard room and to the right of the door leading into it a bar where a slim, cute-looking Yankee dispenses drinks and compounds 'cocktails.' All the cushioned seats in the recesses are full of people eating, drinking and chatting. Squatters, lawyers, doctors, loafers, holders of snug Government berths, actors and *littérateurs* all mixed together, whilst the incessant clatter of plates, and rattle of the huge silver covers of the joints on the mahogany stands which support them as they are propelled to the table of some hungry customer, contrast strongly with the decorous quiet of the 'Wellington' or the 'London.' Selecting a table by the open window and calling for the *carte*, we proceed to the serious business of dining. Will the New Chum order? He will be delighted.

Clear soup, some mullet, stewed pigeon, cutlets *à la Maintenon*, curry, *omelette aux fines herbes*, Parmesan cheese, two bottles of claret and some sparkling Moselle.

'Yes Sir! Thank you,' and we sit down.

New Chum here observes a black-browed, wavy-haired, flower-in-buttonhole'd gentleman at the middle table gazing at him with eyebrows alternately raised and depressed. 'Who's that?' asks he. 'That, Sir, is Barry Sullivan, the actor and lessee of the Theatre Royal which adjoins this building. He is a good actor and can play every part he takes with an ease which compensates in a great measure for lack of genius. His Richelieu, I think, is his best character. He is a careful manager and spares no expense to make his theatre attractive. The corpse-like individual with the deep wrinkles each side of his mouth is Charles Young, the comedian and another of the Royal Company.' 'Does Sullivan play tonight?' New Chum enquires. 'No; Jefferson plays Jesse Rural; if you never saw him you had better come.' 'Delighted,' returns New Chum, helping himself to stewed pigeon. In the pause after the discussion of the parmesan, New Chum asks if the *café* as well as the theatre belongs to Sullivan? No! there is a rather curious story about that same *café*.

Suffice it to say that the theatre and *café* originally belonged to one person, a tragedian whose name, famous here, is not altogether unknown in London; and that from his hands they somehow passed into those of a Mr. Ambrose Hawke. See, there is the gentleman in question entering the room; he has his cloak over his arm; he hardly ever appears in public without his cloak. And mopping his sickly face with a yellow bandana, he orders a steak and a glass of ale. He was originally a bill-sticker, I believe, and from lending small amounts at high interest became possessed of a sum sufficient to enable him to purchase houses and shops in, at that time, rising Melbourne. The discovery of the Victorian goldfields and the consequent influx of people into the city raised the value of his property to such an extent that he is one of the richest men in Melbourne. He looks carefully after his belongings too, does Mr. Ambrose Hawke; if we were to watch we should see him lurking about pit and dress circle entrances, now and then casting careful eyes into the house from the orchestra and sniffing at the check-takers with suspicion in his dull eyes, fearful lest a stray shilling should find its way into other pockets than his own. Nevertheless, to do him justice, he is liberal at times and seldom refuses his name to a subscription list or his guinea to a charity. New Chum here voting for 'coffee and weeds,' we adjourn to the smoking-room and having carefully sugared his mocha and lit an undeniable Havana, the newcomer admits with a half reluctant sigh, 'By Jove; I couldn't have dined much better at the "Wellington."' Keeping him to his promise of seeing Jefferson, we drag him away as soon as his first cigar is over, and passing through a door at the end of the smoking room, after some monetary confabulation with a hermit in a gigantic bandbox outside we find ourselves seated in the front row of the Royal dress circle. New Chum refers to the bill and naturally asks 'who's Jefferson?' Jefferson, my friend, was the original Asa Trenchard to Sothern's Dundreary[25] and entirely differs from Buckstone in his reading of the character. He makes the young Vermonter quite a hero instead of a fat, ridiculous Yankee who has not a civilised idea. This is fortunate for the success of the piece here as Dundreary is played by an affected clown who can neither dress like a gentleman nor act like one. Jefferson plays Jesse Rural tonight. It is the character of a benevolent, simple country parson – a modern Vicar of Wakefield – who, coming up to London on a visit to his pupil, now a fashionable young man, and finding him involved in scrapes and 'situations' of all kinds, benevolently tries to get him out of his difficulties without the young man being aware of the part his old tutor is playing. The inevitable consequence is that the unfortunate man is involved in a seven-fold net of difficulties to the horror and amazement of the bewildered tutor. The piece was played very badly by all but Jefferson who was delightful. In the last act where, having succeeded in spoiling two matches, mortally offended everyone and caused everybody to elope with the wrong person, he is bitterly upbraided by his whilom pupil as being the cause of the mischief, the burst of half-childish, self-reproachful grief which breaks from the old man as he endeavours to show that what he did was dictated by his love for his 'boy,' called forth a torrent of applause and caused even the phlegmatic New Chum to exclaim, as we left the house for air, 'By Jove, what a sensation he'd make in London!'[26]

Come downstairs New Chum and thou shalt see the Vestibule and Melbourne life! Turning down the stairs and passing through a bar and a small door we find ourselves in a large hall open at one end to Bourke Street and closed at the other. On either side run covered bars behind which some twenty or thirty girls dispense with lightning-like rapidity the 'Brandies hot' 'Glasses Ale,' 'Cold without,' 'Colonial Wine,'[27] 'Nobblers for five,' 'Sherry and Bitters,' 'Champagne,' 'Two glasses Claret,' 'Maraschino,' 'Curaçoa,' 'Dark Brandy' etc. etc. which smoking,

---

25 The character in the play *Our American Cousin*, in which the actor, Sothern, made such a hit, first in the United States and subsequently at the Haymarket Theatre, London, then under the management of the popular actor-manager Buckstone, who played the part mentioned above in the same piece. The play had a long and successful run at the theatre in question during the early sixties.

26 The actor in question subsequently achieved a great success in London. Also see note [17] as to his appearance in Hobart in *The Ticket-of-Leave Man*.

27 The Australian wine industry, now of such vast dimensions, was in its infancy when the above description was written.

expectorating men and boys call for on all sides. Melbourne is a dreadful place for drinking; if one meets a friend, the first salutation is, 'How d'ye do! Come and have a drink!' and this in all grades of life. I have seen two doctors, a distinguished lawyer, and a member of Parliament all partaking of 'nobblers' at the bar of an hotel at 11.30 a.m.

Let us stand aside a little and watch the crowd; what a curious one it is! Nearly two hundred people, all smoking and some drinking. White-coated waiters shoot now and then like meteors through the mass bearing coffee to some of the more quiet and less rowdy frequenters of the place; these, sitting at little marble tables, smoke and drink with a philosophical air. At the furthest table from the door sit a knot of Government clerks – young Podgers of the Treasury and Pippin of the Chief Secretary's Office. Beside them, sunk in drunken slumbers, reclines Tom Banbury of the Customs.

Banbury is a generally debased young man; he is nearly always drunk. The common enquiry of his compatriots, when out on the loose, on entering some more than usually vicious den, is 'Seen Banbury?' 'No!' 'Oh! Then I suppose he's drunk!' He is in that happy state now. Some two more friends of the group coming up and amusing themselves by fencing amicably with sticks over the ebriate's head, he is at last aroused to a sense of his position and, staggering up, dives into the little door just behind him where the beautiful girl in mauve silk is standing. That is the door into the Ladies' Refreshment-room, vulgarly termed 'The Saddling Paddock,' and many a merchant's clerk and tradesman's shop-boy has dated his downfall from the day when he entered it. Melbourne, I grieve to tell New Chum, is not a virtuous city; indeed for its size and population it is the most vicious in this half of the globe.

The beautiful girl sitting alone in the theatre, at once attracting the attention of New Chum, who had remarked that she was the most ladylike woman he had seen since he landed by Jove! was the 'Sydney Pigeon,' a pretty 'horse-breaker' of some notoriety; while the elegantly dressed women who parade Collins Street at noon, bowing to nobody, are akin to the objects of the 'Seven Belgravian Mothers'' abuse.[28] Poor girls! They are more to be pitied than blamed. Sent out here by the shipload as governesses, nurses, ladies' maids or what not, deluded by false representations of theoretical philanthropists into leaving friends in England for the chance of employment in the Colonies, they find out their mistake when it is

---

28   See Chapter 7.

too late and are compelled to save themselves from a miserable death by a life of vice. If the class of benevolent ignoramuses who advocate female emigration and offer bonuses to women to leave their families and friends did but know the true state of matters here, there would be fewer cases like that of the poor girl above who sitting clad in silk and velvet with jewels on her breast, but despair and shame at her heart, endeavours by weeping at the fictitious grief of another to forget her own alas! too real sorrows!

New Chum, sick of the tobacco smoke, proposes a stroll up the street into the air. What is the time? Ten o'clock. By Jove! we shall just be in time to see little Clelia Howson in the burlesque at the Haymarket; so leaving the crowd of smoking, expectorating and blaspheming Australians who choke the vestibule, we saunter up the street.

More people again, more smoking, more expectoration, more noise and riot! The pavement rather resembles Wych Street or the purlieus of the Haymarket in London at two in the morning than a respectable thoroughfare at ten post-meridian. Here is a mob of station men from the Murray, booted and breeched, all smoking intensely. They are computing how much money they will spend on drink and debauchery before they go back to beef and stock-riding. Next come, reeling down the road, four sailors from some passenger-ship now in harbour (New Chum's own perhaps) and with vehement addresses to everybody's eyes, limbs, and internal anatomy, lurch into a convenient bar for 'drinks round.' A cab loaded fore and aft with a still more drunken and melodious crew goes flying over gutters and round corners *en route* for Sandridge[29] and the harbour. Suddenly as we pass a dark lane on our left, a woman rushes out with a shrill cry and hurries across the road. Close on her heels comes a drunken and infuriate ruffian who, knife in hand, swears to 'do for her!' if he catches her. He has apparently been attempting it already, for as the wretched creature, wife or paramour, rushes past, New Chum declares that her face was bruised and blackened and her arms bleeding. Ha! the ruffian has run right into the arms of a tall policeman who removes him cursing forthwith. All hail, thou trusty guardian of the night, may thy shadow never grow less!

Presently we meet a group of Celestials, pig-tailed, blue-coated and mandarin-capped, chatting with animation in their jaw-breaking lingo. Well, John, how goes it? 'How yeh! Yoh! Aaaah! G'night!' and with a burst of gutturals they salute us

---

29 See footnote [16].

and pass on. John Chinaman is an honest fellow enough in most cases and works hard. The best vegetables sold in the city are of Chinese growth and in turning an odd penny by the sale of slippers, pipe-lights, handkerchiefs or basket-work he is indefatigable. Up country however he is not so well thought of, for spurious gold 'fossicking' on new 'claims,' thefts, and some most bloody murders have given the diggers rather a bad opinion of John. The great haunt of Chinamen in Melbourne is Little Bourke Street where they have Chinese houses, Chinese signs and Chinese clerks; sell Chinese goods and play at Chinese games, smoke opium and drink tea *ad nauseam*. New Chum expresses a desire to explore this celestial thoroughfare. Not tonight, my dear Sir! if you went in at one end you'd never come out alive at the other! Ask that plainly dressed man with the sharp eyes leaning against the lamp-post yonder what *he* thinks of a stroll down Little Bourke Street after dark. He ought to know something about it; he is Inspector Lynx of the Detective Force. 'Wouldn't advise you to try it, Sir!' says Lynx with a grim smile. 'Bless you Sir! – I beg your pardon but I think you're a New Chum?' New Chum stares and wonders how the deuce he found it out. 'We have more trouble with that street than with all the rest of Melbourne put together, Collingwood included. Why' – but here a shabbily dressed man, who has been lurking on the other side of the road, comes and speaks to Lynx who with a hurried apology moves away.

New Chum continues up street pondering and congratulating himself on his forethought in bringing a revolver with him! Poor New Chum! The sound of music suddenly bursts upon his ears and looking up he perceives a brass band playing at an open upper window. A placard informs him that this is Mohier's Wax-works and invites him to walk upstairs. A crowd round the glowing gas lit window is admiring 'The Bushranger Gardiner' as he appears with revolver, bowie, rifle and thigh-boots complete, the model of an Australian Highwayman.[30] Reflecting that he has seen Madame Tussaud's in London and that this can't be much better, New Chum decides upon not walking upstairs and resisting the entreaties of the benignant phrenologist and proprietor, Mohier himself (whose white hairs stream wildly to the wind as he in vain attempts to persuade New Chum that 'It is de greadest vonder in Melbourne') passes coldly by.

It was well for your peace of mind, New Chum, that you resisted! Your night would have been rendered hideous by the horrors you viewed there. In one

---

30   See Chapter 9 (footnote 39) as to this character.

corner poor Burke and Wills, the explorers, lie in the agonies of death. Further on the rebel convicts are murdering Captain Price[31] (with great *vraisemblance*) in the hulks. Here stand Mrs. Scott, a black man and somebody else, all three concerned in the murder of Mr. Scott and 'in the clothes which they wore at their execution.' There lies the figure of a man with his head split open and bleeding, and his murderer 'with the fatal pickaxe yet in his hands,' stands calmly by, and last, a triumph of modelling and culminating horror, a miserable woman in bed with her throat cut from ear to ear, two Chinamen, the perpetrators of the deed, leering with a sardonic grin on their waxen faces over the couch and the blood 'as natural as can be in red sealing-wax a-running all over the counterpane.' There are, I believe, children living in the house with these monsters; do they ever go into the room after dark? Are they ever disturbed by thinking that the whole collection of gentlemen – and lady – villains beneath are holding high jinks and performing their several little dramas of blood for each other's amusement until dawn breaks? I expect that they are used to the place. Sextons' daughters gambol with skulls, and undertakers' children play at funerals, knock in imaginary nails and take away chimerical coffins with great relish.

We are now opposite the Haymarket Theatre[32] and entering amidst a maze of cabs, cars and carriages, we find ourselves in a similar vestibule to the other, only that it has but a single row of bars. There is more drinking and more smoking, for the house is full tonight. It is the favourite house just now and New Chum remarks that it looks pretty full; it is indeed, my friend, and we shall be lucky if we can squeeze in at the stalls. The burlesque is one of Byron's, *Orpheus and Eurydice*. After much crushing and being sworn at by the men and 'Oh! Dear me'd and 'Oh! Goodness mind'ed by the ladies, New Chum gets a view of the stage. What does he think of it? 'Stunning by Jove' says New Chum with fervour, 'what a jolly little girl plays Proserpine!' Yes, to do Miss Clelia justice, she is pretty and piquante enough and points her jokes with an air that shows she appreciates them. New Chum is enraptured with her of course. Half Ballarat was mad about her and her sister when they played there some time back. All Melbourne has run wild now and 'every fast young man' (confound them) would give his eyes to know the Howsons. Thanks to a father and two brothers, however, the girls are passing the ordeal safely.

---

31   Supposed to have been the original of the character Maurice Frere in Marcus's celebrated novel *For the Term of his Natural Life*.
32   This theatre, named after the well known playhouse, was, some years after the date of this article, destroyed by fire and not rebuilt. Its site is now covered by one of Melbourne's markets.

The father enters now as Pluto. Tremendous applause! At this juncture some half-drunken loafer in the gallery elects to throw a handful of cherry-stones upon the stage. These rattle in all directions and Pluto, addressing the gallery, remarks, 'You shouldn't throw things on the stage, gentlemen, you might strike one of these,' pointing to his two daughters. The only reply to this is another volley and Eurydice being hit, and pretty sharply too, it seems, runs off sobbing and cries, 'You might turn that gentleman out. He's done that two nights!' Instantly Babel arises. Shrieks, groans, whistles, yells of 'Turn him out! Throw him over! Police!' resound on all sides. Deprecatory remarks of 'What a shame!' from the dress circle and fierce, condemnatory expressions regarding the eyes of the cherry thrower from the pit and gallery.

In the midst of this the drunken disturber solemnly rises, and with a parliamentary wave of the hand seems to beseech silence. 'Augh ye old villin! Pitch him over! Hang the infernal scoundrel! Where's the Police? Just let me at him!' are his greetings. Still he perseveres. No use! The House is one universal parrot cage. Such yellings, howlings, whistlings and screechings were never before heard out of Bedlam or the Cockatoo-room at the Zoological Gardens. At length a deft policeman, leaping over the back-seats, collars the tipsy aspirant for oratorical distinctions and bears him off. Eurydice appears again, smiling through her tears, and after five distinct rounds of applause to express its sense of justice, largeness of heart and delight at seeing her no worse, the house suffers her to proceed, whilst New Chum squeezes out of the stalls considerably amused at his theatrical experiences.

What is to be done now? Come and have a drink of course. Passing the long bar for this amiable purpose, we encounter ten or eleven gentlemen all more or less 'cut'. These espying New Chum immediately enquire 'What he'll have to drink?' New Chum, not catching at once the free and easy Australian manner, is about to decline; but remembering the Port Phillip episode thinks better of it and accepts. 'He'll take a little beer,' he thinks. 'All right! Tom, Dick and Harry, what are you going to take?' The wants of the company having been supplied, little Smarte, who has come down from the Billabong with his two year's earnings in his pocket, flings down a sovereign for payment and bows gravely to New Chum over a glass of brandy, the eleventh he has had since he left his hotel. New Chum returns the compliment and bows to somebody else and somebody else bows to him. Then another friend proposes another drink; same ceremony. Then New Chum thinks it incumbent on him to 'shout' another. Ditto repeated.

Smarte 'shouts' again and, before our newly arrived friend has time to look about him, he has imbibed one glass of ale and three 'dark brandies' in rapid succession; naturally he feels some effects therefrom and listens to Smarte, who is telling some tremendous yarn, (Smarte is great at yarns) with a singing in his ears and a mist before his eyes. Smarte is relating some bush story. 'By George, Sir! There were only thirteen fellows in the place and twelve of 'em, "old lags!" They used to call 'emselves the twelve Apostles! Awful villains! All of 'em committed one murder, some of 'em three or four! They tried to murder me one night but, by Jove, I was too quick for 'em! Shot six of 'em on the spot and rode fifty miles to Lake Didawarra with a revolver in each hand and the bridle in my teeth! By God, Sir! Have another drink?'

One of the friends proposes a change of *locale* and New Chum is invited to accompany the crew. Let us follow him gently at a distance. 'Come and play billiards,' says a tall, thin man, Timsby by name, to New Chum 'All r'ght,' says New Chum, who would play at cutting his own throat, 'cockamaroo', or 'blind-hookey' for fifty pound notes in his present, reckless state. The twain, separating from the rest, who elect to 'look in at the Alham,' cross the street to Catabini's. The room is crowded: Jews, Turks, infidels and heretics smoking like several furnaces. By some mysterious passage of half crowns with the marker, Timsby gets the next vacancy at the table (to the confusion of Benjamin Ben-Abednego and Levi Isaacs Esquires who have been waiting for two hours without the courage to tap the marker) and the game begins. New Chum, never a very good player, feels quite out of his depth with Timsby who, after a break of thirteen, coolly suggests as the marker spots the red, 'Suppose we have a skiv on the game, just to give it zest?' 'Two if y' like,' hiccups New Chum who since the imbibition of three more 'nobblers,' ordered and paid for by Timsby, feels very drunk indeed.

The game proceeds slowly, Timsby keeping four or five ahead. New Chum makes a brilliant fluke. 'Good stroke!' cries the marker, 'Forty-four, Forty-seven!' New Chum, inspired by this, plays with more confidence. 'Cannon and Pocket! Bravo!'   plays again – no effects. Timsby plays for an easy stroke but misses, and, after some cannoning, New Chum misses his ball, flukes all round the table with eminent success, pockets red and cannons. 'Game!' cries the marker. 'Well! I am -' (confounded?) says Timsby, producing a sovereign and a shilling. 'Right hand or left?' 'Right,' cries New Chum. 'Wrong by Jove!' says Timsby, handing him the shilling. Going up the street again in quest of 'something to do', they meet Smarte and Company (the former with a bonnet on his head instead of a hat) emerging from the Alhambra – a sort of imitation Argyle Rooms,[33] all in a state of brandy. 'We'll have some oysters!' says Smarte. No sooner said than done; across the road again into a small den, perfumed strongly with shell-fish. 'Oysters for twelve!' says Smarte, 'and look sharp!' 'And porter,' corrects New Chum, 'porter of course! Six bottles of porter!'

Whilst waiting for the viands, two of the party take advantage of the lull to renew a dispute relative to a horse which, being sold by one to the other, did not turn out such a magnificent animal as it was represented to be. 'I'll tell you what it is!' says one, 'I'm not to be done out of twenty notes by a 'Spicer' like that!' '"Spicer" be d----d!' returns the other. 'Oh! hang it! Don't have a row!' interposes Smarte. 'I'll give you peculiar fits in about twos my amiable friend!' remarks Number One. 'You better come and do it!' (volley of pure Saxon) replies Number Two. The only answer that the seller of the horse condescends to make is to grapple the buyer by the collar. Out go the lamps, smash go the dishes and the newly arrived oysters rattle over the floor. Smarte hurls a plate at the spot in the darkness where he supposes the heads of the combatants to be and nearly cuts the eye out of a drunken man who was trying to drink out of the vinegar bottle when the row began. He (the vinegar drinker) promptly splits the bottle over his nearest neighbour's skull and the fight becomes general. New Chum, having fallen peacefully asleep under the table, is rudely awakened by a shower of cold oysters in his face and a heavy boot with a spur in the pit of his stomach. The proprietor of the shop, being used to these little freaks on the part of his customers, attacks the party in the rear and, with the assistance of his barman, kicks the whole *posse comitatus* into the street. Here a policeman swoops down upon and scatters the group; and Timsby, who is not a bad-hearted fellow despite his sharp practice with greenhorns, having elicited from New Chum that he lives at the 'P't Ph'lp Club,' packs him off in a car to that institution where the careful waiter assists him benevolently to his couch. So ends our friend's first day in Melbourne! And when he awakes in the morning with a splitting headache and his face like an unbaked plum pudding from mosquito bites – remembering the money he has spent and ruefully regarding the crushed hat, torn coat and muddy pantaloons that litter the floor – as he rings for brandy and soda, mentally registers the never-kept-vow of New Chums to 'go up the country the day after tomorrow, by Jove!'

---

33   A notorious London dancing saloon in the sixties.

Chapter 9

Life in Melbourne as described by Marcus in the sixties, and by journalists of the present day at Perth, Western Australia. – Description of his place of residence. – First attempt at novel writing. – Second-hand books and prints. – 'The Puff Conclusive.' – 'The Peripatetic Philosopher.' – Accidents whilst out riding. – Reflections upon his own character. – His literary studies. – Bank robbery at Collingwood. – How letters to him should be addressed.

A striking example, both of the accuracy of Marcus Clarke's description of certain social characteristics of the Melbourne of those days and of their reappearance in similar circumstances of recent years, is afforded by the letter of a mining engineer on his way to the goldfields of Western Australia, giving an account of what he saw as he was passing through Perth, during the boom of some years ago:

> Servant girls and barmaids are arriving in swarms from Melbourne and Sydney; they walk about the streets all day in their best clothes with white veils. What strikes you most in a Perth open-air music hall is not so much the excellence of the performance as the unrestrained conversation carried on between the *artistes* and the audience. If the singer is young and good looking, one of the 'boys' will shout out, 'Come up to Coolgardie, will yer?' A dancer, having done a few steps as an encore, when the 'boys' continue shouting, instead of bowing gracefully, walks to the front of the stage and shouts, 'Shut up!'

Again, alluding to the drinking habits of the community the writer goes on to remark:

> Of all the thirsty people I ever met in my life the people of Perth are the thirstiest. You can't sit in an office for ten minutes before the man you are talking to feels thirsty – or you do; and you proceed to the club. I don't know what causes this; perhaps it is the sand – perhaps it is habit.

Let the reader compare the above with the scene in the Haymarket Theatre, Melbourne and the drinking habits of the people as described in Marcus's 'Day in Melbourne' of more than 50 years ago and judge for himself.

A few months after his arrival the promised vacancy in the Bank of Australasia occurred. He was first placed in the Gold department whose function it was to purchase gold direct from the mines, have it melted down, weighed into ingots, marked and shipped to Europe. This involved a trip to Sandridge[34] for the clerk to whom was assigned the duty of seeing the bullion shipped, a trip that Marcus rather enjoyed as he also did the occasional journeys to country branches of the Bank. He was now living in the country at a place called Boroondara[35] about six miles out of Melbourne and occasionally got a day off duty which he could turn to account by seeing a little of the country. His letters of introduction gave him the *entrée* into some pleasant houses, and he speaks of attending the assembly balls that were held on Thursday evenings, but already there were signs from certain expressions in these letters that some of the social conditions were not pleasing to his fastidious taste and in after years became the butt of his caustic wit and satire.

I am told that the following description of his temporary residence (taken from one of his letters from this period) is accurate and that so little is this particular suburb changed, that the picture he drew of the neighbourhood would be immediately recognized by those familiar with it, at the present day:

> A long, one-storied, wooden house with a verandah running all around it, nearly eight feet in breadth and covered with creepers – a large garden in front with peach-trees and vines behind them – a long, white paling at the end of the garden in the

---

34   Now known as Port Melbourne (see previous chapter).
35   Generally designated by its English name of 'Kew.'

middle of which is a gate – the road – a tremendous slope of wooded land and an immense range of purple mountains flung at the end of it – their tops just melting into grey now. On one side the white roofs of Melbourne – in the distance the gleam of the Yarra – and the sea with a white sail on the horizon. On the other, another burst of wood and a gigantic rock, cleft and scarred, as if some giant of ancient days had cloven it with an axe. Below the spur of this, brown woods and white roof, that of the Hunt Club Inn on the Gipp's Land Road. So much for situation!

The room I write in is long, with three low windows opening onto the verandah (an indispensable abutment); the room itself is littered with chairs, a big, cane-bottomed, rocking one being my speciality.

He went on to say that he was at work on a novel, of which he had composed by the end of 1864, four hundred closely written pages. He had at first intended to call it 'Lucas, or a story without a heroine,' and had introduced many incidents and characters of his school-days, 'some of the scum that rose to the top of that scholastic cauldron' adding, 'I think it is good. You must judge in after ages.' This projected novel was never completed, although for a time it figured in his correspondence. Perhaps some of the material was embodied in his first published novel, *Long Odds* (since republished as *Heavy Odds*), although I do not think so, as there is no description in that story of school-life nor of any neighbourhood resembling Highgate – the Highgate of those days.

Great was his delight at discovering that Melbourne was well-supplied with second-hand books and prints, commodities that to natures like his are almost among the necessities of life. 'Unfortunate literati,' he explained, had brought them out in former years and sold them when the place was a 'mass of diggers. I bought all De Quincey's works the other day for a shilling a volume and a copy of the engravings of Callot for five shillings. Does not your mouth water?' Even when at Highgate School, Marcus knew all about the famous Callot (who had left home at twelve years of age to study art in Italy and had made up for want of cash and other difficulties by joining a band of gipsies he encountered on his road).

He sent me a specimen of his contributions to the Melbourne *Punch* with which he was pleased himself, entitled 'The Puff Conclusive,' inspired by the tone of fulsome adulation adopted by the colonial press in its notices of the popular London actor, Charles Kean, then fulfilling an engagement at Melbourne, and is a good specimen of Marcus Clarke's early style of satirical composition:

'The Puff Conclusive' which may be expected to appear in any paper any day this week:

Having exhausted panegyric in eulogizing the separate performances of Mr. Charles Kean, we now propose to speak of his general ability and personal qualifications. Not only is he the greatest actor, who ever trod this or any other stage, but he is the only one. The art of acting was born and will die with him.

He is the Alpha and Omega of his profession. Other men have acquired celebrity upon the boards, at different periods and in different countries, but, compared with him they were puny pretenders, shallow charlatans and impudent impostors. Nature may have bestowed upon each of them some special gift and individual faculty but Mr. Kean is lavishly endowed with them *all*. He is as tall as Barry, as airy as Smith, as regal as Bardon, as precise as John Kemble, as quaint as Harley, as earnest as Macready, as graceful as Kynaston, as sprightly as Dodd, as impressive as Betterton, as original as Dogget, as elegant as Barton Booth, as easy as Havard, as majestic as Siddons, as winning as Eliza Farren, as modest as Powell, as impulsive as Jordan, as genial as Dowton, as racy as Elliston, as humorous as Suett, as perfect as Wilks, and as versatile as Garrick. His voice combines the silvery sweetness of Mrs. Cibber's with the strength of Mossop's, the judicious modulation of Quin's and the flexibility of Bannister's.

He has all the *verve* of Préville, the fire of Clairon, and the immortal youth of Mlle. Mars. His articulation is remarkably distinct and his elocution faultless. He gives to each letter its appropriate sound, to each syllable its fitting accent, and to each number of a sentence its nicely proportional weight and emphasis. He has no mannerisms; absolutely none.[36] No faults – absolutely none. To say that his acting is perfection is to do him a cruel injustice; it goes a long way beyond it. He is a histrionic Colossus, a Thespian prodigy, a theatrical miracle, an interpreter of Shakespeare who dwarfs the poet he condescends to illustrate. Shakespeare is the pedestal, but Kean is the statue on the pedestal.

As to the unfortunate person from whom Mr. Kean derived his name (although an actor of some repute in his day) his fame has been completely overshadowed by that of his son, just as Bernardo Tasso's was obscured by Torquato's; or as the respectable old painter's at Urbino was eclipsed by Master Rafaelle's. What somebody said of somebody else is strictly applicable to Mr. Charles Kean; *Natura lo fece e ruppe la stampa*. And as such, how can we bear to part with him? When he leaves us we shall

---

36   Charles Kean's style of delivery and mannerisms were, if my memory serves me rightly, precisely the actor's weak points.

have to close the theatres. It is quite impossible we can tolerate any other performer. The drama will die the moment he departs; but the ship that conveys Mr. Charles Kean from these shores, will also bear to Europe the harrowing intelligence, that every inhabitant of the colony (Aborigines included), oppressed with an insufferable sense of irreparable loss, has drowned himself and his grief in the waters of Hobson's Bay. *(NB. Home papers please copy!)* …

In addition to many other such effusions as the above he had written a farce entitled, 'What may happen to a man in Victoria,' which had been accepted and played at the Theatre Royal, and in October 1864 had completed a burlesque, 'The Lady of the Lake.' This was produced at the then existing Haymarket Theatre[37] (afterwards destroyed by fire and the site of which is now covered by one of Melbourne's markets); this burlesque, to judge by extracts given in Marcus's letter, abounded in those far-fetched puns that were the almost invariable characteristic of similar productions of the period. Thus before attacking Roderick Dhu, Fitz-James exclaims,

> To draw more bills on Jews I can't afford,
> So on Thee, Dhu, I think I'll draw my sword!

and after he has killed him, continues,

> He's gone; his little game he'll never play more,
> Wanting six feet of earth, he's got a foot of Claymore!

Again, the following couplet has the ring of 'the grand, comic, Christmas pantomime of the sixties' about it:

> I feel like angry Scot,
> That, *coûte que coûte*, I coot kick out the lot!

Some time late in 1864 [1867] he wrote me that he was then contributing a series of articles to the *Australasian* newspaper entitled 'Peripatetic Philosophy,' and described them as being much after the manner of Sala's *Breakfast in*

---

37   The second theatre visited by 'New Chum.' See previous chapter.

Bed, and *Twice round the Clock*, adding (parenthetically) 'I wish I could write for the home papers instead of these colonial ones. I have done nothing but write, write, write since you last heard from me.' This disposes of an assertion I have heard that the first contributions Marcus made to any newspaper were the series of articles entitled the 'Noah's Ark' papers. On the contrary, they were published at a later period of his life altogether. The letter containing the extracts quoted concluded with a rather pathetic reference to the mutability of his own disposition:

> You must excuse this stupid letter. I am in very bad spirits and have nothing to say; you know my mercurial temperament and that in my mental barometer the quicksilver is either up to 70 Fahrenheit or down to zero.

His letters, generally filled with running comments on the books of the day, would have suggested to anyone not conversant with his extraordinary powers of rapidly assimilating what he read, that his time must have been entirely absorbed by literary pursuits leaving none to spare for acquiring the duties of a bank clerk. For in another letter of this period he informs me that he has just finished reading Renan's *Vie de Jésus* and has also been taking a course of Emerson. He continues, 'You should read him. Emerson, Carlyle, Ruskin, Browning, Kant and Bossuet have been my literary pabulum for some time past. Rather a curious mixture but I like incongruities.' He then mentions a scheme for making a living that would enable him to quit the Bank but explains that a more pressing problem awaited his decision, viz, whether he should volunteer for military service in New Zealand where the war with the Maoris was then in progress. He never alluded to this subject in his letters again, but I have since ascertained that not only was the intention quite a serious one but that an accident alone prevented its having been carried into execution. One of his cousins was serving with the British force in New Zealand, but whether by his advice or more probably (as my informant thought) owing to some change in the course of public events, the idea was abandoned.

When I next heard from him he had been thrown from his horse and the letter mentioning the occurrence contained the following reflections on the changes wrought in his own character by his life in Australia:

I am glad, on the whole, I came out. One gets such an immense amount of humbug forced out of one by the force-pump of society here. I used to consider myself quite a small demigod in comparison with the natives (native-born is of course meant) but I have found out that there is a vast deal to be done before I can cry quits even with a Colonial … I, you may remember, was always an effeminate looking, spoilt-boy sort of a fellow, and I am afraid am so still; but a certain amount of harebrainedness (to coin a word)[38] and *penchant* for devilry have carried me through.

Personally, I should have said that there never had been any doubt as to his possession of the qualities in question, doubtless inherited from his North of Ireland ancestors; for delicacy of constitution and sweetness of manner towards those to whom he felt drawn would not have misled anyone with the slightest perception of character as to his courage and self-reliance.

The letter then passes on to other topics and mentions the robbery of a Bank at Collingwood (a suburb of Melbourne) about which it says, 'One of the ruffians was by the blessing of Providence and the assistance of a brass candlestick knocked on the head and the other captured,' and then enquires, 'Has the fame of the Bushranger, Gardiner, reached home? He's quite the rage here. Such a gentlemanly murderer! He was tried at Sydney for murder and triumphantly acquitted amid the cheers of the mob. There are still sixteen distinct highway robberies with violence and two more murders against him, so perhaps the beast will hang at last!'[39]

The letter concluded with the following characteristic petition:

Still direct,

> M. A. Hislop Clarke Esqre,
> Bank of Australasia,
> Melbourne,
> Victoria,

---

38 I copy the passage *verbatim* but cannot discover what word he has 'coined'.

39 See passage in previous chapter where New Chum in passing Mohier's Waxworks perceives 'a crowd round the glowing gas-lit window admiring "The Bushranger Gardiner", as he appears with revolver, bowie, rifle and thigh-boots complete, the model of an Australian Highwayman'.

Some people direct,
> M. A. Hislop Clarke Esqre,
>> Melbourne,
>>> Sydney,
>>>> Victoria,
>>>>> New South Wales,

which is about equivalent to,
> Grosvenor Square,
>> Dublin,
>>> Monmouthshire,
>>>> County Mayo,
>>>>> Scotland,
>>>>>> via Marseille!!!

Chapter 10

Trip to Wood's Point, Gipp's Land. – Incidents of the journey. – Marcus's description of a 'new rush' to a goldfield and Mr Farjeon's treatment of the same subject in his novel, Grif, *compared. – Murder of a Chinaman. – Return to Melbourne. – Experiences of another mining centre. – Marcus quits the service of the Bank of Australasia.*

Whilst in the employ of the Bank of Australasia, Marcus was sent up to a spot called Wood's Point in Gipp's Land, one hundred and twenty miles from Melbourne, where gold had (then) recently been discovered and where the bank authorities had determined to open a branch. He was selected to accompany the newly appointed manager and sent me a graphic account of the journey up, first by coach and afterwards on horseback. They found it rather rough travelling and at the hotels on the road encountered homeward bound diggers very drunk and insisting on 'shouting' drinks all round somewhat in this style:

> 'Well Mate! D--n your eyes, what's yours?' I, who am seated by a log fire, feebly smoking and covered with mud, reply, 'Thanks! I've just liquored up!' 'Oh! that be d----d! There Mate, a nobbler for this b-----!' A 'nobbler' is a stiff glass of brandy and water which I drink. Then more shouting and more nobblers until the manager and I slink off to bed.
>
> About 4 a.m. two ruffians come upstairs and one, very drunk, mistakes the sofa whereon I am courting Morpheus for his bed and, as he has spurs on, I am speedily

awakened but, with the assistance of my chum, eject him. He falls downstairs and attacks all below; there is a scrimmage for some minutes, when someone shouts, 'Nobblers round' and all is quiet. In the morning to horse and away.

The place itself he found intolerable, or very nearly so, 'A regular canvas town; all tents, with here and there some sheds – a regular goldfield.' The rush to it had taken place within a week and there was only a bush road. The latter presented a scene of disorder: 'Carts, families, pigs and saddles all spilt in wild confusion, with now and then a mob of drunken stockmen swooping down like a charge of cavalry.' The inn at which the bank manager and Marcus put up, struck the latter as resembling a bad specimen of a 'public' in a London slum, of one, as he put it, in the Seven Dials (that is, the Seven Dials as he remembered them in the Sixties). The miners ('diggers' as they were called in those days) impressed him most unfavourably, and all that we had read about them in our school days, was, he informed me, 'melodramatic nonsense.'

Mr Farjeon describes the surroundings of a 'new rush', in his novel *Grif* in language which has struck me as being a finished picture of the brief sketch in Marcus's letter:

> Take a few acres of level ground, where in the winter people sank over their ankles in thick mud, and where in the summer they were blinded with the fine dust which an Australian hot wind drove mercilessly in their faces; divide the ground into the narrowest and most irregular of streets and lanes; erect (if it may be so called) upon it a few hundreds of canvas tents, of all sizes and shapes, which in a civilised city would not be thought fit for pigs or poultry; smoke-dry the entire space until the canvas of the tents becomes black and rotten, and hangs in shreds from weak battens and crazy poles; let the wretched habitations be tenanted by gaol refuse, by unscrupulous traders, by dismayed and distressed immigrants who have journeyed over stormy seas in search of gold, by brute faces and kind faces, by flaunting women and ladies of tender rearing; let the spaces be choked up with packing cases, and immigrants' trunks, and crying children, and perplexed wanderers from distant lands; above all, let no vice be hidden – let no shame be shame-faced: and a reasonably correct picture of Canvas Town, Melbourne, in the early days of the gold-diggings will be portrayed.

It was to some such scene of disorder as the above that Marcus Clarke had been sent, for it must be remembered that at the period of which I am writing, not more than some dozen years had elapsed since the first discoveries of gold in Victoria had been made, and that the transition-stage from the pioneer arrangements of the fifties to the orderly conditions of today was scarcely by any means completed as indeed Marcus's letter proves. Amongst his experiences at Wood's Point was the following which I take from another of his letters.

A Chinaman had been killed by one of the 'diggers' just before Marcus's arrival. The murderer, after cleaving open his victim's head with a spade, had returned to his tent and drunk the contents of a bottle of corrosive sublimate (used for sheep) mistaking it for rum. A mate of the murdered man, accompanied by two other men, entering the murderer's tent, found him dying in fearful tortures from the effects of the acid, but, notwithstanding, they strung up the struggling wretch to an improvised gibbet, made of rails, his feet dangling not a yard from the ground. But a troop of mounted police having been sent up, better order afterwards prevailed. After a short stay Marcus and his 'Boss' returned to Melbourne, much to the former's relief.

After a brief interval, however, he was sent to another mining centre, Dunolly, as assistant to the agent of the Bank of Australasia there. He had to ride about and buy gold and could study at his leisure the ways of the 'diggers' and the local characteristics, with the result that he brought back to Melbourne 'two big note books crammed with notes on men and manners' (to adopt his own language) which he subsequently turned to good account. For instance, in his sketch, 'The monster Nugget,' he writes:

> A blazing sun. The white and red heaps of mullock cropping up among the dusty dwarf-gums. The white road leading up to the township. The goats wandering round about. The figure of the Chinaman yonder distinctly outlined against the blue sky, as his yellow body rises and falls with the turning-handle of the windlass. The distant public-house with the stock-horse standing stupidly at the verandah post, while Jem is taking a smoke and 'waiting for the mail.' The dim haze over all and far away in the distant hills, the smoke of a bushfire heavily rising.

He only referred to his position in the Bank of Australasia when it was necessary to explain how he came to be living away from Melbourne. Remembering his dislike of mathematical studies at school, I was not surprised to learn from Mr. Mackinnon's memoir that he (Marcus) 'hated methodical book-keeping,' nor that 'a column of figures was a weariness of the flesh that would depress him for a whole day,' nor, in fact, that though a universal favourite, he had received a friendly hint from the manager that he had better seek some more congenial employment, followed up by the presentation of a quarter's salary in advance and a friendly parting word.

Marcus made literary capital of this incident afterwards, for none understood better than the 'Peripatetic Philosopher' how to amuse his readers by raising a laugh – if necessary – (as in the case in question) at his own expense. The anecdote has already been quoted in Hamilton Mackinnon's memorial volume but as many readers may not have seen that publication, I shall perhaps be pardoned for introducing it here:

> It has always been my misfortune through life not to be a Business Man … When I went into a bank – 'The Polynesian, Antarctic and Torrid Zone' – I suffered again. I was correspondence clerk, and got through my work with immense rapidity. The other clerks used to stare when they saw me strolling homewards punctually at four, and I felt quite proud of my accomplishments. But in less than a week, a change took place. Letters came down from up-country branches. 'I have received cheques to the amount of £1.15.6, of two of which *no* mention is made in your letter of advice.' 'Sir! how is it that my note of hand for £97. 4s. 1¾d., to meet which I forwarded Messrs. Blowhard and Co.'s acceptance, has been DISHONOURED by your branch at Warrnambool?' '*Private*. – Dear Cashup – Is your correspondent a hopeless idiot? I can't make head or tail of his letter of advice. As far as I can make out, he seems to have sent out the remittances to the wrong places. – Yours, T. Tottle.' I am afraid that it was true. The manager sent for me, said that he loved me as his own brother, and that I wore the neatest waistcoats he had ever seen, but that my genius was evidently fettered in a bank. Here was a quarter's salary in advance, he had no fault to find – quite the reverse – but – but – well, in short, I was not a Business Man.

The late Mr. Patchett Martin in an article contributed to the *Temple Bar* magazine, not long after the death of Marcus Clarke, wrote with some discernment, I fancy, concerning this phase of Marcus's career:

> The most toilsome journey often makes the most delightful retrospect, and I shrewdly suspect that the young Genius, who had mistaken his path in life and gone astray in a counting-house was regarded by all alike as an intolerable nuisance, notwithstanding his Horatian verse and his alleged familiarity with the 'tragic passages' of the great Greek dramatist.

Be this as it may, Marcus's connection with the Bank of Australasia terminated
somewhat in the manner he has himself so humorously described towards the close
of the year 1864 or thereabouts. As Mr. Charles Bright has tersely put it: 'He was
about as well fitted to be a judge himself as to be a bank clerk, and the outcome
of that attempt was a foregone conclusion.' And after a short interval and several
consultations with his uncle it was decided that he should try his hand at quite a
different pursuit; one which, although eventually also abandoned as uncongenial,
proved of invaluable service to him in the rich experiences yielded and turned to such
good account in essays and stories dealing with the life and scenery of the Australian
bush. For in Mr. Bright's words, 'Judge Clarke had an interest in a squatting station
in a remote portion of the colony, and thither Clarke was despatched, to learn
the mysteries of pastoral management, and become, it might be, later on, one of
Australia's wool kings. It is to be feared that the breeding of sheep never interested
him to the extent which that absorbing pursuit should have done, but he was busy
breeding ideas which had their outcome later on.'

Chapter 11

Projected theological and philosophical work to be called 'Priestcraft and People.' – The subject not again alluded to in his correspondence but the same ideas introduced in his essay on Civilisation without Delusion. *– He confides his desire for a literary career to his uncle, the judge. – Quits Melbourne for Swinton Station near Glenorchy. – Acquiring his colonial experience. – Adventure with a mutinous stockman. – His continuing interest in literary subjects. – Explanation of the cynical tone of his letters and reference to the vicissitudes of his early life. – Some personal characteristics. – Description of his new surroundings. – Early morning gallops. – Camping out in the bush. – Portrait of a half-caste, native girl. – A sunset scene at Swinton Station.*

Before leaving Melbourne, and indeed for some time previously, Marcus had been collecting the data for a projected philosophical work to be called 'Priestcraft and People,' which was, he explained:

> to take the form of a review of all creeds, beginning with the Egyptian and Mosaic and treating of the Greek, Roman, Brahman and early Teutonic beliefs and concluding with that of the Middle Ages and following epochs down to the present day. It will be chiefly descriptive and reflective (he continues) and somewhat resemble Ruskin's *Stones of Venice*; I mean as regards description, apart from discussion, and will attempt to show the similarity between all religions. I have been reading hard for the past year at the different books needful for details.

This announcement led me to expect that the first public appearance of Marcus Clarke in the field of literature would be in the character of an historical and philosophical writer – in fact as the author of a work the nature of which he had thus foreshadowed.

Of course many such books have appeared during the long interval that has since elapsed. In this connection various well-known, literary names will doubtless occur to the reader – Grant Allen's among the number. The present writer well remembers, in early life, a Liverpool commercial man (of a naturally studious bent) who found relief and relaxation from business cares by composing in his leisure hours a treatise on the 'Philosophy of Primary Beliefs' and other works of a similar character. But the author of a quite recent work of this nature, *The Lords of the Ghostland, or An Account of the Great Religions of All Time*, seems, according to a reviewer, to have really achieved the very object poor Marcus, at the age of nineteen and when a bank clerk, had in view. For this critic remarks, 'Let it be explained that the pages just turn two hundred and that the book is set in large type. Yet in that confined space Mr. Saltus essays to present the nature, evolution and influences of the religions of Hindustan, Persia, Egypt, Babylon, Israel, Greece and Rome,' and adds, 'What is still more surprising is that he does it with more success than could have been believed possible.'[40] Whether Marcus would have been equally successful can of course only be conjectured, but one may with confidence assert, that had he persevered with his 'Review of all Creeds' he would have made something of it; for that brilliant essay of his, *Civilisation without Delusion* undoubtedly embodies some of the results of his studies at the period of which I am writing, although the projected treatise itself was never mentioned again in his correspondence, and no such work from his pen ever made its appearance.

About this time, i.e. during the interval between his quitting the service of the Bank of Australasia and his departure from Melbourne, he confided to his uncle his literary aspirations and found him not 'altogether unsympathetic although unable quite to see how they were to be realised.' So they were abandoned for a time altogether, although, as he informed me, he had been 'writing intently' up to the very eve of his departure. Having at length taken leave of his uncle and such friends as

---

40   *The Gods of the Ancients, The Lords of Ghostland*, by Edgar Saltus. *An Account of the Great Religions of All Time* (Werner Laurie). See review in the *Observer* of February 16, 1908.

he had already made in Melbourne, he proceeded early in the year 1865 to Swinton
Station, near Glenorchy, a 'sheep and cattle run' under the management of Mr. John
Holt in which, as already stated, his uncle, the judge, had a pecuniary interest. It was
situated in the county of Borung, province of Wimmera, on the extensive plains lying
to the W. and N.W. of the Great Dividing Range, and near the western spur of which
the mountain chain is known as the Pyrenees and Grampians, from its supposed
resemblance to those two mountain ranges. The River Wimmera which is, I believe,
in summer little more than a chain of water-holes and sometimes almost dries up,
rising in those mountains and eventually losing itself in Lake Hindmarsh, gives its
name to the district. It is a country of rich, natural pasture but wheat and vines are
now extensively cultivated. The nearest bush town is Glenorchy.

At Swinton Station Marcus was to take up the duties of a 'jackaroo,' or to adopt
the phrase the meaning of which he illustrated in the graphic and amusing sketch
already alluded to, he was about to 'acquire his colonial experience.' From an article
in the *Nineteenth Century Review* and from other sources, I gather that young men
even to the present day come out for the same purpose, 'with that most useless of
all educations, the ordinary education of an English gentleman.' The writer of the
article points out that such a youth has:

> a certain softness of upbringing which gives him wants and desires from which
> an ordinary labourer is free. He is thus handicapped from the start. His one
> qualification for the rough, colonial life, that will make him reticent over failures and
> disappointments, is his pluck. So off he goes to compete in the labour market with
> all the thew and muscle already there. He is not wanted; he is *de trop*. Not only the
> labour class don't want him but the employer doesn't want him.

Now although in Marcus Clarke's time the conditions were doubtless less acute
than at the present day, they differed, I take it, only in degree, and the writer's
words would probably have applied with almost equal force to him. The life itself
was more to his taste than the routine of the Bank of Australasia but a little daunted
him at first, as he has confided to his readers in the essay previously mentioned.
Therein he describes Swinton as the 'Dinkledoodledum Station,' which, as any
philologist could guess by the sound of it, meant 'The valley of the rippling
streamlets,' but where, nevertheless, 'never a rippling streamlet met the eye,' and
the life he led there is touched upon in a half-bantering, half-pathetic strain of an
undoubtedly genuine and autobiographical character:

Oh, that bark hut! Never shall I forget the first day when I, a slim and somewhat effeminate youth, with London smoke not yet cleared from my throat, beheld its dilapidated walls. 'You will sleep here,' said Jack, pointing to a skillion which seemed to have been used as a sheep-pen, so marked was the 'spoor' of these beasts. 'With all my heart,' said I, as that organ sank within me – down, down, down, until I could feel it palpitating in the very tips of my riding-boots.

One of the first problems that confronted Marcus in his new life (not alluded to in the above-quoted essays however) was how to exact obedience from the men. An Australian writer remarks with regard to them:

Like the sailors on board a merchant-ship, the ordinary 'hands' on a sheep-station are frequently a very rough lot. So few are the opportunities of intelligent enjoyment which the men possess that only the roving and ne'er-do-well members of society will consent to adopt the life permanently. The boundary-rider, or shepherd, or bullock-driver, who works upon a station lives by day a solitary life and at night, if he have any companionship at all, it is that of one or two rough customers like himself who under the flaring light of an oil-lamp overhead will play a game at euchre before tumbling on to the stretchers which serve them for beds.

It was not very long before the truth of these remarks was exemplified in the case of poor Marcus; for having been sent one morning to a distant hut where two of the hands lived, to superintend the cutting-out and driving-in of some cattle, he saw by the expression of one of the men's faces that he would not be able to exercise his authority without a struggle. The man was an ex-convict and, when the party went out to drive in the cattle, Marcus observed him watching all his movements with disfavour and noted that he was evidently desirous of seeing him (Marcus) come to grief. Whilst both of them were dodging a very restless bull, the man instead of wheeling his horse to the right and leaving the left open to Marcus wheeled in that direction, the result being that both came in contact with a violent shock. Their horses, half-dazed in consequence, staggered for a moment but that of Marcus, answering to the spur, succeeded in avoiding the bull. A moment afterwards he was aware of a great crash and a thud behind, and looking back saw man and horse rolling together with the bull's horns in the belly of the unfortunate horse. The other men, coming up, succeeded in driving it off and into the enclosure. The stockman, the cause of the mischief, who had himself escaped unhurt, then threw the blame on Marcus, and the latter, justly incensed, both at the accusation and the foul language in which it was conveyed, replied by warning him, that if he did not greatly moderate his behaviour, the balance of his wages should be paid him and he should be instantly discharged.

This threat inflamed the man's passions to such a pitch that he made a rush at poor Marcus with the intention of doing him some personal injury. The latter knowing that in bodily strength and skill he was no match for his powerful antagonist, forced his horse adroitly alongside of him and struck him with the butt-end of his loaded riding-whip a blow that felled him to the ground. For a few minutes he lay motionless, Marcus terribly frightened, thinking he might be dead. But fortunately he had not been seriously hurt, although obliged to lie up for a few days during which he was able to relieve the tedium of his enforced confinement by reading the books sent down to him from the station by Marcus. Eventually he returned to his duties, 'subdued and even civil,' and the incident had the salutary effect of establishing Marcus Clarke's authority with the men, for this one had been the notorious bully of the station.

The element of danger involved in some of the operations forming part of the routine of life on a sheep and cattle run was an attraction – not a drawback – to Marcus Clarke. Despite his slight and somewhat effeminate appearance (as he himself described it) he had been noted at school for his coolness and indifference to bodily danger, in fact for his presence of mind in an emergency. These qualities must have stood him in good stead for very skilful horsemanship and presence of mind are frequently required in heading cattle, the horses being rendered occasionally almost unmanageable by their terror of the infuriated animals. His letters were however seldom taken up with his personal experiences and adventures, but were far more often filled with his impressions of the topics of the day, in particular the latest literary ones, which were treated with an eagerness and interest evoked by no other subject and showing only too clearly where his real sympathies lay. More than once he apologized for the cynical tone he had frequently adopted in them, by reminding me that he had been 'kicked upon the tide of time' to 'sink or swim' at sixteen and gone through as much by the time he had reached twenty or thereabouts as many men have at thirty. Had he not, he asks, among other experiences, been gold-agent at a 'new rush' where amongst the mob of new-comers who had made their way thither in the hope of finding their fortune, there might well be some who would knock you on the head for the gold in your tent if they had the chance? Had he not lived for six or seven weeks at a time in the bush with no companion but an 'Old Hand,' (i.e. an ex-convict) and with blacks encamped within 'cooey' of them? Had he not dabbled in mining speculations, sometimes successfully, oftener the reverse, and when successful squandered the money thus lightly won in 'seeing life' in Melbourne so that it was not to be expected (he concluded) that he should be quite as confiding in human nature as he had been at sixteen! He described himself as rather vain, having all sorts of ambitious notions in the matter of authorship, hoping to 'equal Thackeray in satire and Dickens in description,' and as entertaining 'very heterodox opinions on many subjects on which he should be inclined to write like a literary Ishmael.'

But he was well aware of his weak points, utterly the reverse of self-satisfied or self-complacent and given to deploring his own carelessness in money matters. The only thing in life he cared about, he wrote, was to 'become favourably known as an author,' a longing that was also constantly expressed in early life by his favourite novelist, Balzac. When despondent and under the influence of the feeling that 'All is vanity under the sun', he 'wrestled with his bad humour,' and only used it, he assured me, 'as an incentive to philosophical musings.'

The above reflections were embodied in one of his long, early letters from Swinton and were accompanied either in that or in the following one by a diagram of the station and a description of his surroundings. After enumerating the various buildings and their dispositions, he continues:

It is a very pretty place. The River Wimmera runs through the garden, which is filled with peach and apple trees and vines. Enormous trees cast their shade all around and beyond them is the bush. My room affords through its open windows a glimpse of the distant ranges and of a break in them called 'Hell's Gap,' which, when the sun sets, looks like a gorge of fire. My room is oblong in shape.[41] On the fireplace hangs a machine for supporting whips made of horns fastened to uprights; there repose four whips. This is flanked by two huge boots, which are worn in traversing swamps and during the rains. On the (one) wall hang pictures: 'The Cornflower,' (a young girl with sheaves); a set of cartoons on grey paper (hunting sketches) called respectively, 'The Meet', 'The Find', 'Full Cry', 'The Death'; whilst on the other are fixed a rifle and shot-gun, and underneath them is a sofa with an opossum-skin rug spread over it. A large table stands in the centre of the floor covered with books, tobacco-jars and

---

41   This description refers to his room at the Head Station. The 'bark hut' would be occupied when the work required Marcus's presence at an out-station, but in the above letters he is speaking of his quarters at the homestead.

cigar-boxes whilst another table in the corner holds my desk and papers. Three or four cane rocking-chairs litter the room and on the mantelpiece is a rest for spurs, a pipe rack, a whistle, and the well-known engraving of that picture of Holman Hunt's, 'I stand at the door and knock.' Queer companionship! – whilst pinned to the space between the windows is a copy of the 'Scab Act for 1865.' These said windows are open and lead on to the verandah where I catch a glimpse of young Holt luxuriously smoking and reading *The Three Musketeers*. There are besides two dogs in the room, a terrier and a kangaroo dog. A door to the right gives access to my bed-room … You have no idea how jolly I feel when, in the early morning before sunrise, I get my horse and gallop over the plains at the foot of the mountains, watching the parrots flying from the distant woods and the sun rising over the purple hills; perhaps starting an emu (there are mobs of them on the plains) and getting home in time for breakfast … Camping out in the bush too is very jolly, smoking by your fire, wrapped in your rug; while the numerous birds and insects of the Australian forest are keeping high festival around.

In another letter he writes:

To my right, through the verandah-curtains, I get a glimpse of the river and of the blacks' camp. Beyond the river the plains roll away to the jagged and grim-looking mountains now nearly black against the sinking sun. A delightful breeze has sprung up which stirs the folds of the handkerchief that K (who is buried in the depths of a huge Chinese cane-bottomed chair) has flung over his face.

Holt is leaning over the rails of the verandah and employed alternately in repelling the caresses of two kangaroo dogs who are fawning on him, and talking to a half-caste girl who has come up from the camp to petition for brandy for Tom, the black stockrider who, it seems, has 'big one bruise long um leg, Sah!' She is a fine specimen of a savage, this same half-caste. She is only fifteen years old but has a magnificent *tournure* and feet and ankles as small as a Spaniard's. Her skin is not black but bronze and her dark eyes, white teeth, and long black hair entitle her to be spoken of as 'Budgeree lubra, dat one e-e-h?'[42]

In the stockyard are five colts in the 'tackling,' running round and round and being enticed by a red-shirted stockman and his mate who are looking through the

---

42   Word, in the original, illegible.

rails with an expression of favour towards the boss's 'young 'uns.' Dotted here and there are some fifteen or twenty horses grazing in the paddock.

The sun has just set and the parroquets and laughing jackasses are holding high jinks in the bush behind us and down at the men's huts I hear them laughing at some joke of 'Long Harry's', the cook. Looking into the room behind me I see old Maggie, the housekeeper, laying the cloth for supper, so I must stop, more especially as two figures are approaching the house at a gallop – a tall, bearded fellow on a big grey horse and his daughter on her blood filly Norah. These are our next neighbours, the E----s, and I think F.[43] intends to 'hitch on,' as the Yankees say, with the girl. Poor devil! So, Good Bye!

---

43   One of the squatter's household.

Chapter 12

First results of his leisure time at Swinton. – Rendering into English verse of Horace's ode, 'Ad Barinem.' – Other literary efforts including an essay on sheep shearing. – His views on the prospects of the pastoral industry. – The scenery and climate of Swinton. – A bush fire on the Run, and its dangers. – The hardships and risks involved in fighting it. – The experience subsequently turned to account in a story.

Some months after Marcus's arrival at Swinton, he enclosed in one of his letters a copy of the following verses, viz. a rendering by him into English of the Horatian ode 'Ad Barinem.' He considered, he said, that his lines were pretty close to the original and hoped that I should be able to get them into one of the London magazines but added that he did not ask for the favour of an illustration by my brother, Gerard[44] this time, there being nothing that he could see in them to illustrate. I have never come across them in any published edition of his works and although by no means equal in my opinion to his version of Heine's ballad 'The Sphinx Riddle,' nor even to some of his own lyrics, they will, I think, be found of interest, regard being had to the conditions in which they were produced; for amongst the numerous translations of Horace's *Odes*, this may well be the only one composed by an admirer of the Latin poet, who was at the date of its production a pupil on a sheep and cattle station in a part of the country that was then regarded as

---

44   Father Gerard Hopkins S.J. (See Chapter 5).

the 'back blocks' of Victoria. I sent them, as requested, to the editor of *Once a Week* and to one or two other periodicals of that day but they were not accepted; and I accordingly returned them to Melbourne, much disappointed that my efforts at getting his work 'placed' in London had again proved unsuccessful. I now give the verses in question:

To Barine

For all thy honeyed lover's lies,
For all thy dear, deceitful, sighs,
For all thy pretty perjuries,
Did but one pang of memory grieve Thee!
Were thy pearly teeth less white,
Were thy sparkling eyes less bright,
Had the avenging bolt let slip
But grazed one rosy finger-tip,
My foolish heart would still believe Thee!

But the memory of thy guile,
Of each delusive, siren smile,
Of vows thou mad'st and broke the while,
But serve thy beauty for enriching,
The knowledge of thy old deceit
But makes new-uttered vows more sweet,
When Thou appear'st the throng among,
A crowd of lovers old and young
Proclaims Thee still bewitching!

You vowed your heart was wholly mine,
With lover's looks and phrases fine,
Vowed by yon stars that silent shine,
By Heaven, where cold Death cometh never,
Vowed by your mother's funeral urn,
By all the oaths those lips could learn,
Yet – tho' I know Thee false as fair,
Thy beauty hath a charm so rare –
I cannot choose but love Thee ever!

I tell thee, Sweet, the piteous sight
Of all thy lovers, left and right,
To Venus' Self doth give delight!
Her saucy nymphs with glee throng after,
Praising the power of thy smile,
And heartless Cupid, who, the while,
With cruel joy his whetstone turning,
Sharpens his love-dart keen and burning,
Applauds with floods of rippling laughter.

This is not all; – forewarned in vain –
Daily some stripling fills thy train,
Each new-fledged gallant boasts a chain
Forged by thy cruel, fairy fingers;
Old loves upbraid thy fickle heart,
Yet cannot – if they would – depart,
For each by Thee for loving chid,
But loves the more, the more forbid,
And near his naughty mistress lingers.

Fond mothers watch with anxious eye
Their bumpkin sons when Thou art nigh,
Old gallants tremble while they sigh,
Lest thy charms force *them*, too, to marry!
Each pretty bride with anger burns,
With fear grows red and white by turns,
Lest – despite kisses, vows and sighs –
The subtle charm that in Thee lies,
Should lure her lord with Thee to tarry!

His pen was always busy. He next wrote a love song in French (a copy of which he enclosed) and a skit in verse on the curator of the Melbourne Botanical Gardens who fancied that he had discovered a great lyric poet in the person of a certain Mr. Jenkyns at Geelong. The latter appeared in the Melbourne *Punch*. He had, he informed me, also written an essay, 'A Day in the Bush,' but asked whether he should not rather call it, 'The Golden Fleece, or Melibœus at the Antipodes' or 'some other Salanesque name?' I never heard more of this essay, nor of one or two stories casually mentioned, the outlines of which he had briefly sketched in the same letter, but it is clear enough that at this period of his life, he was busy emulating the spirit of the subject of Burns' lines, 'A chiel's amang you taking notes,' and that he subsequently turned these notes to good account. For I notice, among other articles contributed by him to the London *Daily Telegraph*, (when acting as their Melbourne correspondent some years afterwards) one on sheep-shearing in Australia commencing thus, 'My friend, Melibœus – not the same concerning whom Virgil in ancient, and Mr. James Payn in modern times, so sweetly discoursed – lives at Pine Plains Station on the Wimmera River, Victoria, and once a year he holds jubilee. The 'shearing' is the year's event on a sheep station … Sooth to say the operation is a serious one, more especially if, like Melibœus, one owns thirty thousand sheep.'

And then follows a description of the process as practised in Marcus Clarke's time and in the district which he knew (omitting no details) such as could never have been penned by anyone not practically acquainted with his subject and showing that he must have taken an active part in the operations himself. At this time indeed, and in spite of certain evidence of literary activity, he appeared to be taking an interest in his new vocation, and from the tenor of some of his letters one might have supposed that he was becoming reconciled to it. For he occasionally quitted the field of literary or philosophical speculation for the discussion of more practical topics and dwelt in an airy strain on the prospects of the pastoral industry. Whether the calculations contained in some of his letters were of any real value I have no means of judging but, like everything that came from his pen, they were at least expressed with admirable lucidity and made very pleasant reading. Indeed a perusal of them would, I fancy, have gone far to convince Mr. Desmond Byrne that he was exaggerating when he wrote concerning the life that Marcus led at Swinton, 'All the day and half the night were dreamed away in literary thought.' Some real work was exacted and was performed by Marcus as I shall presently show … Referring to the aspect of the country in the neighbourhood of Swinton, he writes in one of his letters:

> If you want wild scenery I fancy I could show you some in these hills. Our scenery is not very grand but it is very wild. Gum trees, ferns, prairies, plain, about here at least; though Australian scenery may be described as a rule to be 'toujours Gum.'

He related his experiences with sheep which, if amusing to read, were probably far from being amusing or congenial to him in reality, and commented on the heat that he was then enduring:

> At this moment the temperature in this apartment – doors and windows open – is 110! In the sun it is 120! There is a hot wind blowing! Water is only to be found in the river and we have had no rain for four months. In fact so bad a season has not been known for years.[45] Many squatters are ruined; sheep and cattle are at a discount whilst the only thing left for their owners to do is to drink Bass *ad libitum*, smoke *ad nauseam*, and to curse the climate.

He advised me if we ever experienced such heat in England to wear a pugree (a novelty in those days) adding, 'If you start one at Brighton or Folkestone you will perhaps be taken for a returned Australian and if you only throw in a word or two about sheep, Murrumbidgee mining shares, the Black Hills of –' but at this point he had obviously been interrupted for the sentence was never completed. He had previously written me on the subject of sheep-farming, 'In short it is admitted on all hands that sheep-farming pays better than any other business, and in twenty years Australian uncles will have supplanted Indian uncles on the stage.' But now he was beginning to see something of the drawbacks of sheep-farming and to realise the nature of those 'ups and downs' described in one of Rolf Boldrewood's novels (published originally under this title, I believe, but subsequently renamed *The Squatter's Dream*). So that it was no surprise to anyone acquainted with the mutability of his disposition to learn not very long afterwards that 'he was tired of sheep, sheep, sheep, plain, plain, plain, sun, sun, sun, and bush, bush, bush.'

There came, too, an account of an exciting and very uncomfortable experience thus described:

> We had a fearful bush fire in the ranges last week. I was there for five days and nights without taking my clothes off. We had to fetch water seven miles on horseback. The men and myself were nearly dead with heat and want of water. I hope that it may never be my lot to be present at such another. The fire burned nineteen miles of

---

45   Interesting in view of the fearful drought of recent years.
46   Probably square miles is intended.

country and sixty-two miles of fencing besides raging in the mountains; it is burning yet, I believe, up-country; but it has passed our run.[46] There is no spectacle, save perhaps that of a burning city, so grand as a bush fire. Imagine the trees and scrub high above your head blazing – all the ranges, as far as the eye can reach, one mass of smoke and fire. Birds flying away screaming, herds of cattle and horses, wild with fright, rushing madly from the flames and the roaring of the advancing fire sounding like a mighty sea. We had to burn before it and then put out the flames, hard work with the thermometer at 102 in the shade!, so that when the fire reached us it died out for want of nourishment. We had seven hundred sheep burnt, besides several mobs of cattle and horses. The first night we camped out in a gully of the mountains called 'Hell's Gap' and a mob of some two thousand cattle dashed down the gully through us.[47] You should have seen our plight when we looked at each other! I was bowled into a mud-hole and came out as black as the ace of spades. Several of the men were much bruised and one poor devil of a black fellow was gored and disembowelled. The fire came down on us so quickly that we had to leave his body which was burnt, I believe. Holt is away at the fire now; i.e. at such portions of logs, trees etc as have not died out. I wish him joy of his job! I am completely done up.

Undoubtedly Marcus Clarke had the faculty (which he shared with so many novelists of note) of turning all his personal experiences to account in his writings and this bush fire became the subject of one of his stories of Australian country life. He describes therein how he and friend were watching from the verandah one hot afternoon, 'the eagle-hawks float and pause in the cloudless, blue sky' when the fire-alarm was sounded and concludes:

After pulling down by main force half a mile of fence, thus blowing up communication (the bush-fence of Australia is made of trunks of trees drawn together by bullocks and then interlaced with cut branches) we got the enemy turned away in the ranges. There he blazed for nine days until he got over the other side of the mountain and we saw him no more. During four days the fire lurked round us. The air was pungent with the aromatic odour of burnt gum leaves, the blackened branches and saplings striped our clothes as we walked, while the ashes lay ankle-deep on the black, hot earth. All night the mountain gave out a dull light, while here and there along the range a

47   See previous chapter for mention of this place.

burning tree would flame like a torch and the embers of the red-hot stumps glow fiery red like danger lights. The birds had all gone. The kangaroos and cattle had fled.

Even the dingos were afraid to pass that blackened and desolate forest … But on the tenth day after, a big rain fell and in less than a week all the burnt ground was green as emerald beneath the grey, dead trees. I came down to Melbourne so soon as this happened, the richer by a strange experience, in which the picturesque memories of the burning forest at night – one of the grandest sights in the world, believe me – blend strangely with recollections of burned hands and a longing for pure water unknown even to Sir Wilfrid Lawson.

Chapter 13

Drought at Swinton. – Homesickness and occasional fits of depression. – Local topics. – A murder on the Run. – A ride into the wilderness. – Removal to Ledcourt Station near Stawell. – Mark Twain's opinion of the climate and neighbourhood. – Marcus's own impressions of the scenery. – The requisite qualifications for a pioneer squatter. – Forecast of the prospects for squatters in Victoria. – His picture of the mining township of Stawell. – Comments on the outbreak of hostilities in Europe: (The Austro-Prussian campaign of 1866). – Sickness at the station. – Marcus a general favourite; the heart and soul of local entertainments. – A regular attendant at the church and frequent visitor at the state school.

Drought is naturally a subject frequently referred to in the pages of Australian writers and it figures in some of the letters I received from Marcus at this period, for a spell of that great drawback to the Australian climate was experienced during his first summer at Swinton. The change from a town to a country life and the novelty of the surroundings had at first yielded nothing but pleasure to his receptive and eager nature, but in course of time a reaction of feeling set in, and his letters gave the impression that he was either becoming homesick or brooding over the early troubles of his life. For in one, written during the drought, occurs the following suggestive passage:

> Oh! how I long for a sight of green grass and of a pretty English girl in a morning dress. Oh! for a spring day in England! My plan of life was an easy going existence

as attaché to the embassy at Paris or Vienna, with a connection among the literary people ... Perhaps I had hoped also to achieve fame as a novelist myself, and now by some hard fate all is changed and I am cast out like a leper into the wilderness.

The pathetic ring of these words seems to suggest Browning's well known lines,

> Oh, to be in England
> Now that April's there,
> And whoever wakes in England
> Sees, some morning, unaware
> That the lowest bough and the brushwood sheaf,
> Round the elm-tree bole are in tiny leaf
> While the chaffinch sings on the orchard bough
> In England – now!

However this was probably but a fleeting mood for, when urged by a friend at the station (not very long afterwards) to return to England, he replied that in his opinion such action would be folly and doubted, for his own part, whether he could ever settle down to a London life again.

He seldom alluded to Glenorchy, the 'Bullocktown' of his stories wherein it is described as 'situated ... on ... something that is a flood in winter and a mud-hole in summer,' which 'for general purposes the inhabitants ... called ... a river,' and to which 'those intelligent land surveyors that mark "agricultural areas" on the tops of lofty mountains, had given ... a very grand name indeed'; but his letters occasionally referred to subjects of local interest. Thus he mentions a murder that had been perpetrated in the district remarking, after giving details, 'It is a true story and was told me by a trooper exactly as I have described.' Unfortunately the part of the letter containing the story has been destroyed but the remaining half sheet has the following:

> Apropos of murder a travelling jeweller and his mate were robbed and murdered *on our run* about five miles from where I write this. Their bodies were not found until eight days afterwards. I must have passed the place twenty or thirty times during the interval, but the victims were so admirably concealed in a clump of wattles that had it not been for the stench and the presence of an unusually large number of eagle-hawks, they might have remained undiscovered for years.

And then he went on to give me an account of a strange personal experience of his (amplified in a subsequent letter):

> I have been a month away at Fort Bourke[48] the furthest settlement. It is eight hundred miles from this. A friend of mine and I rode up with two horses apiece. It is a magnificent country but all beyond is the howling wilderness. We were without water for twenty-four hours on one occasion and for thirty-six on another.
>
> All the back country is dried up. Indeed some of the squatters have deserted the runs. We have had no rain for nine months. I have an idea that I shall take stock up to Fort Bourke or else to Nicol Bay (the extreme point of civilization) as one may get one hundred square miles of country for ten pounds a year. If I do, in five years I shall be worth at least twenty thousand pounds (£20,000) but then those five years! Five years banishment from all society, from music, literature, and from all that makes life endurable! I am hardly willing to go.

The letter from which the above is taken concluded with a characteristic reference to a ministerial crisis in Melbourne and the retirement of the then Governor of Victoria, Sir Charles Darling, conceived in the witty vein which won him so much favour as the writer of light literature a few years afterwards … In June 1866 he was transferred to another station, named Ledcourt, managed by Mr. Holt's brother, about twelve miles distant from the town of Stawell. A chain of mountains, the Dividing Range, traverses the greater part of Victoria from east to west and in the neighbourhood of Stawell is known as the Pyrenees and Grampians. During the spring the country is covered with brilliant verdure turned, as the summer advances, into a natural hay; excellent food for stock and in the vicinity of the volcanic hills the soil is extremely rich; now planted with vineyards and producing exceptionally fine wines. The hills themselves are frequently full of mineral wealth and the climate of the mountainous districts very agreeable.

Indeed Mark Twain writes of both the scenery and climate of this neighbourhood with enthusiasm:

> In some countries an indolent, unsheltered drive of an hour and a half in such conditions (noonday; no wind; the sky without a cloud, the sunshine brilliant, and

---

48   See Chapter 15.

the mercury at 92° in the shade) would be a sweltering and prostrating experience; but there was nothing of that in this case. It is a climate that is perfect.

Stawell lies to the S.W. of Glenorchy on the southern side of the River Wimmera and nearer to the Grampian Range which contains numerous cones and extinct craters. (Mark Twain mentions a curious group of boulders called 'The Three Sisters.') Marcus described Ledcourt as being up in these hills and as being 'a most fearfully rocky, rangy mountainous spot surrounded by magnificent scenery. 'It is almost worth while to come out to Australia,' he continues,

> to see the sun rise and set over these mountains. We have all kinds of game, ducks, cranes, peewits, kangaroos, bandicoot, possum, native bear, *et id genus omne,* but the riding after cattle in the hills is terrible work. Some of the names of the so-called 'Gaps' would surprise you.
>
> We have 'Mount Misery,' 'Hell's Gap,' 'Hell's Mouth,' 'The Devil's Den,' and other choice specimens of nomenclature, including 'Thunderer's Flat' and 'Dead Man's Gully.' The sayings and doings are much the same as in the other place so I won't bore you by recounting them.

The hankering to try his fortune in the half-settled country to the north had not left him and the letters from Ledcourt sometimes dwelt upon the chances for those not afraid to venture. But to achieve success hardships would have to be encountered, for he wrote that to manage an estate or a 'run' in the northern districts:

> I must use up all my little capital and lead a terribly hard life for some years, but it is a certain fortune in the end. You must remember that a squatter in new country has to take tea, flour, sugar and stores for at least three years' consumption; has also to take with him a blacksmith, carpenter and some ten stockmen; has to build his own house, clear his own ground, look after his sheep or cattle, protect them from wild dogs and be prepared for fights with the natives. But, if he succeeds in all this, after five years he will have some forty thousand sheep, some nine thousand pounds worth of wool and a station worth thirty thousand pounds. Unless a man knows thoroughly the practical part of working a 'run', he will never do in new country. Station 'hands' have great respect for a man who, if they won't work, can jump off his horse and show them how he wants the work done. I am inclined towards 'back country' moreover from the fact that the squatters' government leases will be up in 1870 – and that there

is more than a probability that the land will be rented in small blocks as farms, which will virtually put an end to squatting in Victoria. *Then* the owners of one hundred square miles of fine country and fifty thousand sheep will find a ready market for their wool, and their land will double in value.[50]

I had gathered that these views of Marcus Clarke's about the land in the neighbourhood of Ledcourt were correct, for it is described in modern handbooks as a district formerly pastoral but now largely given up to agricultural pursuits and to the fruit-growing and wine-producing industries, and I have since been informed on the best authority that this forecast of his has practically been absolutely verified. 'Sometimes, however,' his letter concludes, 'when coming home tired and sore with three days' camping out and hunting for cattle, or twelve hours in dusty sheep-yards running ten thousand ewes through arsenic water for foot-rot, or a day's perilling of one's life in a stock-yard handling young horses, I think of cutting the whole concern.' This fairly bears out Hamilton Mackinnon's statement that Marcus eventually disliked the life and expressed himself to that effect to a neighbouring squatter, averring that the work he was engaged upon, could be better done by a few chimney-sweeps.

Stawell is a market town and an important loading station for grain and wool and the surroundings are said to be attractive, but this is how it struck Marcus Clarke:

> The mining township of Quartzborough, or as it is called in the vernacular, 'Grumbler's Gully,' is situated about twelve miles from Bullock Town.[51] The first impression of Grumbler's Gully is, I confess, not a cheering one. I think it was Mr. Caxton who replied when asked what he thought of his new-born infant, 'It is very red, ma'am'. The same remark would apply to Grumbler's Gully. It is very *red*. Long before you get to it you are covered with dust that looks and feels like finely-powdered bricks. The haggard gum-trees by the roadside – if you can call it rightly a roadside – are covered with this red powder. The white near leader seems stained with bloody sweat, and the slices of bark that, as you approach the town, fringe the track, look as though they were lumps of red putty, drying and crumbling in the sun. On turning the corner, Grumbler's Gully is below as a long, straggling street, under a red hill that

---

50   MC is referring to 'fine country' beyond the boundary of Victoria; to the district lying to the N. and N. W. of that state.
51   'Bullock Town' is Glenorchy whilst 'Quartzborough' or 'Grumbler's Gully' are identical with Stawell.

overlooks a red expanse of mud flecked with pools of red water, and bristling with mounds, shaft-sheds, and wooden engine-houses. The sun is sinking behind yonder mighty range, under whose brow stretches that belt of scrub, and marsh, and crag that meets the mallee wilderness, and minor mountains rise up all around us. Grumbler's Gully is shaped like a shoe with a lump in the middle of it, or rather, perhaps, like one of those cock-boats that children make with folded paper. It is a ridge of quartz, rising in the midst of a long valley surrounded by mountains....

Around are solemn, purple hills, with their hidden mysteries of swamp and wilderness; and here, on the backbone of this quartz ridge, in the midst of a dirty, dusty, unsightly mud-patch, punched with holes, and disfigured with staring, yellow mounds, are fifty or sixty straggling wooden, iron and brick buildings, in which live people of all ranks of society, of all nations, of all opinions ...

Nevertheless, (as I think I am right in assuming) it was from his residence at Ledcourt that Marcus Clarke derived his appreciation of the mysterious attraction of the Australian bush. The surrounding mountain-ranges and wild scrub become to him a source of inspiration from which he drew the material for much of what is best and most artistic in his work.

Not very long after his arrival at Ledcourt the news of the outburst of war in Europe and the resulting panic in the City of London reached him and was thus commented upon, 'Panic! wars and rumours of wars! Overend, Gurney and Company, and the Agra and Masterman's Bank all smashed and war in Europe!' He went on to explain that his sympathies naturally inclined to Austria but that a fellow-pupil, who was a Hungarian, had assured him that from personal experience he knew the Austrians to be 'Brutes in manners, demons in morals, and the two characters alternately in politics!' Reverting to personal topics he begs to call my attention to an enclosure in the letter, a photograph of himself, which, he said, looked like that of 'a groom out of place or one of Leech's hunting men with a brown coat instead of a red one.' Affairs at the Station were, he explained:

rather at sixes and sevens. We have got a house-full of sick people here at present. The overseer has had his leg broken and several ribs also by a fall from a colt which he would persist, contrary to my advice, in riding; whilst Holt has an attack of ague from camping out in a swamp while shooting wild geese. So that the work of the place mostly devolves upon me. The stock-rider, 'Black Harry,' has had his skull fractured by one of the blood fillies and I have ridden thirty-seven miles for a doctor. He died, however, this afternoon.

One may here perhaps appropriately insert a passage from Mackinnon's memoir referring to this period of Clarke's life:

> Marcus Clarke was a great favourite with everybody, and was the life and soul of every local entertainment in the shape of concerts and balls, in all of which he took part with great zest. He was also at that time a regular attendant at the church and a frequent visitor to the local State school, in which he took a lively interest, giving prizes to the boys. He was, moreover, an omnivorous reader, getting … all the best English magazines and endless French novels from Melbourne regularly.

Chapter 14

The campaign in Bohemia of 1866. – Austrian and Russian Cavalry. – Striking opinion expressed by Marcus on the potential value of Australian stockriders as irregular or light cavalry and its vindication by the war in South Africa, some twenty four years afterwards, and in the recent war in France. – Sundry equestrian feats described and the manner of their accomplishment explained. – Confirmation by Mrs. Campbell Praed and others. – Marcus's admiration of Gustave Doré's work and his comments on F. Sandys' illustrations in Once a Week. *– A modern art critic on the latter. – Winter at Ledcourt; a tempest raging. – The station cook a 'Glass-Button' Mandarin. – Allusion to Carlyle.*

Discussing on another occasion the campaign in Bohemia of that year (1866) when the news of the collapse of the Austrians (despite the excellence of their cavalry) had reached Victoria, he points out how the skilful horsemanship of the Australians might be turned to account for military purposes, an opinion in the nature of a prophecy which the war in South Africa and since then the great war in France both strikingly corroborated:

> You say [he writes] that the Hungarian Hussars are the finest body of cavalry in the world. You are wrong. The Tcherkessian Guard of the Emperor of Russia bears the palm. The uniform alone costs seven thousand roubles and each horseman has lived from boyhood in the saddle.

He was thinking doubtless of the Cossacks of whom an Australian war-correspondent during the Russo-Japanese war has written from personal observation,

> Every man there was a horseman to the marrow; not merely a fellow who knows how to sit astride a horse and keep from falling off, but men who knew how to push a good animal to the uttermost limit of its capacity without quite overdoing it. There was not one of them who could not handle a charger fresh in from the wilds and break it. They 'mouthed' their own mounts, broke them, groomed them, bedded them, made companions of them. They knew every trick of temper, every vicious and every playful habit within the hide of their equine chums and they seldom put hand or heel to them in seventy miles.

Marcus's letter continues:

> I am rather inclined to fancy that Australia could furnish magnificent, irregular cavalry. You remember the feats we used to admire at school in the works of Mayne Reid and others.[52] I will bet that an Australian stock-rider will beat a Mexican *ranchero*, *torrero*, or *gaucho*, into fits.[53] I myself, who am but a poor horseman compared to some, can pick up my hat from the ground at full gallop. This is an easy task though it looks a difficult one. The manner of doing it is this. Take your horse well in hand and start him in an easy canter. Hold the reins with the left hand as high up as possible and grasp the mane with the left hand (holding the reins) about seven inches from the horse's ears. Take both feet out of the stirrups and draw up your left leg until the heel of your boot catches the cantle of the saddle; then bend down quickly to the right side, holding on to your horse by the left hand on the mane and the left foot round the cantle of the saddle. You will be perfectly safe and will find that you can touch the ground with your right hand and regain your erect position without difficulty. The nerve is the only thing requisite. I can also jump on and off my horse at full gallop. This is also easier than it would seem. Hold up your reins in the right hand, take your feet out of the stirrups and pass your right leg over the pommel of the saddle and *under* your right arm. You will then be sitting sideways on your horse, with your

---

52 He is alluding to *The Adventures of Two Englishmen in the River Plate* or some similar title; the book mentioned in a previous chapter.

53 Probably *Estanciero* is intended.

feet to the left side. Keep a firm hold of the mane and reins with the right hand and jump with both feet together *with* the horse. You can run by his side (holding the mane) for some yards with ease. Then seize the mane with your left hand and spring upwards to the saddle without using the stirrups. At the same moment leave go with the right hand and catch the cantle of the saddle. You will regain your seat with ease. You may fancy that I am boasting of my horsemanship. These things are considered nothing here.

Mrs. Campbell Praed, in her charming work *My Australian Girlhood,* refers to an old stockrider of her acquaintance which goes far to confirm the above, if there were any need of confirmation:

His natural home was a horse's back, and he was a beautiful sight when mounted on a young colt. First, he would take off his hat and blind the creature by putting it in the cheek-band of his bridle; then he'd catch the near-side rein with his right hand, draw the off-side rein into the horse's neck and hold the two reins and the near-side ear in his left hand – the horse would never buck as long as his ear was held – and then with the right hand on the pommel and a foot in the left stirrup, he would spring up in a second, and gripping the saddle with his knees, his long, lean body balancing with every movement of the horse's body as though he were growing out of it, he was ready for anything that might happen.

Mr. George Sutherland, too, speaks of the extraordinary command over his horse possessed by the bush roughrider and gives one or two examples, but apart from the testimony of Australian writers, I have learnt from one who has lived the life that my friend did not exaggerate, such accomplishments being common with the finished bushman and having their practical value, although to us they may sound too much like the feats of the circus and the tricks of the *haute école*. More interesting is the vindication of the soundness of Marcus Clarke's judgment on the potential military value of such accomplished horsemen afforded by recent events. It is sufficient to cite the testimony of the *Times* correspondent in his account of the review held by H.R.H. the Prince of Wales at Melbourne in May 1901 [54]

---

54   During their visit to the Australian states to open the first Commonwealth Parliament (of that year).

> When their Royal Highnesses entered the parade-ground [his letter ran] behind and
> before them was an escort consisting of a vast collection of Australian cavalry and
> mounted infantry. We have learned their value during the war which has cemented
> the unity of the Empire. A truly inspiriting picture was presented by the war-like
> troopers, some of them war-worn. Perfect riders mounted on beautiful horses, they
> looked ideal soldiers for a rough country, sitting proudly in their saddles ... I shall
> never lose the memory of the sight ... The final scene, after the mounted men had
> advanced in review order and had given the royal salute, was very striking and left the
> impression that some of the finest soldiers in the world exist in Australia.

It is only right to mention here that one of Marcus Clarke's own sons saw service in
the ranks of these same 'ideal soldiers,' despatched by the Australian Commonwealth
and the Dominion of New Zealand to aid in the fight for the safeguarding of the
British Empire in South Africa.

To revert to subjects of a more peaceful character and as an example of the continued
interest taken by Marcus in literary and artistic matters whilst leading this out-door
country life, take the following from one of his letters of this period:

> Have you seen Gustave Doré's illustrated *Don Quixote* and *Bible*? They say he
> draws from memory and can carry away a scene in his head and produce it
> upon paper to the smallest detail. *A propos* of illustrations what a vile, ultra-Pre-
> Raphaelite affair is the page-sketch of Helen and Cassandra in *Once a Week* for
> May by F. Sandys! I admire Sandys as a rule but in this instance he is hideous;
> Cassandra looks like an enraged fishfag. The only good point in the picture is the
> mirror with Cassandra's foot upon it. By the way, too, the sandals of both ladies
> are Roman, not Greek or Trojan!

This shows him to have been something of a judge of 'Black and White' work (as
well as of such details as Greek and Roman shoe-gear) for in a review of the art
of the period I find a good deal concerning Sandys' illustrations to *Once a Week*
and other periodicals; the writer stating that some of his (Sandys') work compared
favourably with that of Millais.

Referring to the articles for publication in London which he had previously
forwarded to me, he writes, 'Don't have my name put to them at full length; only
the initials "M.C." as some of the people here might know themselves and not

relish the portraiture.' Then, turning to his immediate surroundings at the time of writing, he continues:

> This is the winter season here and we are in the midst of one of the tropical storms that make up our winter. The rain is coming down in torrents, the wind is howling and the trees are crashing and Tommy, my Chinaman cook, has made me a blazing fire – though yesterday was hot enough to roast a bullock. It is a curious thing that Australian cooks are nearly all Chinamen, as ships' cooks are nearly all Niggers. A question for philosophers this! Tommy, however, is, or rather was, a 'Glass Button Mandarin' (whatever that may be in the Flowery Land) and is, moreover, an excellent cook. His English is most curious. In serving dinner he enumerates the various articles thus – 'Roast Bee – Ver'good, Sar! Pair duck! Corfee! Bread pooney – Ver'good! Bottle wine, Sar! Bring-em brandygrog baccy, Sar! after dining that, A-a-h!' which means, 'Roast Beef, Coffee, Bread-pudding etc etc.'

Here the enumeration of the various dishes breaks off and the letter concludes with characteristic abruptness by a reference to an item of views of a literary character,

> 'I see Carlyle has been made a Scotch don,
> 　　　　In haste,
> 　　　　　　　　Your affectionate Chum,
> 　　　　　　　　　　Marcus Clarke.'

Chapter 15

The monotony of station life and its effects on Marcus's spirits. – His method of obtaining relief. – The hot winds and early morning. – An adventurous ride to Fort Bourke. – The bush scenery at night. – The influence on Australian literature of the idiosyncrasies of the scenery and the inspiration it afforded to Marcus Clarke.

As time passed and the novelty of his surroundings wore off, Marcus began to find his occupation a monotonous one:

> I cannot describe to you (he writes) the curious feeling that comes over one after some months' stagnation here. You have heard, of course, of diggers, bushmen, and others going down to town and drinking buckets of champagne, eating banknotes, etc. I used to laugh at this, but I cannot do aught but pity them now. I can easily understand the feeling that prompts to these absurdities. A wild desire to spring up and shout, or run, or do something wild and extravagant, seizes one at times, a desire to do anything that will throw off the insupportable feeling of stagnating energies and stagnating blood that comes over one.
>
> Often after being out all day in the solitary bush, where nothing is seen save the wide expanse of green or brown bush, the long, low-lying swamps with cattle feeding lazily beneath the burning sun, the jagged and rocky mountains glowing in the heat, the brakes of scrub and matted underwood, the silent, sluggish creeks and the wide, shimmering plains, I have returned hot and weary, my blood boiling in my veins

from the fierce heat which has permeated my body all day, and after supper and a pipe, when the sun has gone down, the moon is bright and all the myriad noises of an Australian night are chirruping, chirping, crying, calling or croaking from bush, morass, swamp, creek, or mountain, I have felt a sudden exhilaration seize me, a sudden, wild sort of inspiration rush over me, and have left my friends, rushed to the stable, saddled my horse and galloped for hours over the plains, shouting and urging my horse to his top speed, heedless of holes or landslips, rocks or stones, and have returned at two or three in the morning with my horse in a foam and myself utterly exhausted. I don't know why I should have these berserker fits but it must be the need of some excitement or the effect of the heat upon the blood.

Does not the feeling he describes as impelling him to go forth in the night seem reflected in the following passage of Mr. Brunton Stephens' fine poem 'Convict Once'[55]

> Oh, summer night of the South! Oh, sweet languor of zephyrs love-sighing!
> Oh, mighty circuit of shadowy solitude, holy and still!
> Music scarce audible, echo-less harmony joyously dying,
> Dying in faint suspirations o'er meadow and forest and hill!
>
> I must go forth and be part of it, part of the night and its gladness;
> But a few steps, and I pause on the marge of a shining lagoon
> Here then, at length, I have rest; and I lay down my burden of sadness,
> Kneeling alone 'neath the stars and the silvery arc of the moon.

The letter continues:

By the way, you have no notion what a sensation the hot winds and sun give me. The worst time is in the early morning. If one has been out in the early morning and enjoyed the cool air, on a sudden the sun rises fiercely hot and the air changes all at once to the blast of a furnace mouth. One is obliged to go under a tree for shade, but after some hours of this one gets thoroughly baked and I, at least, feel a positive

---

55   Mr. J. Brunton Stephens like Marcus Clarke himself was British born, and emigrated to Queensland.

pleasure in the heat then. One moves one's hands though the hot air and draws deep breaths of the hot wind. One's blood seems rarefied, one's perceptions clearer, and a sort of delightful languor then comes over one, which is succeeded by a complete reinvigoration, if I can say so, of the body.

The blood boils at fever-heat, the heart beats rapidly and a strange enthusiasm seizes one. You shout, spur your horse and rejoice in the hot blast that sweeps past you as you gallop beneath the burning sun. I can understand the hot blood of the South now. By Heavens, one could attack an army while that feeling lasts! It is glorious!

We read in that sketch of up-country life of his previously quoted, ('In a Bark Hut') that:

It is proper to boast of the Australian summer. Those who have lived in tents, camped by rocky water-holes, kept dew-sprinkled watch beneath the yellow moon, and ridden through fiery noons hard upon the tails of the head-long herd, can with justice boast of the wild intoxication of that burning ether … Tell me what draught of love or wine compares with *this* – the champagne nectar of a hot-wind gallop?

But the language of his letter seems to me more impressive because more spontaneous; and penned immediately after experiencing the very sensations he was then describing.

According to the handbook for Australia, land in the central and northern districts, although subject to drought, is, perhaps, the best in the world for the rearing of fine-woolled sheep. Probably Marcus Clarke would not have succeeded as a pioneer squatter. Nevertheless the account of his adventurous excursion into the unsettled country beyond the River Murray (unsettled in those days) briefly alluded to in his previous letter will, I think, be found interesting, if only for the proofs it affords of his pluck and independent temperament. I give it in his own words:

I started from Ballarat with two horses, riding one and leading the other. All went well until I reached the northern territory[56] The drought there had been so bad that all the settlers had left their stations and the country was deserted. I had to travel

---

56   He is not alluding to the so-called Northern Territory on the northern seacoast of the Australian continent but merely to the district beyond the river Murray.

two hundred and fifty miles through this desert or go round nearly three hundred. I decided to go straight on and calculated on being able to do it in a week. I did not know the country but the track was plain enough, they said. On the first day I missed the waterhole where I should have camped, so that I and my horses were without water for that day. The next day one of the horses, a grey stallion I gave sixty pounds for in Ballarat, began to knock up. I felt rather in a stew as there was less water than I expected and the heat was awful. I need not tell you all my shifts but I was forty-eight hours without water! and the day before I reached Fort Bourke the 'entire' refused to go on. I left him with my valise, rugs etc., and pushed for Fort Bourke. I reached it at 2 a.m. and didn't I have a drink of tea and a smoke! My tobacco had run out. I went back next day and found 'Tomboy' (the grey) nearly dead not five yards from the place where I left my swag! We got him round however. Everybody said, 'What a fool you were to go through the deserted country!' But it was an adventure!

The aspect of the country was fearful. Brown, burnt-up and sweltering under a broiling sun! Endless plains of short, brown grass or huge tracts of mallee and wattle scrub with patches of sandy heath, then a bend in the bed of the dried-up river with some primeval gums around it. Then again the rolling plains, the bush, *par excellence* the huge gumtrees, the thick tangled undergrowth, huge ferns, immense and monstrous forms of vegetation, hideous belts of impassable scrub, the lair of the snake and abode of the devilish looking iguana. Then again the wide plains with the track running on through the midst, marked by the bones of bullocks, cattle, and wild dogs, and now and then the ashes of some traveller's campfire. Not a living soul did I see and not even a bird except the crow, the whole of the seven days! The country looked accursed!

Before I returned, however, we had three days heavy rain (there had been none before for sixteen months) and the surroundings changed as if by magic. Green grass, huge lagoons, flocks of turkey, wild duck, parrots, the emu far away like a horseman on the horizon, the herds of wild cattle who, as they sniff your horse, wheel round with snortings and scamper off into the boundless plains, bullock drays and horsemen, waggons, flocks of sheep and cattle, all going back to their *lares and penates*. I went up to buy country – there is eight-hundred square miles of it! – but the specimen I had in my seven days was enough! The country is well adapted to stock but the drought is ruinous.

Such an experience as the foregoing and the night rides round Ledcourt may help to explain the extraordinary effect on Marcus Clarke's imagination the scenery produced. They may account for his reference in 'Holiday Peak' to the 'indescribable ghastliness' of 'the mountain bush at night,' to the 'grotesque and distorted trees, huddled here and there together … like whispering conspirators. The little open flats encircled by boulders which seem the forgotten altars of some unholy worship. The white, bare and ghostly gums gleaming momentarily amid the deeper shades of the forest. The lonely pools begirt with shivering reeds, and haunted by the melancholy bittern only.' In another well known passage he has described the sensations of a solitary horseman when

> riding through this nightmare-landscape, a whirr of wings and a harsh cry disturb you from time to time, hideous and mocking laughter peals above and about you, and huge grey ghosts with little red eyes hop away in gigantic but noiseless bounds… the mare lengthens her stride, the tree-trunks run into one another, the leaves make overhead a continuous curtain, the earth reels out beneath you like a strip of grey cloth spun by a furiously-flying loom, the air strikes your face sharply, the bush – always grey and colourless – parts before you and closes behind you like a fog

and the rider feels himself become

> drunk with the wine of the night and losing your individuality, sweep onward a flying phantom in a land of shadows.

The influence of Marcus Clarke on all subsequent writers who have described, in their turn, the scenery of the Australian bush, cannot, I think, be disputed. For instance, the following passage from one of Tasma's novels reads like an unconscious plagiarism although the similarity of thought is probably accidental:

> Is the monotonous, grey level typical of the life that is beginning for her from today? Will the only breaks be as harsh as the line of gaunt gum trees ahead, twisting themselves like tortured souls out of their shreddy bark? The only goal as far off, as impenetrable, as the horizon that bounds them?

Many of her descriptions of the scenery, of the slight but significant changes of colour in the spring foliage, the monotony of an up-country township, or the composition of the gay throng on the Melbourne race course recall his essays and bush stories. Again, Mark Twain mentions a bush road that led through a 'forest of great gum trees, lean and scraggy and sorrowful,' and goes on to describe how these 'sad gums stood up out of the dry, white road, pictures of patience and resignation.' And this, too, in the Wimmera country.

There are of course other writers who point out the more beautiful aspects of nature in the island continent. Mr. Thomas Heney, for instance, describes in one of his stories a flight of cockatoos,

> whose every movement was in concert, so that at one instant a cloud of pink and blush-rose spread out before the traveller, then a wheeling curve sent upward a mass of snowy white as the eager wings opened and shut; next, as the birds sank below a near rise, their backs and upper wings presented a plane of slate.

But all unite in impressing their readers with the sense of solitude and are inspired by Australian scenery. Mrs. Campbell Praed speaks of the effect produced by the ghastly shadows of the grass tussocks and spinifex bushes in the moonlight on the plains of Queensland and dwells on its weird fascination. The two first writers to place on record emphatically that fascination were Lindsay Gordon and Marcus Clarke.

Chapter 16

Marcus Clarke's views on the subject of the future prospects for 'squatters' in Victoria. – Partial confirmation of the soundness of his opinion afforded by Francis Adams' work, The Australians. *– Marcus resolves to join the colonial mounted police.*

After his expedition to Fort Bourke and before the close of the year 1866, Marcus believed himself to have some chance of obtaining a small post in the Civil Service of the State (presumably through his uncle's influence) and almost simultaneously he had been asked by a friend to join him in a sheep-farming venture in the Western district.

> I am thus debating (he explained) between civilized attire, cigars, claret and a subscription to the Union Club Balls, Governor's levées and Melbourne life, and sheep-farming, cattle-hunting, horse-breaking, duck-shooting, and a share in twelve thousand sheep. Christmas will decide. I have given up the notion of going to new country. Too much hard work and absence from all that makes life tolerable. And as to buying a station in Victoria, that is out of the question.
>
> I will give you the reasons. The original holders of government land, the first 'squatters,' became proprietors of their 'runs' under these conditions: They went up country; took up as much land as they chose; (even three hundred or four hundred square miles) and paid to Government some fifty pounds a year as lease for the same. As stock became more valuable, these persons sold to others; i.e. sold them their stock, receiving a little more than the real worth of it as 'goodwill' for the land, the

next buyer still paying rent to government. The leases run to 1870, when all these lands will be put up to auction, to be sold to the highest bidder.

Now it must be evident to all that land (carrying twenty thousand sheep and costing, say £20,000) will not be worth as much in 1867, 1868, or 1869, as it was in 1866, for there is less time to be got out of it. Consequently a man who buys a 'run' in 1866 must sell it in 1869 at a loss, or run the risk of losing it in 1870.

In 1869 all squatters will wish to sell. As a matter of course stock, which is sold with the land, will fall in value. There will be a panic; crash will go to the banks! (These do the chief business of lending money to squatters upon mortgages of their lands.) Money will become scarce, the lands go up to auction, and the ready-money capitalist step in and secure, say, fifty thousand acres at one pound an acre, which may be worth in 1873 (when confidence has been restored) five pounds an acre! This must be the infallible result! Therefore I am waiting; determined to make as much money as possible up to 1870, and then buy. Not only shall I be able to sell in a few years at a profit; but even if I hold on, I shall own an estate which I can afford to improve and make carry double the usual number of sheep by artificial grasses, etc. At present men won't improve because of the uncertain tenure. There is immense room for improvement in working stations; these pig-headed fellows won't see it but *I* do! For instance, some three or four hundred sheep die every year from carelessness or neglect; this is a small item in twenty thousand sheep, but why should it be an item at all? Stores etc. are wasted in a frightful manner.

In driving cattle, should one lag behind, off jumps a stockman and cuts its throat! This is the result of 'making hay while the sun shines.' Of course the squatters must make a profit before 1870, or they are ruined. Consequently the plan is to get as much wool as possible off the 'run' and then sell. This is a very short-sighted policy. The 'run' that my friend has bought is all purchased out and out and is in the heart of the finest country in Victoria. If he can only make it pay him for his outlay and will take my advice and buy more in 1870, his fortune and mine will be made.

Those acquainted with the technicalities of the subject and with the actual historical facts will be the best judges of how far this forecast of Marcus Clarke's may have been verified by the events, but a passage in the late Francis Adams's work, *The Australians*, seems partly to bear it out:

The old reckless overstocking, coupled with the old reckless expenditure, and backed up by the droughts, have ruined him (i.e. the squatter).

Mortgage upon mortgage have made him slave of the big pastoral syndicates or of the banks. Often the banks and syndicates are one. They have put their heavy hand on to him: if he was worth retaining as the manager of his one-time station, retained him: if he was not, thrust him out, and substituted a man of their own. All the old profuse hospitality, the hunts and dances and four-in-hands of the squatter 'kings', live now but as a dim tradition. Pastoralism can now only be made to pay on a vast scale.

I am informed that very much the same economic changes have since taken place in Queensland. But the plan mooted by Marcus of joining a friend in the western district of Victoria and participating in his venture was abandoned, or was perhaps never seriously intended.

It was evident from his next reference to the subject that he had begun to feel he was not adapted to the pursuit of sheep-farming. Certain political difficulties were at that time looming on the Australian pastoral horizon and these were perhaps put forward in his letters as a colourable pretext for abandoning the calling. Such a passage as the following gave one that impression and seemed to foreshadow another change of profession:

> In one of my letters I spoke of buying a share in a station in Victoria. The Minister of Lands has, however, made such a terribly anti-pastoral speech and evinces such determined enmity to squatters that Victorian property has fallen to 50 per cent in the market. So I judged it advisable to postpone all my intentions of going in for squatting until I should see how matters shaped … I may go to New South Wales and take up a station or go to Guichen Bay or Queensland or go in for new country.

In a letter written some time afterwards an alternative scheme was put forward, that of joining the Mounted Police. The late Mr. Patchett Martin writes in his *Beginnings of an Australian Literature*:

> It is a somewhat singular fact, that Gordon, whom Marcus Clarke ranks as the founder of Australian poetry, and Henry Kingsley, whom I consider to be the founder of Australian fiction, should both have been Mounted Policemen. Australian literature, it would therefore seem, originated not in the student's library but in the trooper's saddle.

Marcus thus described his prospects if he joined the service:

But though the billet is a good one I should have to go to some infernal hole on the border and perhaps get shot by some old 'lag'! ... I may perhaps accept it. Heaven knows! .... You must not confuse the mounted troopers with the home police; they are quite another kind of cattle. The inspectors and superintendents are all gentlemen, most of them old army men, and a troop is not by any means to be despised. One gets a house, a servant and four horses free; and in the non-settled districts is pretty well 'monarch of all one surveys.'

Captain Standish, the chief, was in the Royal Horse Artillery and is a friend of my people at home. His offer is rather a compliment than otherwise. But there will be no station quarters, no comfortable escort duty, no government balls for me. I expect that I shall have to go 'high up', and may possibly even have the 'Black Police.' (A term applied to the Queensland native mounted police, to which force Marcus was probably alluding.) Needs must, however, when the old gentleman drives! I often wonder how my life will end; the beginning of it is strange enough, God knows! What a change from all my old plans and hopes; the Foreign Office, jollity, good society, hunters, crack balls and diplomacy!

Marcus never joined either the Victorian or the Queensland mounted police. He did, however, as will be seen, accompany some friends on a sort of amateur prospecting expedition into the western districts of Queensland and it was attended with disastrous results. This was the last experiment of the kind he ever made and it took place just previous to his settling down to a literary career in Melbourne.

Chapter 17

Marcus Clarke's promiscuous reading at Swinton and Ledcourt. – His admiration for the works of the Russian novelist and poet, Mikhail Yurevich Lermontoff. – Some characteristics of early Russian literature. – Parentage and early life of Lermontoff and of Marcus Clarke compared. – The similarity of their literary gifts and views of human nature. – The early death of each of them. – Study of Balzac's novels by Marcus. – Criticisms on Sterne and Trollope. – Confirmation of his strictures on the latter by distinguished writers of recent times.

Mr Desmond Byrne, referring to this period of Marcus Clarke's life, remarks that:

> Just as he wandered alone over fern-hill and creek-bed, plain and mountain range, and absorbed impressions of a scenery at once repulsive and fascinating to him, so he dipped into all kinds of literature without method or set purpose. But he preferred fiction; and as the consignee of an endless succession of French novels, he became a marked man in the eyes of the village postmaster.

There fell in this way into his hands a story by a certain Russian author which fired his imagination and left a deep and lasting impression on his mind although he could only judge of it by a translation. The title of it was *A Hero of our Times*, one that might, I think, have been more happily rendered as 'A Modern Hero of Romance,' and the author of it, whose grace of style and keen insight into character (as revealed in this story), had so charmed Marcus, was none other than the well known, early Russian novelist and poet, Mikhail Yurevich Lermontoff.

Russian literature was in those days more or less of a novelty and, according to a distinguished German critic, the knowledge of it among the reading public of Western Europe had not advanced until long afterwards beyond 'the general and the vague.' Indeed, even at the present day, I noticed that the reviewer of a recent work of Mr. Maurice Baring – *Landmarks in Russian Literature* – prefaced his remarks on it with the words, 'It is time that English people knew more – knew something, we might almost say – of Russian Literature … Gogol, Tourgeniev, Dostoievsky, Tchekov, convey little or nothing to the English mind.' [57]

Reviewers of Russian literature style Pushkin and Lermontoff the pioneer romance-writers of their country and assert that nowhere is the life of the people more clearly reflected in its literature than in Russia. Lermontoff, however, only portrays the life of the upper class, and being himself an intense admirer of Lord Byron, his hero is cast in the Byronic mould. The scene of his story *A Hero of our Times* is laid in the Caucasus to which province Lermontoff himself had been banished by the Emperor Nicholas and where he ultimately met with his premature death, having fallen, like his friend, Pushkin, in a duel, and having, just as did the latter, divined his fate, with a prescience bordering on the supernatural, beforehand. Indeed he composed some most striking and prophetic verses on the subject, of which a beautiful translation appeared some years ago in the Paris *Figaro*, subtitled 'Le Songe.'[58]

In the fascinating but *blasé* man of the world who figures as the principal character in Lermontoff's romance we have presumably a prototype of himself, for, according to the German critic previously quoted, Pushkin's and Lermontoff's characters 'sprang from the innate sympathies of their creators with the educated minority in Russia.' The type, it seems, was often to be met with in that country at that period: 'Half child of nature, half the *mauvais sujet* of a restless civilisation … a past master in self-analysis, a terrible vivisector in the mental and moral domain.' And Russians of the educated class are stated by the same authority to be 'experts in deciphering character; thought-readers, enquirers, mystics.' A modern instance of this propensity was afforded by Captain Klado in his book *The Russian Navy in the Russo-Japanese War*; for in that author's words, 'The Russian is naturally a dreamer, for this is a failing which is characteristic of our race.'

---

57   See *Times Literary Supplement*.
58   See *Le Figaro*, October, 1893.

Now such traits were precisely those that would appeal to Marcus Clarke, and finding something of the kind in this story, he read it with the most profound attention and delight. He remarks that it well repays perusal, if only for the charming descriptions of scenery in the Caucasus to be found in it. Whether he even read the history of the author's own short and stormy life I do not know, but in one of the last letters he ever wrote me he dwelt on the similarity of Lermontoff's view of life and human nature with those of his own. It is singular that, like Marcus Clarke, Lermontoff should have been the son of a wealthy widower who lost his wife when the boy was but three years of age and brought him up in an injudicious manner; that both should have had to leave their native country in early manhood, Lermontoff, the Russian guardsman, having been banished by the Czar to the Caucasus, Marcus Clarke led by the force of circumstances to quit England for Australia; that both were very young when they began to write; that both should have died before attaining middle life; and that each of them, in their different manner, should have divined beforehand that their life was not to be prolonged. Both of them were exceptionally gifted and both had apparently somewhat similar weaknesses of character. The outward appearance of the hero of Lermontoff's novel is the subject of an elaborate description in the course of which the reader is informed that when Petshorin smiled, his eyes 'expressed no sympathetic accompaniment, the sure sign of a perverse nature or of some deep and incurable sorrow.'

Now this was a peculiarity of the Czar Nicholas I's eyes (noticed by Lady Eastlake and others who wrote of him) that, 'His mouth sometimes smiled, his eyes never.' Such a personal feature in the dreaded Czar was not likely to have escaped the keenly observant Lermontoff, who had been an officer in his bodyguard. To return to the 'portrait of Petshorin,' the reader is told that 'His glance which was wandering, was nevertheless grave and penetrating, producing the effect of an indiscreet question, and would have been positively importunate had it not likewise expressed tranquillity and indifference.' The influence of this Russian author on Marcus Clarke is apparent in some of the latter's stories but he only once mentions him by name. He has however a spirited ballad, 'The Bridal of Bela,' describing an elopement in the Caucasus, of which the subject and the name were derived from Lermontoff's writings. It originally appeared in the 'Noah's Ark' papers. The direct reference is in one of Marcus's short stories, 'Playing with Fire':

> The Russian novelist Mikhail Lermontoff said that he 'hated men, to prevent life becoming a hideous tragedy.' May we not add that, if we can succeed in despising them, it becomes a most ridiculous farce?

Here are the names of some of the books mentioned casually from time to time in his letters from Swinton and Ledcourt by Marcus as those he had been recently reading and about most of which he had something interesting to say: Tennyson's *Maud*, and *Idylls of the King*; *The Reminiscences of Captain Gronow*; Renan's *Vie de Jésus*. And the following works of fiction, French or English: Michelet's *La Sorcière*; Andersen's *Improvisatore*; *Charlie Thornhill*; *Ella Norman*; *Guy Livingstone*; *Armadale*; *Our Mutual Friend*; *Half a Million of Money*; *Kestrels and Falcons*; *The Race for Wealth*; *The Second Mrs. Tillotson* (a title that recalls that of a comparatively recent play *The Second Mrs. Tanqueray*); *Never Forgotten*; *The Village on the Cliff*; Arsène Houssaye's *L'amour comme il est*; Victor Hugo's *Travailleurs de la mer*; Paul de Kock's *Un tourlourou*; George Sand's *Adriani*; Balzac's *Peau de chagrin*; *Eugénie Grandet*, *Gobseck*, and *La recherche de l'absolu*. In a letter in which some of the above occur, I find the following criticisms:

> Let me see if I can say something that may interest you. You speak of *Kestrels and Falcons* disparagingly; *I* like it. It is very well written and takes somewhat the same view of womankind that *I* do. It may not be *natural*. Unfortunately I number so few peers or even baronets among my acquaintance that I am hardly qualified to sit in judgement upon 'high life' novels. The workings of the passions, however, and notably of feminine passions are, I imagine, much the same of the world over; and though Lady Clara Vere de Vere may not break her husband's head with a broom-handle when she discovers his infidelity as Moll Flagon or Doll Tearsheet would, yet I should suppose that the feelings which influence both of them would be much the same. Their manner of expressing those feelings is, of course, as different as education, that *real* second nature, can make it.
>
> Perhaps you find fault with the action of the characters. There is something rather 'Eugène Sue'-ish about it; but why? Sue, a man of the world, a man of success, a man of wealth, a man of society and a man of *bonnes fortunes*, was the leader of a school who dare to depict 'high life' as it *is* and not as it ought to be. There is as much lack of virtue among the upper and middle classes as there is among the lower. Granted that it is not so visible. A woman brought up in St. Giles and a 'casual' born in Field Lane take very little heed to conceal their natural bent. But among country people, peasants, plough-boys, milkmaids etc. there is more actual virtue than among the class of which Lord Deucease who 'keeps' two mistresses (one for town, the other for country); the Marquess of Steyne who has a harem in Park Lane; the Hon. Rook who goes to Ascot with two *danseuses*, a lady of easy virtue, and Tom Pigeon, (who is to be plucked in the evening) the Duchess of Quiverfull, who hawks her twelve marriageable daughters

all over London and whose respected husband has three illegitimate children by his housekeeper at Horn Park – are burning and shining lights.

My dear fellow, women are not a bit more virtuous than they were in the days of Nell Gwynne, or the Duchesse du Barry; they are more prudent, that is all! … As touching *A Race for Wealth*, it is pretty good *as far as it goes.*

This story was then appearing in serial form in a London periodical (*Once a Week*, I fancy) anonymously. Marcus, after some desultory criticisms, concluded by saying that he was sure it was written by a woman. (It was of course the work of the well-known and then popular novelist, Mrs. Riddell). He concludes this letter, after discussing further literary topics, by expressing his admiration for those verses of Charles Kingsley's commencing,

> When all the world is young, lad,
> And all the trees are green;
> And every goose a swan, Lad,
> And every lass a queen;
> Then hey for boot and horse, lad,
> And round the world away!
> Young blood must have its course, lad,
> And every dog his day.

It has been asserted that Marcus Clarke's novel, *For the Term of his Natural Life* was the result of his study of Balzac. Unquestionably, Balzac was a favourite novelist of his, just as the author of *The Three Musketeers* was of R. L. Stevenson's. Francis Adams, in his review of *His Natural Life*, a novel to which I have devoted a separate chapter, says:

> Clarke's debt to Balzac is a large one, a far larger one that can appear to anyone who had not studied the work of the Australian writer as a whole.
>
> Clarke had enough of the infallible instinct of genius to see what was really wanting in him, if he was to attempt the achievement of anything satisfactory … Rising from a course of Balzac, thoroughly imbued with the literary method of the man, he wrote the first draft of the story.
>
> Then the influence passed and he was left facing the unequal results of his work.
>
> A certain classical sense … saved him from Balzac's pedantry if he was unable to fathom Balzac's profundity …

Now, as we have seen, Marcus took to reading Balzac whilst living in the bush at Swinton and Ledcourt, years before he himself wrote novels and cannot therefore be said, with any degree of accuracy, to have composed his well known story of convict life 'after rising from a course of Balzac thoroughly imbued with the literary method of the man.' This was a mere assumption on the part of Mr. Adams and an incorrect one.

In after years Marcus admired more particularly *Le père Goriot*, and indeed there are some passages in that story that would be sure to commend themselves to his mind, for they might have been the coinage of his own brain: that, for instance, describing Madame Vauquer's obstinacy in mispronouncing the word *Tilleuls*, although she boasted an aristocratic maiden name and although her attention had been frequently called to the error by her boarders. Or the one in which her hopes of becoming Madame Goriot are thus conveyed to the reader: 'Madame Vauquer se couch le soir en rotissant comme une perdrix dans sa harde au feu du desir qui la saisit de quitter le suaire de Vauquer pur renaitre en Goriot.' The character of Vautrin is frequently referred to in Marcus Clarke's stories.

A reviewer in the *Times* once pointed out that it was an error for the admirers of Balzac to plume themselves on his being so hard to translate. Marcus had quite mastered his peculiarities of style before he left Ledcourt although he had found them rather puzzling at first, and it has been asserted that he had become so infatuated with the French author as to have debauched the minds of Mr. Holt's boundary riders with his too realistic pages!

But to translate at sight and *viva voce* with sufficient rapidity to hold a listener's attention is an irksome task, as all must be aware who have tried it, and Balzac's novels do not lend themselves much to the kind of thing, nor, should I have imagined would they have at all interested the boundary riders. Still, I have been informed that Marcus really was in the habit of thus entertaining them. When Charlotte Bronte first read Balzac she thought he was going to be 'painfully minute and fearfully tedious,' and it was only subsequently that she entered into the 'mystery of his craft' and discovered 'where his force lay', namely 'in the analysis of motive, and a subtle perception of the most obscure and secret working of the mind.'

Marcus's essay on Balzac was the direct outcome of his study of the author at Swinton and Ledcourt. Since the date of its appearance so much has been written about the French novelist in question, and that by those well acquainted with France and French literature, that to a reader of to-day, ignorant of the circumstances in which it was produced and even of the date of its publication, it might perhaps appear boyish and crude. But there are two remarks in it worth noting; the first, that 'the great names of the French literary world are bandied about on all sides but they are but names' was at least true *when he wrote it.* The second, that 'to the easy-going *dilettante* author who thinks to step into fame and name without an effort, the life of Balzac will seem terrible. It was one long struggle with debt and difficulty' is as true and forcible now as ever and has been made by many other subsequent critics. Thus, Mr. Arthur Symons concluded an article in the *Fortnightly Review* some years ago with the words, 'The life of Balzac was one long labour, in which time, money and circumstances were all against him.' In one of his letters Marcus had informed me that it appeared to him from the novels he had been reading at Ledcourt that the general characteristics of French fiction were, 'Some woman *incomprise,* some lover and some cruel husband': 'Alfred! Alfred!' s'écrie la jeune femme. 'Par ici! Embrasse moi! Ah! tes lèvres sont sèches et fiévreuses! embrasse moi! ou je meurs! je meurs!', with more in the same strain.

Marcus was fond of trying his hand at French composition and when a few years afterwards residing at Hawthorn (a suburb of Melbourne) contributed a translation into French of the nursery rhyme 'Old King Cole' to the Melbourne *Punch*, not unlike Thackeray's rendering into English of 'Le roi d'Yvetot' in his *Paris Sketchbook.*

While still at Ledcourt, Marcus composed some verses commencing,

> Let Wisdom sitting side by side with sorrow
> The cypress with the laurel twine,

of which he sent me a copy with the remark that they had been set to music by a friend at the station, the air resembling the ballad in *Masaniello* commencing 'Behold how brightly breaks the morning!' which readers of Du Maurier's novel *The Martian* may remember was sung by the hero of the story one Sunday morning on the boulevards to an admiring audience on behalf of a poor woman who had begged of him and on whom he had taken pity.

In another letter of this period there are some interesting remarks on literary worthies of past times – interesting, at all events, from a biographical point of view from which I extract the following, but with more than a little hesitation, for in the light of Mr. Walter Sichel's recent, brilliant, work on the author of *Tristram Shandy* and his appraisement and that of other literary students of Sterne's genius, they may well appear very crude and biased. Be it remembered, however, that Marcus Clarke dashed them off in a letter to a friend written during his leisure moments when a pupil on a sheep and cattle station in the Australian bush, and was, moreover, only some twenty years of age at the time. The passage runs as follows:

> You speak of Sterne and *The Sentimental Journey* – I used to admire it hugely but find that he has copied wholesale from Rabelais. Moreover his sentiment is all claptrap. Like *Paul et Virginie*, the book is composed of sentiment and sensualism so artfully mixed that it is difficult to tell where one begins and the other ends. Sterne is humorously indecent. The horns of the satyr peep forth even amidst the choicest retreats of sentiment … But I cannot help admiring *The Captive* and *Maria* and *The Ass and the Macaroons*. But the intense conceit of the man himself spoils it all. He seems to say, 'See how tender-hearted I am! how virtuous I am! how fascinating I am!'

I note that a reviewer of Mr. Sichel's book makes the following, among other, observations:

> It is a curious thing but I never yet met an English woman who admitted caring for Sterne, and even among men it is a silly fashion nowadays to decry his writings as vulgar plagiarisms. Sterne has been far more plagiarised upon than ever he plagiarised. Yet human nature underlies all Sterne's work, even his distortions. The pathos of his humour is unsurpassed.

I am certain that whatever one may think of the value of Marcus Clarke's opinions on matters of literature and art, they were at least original. If he wrote about Sterne as he did, it was because, at that time at all events, that was how Sterne's style and mannerisms struck him. He was no parrot repeating the literary opinions of others, nor had he any opportunity of studying them at this period of his life had he been the least that way inclined. I fancy that in after years he somewhat modified his views about Sterne and I believe that he assisted in starting the Yorick Club in Melbourne.

The letter from which the criticism on Sterne is taken continues: '*The Village on the Cliff* is clever but, to my mind, bread and buttery and flat' – and then referring to a novel of Trollope's appearing in serial form in the *Cornhill Magazine* at that time (but the name of which is illegible) he exclaims with his usual delightful candour and directness, 'Trollope is simply Trollopian. The only fresh character in the story is Sophie Guardeloup. Everyone else is an old friend. I am sick of manly, honest clerks in post-offices and "loving, womanly" but "deserted" parson's daughters. Cannot A. T. give us an *amour* between a Dean and a dairy-maid, or tell us how the wife of the Bishop of Barchester intrigued with the bell-ringer of the Cathedral and the result? His characters never sin but only are going to. His cup of Circe is but lemon kali or toast and water at the best, his wildest revelry a church tea-meeting, his maddest debauch a flirtation with a pew-opener during the voluntary. He is the poet of conventionalism.' These strictures on the limitations of a famous and popular mid-Victorian novelist, however youthfully and boisterously expressed, have been fully confirmed by later and more distinguished critics since. Not very long ago, Mrs. Alice Sedgwick wrote in the *National Review*: 'If Trollope insists too little on sin, he may be accused of insisting rather too much on mediocrity.'[59] Mr. Herbert Paul's article on Trollope and other mid-Victorian novelists at the time of the Diamond Jubilee may be cited as another instance and a later critic says:

> There was no sign of life or spontaneity about any of the later Trollopes, and his public, – or the great bulk of his public – did not want any. They were happier without it. It was enough for them to gaze year after year upon that never-ending series of social photographs, each of them undistinguishable, save by the merest superficial differences from the last.

Again, the late Sir Leslie Stephen commenting on Trollope's heroines who 'haven't a thought beyond house-keeping or making a respectable marriage,' rightly puts his finger, I think, on the very weakness in the novelist that had irritated Marcus and outraged his immature but sound ideas as to the human interests and emotions a great master of fiction should depict:

> By the excision of all that is energetic, or eccentric, or impulsive, or romantic, you do not really become more life-like; you only limit yourself to the common and uninteresting. This misconception injures Trollope's work and accounts, I suspect, for the decline of our interest ... Barsetshire surely had its heroes and its villains, its tragedy and its farce, as well as its archdeacons and young ladies bound hand and foot by the narrowest rules of contemporary propriety.

---

59   *National Review*, March 1910.

I have merely given these instances as one and all vindicating the soundness of Marcus Clarke's youthful but able, critical faculty in literary matters at this period of his life.

Chapter 18

Mining ventures and instances of lucky hits. – The romance of discovery in the development of Australia's mineral resources. – Supposed impending discoveries at Ledcourt Station. – Marcus pays a flying visit to Melbourne but rejects offer of employment in a bank. – 'Halting between two opinions.' – Reflections on his own temperament. – Longing for intellectual society. – Australian types and Australian slang of the period. – Mark Twain's views on the origin of the latter. – Marcus Clarke's literary beginnings. – His nom de plume of 'Marcus Scrivener.' – Whence derived. – Adopted at this time but afterwards discarded.

Marcus Clarke's letters were of course not entirely filled with his opinions on the books he had been reading, although literary subjects and the occasional exposition of his religious views and personal philosophy formed the bulk of their contents at this particular period.

Stawell (the nearest township to Ledcourt Station) being a mining centre, mining shares would naturally be the medium for those living in the district who were speculatively inclined. Thus he writes on one occasion. 'I have just bought a fifth share in a quartz reef here. It cost me thirty pounds.' (This was before the days of Australian mining companies with shares of the nominal value of five shillings or even of a far smaller denomination.):

If they strike gold, it will pay me at least sixty per cent, if they don't – I lose my money. I heard yesterday that in the next claim gold has been struck at a depth of fifty-five feet and that the mine is paying ninety pounds per share per week. By the look of the thing the vein runs immediately below our shaft. If so, we must strike it. If it then takes a downward dip our returns will be enormous.

But that is almost too much to hope for. I know an instance of a man at Beechworth who paid one hundred pounds for a share and in three days received eighteen hundred pounds a week for seven months. Of course many men have sunk hundreds in reefs and got nothing. It is all a lottery!

Australian writers give many such instances. Mr. Sutherland tells a story of a man who invested his last five hundred pounds in a mine in eastern Victoria which gave him an income on that share of ten thousand pounds a year for ten years afterwards. There are one or two striking instances given in the small school history edited, but not written, by Marcus Clarke himself and which appeared under his name. (*History of the Continent of Australia and the Island of Tasmania*):

> A bushman wants a light for his pipe and fires his tinder-box with a spark struck from a bit of quartz and the back of his old knife. The quartz lump is found to be speckled with gold, and the discovery of the goldfields of Victoria is the ultimate result. A shepherd, idly wandering after his flock over the scrubby flat limestone plains of Yorke's Peninsula, in South Australia, is drowsily watching the large holes made by the wombat and the wallaby. He picks up a small piece of green-looking stone which had been scratched up by these animals in the operation of forming these holes. It is green carbonate of copper; and his employer, Captain W. W. Hughes, subsequently opens up the magnificent *Moonta* copper mine, which is found to be even richer and more extensive than the *Burra Burra*, a mine which a few years before had been turned up by the wheel of a passing bullock-dray! The stories of such incidents in the development of the mineral resources of Australia are endless.

Towards the close of his stay at Ledcourt Marcus informed me that some mineral discoveries had been or were (it was believed) on the point of being made on the property itself. His intention was to await the result of these possible discoveries before coming to any resolution about leaving. For without having previously put it into so many words, his letters had made it sufficiently evident to me by this time that he was longing in his heart for some more congenial occupation. He enjoyed the open air life and the riding about the country but felt that his literary gifts would have no scope in such a career if it were to be his permanent vocation.

A brief visit to Melbourne had given him another opportunity of talking over matters with his uncle. Whilst on this visit an offer of a situation in a bank then about to start business had been made to him, and a friend had applied for his co-operation in a joint venture in Queensland. Neither alternative commended itself to his mind; the first being dismissed with the characteristic remark, 'This offer is tempting in the way of salary but I don't like banks.' He dwelt upon other possibilities that he had thought of and concluded by saying:

> So you see I am, as of yore, halting between two opinions … This colony is going to the deuce as hard as an insane ministry, a reckless Assembly, an idiotic population and a triumphant banking interest can drive it. *Pour moi*, as long as I can exist, I am thankful.

'Existence' at this epoch probably meant for him a quiet, easy-going life with leisure to study his favourite authors.

He expressed his regret that he could not take much interest in the people he met but supposed that, as he did not adorn his conversation with strange oaths, had no taste for brandy or 'Fly-Loo' (betting sovereigns on which lump of sugar a fly will first settle), was but a passable billiard-player, and disliked talking about his own adventures, besides cultivating a few ideas above sheep, cattle, horses and dogs, he was unable to appreciate the doubtless excellent qualities of the colonial youth nor did he suppose they much appreciated him. He regretted the expensive tastes he had acquired in early life when all their circle of friends believed his father to be a wealthy man and pleaded with much force the following considerations that should be taken into account before his conduct was severely judged:

> I do not wish to excuse my reckless extravagance, but put yourself in my position. My whole tenor of life was changed in a moment. I was forced into a career utterly uncongenial to my tastes. I was somewhat of a 'swell' (God help me!) – I was sent to the land of radicals and mob-law. I was fond of art and literature; I came where both are unknown, I was conversant with the manners of a class; I came where 'money makes the gentleman'. I hated vulgarity; I came where it reigns supreme … I see daily before me a pit into which I dread to fall; the pit of vulgarity, ignorance, slovenliness and radicalism. In a word I dread lest I become like others. I have a fatal facility for adapting myself to my company and am in hourly terror lest I fall into that most

degrading of all states, the state of the man 'who can be the gentleman when he likes.'
The consequence of this state of things is that my mind is becoming cynical.

I say bitter things, laugh uproariously and sigh despondingly. I am Heraclitus and
Democritus rolled into one. I ride hard because I don't care about a broken limb. I
play hard because I don't care for money. But thank God! I don't drink hard. Drinking
is the curse of the place! I never could see any pleasure in getting drunk.

I am cool in manner, partly natural and partly artificial, I am egotistical because I
see no one that I like better than myself, I am reckless because I cannot bear to see my
inferiors in mind excel me in bodily exercises.

He never was nearer the truth about himself, for in his school-days the foregoing had
been a marked feature of his character. In a subsequent letter he observed that he
had 'raved rather too much against Australia,' painted in fact too gloomy a picture:

I liked the life well enough at first. A walking tour is pleasant for six weeks; so is
salmon-fishing in Norway. But wet feet and twenty miles a day for life!

The excitement of the life is very well at first but, when it palls, it becomes worse
in proportionate ratio to its first pleasing. Flat champagne is ten times more insipid
than fresh water, and having done all the cattle-hunting, stock-riding etc., I want to
fall back upon cultivated society, upon books, music,

    Cigars and chat,

    Champagne and chicken and all that,

and lo! they are not!

He proceeds to sketch Australian society, his impressions of which and the specimens
he gives of the current slang of that period will, at this distance of time, be probably
found of interest:

There are some very jolly, gentlemanly fellows in Australia ... The squatter *par
excellence* is usually a younger son, an ex-captain of some crack regiment, an ex-
gentleman-farmer or such like. Read Kingsley's *Geoffry Hamlyn* it will give you an
excellent idea of what I do every day of my life. How can I describe to you Australian
society? ... The slang is different ... The Australian calls a herd of cattle a 'mob of
cattle'; a compact little mare 'a little nugget of a mare'; a vicious horse is 'a regular
nut and no flies'; a man who stands brandy to his friends at an inn, 'shouts drinks for
the crowd'. A betting man 'goes his death' upon his favourite horse; a man drinking

beer 'puts himself outside his malt'; a poor-looking, ill-bred horse is a 'scrubber'; a man who boasts is a 'blower' or 'blow-hard' … In the Bush, if you invite a stranger to partake of supper, you say, 'Hullo, mate, come in and sport your dover!' (A 'dover' is a knife.) A man who tells a good story of his own exploits is a 'single-handed pitcher.'

An Australian drinks 'Hyson's Skin' and smokes 'Barretts' Twist'; if he carries his knapsack or blankets on his back, he 'humps his swag'; if he works lazily, he does the 'real Government stroke' (borrowed from convict days, this last). If he robs a man, he 'sticks him up'; if he spends fifty pounds, he 'knocks down fifty notes'. If he takes the nonsense out of a buck-jumper, he 'lambs him down with the raw hide'; if his horse bolts, 'he makes tracks for glory'. If the wind blows hard, it is described as 'coming it hard from the tombs'. I could go on for hours! All these expressions are quite different from those in use at home.

The remark was true enough at the time but since then most, if not all of them, have been incorporated, one by one, into the vocabulary of our familiar home-slang and have long since lost the charm or the flavour of novelty. The late Professor Morris of Melbourne University published a dictionary of Australian words which the *Times* compared to a 'permanent photograph of a certain stage of growth,' and designated as a 'contribution of distinct value to English philology,' and a 'useful companion to the readers of Australian novels'.

Marcus Clarke's letter shows that he had supplied his friends in England with the nucleus of such a dictionary years previously. Mark Twain points out, in his account of his visit to Australia, how the natural features of the country and the strange native animals would be sure to beget a local slang, selecting as two favourable examples, 'The Never-Never Country', and the phrase, 'She lives in the Never-Never Country', meaning that the lady alluded to is an old maid. Marcus Clarke's letter continues:

Australian Society may be divided into squatters, Government officials, and reefers or miners. The squatters are the aristocracy of Australia. They hold much the same position that the southern planters did in America. The squatter lives upon his station half the year and comes to town when his 'clip' or cattle are sold. He prides himself on being well dressed. He sports the neatest of cord breeches and black boots or white pantaloons. His white straw sits jauntily over his brown face, bushy beard and everlasting cigar. He drives a high buggy with the most spirited horses that money can procure. He is always giving his friends champagne lunches or making 'one' for some pleasure or race trip. He keeps a race horse or two. He is lean, brown, quiet, gentlemanly and smoky. His discourse is flavoured with the perfume of the finest *Cabana*; his white silk coat smells terribly of the noxious weed. He undertakes a ride of five hundred miles as calmly as ordinary mortals in London go to Paddington by 'bus. His skin is impervious to mosquito bites and his *gluteus maximus* is as hard as the saddle it rests upon …

The Government official is a hybrid between a second-rate swell and the Indian Nabob of stage memory. He is irritable, yellow and moist. He is given to Government balls, brandy and soda, 'doing bills' and shirking work. He is the essence of Podleism. He has been perhaps one of the *upper ten*; his great-aunt's grandmother was wife to the brother-in-law of the Governor's cousin's uncle and he claims a relationship with the aristocracy as his brother married a Paget. He wears yellow gloves and a pugree round his hat and drives a 'buggy'. He finally goes home or dies of D. T. from brandy and water on the brain …

The 'reefer' is an authority on mining. He may be seen about the offices of brokers. He converses upon 'slabbing', 'driving', 'deep-striking', 'bottoming', 'quartz-crushing', and a machine for the working of 'tailings'. He dresses somewhat in American fashion. He is either worth eighty thousand pounds or nothing. His 'claims' pay him seven hundred pounds per week. He eats and drinks of the best. He is vulgar, smart, and wears much jewellery. He travels in the trains to Ballarat and plays euchre and brag or poker all the way up. He tosses for sovereigns for hours together. He drinks much, he smokes much, he does everything at railway speed. He is generous to a fault, but too sparing of his h's. He sends to a charity a cheque for five thousand pounds signed 'John Smith, X. His mark'. He is the product of the lucky digger multiplied by the Yankee speculator. He detests squatters, is ultra-radical in politics, goes in for *Free Selection before Survey*, *Miner's Rights*, and general subservience to the *Almighty Dollar*.

With regard to the foregoing delineation of contemporary Australian types I must point out that in his essay on 'Squatters Past and Present', Marcus draws a different portrait of the old fashioned squatter. Perhaps both types were then to be found and the one sketched in the letter above was derived from observation at first hand of Mr. Holt's neighbours at Swinton and Ledcourt.

Referring to an observation of mine concerning his literary abilities and inclinations, he replies:

By the way, what you say of my literary inclinations is very true; I want stirring up. I think that I can write but have no time, and seldom alas! inclination. I have written plenty, but at my age, experience is not yet. Up to twenty-five we get our ideas of life from books; afterwards from men. As some French author says, 'If only youth knew or old age were able' … I will send you by next mail a photo of the stations.

That he had already 'written plenty' was perfectly true, for we know upon the authority of Hamilton Mackinnon that, instead of retiring to rest, Marcus was in the habit of spending part of his nights both at Swinton and Ledcourt in literary work, for the most part probably in filling up notebooks with memoranda concerning the salient features of his environment, as he had done at the gold-diggings when in the employ of the Bank of Australasia, and in composing stories.

Some of the results of this burning of the midnight oil appeared in the *Australian Monthly Magazine*, a periodical of that day edited by Mr. W. H. Williams, and these were signed 'Marcus Scrivener'. This was a nickname given him at school by my brother Gerard and he adopted it at first as his *nom de plume* but subsequently discarded it for that of the initial letter, 'Q', with which he signed his articles and stories, because that initial had been used as the stock-brand at Swinton and Ledcourt stations. Finally, as success came to him, this signature was also dropped and his own proper name substituted.

Chapter 19

Personal Popularity of Marcus Clarke at Swinton and Ledcourt. – Visit of Dr. Lewins to Ledcourt Station and the result. – Dr. Lewins' scientific attainments and materialistic views. – His influence on Marcus. – The essay Civilisation without Delusion, *and ensuing correspondence with Dr. Moorhouse, Anglican Bishop of Melbourne. – Opinions of Mr. Desmond Byrne and Mr. Brazier. – How the essay came to be written. – Marcus Clarke's own religious ideas as expressed in his early letters and subsequently in his miscellaneous writings.*

Mr. Hamilton Mackinnon in the brief space allotted in his biography to this period of Marcus Clarke's career dwells upon his popularity with all with whom he came in contact – a popularity fairly earned by his pleasant, winning manner and the general grace and brightness of his character. There are some still to be found who cherish his memory, from their acquaintance with him in those days. No one indeed who had known him in early life could be surprised at learning this, for, as I have tried to convey, there was an indefinable charm about him in boyhood that has remained in the memory of all who knew him at school to this day. 'Do I recollect Marcus Clarke? Very well indeed. I understand that he made a name for himself in Australia. I remember him because he was a particularly bright, amusing boy.' When I have addressed myself to his old schoolfellows some such answer has been invariably forthcoming. And I gather from various sources that his fellow clerks in the Bank of Australasia at Melbourne were of much the same opinion.

Nevertheless, and notwithstanding this general popularity, it appears to have gradually dawned on Mr. Holt that, as Hamilton Mackinnon puts it, Clarke's services 'as a "hand" on the station' were 'not of countless price.' In the words of the writer in the *Cosmos* magazine,

> Clarke thoroughly enjoyed the free life of the bush, but, as might have been anticipated, never set earnestly to work to master pastoral mysteries, viewed as money-making business. He was found poring over a fascinating volume when his attention should have been occupied with books far less entrancing, or enjoying a solitary ramble on the hills when he was wanted among the lambs or in the woolshed. There were occasional visitors at the station, and by one of these (Dr. Lewins), who had been Staff-Surgeon-Major to General Chute during the New Zealand war, the eccentric youth at the homestead was appreciated at something like his true value.

So that when this Dr. Lewins, himself a man of intellectual power and scientific attainments – possessed moreover of influence with the press – offered to procure for Marcus, by whom he had been captivated and impressed, a position on the staff of the Melbourne *Argus*, no objection was made by Mr. Holt.

Mr Hamilton Mackinnnon refers at some length to the materialistic views of Dr. Lewins and to his success in making a convert of Marcus. As proof he cites an article on 'Positivism' supposed to have been written by the latter not long after his having made Dr. Lewins' acquaintance. According to a certain rumour, this article eventually appeared in a London review, the proprietors of the *Australasian* to whom it was first submitted, having declined to publish it.

Whatever the truth may have been as to the effect on Marcus Clarke of coming in contact with a distinguished sceptic of the Huxley type, the following extract from a letter of his written at this time proves that if he had changed his religious opinions in consequence of the arguments of Dr. Lewins, the change had not taken place without his undergoing considerable mental disturbance. For alluding to my brother Gerard's adoption of the Roman Catholic faith, he writes:

> I am not surprised … I always thought he had a leaning that way. Indeed, for an imaginative, clever *and yet timid mind* (the italics are his own) the Romish Church is the only one which satisfies; the others are but 'leather and prunella.' Protestantism in its purest form is simply a religion of the intellect; it offers no safeguard, no 'rock of defence'; it stretches forth no helping hand to the sinking, struggling wretch who feels

the waters of scepticism closing o'er him. Protestantism is like a gothic building on a barren shore, stern, cold, icily regular, freezingly beautiful. Romanism is a gorgeous Moorish palace, deep-embowered in foliage, surrounded with glowing flowers, brilliant colours, and viewed by the light of a tropical sunset. Protestantism is as a stern master saying, 'Believe or Perish!' Romanism is as a loving Mother crying, 'Here is Refuge! Here is Peace! Here is Love!'

For a man who feels that he must believe something, that he must have some standing-place amid the shifting sands of infidelity, rationalism, spiritualism and scepticism, the Protestant Church seems cold and dismal and its teaching but as the apples of Sodom that turn to ashes in the mouth. Romanism calls aloud to him, through her hundreds of agents, saying, 'Come! Believe! Put your trust wholly in me! Give yourself up to me, I will save you!' Happy is the man who *can* believe! I cannot, but am no desperate destroyer; no denier of God and Heaven! I am rather as one who, wandering through the pleasant gardens of Faith and implicit belief, has stumbled upon the stern rocks that border them; the rocks of Reason and Practicality and Materialism, and stunned by the fall is no more able to return to the pleasant paths and rest with heart at ease upon the dewy turf but, must cling to the rugged and sharp stones around him lest he fall into the raging sea of despair and utter incredulity that boils and seethes beneath him.

I am no advocate for the writing and publishing of infidel books. For they can but destroy; they cannot build up. The most ignorant peasant that prays to his wooden image of divinity is happier and perhaps nearer salvation than the clever, scornful and intellectual materialist whose stern logic tears away all the sweet, delusive ornamentation of belief, whose ruthless hand plucks away the many-coloured garment of religion and shows to the awe-stricken crowd that she is but a figure of dry bones and that life is not in her. Belief in something is essential to happiness and the man who destroys the sincere faith of one of these little ones, better were it for him that a mill-stone were hanged about his neck and that he were drowned in the depth of the sea.

A couple of years previously he had written that although he considered the Roman Catholic as 'the most picturesque and splendid form of belief,' and had himself sometimes felt tempted to adopt it, he rather 'inclined to the mystical in religion.' So that Mr. Desmond Byrne's view that 'the spiritual side of his nature was an undeveloped, almost a barren field,' and that 'in dealing with religion, his characteristic independence developed into a stiff intellectual pride, and from that into a recklessness which disregarded alike his public reputation and the feelings of others,' is quite an erroneous one with regard to the period of his life with which I am now dealing and as I think I can show, not fully justified at any other.

It was doubtless suggested by the notorious controversy between Marcus and Dr. Moorhouse, the Anglican Bishop of Melbourne, the merits of which Mr. A. W. Brazier has more justly appraised than previous writers in his interesting monograph, *Marcus Clarke: his Work and Genius*. 'The fact is,' says Mr. Brazier, 'he (Clarke) was a deeply religious man. Your irreligious man is he who, being too lazy, or too cowardly, to face the great questions that mankind has to face, each man on his own individual responsibility, takes refuge in a dogma, because it is conventional, orthodox, convenient; or who, like Gallio, 'cares for none of these things,' and adds, 'I would like to ask the young authors of this Society (the "Australian Literature Society") if they are prepared to pass through the fire for the sake of what they believe to be true in their very hearts – as Marcus Clarke did.'

In this connection I must anticipate and refer more fully to the episode in question, the publication of his essay *Civilisation without Delusion* and the correspondence between the bishop and himself that ensued. A regard for his own interests, professional and social, would probably have induced him, had he paused to consider, to refrain from publishing it. For whatever might be thought of it now, the publication of such an essay at that date was surely a violation of his favourite maxim concerning the folly of wearing one's heart upon one's sleeve for daws to peck at. For not only was the subject of a highly controversial nature but the opinions expressed or implied such as Marcus must have foreseen were almost certain to give offence. It is true that such an essay if it had first seen the light at the present day would probably have evoked but a very mild sensation.

Mr. Walter Murdoch in a thoughtful article contributed by him to the Melbourne *Argus* some years ago pointed out, forcibly enough, what an exaggerated importance had been attached to it.[60] Alluding to the 'almost gallic vivacity' of Marcus Clarke, he refers to the notorious pamphlet, *Civilisation without Delusion*, the merits of which he sums up as follows:

> It is impossible to take it seriously; no man ever entered the field of theological controversy with an equipment so ridiculous. He has had time, it would seem, neither to read nor to think about the subject at all; and yet, armed with a few shreds of

---

60   See Melbourne *Argus*, October 22nd, 1904.

irrelevant information and half-a-dozen ancient arguments, he steps out jauntily to demolish Christianity. Well, his pamphlet can be read from start to finish without fatigue. That is all that can be said for it; but in the circumstances it is a great tribute to his literary art that we can say as much.

To me its interest is chiefly retrospective. For the views expressed in it are clearly the outcome of those theological studies pursued during his leisure hours when a bank-clerk; and doubtless continued at Swinton and Ledcourt where his evenings and part of the night were devoted to literary pursuits.

As previously mentioned, he had been engaged in studies for a projected work to be entitled, 'Priestcraft and People,' which was to have been a 'review of all creeds from the earliest ages down to modern times. It would, (it will be remembered he wrote me) 'demonstrate by description, apart from discussion, the similarity of all religious beliefs,' and by its 'descriptive and reflective character' resemble Ruskin's *Stones of Venice*. Although this daring project obviously came to nothing, (for no such book was ever published of his composition) the notes he had taken when planning it furnished of course the material upon which he drew for the essay in question. Probably the latter was a condensed summary of these notes which, he assured me, were 'the result of twelve months' hard reading.'

Since the appearance of Marcus Clarke's essay, a stream of literature on the same or analogous subjects has been set flowing and given to the world; as witness such works as Dr. Frazer's *Golden Bough*, *The Tree of Life* by Ernest Crawley, *A Study of Religion*, and countless others[61] but at that date and place the subject was comparatively novel and the sensation created by its appearance enhanced, as already mentioned, by the correspondence with the then Bishop of Melbourne that immediately followed. 'Conceive my soul-felt joy,' wrote Marcus to a fellow-journalist at the time, 'when I saw those revered gaiters actually getting over the "ropes," and beheld his Lordship throw his shapely shovel hat into the ring!'[62]

Doubtless the chance thus afforded to one of Marcus Clarke's temperament of engaging in public controversy with an opponent of the social standing and distinction of Dr. Moorhouse was too tempting to be resisted and quite carried him off his feet, metaphorically speaking. And it is impossible to read the correspondence

---

61   *The Belief in Immortality and the Worship of the Dead*, by J. G. Frazer (Macmillan).
62   See article entitled 'An Australian Novelist' in *Temple Bar Magazine* for May 1884, by Arthur Patchett Martin.

without feeling that, as a controversialist, Marcus had the best of it. Nevertheless, I maintain that the latter's real feelings on the subject of religion are more accurately reflected in his early letters and certain passages of his miscellaneous writings. Who can doubt, for instance, that the man who wrote

> The lonely horseman riding between the moonlight and the day sees vast shadows creeping across the shelterless and silent plains, hears strange noises in the primaeval forest where flourishes a vegetation long dead in other lands, and feels, despite his fortune, that the trim utilitarian civilisation which bred him shrinks into insignificance beside the contemptuous grandeur of forest and ranges coeval with an age in which European scientists have cradled his own race

– who can doubt, I say, that the author of this passage and of others, including that in his letter to the bishop describing his own consciousness, when alone in the Australian wilderness of the presence of the 'Awful Spirit of the Universe' – was a believer and a spiritually-minded man, however unorthodox?

What has he told his readers elsewhere in his writings? Take, for instance, that passage in the 'Noah's Ark' papers in which an Irish member of the circle closes an argument on the subject of immortality by exclaiming, 'Talk no more! As my own poet, he, whom ungrateful Ireland allowed to die of starvation in Meath Hospital, says,

> 'Tis idle! we exhaust and squander
> > The glittering mine of thought in vain;
> All-baffled reason cannot wander,
> > Beyond her chain.
> The flood of Life runs dark dark clouds
> > Make lampless night around its shore;
> The dead, where are they? In their shrouds –
> > Man knows no more,'

a quotation, which, although apparently throwing doubt upon the doctrine of the immortality of the soul, is introduced by way of rebuke to previous speakers who have carried on the discussion with a certain levity of tone, and to raise the debate to a higher level. And, incidentally, a quotation which throws a sidelight on the wide range of Marcus Clarke's reading and culture, for until comparatively recent years but scant attention was accorded to the work of the unfortunate poet, James Clarence Mangan, author of the above lines, of whom an interesting account appeared in *T. P.'s Weekly* some years ago, including an until then unpublished poem of his.

Additional and more conclusive evidence with regard to the religious opinions of the author of these same 'Noah's Ark' papers is to be found elsewhere in them. For instance, take the following extracts from the same debate or one on a kindred subject:

> The Parson. – Kyfax, you are in a parlous state!
>
> Kyfax. – The happier are you, Sir, who believe and hope; I only doubt. If I could only be sure of disbelieving I should feel more comfortable …
>
> The Parson. – All forms of religion are worthy of consideration … I affirm that the Christian faith is good, merely because it *is* a faith; the religion of Mahomet is good merely because it *is* a religion: Buddhism and Judaism are good, and equally good is the religion of the wild Indians who worship God in the depths of their forests. The religion of rappings, flat irons and tumblers of tepid water, is merely contemptible.
>
> Noah. – What do you mean by the word 'contemptible?' A contemptible thing is merely contemptible to *you*. Your God, as a great man said, may be my devil.
>
> Marston. – 'By your fruits,' said the great Teacher, 'you shall know them.' Any faith which helps its votary to live purely and unselfishly is sufficient for me. Out of the milliard creeds for which poor human beings have suffered and died, who shall presume to say which is the true one?

There follow some interesting comments on the worship of the sun by the Persians and the discussion terminates with the following appeal from Noah to those who have taken part in it. 'It is starlight. Go and look up to heaven, and count the stars. You cannot.' To which Marston, the last previous speaker, replies:

> And when we realise that these endless ranks of solar systems have all their following of planets and satellites (probably filled with living beings), that the milliards of suns are endlessly various, that all the complicated motions of their different systems (of one of which our trifling earth is part) are all accomplished in perfect order, we shall then, perhaps, begin to comprehend how incomprehensible is that Great God of whom we all speak so flippantly.

Surely no fair-minded critic, after reading the foregoing impressive words, can entertain a doubt that the writer of them must have been a man of deep religious feeling at heart, however startling some of his ideas may have appeared at first sight to the thoughtless, the superficial, and the narrow-minded. A man of deep, religious feeling I repeat; not the smart and cynical sceptic they have been led to suppose. The easy audacity of the essay *Civilisation without Delusion*, and the undeniable flippancy of tone that marked one or two passages in the author's replies to the Bishop of Melbourne's remonstrances may perhaps have justly given offence at the time; but the extracts from his early letters to me and from his published writings of a later period prove Marcus Clarke to have been quite other than was supposed by those – and they were numerous – who formed their opinion of him in this respect from one or two aspects of the unfortunate episode in question.

Chapter 20

An underpaid letter supposed to have been tampered with during its transit by the Post Office officials. – Enumeration of the punishments by torture that might be inflicted upon the guilty parties. – A speculative transaction in sheep followed by one in mining shares. – His aspirations for a simple life, as expressed in the 'Noah's Ark' papers a few years afterwards.

The letter, from which I have given extracts in the previous chapter, drifted towards its conclusion into a lighter vein and continued, 'but I am getting prosy – and religiously prosy – which is the worst kind of prosiness,' and passed on to an entirely different subject, that of a letter of mine for which he had been charged double postage, amounting to the sum of half a crown. Assuming that the postage stamps originally affixed by me had been surreptitiously removed by some post office clerk, he recommended me to subject the guilty official to the following ordeal for having thus tampered with them:

> Have his blood! Break him on the wheel! Rub cayenne pepper into his wounds! Pour molten lead into his navel! Bake his head in an oven! Scrape his backbone with broken glass! Fry him over a slow fire until his brains bubble and his marrow distils, drop by drop, and his eyeballs burst with heat! Deliver him over for vivisection! Place him in a barrel with two mad cats and roll him down hill! Tear out his nails and break his bones, inch by inch. Crack his joints and pump water into him until he bursts – but *don't* kick up an official row because I have destroyed the envelope and can prove nothing!

Another letter containing an account of a certain freak of his may perhaps be appropriately introduced at this point as an illustration of his boyish high spirits and love of adventure at this period of his life:

Soon after I wrote my last letter to you I went to Ballarat in order to purchase two hundred head of fat cattle for the station. After three or four days humbugging in cattle yards up to my knees in mud, I succeeded in doing this, and on the evening of the purchase was indulging myself after my labours with a quiet game of billiards at the 'George.' I was playing with the marker and not paying much attention to the game, when I heard a conversation at the next table which caused me to think a little.

The conversation was between two squatters who, it seemed, had come to Ballarat for the same purpose as myself, namely, to buy stock. One of them, it appeared, was either an agent or something of the kind and he was complaining to his friend that he had promised to forward a certain number of sheep to his correspondents and was fifteen hundred (1500) sheep short. 'I don't care how much I give, or whether the sheep are sound or not,' said he, 'but I must have them by tomorrow night.'

Now it so happened that in my wanderings through the saleyards in search of cattle, I had come upon a mob of about two thousand sheep which were 'fluky' (a peculiar disease which it would take me too long to explain and interest you little). 'Now if I can get these sheep,' thought I, 'I can sell them to this fellow at a profit, as I know there are no more in the market.' (There would be plenty in a day or two, but at this moment this was the only flock unpurchased.) I went out of the billiard room, ran down to our agent's house and agreed with him to purchase the flock at seven shillings and sixpence a head, provided he would have them in his yards at 10 a.m. next morning. I must tell you that I had not a rap and did this solely 'on spec.' Of course, as I had just handed him over a large cheque for the cattle, he was quite easy in his own mind as to my solvency.

At 10 a.m. next day I was in the yards and saw my purchase, fat sheep but very 'fluky.' 'If the fellow is much of a judge,' I thought, 'I am done!' However at 12 (meridian) in comes my friend of the night before.

'Sheep for sale?' says he. ('All right,' I thought, 'there are now no more in the market or you would not be here.')

'Yes,' said I.

'How much?' says he,

'Thirteen shillings a head,' says I.

'Nonsense,' returns my friend, 'the sheep are fluky.'

'I know that but they are the only mob in the market and they won't go for less!'

We had some bargaining and finally agreed to twelve shillings a head, on condition that he took the whole flock. He gave me the money on the spot and took delivery of the sheep, whilst I walked over to the agent and paid him seven shillings and sixpence a head, thus pocketing four shillings and sixpence a head for the flock, making a total of four hundred and thirty three pounds and some shillings for my morning's work. I never made so much money in my life before.

The sheep were barely worth seven shillings and six pence a head, but I knew that he must have sheep and so made my own terms. Such a chance might not occur again for a hundred years. You may imagine I was in high feather and started for Melbourne that night, well equipped with the sinews of war.

My luck however did not stop here. The train left at 4 p.m., and as I was waiting on the platform I saw a fellow who was in the Bank of Australasia with me rush down to the telegraph office in violent haste. We interchanged greetings and I asked him what was up?

'Oh,' says he, '"Wombats" (the name of a mine) have found a "lead" this afternoon and we are telegraphing to the Melbourne branch to buy shares.'

He had no business to tell me this, as I was no longer in the bank, but I suppose he thought, 'No harm.' Having just made such a lucky hit in *sheep*, I thought I would try my luck in *shares*; having become possessed of a piece of intelligence which the Melbourne brokers would have given their ears for.

I got to Melbourne at 12 p.m. (sic.) and intended to go to the brokers the first thing next morning. But, as luck would have it, going into the Café Royal for a smoke, I met a man named H. who dabbled largely in shares. I conversed with him and with a diplomatic skill which would have made my reputation for ever in the Foreign Office, brought up the subject of shares.

'I can sell you some if you like,' said he. (He was always ready to 'pigeon' a green hand, as I knew)

'What are they?' said I.

'Wombats', he replied.

My heart jumped.

'They are doing A.1,' said he, 'a capital spec.'

Now I knew this was a lie, as they were very low in the market.

'All right, my boy!' said I, 'I have just made three hundred pounds in the bush; I take the shares and risk it!' We exchanged an agreement to that effect and parted; he, thinking he had got rid of a lot of useless scrip, and I hugging myself for joy. Next morning I went to his office and got the scrip and found by going over to the brokers that my three hundred pounds was worth three hundred and seventy-five pounds. I held on until noon next day when I sold for four hundred and thirty-seven pounds, six shillings (minus brokerage). The whole town was wild about 'Wombats' and, had I held on for three or four days longer, I could have realised over five hundred pounds. You see the chances one has in this goldmining colony!

Don't think however that I am in the habit of making lucky 'coups' like the above; if I were, I would soon come home a rich man! It was through simple luck; as, if I had lost the sheep, I should have had to draw bills to pay the cost of my purchase, as I bought them purely 'on spec,' and when one has money to spare one can make anything in shares, that is, if you know the 'ins and outs' of mining, which my banking experience gave me some insight into…

You will perhaps think that this story is a yarn; or, at least, much exaggerated, but I give you my word that it is true. I labour under the dread that you imagine I am romancing … but I am not.

Neither did I think so, for retailing anecdotes intended to depict his own ability and smartness, had never been a weakness of Marcus Clarke's. He was too perspicacious to practise what he despised and ridiculed in others but I remember the doubts that beset me as to whether such lucky hits would bring him much luck in the long run. 'Easy come, easy go' is a proverb with more than the customary grain of truth in it, and such flukes probably only increased (if they did not engender) a natural propensity to carelessness and recklessness in money matters on his part.

A few years afterwards he wrote in the 'Noah's Ark' papers,

'Ah, me; what injury has not 'commerce,' with its hurrying, extravagant, time-bargaining fury not done the English character. How few men in this nineteenth century that we are so proud of can enjoy the simple pleasures of living. We are all for town life, for hot rooms, gas, and shoddy. How many men of your acquaintance are aught but bored to death by a country walk? …

When I am rich – that is, when I am out of debt – I shall contrive to earn 30s. a week somehow, and live upon it – in the country …

Just now there seems to be nothing so excellent as peacefulness and temperance and the smell of newly turned plough furrows. My office holds me one side, my newspaper beckons me from another. I have a book to write, a play to finish, a bill to meet, a creditor to satisfy. I do not live. I am in too great a hurry.

Chapter 21

Effect of Dr. Lewins' visit to Ledcourt. – Marcus Clarke abandons the idea of joining the mounted police. – His cousin's letters from England. – His own carelessness and forgetfulness of dates. – An unfulfilled promise. – Interval in our correspondence. – His appointment to a position on the staff of the Melbourne Argus. *– Close of the private period of his career.*

Dr. Lewins' visit to Ledcourt Station had evidently quite unsettled Marcus Clarke. For from that date onwards his letters, in whatever spirit they were indited, never varied in referring to the probability of a coming change in his way of life. Following on his amusing denunciation of the supposed purloiner of the postage stamps, came a letter commenting in the same farcical strain on the fact mentioned in one of mine that a ball had been given at his old school:

> A ball at Highgate schoolhouse! Imagination refuses to picture it! I could understand a musical *soirée* at the Deaf and Dumb Asylum, or a gymnastic exhibition at the Orthopedic Institution – but a ball at Highgate schoolhouse! Ye gods defend us! *Dii avertite omen*!

And then followed a half sheet of clever nonsense concluding with the reflection, "'Never mind! 'Tis but a dream! And I am servant in a Highland family!'" as that celebrated dramatic author, Marcus Clarke, says in his burlesque, *The Lady of the Lake.*' But, after this final sally, the writer's style sobered down and, although in subsequent letters he sometimes adopted a light tone, he never seemed able to 'recapture the first, fine, careless rapture.'

Discussing the relative merits of British and Australian horses, he sums up in favour of the latter with a remark about the different conditions obtaining in the two countries and an apposite quotation from Lord Byron. 'But then, to be sure, our roads are different from "Thine incomparable road, Macadam!"' This letter, like most of his at that period, was written in instalments, and towards the end of it he describes the first part as having been penned 'with an assumption of gaiety that I am far from feeling,' adding nevertheless, 'I daresay, however, that by next mail-time I shall be in better spirits ... Many thanks for the trouble you have taken about my scribblings; they really are not worth it. The thermometer is 112 in the shade today and the ink consequently like mud. I was riding yesterday from 6.30 a.m. to 8 p.m. and the thermometer was at 165 all day in the sun! Be thankful you are not in Australia!'

In a subsequent letter he referred again to the prospects of sheep and cattle farmers.

> If I choose to go into squatting in Queensland or elsewhere, I am sure of an independence; say at least fifteen thousand pounds in six or seven years. But I don't choose! What can compensate a man for the wasting of the best years of his life in money grubbing? I fear that my Bohemian blood is too strong in me and that I must have change!

Nevertheless he gave me to understand that he had refused the 'police arrangement' and decided to remain at Ledcourt until something definite was known as to the value of the supposed mineral discoveries. Alluding to his relatives in England, he informed me,

> My friends are all dispersed and I get letters from my cousins, who are becoming desperate swells, dated 'Aston Hall,' or 'Badminton' or 'Sevenoaks,' and full of trash about balls and hunts, *levées*, and suppers, whilst aristocratic names pelt about my plebeian head in a hailstorm of Debrett! Confound their jollity and roistering! If they were only hard up, 'in the bench,' or 'going through the court,' I could be as affectionate a coz as ever breathed, but what sympathy have I with these 'tenth transmitters of a foolish face'? I suppose the news that Army men have to tell, however, is not very piquant and I must endure ...

It must have been about this time that Marcus gave expression to those views of his regarding the nature of the business he was learning to a neighbouring squatter who had asked him to dinner (related by Hamilton Mackinnon), the conclusion

Marcus had arrived at being that 'Sweeps could do the work as well, if not better!' He probably felt that his days of apprenticeship to the pastoral industry were drawing to an end. The writer in *Cosmos*, referring to Dr. Lewins' visit to Ledcourt says,

> When the doctor returned to Melbourne he sought the help of friends in leading positions on the metropolitan press to gain for his *protégé* the opportunity of starting on a literary career, and sometime in the year 1867, Marcus Clarke made his *début* as a journalist. He was regularly engaged on the *Argus* staff, and besides writing articles for its columns, undertook the business of theatrical critic.

A letter to me dated 'Ledcourt Station, February 14th, 1867,' (the very month assigned in Mackinnon's biographical notice as that in which Marcus Clarke joined the *Argus*) commences thus:

> You see that I am here yet, but I shall not be here next month. Where I shall go to is at present, with several other matters, 'in the womb of time.'
>
> 'Tonight my heart is light,
> No dirge will I upraise,' as Edgar Allan Poe says,

and then follows this characteristic remark about dates which shows how easily Mackinnon might have been led astray if he trusted to Marcus himself for such information:

> Many thanks for the sailor twins by your brother (alluding to a pen-and-ink sketch by Arthur Hopkins which I had sent him). Henceforth I shall date your letters by their vignettes. For my own part, when you talk of 'your letter of September or January, or February,' *I* don't in the least know what said letter was about, being one of the most forgetful of mortals *as to dates* that ever hunted in an almanac. Indeed, what can you expect from people like us squatters who, 'under the shade of melancholy boughs, lose and neglect the creeping hours of time' …
>
> My uncle is going to England upon his pension after next Christmas and wants me to go with him. I shall not go however; for I see nothing to be done at home and don't care, after choosing of my own accord to come out here, to return and confess that I have done no good by coming … I promised you a photograph of the station. The photo is in my desk but I have had no opportunity of ascertaining the postal regulations concerning packages and parcels, so one day next month I will find out all

about them and send it to you by the next mail … Don't be afraid of my fading from human sight; I shall take care that your letters shall be forwarded.

But the promised photograph of Ledcourt Station never arrived, and an interval of several months elapsed before I received another letter from him.

When, at length one reached me, it bore the Melbourne postmark and was written on paper headed *Argus* Office. It ran as follows:

My dear Cyril, Don't start at the address! I am now on the staff of the *Argus*, our chief paper here. I have just received your letters – about five in a bundle and must state reasons for not replying before.

In the first place I have been three months up in the bush. In the second I have been down with ague-fever and all sorts of disorders. To explain: I left Holt's place and went up with five more fellows on an expedition to Queensland. I need not detail all the miserable failures. Suffice it to say that we lost about three hundred pounds each; that our horses died and our cattle were drowned by floods, that fever set in and that we were all taken ill. One poor devil, the Hungarian, Max Kabat, died and was buried in the bush. I reached Adelaide in rags and, after waiting some time, got some money remitted and came up to town.

The *Argus* people were in want of a theatrical critic and I accepted the post at a salary of three hundred a year.

(We have seen above that he did not by any means obtain this position in the casual manner intended to be conveyed by this passage but simply through the influence of his newly made friend, Dr. Lewins.) 'I write also reviews and leaders,' (the letter continued),

The life is well enough but at the end of the year I intend to come home and go in for authorship. I am sick of the bush and the colonies … They want to keep me but I don't believe in staying … People say that I look ten years older after this infernal Queensland business. I feel a hundred! … I am afraid that this is a most stupid letter but I am not 'i' the vein'… I am so unwell and shaken that I cannot settle to anything and have to grind out my literary work at the cost of nervous tissue! …

Write to me by every mail! You have no idea how your letters cheer me up! … What a life I have had! Bank clerk, gold buyer, squatter, overlander, play writer, author and man of means! Share buyer and speculator too! *Vive la bagatelle!* If I had only saved the money I have made! Lord, what fools these mortals be!

P.S. The enclosed are criticisms and reviews cut out at random; the 'Balzac' and 'Doré' are the only things worth a rap in a literary sense.

The foregoing are extracts from a letter I received from him towards the end of the year 1867 and show that during the interval between Dr. Lewins' visit to Ledcourt and his (Marcus Clarke's) becoming a member of the staff of the *Argus*, he had formed one of a party travelling overland from Victoria into Queensland to see for themselves what the prospects might be for settlers there; an expedition that proved a disastrous one. Marcus made his way to Adelaide, as we have seen, where he arrived in an exhausted and dilapidated condition and whence (after a rest and refit), he proceeded to Melbourne and obtained the employment for which he had doubtless been hoping from the date of Dr. Lewins' visit to Ledcourt. As to the supposed impending mineral discoveries there, he never alluded to them again.

We have now reached a point in Marcus Clarke's career that seems to mark the close of what – for want of a better designation – I may term the private period of his life. For from this time onwards he gradually emerges from obscurity, becoming known first as a journalist, a purveyor of light literature, and a clever hand at a short story. Then he figures as an historical writer whose speciality is neither that of regular history nor yet historical fiction, but a faculty for selecting certain incidents from the records of early colonial days and presenting them in a new light – that of entertaining narratives. Further developing this faculty he next employed it in searching the records of the formerly notorious convict settlement in Tasmania and found therein material for one of the finest English novels of the nineteenth century. He never perhaps quite attained to this level again but wrote many brilliant essays, amusing verses, and strange and fascinating short stories.

The later years of his comparatively brief life were chiefly employed in writing for the stage. Most of his work in this branch of literature consisted of burlesques and the librettos of comic operas. This would seem to imply a decline of literary ability but the motive for taking up work of this kind was undoubtedly a pecuniary one. He found adapting popular novels and converting them into stage plays, and even writing original plays of his own, an easier and more rapid means of earning money than that provided by regular literature. From this point of his career onwards, at all events, i.e. from the date of his return to Melbourne to start as a writer on the press, his life becomes that of a public journalist and popular author, and it is only very occasionally that his private letters add anything fresh to what is already known about him or throw any fresh light on his character.

Chapter 22 (i)

Commencement of a literary career in Melbourne. – Natural qualifications for journalism.
– Extraordinary enterprise and industry. – Editorship of the Colonial Monthly. – Names
of some of the contributors. – Severe accident whilst out riding. – Misconceptions of foreign
critics. – Personal appearance at the age of twenty-two. – The Melbourne Club and social life
in Melbourne at this period.

As compared with the results of his two previous attempts at earning a livelihood, the one finally adopted, that of journalism, proved almost from the first, a brilliant success. Mr. E. La Touche Armstrong, Chief Librarian of the Melbourne Public Library, with which institution, some two years after his return to Melbourne, Marcus Clarke became connected for the rest of his life, writes, it is true, with regard to Marcus's achievements in this branch of literature, 'Regular journalism, however, was little more palatable to his mercurial temperament than had been his other attempts to earn a living and he soon became a freelance instead of a regular member of the staff.'

Mr Armstrong is here alluding to Marcus Clarke's loss of his position of theatrical critic to the *Argus* not so very long after his appointment thereto. His duties in this capacity came to an abrupt termination for the following reasons (as explained by the writer in *Cosmos*):

> He was deputed to furnish a notice of a concert at one of the Melbourne halls. It
> was a second-rate programme, and as most of it was already familiar to the gentle

reporter, he thought he could write about it quite as well without experiencing the tedium of attending, as if he had sate there the evening through. So he spent the hours pleasantly with two or three congenial companions, and having satisfied his conscience so far as to verify the fact of the concert having taken place, he penned his paragraph. There was one particular song which he knew was always detestably rendered by the performer whose name was set against it in the programme, and Clarke made the most of his chance of slating him. His criticism was vigorously written, of course, but it unfortunately happened that on this occasion the condemnation was hardly merited. The first thing that Clarke's eyes lighted on in the morning was a notice of the same concert in a rival paper, stating that Mr. So-and-So was unhappily prevented from fulfilling his engagement by a severe cold. Clarke ... was little surprised when he received a notification from the newspaper office, informing him that his services on the reporting staff would no longer be required. He still continued, however, to do valuable work as a contributor, sometimes with a *nom de plume* and sometimes without, and it was not till a few years afterwards that his connection with the *Argus* and *Australasian* was permanently severed, and his services transferred to the *Age* and *Leader*.

I have read that what is required in the mind of a journalist is that it should adapt itself to the work with a quick grasp of facts and a light touch. These qualities came like a second nature to Marcus Clarke, and combined with a keen sense of humour and happiness of expression, invested what he wrote with an unfailing charm.

Lord Rosebery during his visit to Melbourne noticed and admired his (Marcus's) literary gifts, and very naturally so, for judging by His Lordship's speeches and writings, his own mind and that of Marcus Clarke were cast in somewhat similar mould. But although the latter, no longer immersed in the uncongenial work of a bank nor in the almost equally uncongenial tasks of a sheep and cattle station, was now in his element, his life henceforward was one of fairly arduous toil, no inconsiderable part performed, like that of his favourite author Balzac, when other men were asleep. For in the space of time comprised between his return to Melbourne when barely two and twenty and his death at the age of thirty-five, he had, in addition to his ordinary journalistic work, and subsequently to his work at the Public Library, published numerous essays, historical narratives, novels, verses and plays, a record of unceasing industry.

Yet, strange as it may appear, I have read that after his death, a charge of want of industry was brought up against him in certain literary circles in Melbourne. With far more justice and insight, the Right Hon. W. B. Dalley referred, in an article contributed by him to the *Sydney Morning Herald*, to the 'vast amount of literary work which this accomplished man must have performed – work that has no enduring place – demanded day by day and containing in its essential elements of intensity and unpremeditation all the blemishes and sometimes the beauties of such labour.'

A writer in the *National Review* rebutting a similar charge concluded his article by saying that he wrote in no spirit of vainglory but to show the untruth of the 'charge of idleness that is so frequently and unwarrantably brought against the freelance struggling to secure some foothold on the slippery steps at the top of which sits success.' In the case of Marcus Clarke there were possibly two causes which may partly account for such a charge having been brought, although looking at his life-work as a whole, surely without foundation. Mr. Armstrong mentions one of them.

> His literary work was his life's work, and to it his Library work was entirely subordinate. The visible records of his ten years' work in the library are some badly kept minute books, and a worse than badly kept catalogue of bibliographical works that were his special charge. Neither Marcus Clarke's temperament nor training rendered him suitable for the real work of a Librarian…. The drudgery of the routine work, which is essential for any Librarian, was not a thing that he would attempt…. After ten years' apprenticeship, the letter that he wrote in applying for the office of Public Librarian, was one that might have been written by the veriest tyro.

The other may perhaps have been the notorious fact that he had found the task of completing his story *For the Term of His Natural Life* within a fixed period a very trying one, the publishers of the serial in which it originally appeared having experienced considerable difficulty in getting the successive instalments in proper time, and having been compelled to resort to sundry devices to accomplish their object.[63]

The fact is that Marcus Clarke was essentially a writer of short stories, light plays, humorous or sentimental verse, essays grave and gay; and that the conditions of his life rendered these more easy of execution than a lengthy and laboriously worked up novel such as the one referred to. In the earlier years of his career as a literary man, so energetic was he that he purchased, with the assistance of a friend, the periodical that had first given to the world his bush stories (composed at Swinton

---

63   The *Australian Journal.*

and Ledcourt). Having changed its name from the original *Australian Journal* or *Australian Magazine* to that of the Colonial Monthly, he became joint editor with the late J. J. Shillinglaw of the said periodical. The following is an extract from the *Weekly Times* (a Melbourne journal) in reference to it:

> In the sixties there flourished in Melbourne a well known magazine called the *Colonial Monthly*. Edited by Marcus Clarke, it had, for its contributors the chief literary lights of the time. Among these were the poets Gordon, Kendall, Horne and McCrae, a quartet of singers no literary combination in the Commonwealth has perhaps equalled since.

A warm friendship sprang up between them, especially between Marcus Clarke and Adam Lindsay Gordon, whose verses (afterwards as familiar as household words to that generation of Australians) were just then becoming popular.

Marcus's first novel appeared in serial form in the *Colonial Monthly*, but owing to a severe accident he met with, he was unable to complete it himself. This his friend, the late G. A. Walstab, accomplished, but whether quite in accordance with the author's plan cannot be exactly determined. The accident is thus described by Hamilton Mackinnon:

> Clarke had, in company with the late Walter Montgomery, been out to a meet of the hounds, and on their return home he was dared to take a fence. In his usual reckless way he charged the timber, which the horse failed to negotiate, the result being a hard hit, a bad fall, the horse injured, and the rider rendered senseless by a kick on the head from the struggling animal. So severe was the blow that many days passed before the patient recovered consciousness, and to his dying hour he carried the mark, an indentation at the back of the skull, easily discernible.

I believe that both Professor Nordau in his work on degeneration and Signor Lombroso have ascribed the genius of Marcus Clarke to this untoward accident. (Lombroso says, 'Lesions of the head and brain are very frequent among men of genius'.) Unfortunately for this extraordinary theory, Marcus Clarke's mental powers developed very early in life, and far from enhancing their value, this mishap permanently injured them. For Mackinnon's account continues, 'And ever afterwards he occasionally betrayed symptoms indicative of the shock his nerves had received, his memory at times, and suddenly, utterly failing him.' Marcus only referred to this severe accident very briefly in a letter to me dated August 15th 1868, but which contained other and interesting news about himself. The letter in question was written from the Melbourne Club of which he had shortly before this time been elected a member. 'I have had several letters from you and have been, for the first time since I left England, guilty of the sin of silence.' He had indeed always written regularly except during the interval between his departure from Ledcourt for Queensland and return to Melbourne to join the staff of the *Argus*.

> The reason is a valid one. I have been as nearly dead as it is possible for a man to be. I was thrown from my horse over a jump, and got concussion of the brain, during which I could neither write nor read.... I am at present in rather good circumstances. I am making a decent living by article writing and hope shortly to see the *Colonial Monthly* a success. I write leading articles for three dailies (say, I write five leading articles a week), write theatrical criticisms, edit the magazine, and contribute an article to a weekly paper, and in all I make an average of fifteen pounds a week. I have read *On the Heights*, to which you refer (a translation of Auerbach's well known novel *Auf der Höhe*). It is good and true, which is better than good.... What do you think of Reade and Boucicault? Read *Griffith Gaunt* – the best of Reade's books I think, very powerful and clever.

He went on to criticize a then recently published poem of Swinburne's in rather strong language, adding however, as a saving clause apparently, 'Nevertheless the "Hymn to Proserpine" is very fine. So is *Chastelard*.... Edmund Yates is progressing favourably.'

The latter, whose novels were then attracting a good deal of attention, was an old Cholmleiian (as those who had received their education at Sir Roger Chomley's school, Highgate, were called) and of course excited our interest. Then, alluding to an article on 'friendship' that had recently appeared in the *Saturday Review*, he expressed the pious hope that if we met again, 'Although possibly – probably – both much changed, we should not mutually hate each other,' and concluded by asserting that recent events and experiences had so changed him that, although only twenty-two, he felt a hundred. 'You would hardly know me; wrinkled and hard-set.'

If so, this must have been entirely owing to the severe physical shock he had so recently sustained and have been but temporary. For his personal appearance as well as his manners and individuality are thus described by a contemporary journalist (Mr. Charles Bright) who made his acquaintance a little while previously to the accident in question.[64] *En passant*, I may remark that Mr. Bright's description of Marcus Clarke's personal appearance at this period (probably about the beginning of the year 1868) closely tallies with my own final recollection of him just before he sailed for Melbourne some five years earlier:

> It seems but the other evening, yet is nearly eight and twenty years ago, that, seated in the lounge of the Café de Paris, – Pond and Spiers' Melbourne success, before the firm migrated to London – a fellow-journalist by my side remarked, in an undertone, 'That's Marcus Clarke,' as a slight, boyish figure daintily attired, hastened past and disappeared through the swing-doors leading to the dress-circle of the Theatre Royal. I had heard of him as a recent notable addition to the literary staff of the *Argus* and *Australasian* but had not previously seen him. Later on that same night he reappeared with Walter Montgomery, the actor, who, in his *grand seigneur* style, brought him up, remarking 'Charley, my boy; you ought to know Marcus's; and the introduction was duly celebrated in the customary style. I noticed as a peculiarity of the newcomer that he partook of absinthe, a drink rarely called for by any but Frenchmen, and I asked if he liked it. 'Not particularly,' he said, 'but I'm experimenting with it. They say it'll drive a fellow mad in a month and I want to find out if that's a fact. I've tried opium-smoking, and rather like that. There are a lot of lies told about these things, you know, and we have scriptural authority for proving all things and holding fast that which is good. I can't say yet if absinthe be good, or not.' His voice was pleasant to listen to, and he appeared to have a slight difficulty occasionally in getting out his words – not a stutter, but an approach to it – which, like Charles Lamb's fully-developed stammer, gave an added charm to his talk. Still, I cannot truthfully affirm that I was greatly attracted by him that first night of our acquaintanceship. It was distasteful to me to find so young a man – he was then about one-and-twenty – so cynical and, apparently, so *blasé*. When I came to know him better I discovered that much of this cynicism and indifference was but skin deep. At heart, he was open to all human sympathies and alive to every generous aspiration, but it took time for an outsider to get there, and at first one was apt to be misled by his affectation of satiety and recklessness.
>
> The likeness, accompanying this article … gives a good idea of the author of *His Natural Life* during the latter portion of his career, but differs greatly from his appearance

---

64   See article in *Cosmos* magazine dated April 30, 1895.

when he first made his mark in Melbourne journalism.[65] At that time he had no hair on his face, save a soft, silken, light brown moustache, and his clear-cut features and beaming eyes were almost feminine in the beauty of their aspect. He was considerably below the middle height, yet of singularly symmetrical figure, and looked in his carefully-fitting costumes, as a full-sized British dandy of the period might look if viewed through the wrong end of an opera-glass…. It was a noticeable fact that those who only knew him from his writings always pictured him as a big man, physically, and were astonished when brought into personal contact with him. One memorable instance of this delusion came under my own immediate cognizance. Towards the end of 1870 a number of indiscreet friends persuaded me that I ought to be in Parliament, and I was nominated for one of the metropolitan constituencies.

Opposition was expected and a friend, who had never seen Marcus Clarke, suggested him as chairman of the meeting.

I had to explain that a less likely Boanerges could not well have been suggested.

As already mentioned, Marcus had, sometime early in his literary career, been elected a member of the Melbourne Club. What this membership implied at that date (1868-69) is very clearly set forth by the late Mr. H. M. Hyndman in the first volume of his autobiography:[66]

I have always remembered my sojourn therein (i.e. at the Melbourne Club), off and on for two years, with the keenest pleasure. I became very intimate with many of its members and I saw from the first, what not a few Englishmen coming out to the Colony failed unfortunately to recognize, that, before the gold fever and spirit of adventure drew them out to Victoria, many of these *habitués* had seen and enjoyed pretty nearly all that was to be seen and enjoyed of European Society.

Whilst of Melbourne itself as a capital he adds,

---

65   Identical with that forming the frontispiece of Mackinnon's *Memorial Volume*.
66   The Record of an Adventurous Life by H. M. Hyndman.

I have been a great deal about the world and I have moved freely in many societies, but I have never lived in any city where the people at large, as well as the educated class, took so keen an interest in all the activities of human life, as in Melbourne at the time I visited it. Art, the drama, music, literature, journalism, wit, oratory, all found ready appreciation. The life and vivacity of the place were astonishing.

Such was the public, then, to whom Marcus Clarke had to address himself, and therefore, in so far as it depended upon circumstances of that kind, he must be considered to have been fortunate in his environment.

Chapter 22 (ii)

For the Term of His Natural Life

No mention of this remarkable novel usually to be found in the works of critics or reviewers of fiction during the Victorian era. – Some independent appreciations by Australian and English writers. – How the story came to be written; 'an overmastering inspiration.' – Delay in completion. – Gradual recognition of the author's genius. – Adaptation of the story to the stage and press comments on the dramatised version. – Period and scene of the story. – The British Penal Code during the earlier half of the nineteenth century. – Comparison of the story with Victor Hugo's Les Misérables by an Australian critic. – The author's restraint. – Other novels dealing with criminal life. – The present aspect of the derelict convict settlement. – Memories of the past. – The enduring human interest of the story.

I have been unable to discover in the numerous reviews dealing with the fiction of the Victorian era any mention of the novel *For the Term of His Natural Life* although the reviewers found plenty to say about *Wuthering Heights* with which

Lord Rosebery has compared it. One of them, referring to Emily Bronte's novel, considered the latter inferior to *Treasure Island* because in his opinion a greater effect had been produced in Stevenson's story without the introduction of a single violent expression, a result possible only owing to the fact that Stevenson was a great literary artist. If this view be just, it applies with equal force to Marcus Clarke's book of which the reviewer makes no mention. Nevertheless, *For the Term of His Natural Life* will bear comparison with any great work of fiction, although the reader cannot, in Lord Rosebery's words, 'but be harrowed by the long agony of the story and the human anguish of every page.'

Under the heading of 'Reprints', the following notice of it appeared in the *Times Literary Supplement* for April 25th 1912:

> *For the Term of His Natural Life*, by Marcus Clarke,
> Macmillan's Shilling Library
> This novel of the British penal system as it existed in Norfolk Island and at Port Arthur during the forties has been reprinted over and over again, and is not only the chief product of the brief career of the Australian novelist and dramatist (1846–1881) but remains still the most famous novel that Australia has produced.

If, in some respects, it was a drawback to the author that he was domiciled in Australia, there were even from a literary point of view, certain compensatory advantages, especially with regard to such a work of fiction as this. For without previous study of the government records and topographical conditions on the spot, this drama of convict life in Tasmania could never have been composed. Indeed one Australian critic, by no means disposed to magnify Marcus Clarke's achievement, remarks in this connection:

> One inclines to believe then that much of the force of *His Natural Life* must have lain *perdu* in the records on which Clarke based his story. But Clarke had a fine faculty of dramatic insight and dramatic expression. Given the ore he could refine it, given the situation, the scene, the men, he could bring all the contours and contrasts, into prominence.

Mr. Hyndman, however, to whom this qualified praise would probably not have commended itself, takes another and a broader view of this aspect of the novel in question, for in his reminiscences of his visit to Australia he refers to it in the following telling passage:

> This is an awful book. Some one speaking of it the other day said it was a mere reproduction of official records. This is quite unfair in every way. The novel is in its line a masterpiece of horror. It is not mere photography: it is an artistic presentation of events so terrible in themselves that it needed a craftsman of much more than ordinary skill and imagination to bring them within the scope of literary art at all. The story is based upon incidents many of which actually took place in those hells upon earth Van Diemen's Land and Norfolk Island. So hideous were the details ... that I believe the original records were deliberately destroyed, as being contrary to public morals that such things should ever see the light. But Clarke's tremendous book remains, telling, alike by what it recites and what it suppresses, the frightful truth. I defy anyone to read it through without feeling as he lays it down that he has been perusing what is not far, if at all, removed from a work of genius. This is the more remarkable inasmuch that Clarke's turn seemed to be towards light and witty comment on the topics of the day. *His Natural Life* shows that, as I suspected, much greater power than he himself knew lay below the surface of his ability. He never did himself full justice. But this novel of his will live by sheer force of its terror-inspiring delineations long after his other work is forgotten.

Mr. Charles Bright, a distinguished Australian journalist of that day, whilst paying a generous tribute to its literary merits, has given the following interesting account of the origin of the story:

> It is a keen satisfaction to me now that I was among the first to publicly appraise at something like its real worth that thrilling romance, *His Natural Life*. This work, which has given Clarke an enviable reputation the wide world over, owed its genesis to the fact that his health had broken down, and that he was anxious to pay a holiday visit to Tasmania. His marriage with a charming actress of the day ... took place in 1869, when Clarke was just three-and-twenty, and it was the following year that he meditated his notable holiday trip. How were the means for such a dissipation to be provided? He resolved to draw upon the bank of his inventive genius, and succeeded, with fortunate results, for all time. He proposed to the proprietors of the *Australian Journal*, a magazine to which he had already contributed many a brilliant page, that they should advance him the wherewithal to enable him to travel through

the old convict island and rummage the musty records at some of its ill-favoured prison depôts. He took a few weeks for the task, going to work with a will born – who can doubt it? – of an overmastering inspiration. The story which resulted from this excursion appeared in due course in the columns of the *Australian Journal*, and although it was disfigured with many mistakes, which were rectified before its second publication, the genius of its author was thenceforth regarded as an assured fact by all who trusted to their own insight, and waited not for the stamp of English approval. I had been previously closely associated with Clarke in one of his literary enterprises – the publication of a satirical weekly journal entitled *Humbug* – and my estimate of his ability was an exalted one. But I must confess I had never credited him with the possession of powers such as those manifested in his *magnum opus*. He had written short stories of the Australian bush of such rare excellence as to secure him generous words of recognition and praise from literary men of the highest standing in distant parts of the world. But few conceived that he had either the capacity or tenacity of purpose to construct an elaborate plot, introduce a multitude of diverse characters, and present scene after scene of absorbing interest at such a high artistic level as is attained and maintained in his great fiction.

That the story was not completed without considerable effort on the part of both author and publisher is evident from the account given by Mr. A. H. Massina to a representative of the Melbourne *Herald*, (reproduced in its issue of March 2nd 1909):

> The *Australian Journal* was first published by Mr. Massina, one of the best-known printers & publishers in the Commonwealth, founder of the firm of A. H. Massina and company forty years ago. Marcus Clarke, Adam Lindsay Gordon and George Arthur Walstab were writers who did some of their best work for his publications. How the story *For the Term of His Natural Life* came to be written is crisply told by Mr. Massina:
>
> Clarke came to me one day and said, 'Massina, I want £50.' 'Oh', I said, 'You've had enough out of me. What more do you want?' '£50,' replied Clarke, 'I can write a story for your journal. I am going to Tasmania to write up the criminal records and I'll do the story for one hundred pounds.' We jumped at it. Now Clarke was going to write that story in twelve monthly sections. At first he wrote enough for two months, then enough for one month, and got down to very little. In fact we had once to put it in pica type, instead of brevier to swell out the size of that month's contribution. But on one occasion he had nothing ready and we had to go to press with an apology to our readers. Finally we had to lock him in a room to get his matter written.

Cheap editions of the novel have been published both in Australia and England, the British edition by Messrs Macmillan, and the story has been dramatised and represented on the stage. In a review of the latest dramatic representation the *Australasian* referred to the gradual victory achieved by the story both in Australia and at home.

> The finest story ever written in Australia can hardly fall short of being a successful play, though like many other strong romances *For the Term of his Natural Life* suffers something in dramatisation ...
>
> It is worth while noting that in the period between the first and latest dramatic production of this celebrated romance, Australia has in art and literature practically found herself.
>
> Until Lord Rosebery ... read and recognised its merits and practically introduced it to the world of novel readers as something quite beyond the common, Marcus Clarke's story had, even in its own land, but a limited vogue. From that moment it became a classic amongst famous novels – Australia's first and greatest contribution to the world's fiction.

Commenting on the performance, the writer continues:

> It is almost impossible for reasons already stated to satisfy everyone, or even a small minority, provided they have read and thought, with a stage version of Rufus Dawes.
>
> Every tourist who pays a visit to Port Arthur to-day, who walks along Eaglehawk Neck, or lands upon the lone island of the dead, feels that step for step with him moves always that ever-living figure of the self-condemned convict, whose transformation from splendid courage to the reaction of ungovernable, hopeless desperation are the power of the story. If you feel so about the more than shadowy man of the imagination, you give the best of actors a tremendous task in striving to represent your ideal ...
>
> Mr. Duggan, in overdoing the tyranny of Maurice Freer, missed something of his masterful personality, for the character had distinctly two sides.
>
> Popular opinion defines it as a portrait, but those who had the best chance of judging say that the Superintendent of convicts supposed to be represented was a man who acted habitually from method, and never from personal caprice. We are apt to forget, too, that those who came under his iron discipline were not all of the type of Rufus Dawes.[67]

---

67   Ex *Australasian*, March 13, 1909.

With regard to the scene of the story, the locality had, previous to the appearance of Clarke's novel, figured in fiction. Edmund Yates had alluded to the convict settlement of Port Arthur, Tasmania, to the bloodhounds kept on the Eaglehawk Promontory and to the severe search of all outward bound vessels practised there, in one of his novels, *Nobody's Fortune*, but the absence of details and other indications show that he can never have visited the spot and merely wrote of it at second hand.

Again, as to the facts recorded, although whilst engaged on his sad story of suffering and despair, the author of *His Natural Life* might have exclaimed in the words of Charles Reade on the subject of his well known novel, *It is Never too Late to Mend*, 'I will make people feel … They read of an occasional outrage in an asylum or prison, say "How shocking!" and forget all about it; I will bring it home to them; they shall feel. They shall see how these facts touch them individually,' nevertheless, as has been fully recognized, he (Marcus Clarke) never overstated his case.

Great ameliorations have been introduced into our criminal code, more especially since the year 1864. In the earlier half of last century, a recent historian expresses the opinion that:

> The most gruesome records of all Europe, from the battle of Waterloo to the death of William the Fourth, were in the Newgate Calendar. Nothing in Turkey under the Sultan Mahmoud, nor in Egypt under Mehemet Ali, could vie with it in horror, though everything was done at Newgate in the name of law and justice. Looking back at the time Lord Ashley began his labours, one is struck with the want of sensibility of the nation at large.[68]

Even in our own day the writer of a work entitled *Prisons, Police and Punishment* designates 'the prison, as it has hitherto existed,' as 'simply a hardening institution, which inures folk to crime and the criminal life, and deliberately renders them unfit to become decent and useful members of society. It is an epitome of folly and wickedness. In the prison, the State is seen, like an evil stepmother, beating its own children – whom it has reared in poverty and ignorance, and among conditions which must inevitably lead to crime – beating them for its own sins and neglect, and confirming them in their hatred of itself and each other … And if … it seems strange that honourable and sincere men should lend themselves to the deceits,

---

68   *Victoria, Queen and Ruler*, by Lady Emily Crawford [1903].

the barbarities, the wilful blindness which we see daily displayed in our courts; if we wonder that … they should be capable of such hardnesses, stupidities, such real ignorance of human nature, as many of them betray; we must remember how paralyzing to all authentic human thought and feeling is the connexion with so rigid an institution as the Law – how inevitably it causes the mind to lapse into habits and formulae, which … are in general a legacy of the barbaric past.'[69] Whilst a Colonial Judge, acquainted with the conditions obtaining at the period portrayed in *For the Term of His Natural Life* has written of them:

> The student may read for himself … the details of a condition of society where women were openly sold in the market place, where the rum bottle was the only currency, where the lash resounded daily in the barrack square and the gibbet was never disestablished, where licentiousness and drunkenness – parents of every sort of evil – were nearly universal and where the favours of an irresponsible ruler were bestowed on cringing and fawning slaves.

One of the characters in the story in whose delineation the author has displayed much skill and observation is thus alluded to by Mr. Desmond Byrne, in his work on Australian writers:

> But what could be more luminous than the portrait of Sarah Purfoy, the clever, self-possessed adventuress with the single redeeming quality of an invincible love for her worthless and villainous convict-husband?

She is nursemaid to the infant daughter of the officer commanding the troops on board the convict ship and is introduced in a graphic passage describing the child's endeavour to recover her ball from the part of the deck reserved for the convicts to take exercise:

> but even as she turned, from under the shadow of the cuddy glided a rounded white arm; and a shapely hand caught the child by the sash and drew her back …
>
> The convict raised his eyes and saw a young girl of eighteen or nineteen years of age, tall and well developed, who, dressed in a loose-sleeved robe of some white

---

69   *Prisons, Police and Punishment* by Edward Carpenter.

material, was standing in the doorway. She had black hair, coiled around a narrow and flat head, a small foot, white skin, well-shaped hands, and large dark eyes, and as she smiled at him, her scarlet lips showed her white, even teeth.

He knew her at once. She was Sarah Purfoy, Mrs. Vickers' maid, but he had never been so close to her before; and it seemed to him that he was in the presence of some strange tropical flower, which exhaled a heavy and intoxicating perfume.

The scene in the ship's hospital between this woman and her fever stricken and unconscious convict-husband is remarkable for the intensity of feeling, and knowledge of human nature apparent in the author's portrayal of it. The description of the outbreak of the mutiny on board resembles in some respects Hogarth's well known pictures (which had so much impressed Marcus in his boyish days) in that some details which at first sight appear unnecessary and repulsive are found on closer examination to assist in making-up a most effective *tout ensemble*. Due allowance being made for the time occupied in reading it, one seems in this chapter to be gazing on a series of what were formerly known as 'dissolving views', but which may better be described to the present generation as cinematographic pictures, only these cinematographic pictures are reflected in words; their effect being however identical, for they paint for the reader each successive phase of the struggle. In Book the Second one cannot fail to be struck with the chapter entitled, 'The Topography of Van Diemen's Land', in which the causes for the salubrious climate are set forth with admirable lucidity and the oppressive character of some of the scenery in the vicinity of the convict settlement depicted.

In a letter received from the author's widow from Sir Donald Wallace, who accompanied the Royal party on their visit to Australia, she was informed that they had been most anxious to visit the scene of the novel but that owing to pressure of engagements and lack of time this had been found to be impossible.

In the portrait of Sylvia Vickers we see the type of female beauty Marcus always admired. She is a replica of the young girl who had so much impressed him on board the *Wellesley*, during the voyage to Melbourne in 1863 and whose appearance is described in his letter relating to that voyage: 'Her little figure was as upright and as supple as a willow rod; and her innocent, delicate face was framed in a nimbus of that fine golden hair – dry and electrical, each separate thread shining with a lustre of its own – with which the dreaming painters of the middle ages endowed and glorified their angels.' Her quaintly expressed note to Frere apologizing for her rudeness is very natural in so isolated a child and his reflections on reading it

equally so for a man of his character: 'I wonder what book she took that out of? …
'Pon my word she must be a little cracked. Gad, it's a queer life for a child in this
place, and no mistake' …

Book the Third containing the chapters entitled 'The Work of the Sea' and 'The
Cyclone' may well be studied for the sake of the brilliant descriptions of natural
phenomena embodied in them. 'It has been sometimes assumed,' says Mr. Bright,
'that Clarke would have accomplished greater things in literature had he remained in
England, but I cannot share in that opinion. The sudden wrench by which he was
extricated from his youthful environment and sent to the opposite side of the globe
among completely fresh surroundings gave him, I believe, a higher purpose in life, and
enabled him eventually to write a better book than he could otherwise have produced.'

Francis Adams considered that Marcus had applied the *limæ labor* to the story
and had not only done this but (what is so much more difficult still) set upon
'loading all the rifts of his subject with ore' to the best of his ability. In neither
operation had he been wholly successful:

> That was not possible to him; but he was successful enough to end with having
> produced one of the few remarkable English novels of his time – one of the few which
> have won for a man a place, however small, in the crowded fane of our literature.

And Mr. Walter Murdoch points out with reference to the unhappy convict, the
central figure of the story, that:

> the picture of this mere human soul, in the vicissitudes of his struggle with the system
> – the system whose shadow hangs over the story as the shadow of necessity hangs over
> a tragedy of Æschylus – has a grandeur of outline that raises its maker almost to a
> level with Hugo – the Hugo of *Les Misérables*. In one point he compares favourably
> indeed with Hugo; with that author's leaning for the grandiose he has no sympathy;
> his art is everywhere restrained. And in his method of handling his material – in what
> the French call *documentation*, in the patient, laborious working up of his historical
> evidence – he is the co-mate not of Hugo, but of Flaubert and Zola, and of the
> great master of all who employed this method, Defoe. Not Defoe himself, collecting
> his materials for the *Journal of the Plague Year*, worked more diligently or to better
> purpose than Clarke with his records of the convict system. The idea of such a book
> being written by a careless Bohemian, writing as the mood took him from day to day,
> is merely preposterous. The book was written by a great and serious artist in love with

his art, patient, sedulous and industrious in pursuit of it. His reward is a book that lives. It is not a story with a moral 'thrown externally over it', in Stevenson's phrase, 'like a carpet over a railing'. It is not a 'novel with a purpose', which becomes valueless when its purpose is accomplished. The transportation system has passed, but man's inhumanity to man remains, and Clarke's great sermon is still of universal validity.

The inherent truth of these words is borne out at the present time by the fragmentary glimpses obtained by the public of the sufferings of the British prisoners of war in Germany and the agonies already recorded of the victims of their inhuman conduct in Belgium and French Flanders in the early days of the German invasion.

Dr. Patrick Moloney, in a short biographical memoir of the author of *His Natural Life*, a work which 'may fairly be said to have placed Marcus Clarke on the topmost rung of the Australian ladder of fame', mentions that the novel has been translated into several foreign languages. Proof of the author's genius is surely apparent in his intuitive perception of the fact that a study of the prison records at Port Arthur would in all probability yield material for a powerful romance that yet would be the very essence of realism. Hence his eagerness to proceed to Tasmania for the purpose of research and examination of the prison records and surroundings. No sooner had he set to work than he discerned the history of human anguish latent in them and evolved from their bald statements the narrative which eventually captured the imagination of the reading world. The following passage from a small work of great interest, *Confessions of a Journalist*, well illustrates my meaning:

> I have heard novelists complain of the paucity of dramatic incident in actual life, and I have heard readers complain even more bitterly of the scarcity of real dramatic incident in the modern novel ... The fact that human nature is not quite so black as it is painted, is a tribute to our innate goodness and a sign of the deplorable lack of experience on the part of most modern writers. Every hour of the day's history thrills with humour, drama and pathos, but it takes place far away from the sumptuous sitting room where writers with large circulation imagine and circumvent impossible deeds of villainy.

Very different to the calculating and commercial spirit which prompts their melodramatic and artificial productions was that inspiring the author of the stern and sordid tragedy *For the Term of His Natural Life.* Some resemblance to it might perhaps be expected in it to other stories concerned with criminals, such for instance, as that well known one by the Russian author Dostoieffsky, *Crime and Punishment.* But whereas the latter traces the gradual detection of a murderer, the author of the Australian novel relates in the form of fiction the actual sufferings of the Tasmanian convicts, with the graphic touch of a Defoe.

Some years ago a novel was published entitled *In Steel and Scarlet*, dealing with military life and imbued with a spirit of, as it seemed, rather hopeless misery. But whereas the trials of the unfortunate life-guardsman, even if possible, must have been quite exceptional, those of Rufus Dawes at the period assigned were by no means unusual amongst the convicts at Port Arthur. *Fettered for Life*, the work of a well known novelist, Frank Barrett, is partly concerned with Dartmoor Prison, but although the titles of some chapters recall those of Marcus Clarke's story, there is no resemblance in their contents beyond the identity of the subject. Moreover, the date of the action and the locality of Barrett's story are far removed from those of the fierce Tasmanian tragedy. Another story, *The Inimitable Mrs. Massingham*, although the scene is partly laid in New South Wales in the old convict days, bears no resemblance, being a romantic tale of love and adventure. Other works of fiction and of philosophy also, connected with the subject of crime and prison life doubtless there are in abundance; but nothing would be gained by an enumeration of their titles, or the nature of their contents. There is an originality and distinction about Marcus Clarke's novel that stamps it as unique of its kind.

When it was first published (for it has run through various editions) the convict settlement in Tasmania was still in existence, although the number of inmates had dwindled to small proportions. But in 1877 it was finally abandoned and at the present time, as is evident from articles in the press and from Mr. Archibald Marshall's interesting work *Sunny Australia*, the very prison buildings are little more than ruins:

> Port Arthur itself … bears so much an air of the past that, in its beautiful setting, it makes the same impression as the remains of far more ancient days. Though not so far removed in time, the clank of chains, the tramp of heavy feet, the curses, the groans, the sharp words of command, are as completely silenced as the sandalled footfalls and the uplifted chants that echoed in some now deserted, grass-grown cloister of the Old World. The old convict life is as dead as the old monastic life and the stones that sheltered it have as interesting a tale to tell … From the top of the hill the settlement lay stretched out before us facing the blue waters of the tree-encircled bay. On its edge

were the ivy-covered ruins of a great, stone-built church, lacking nothing in the way of picturesqueness. It had been a massive building of considerable dignity, designed by a convict architect, built by convict masons and carpenters ... The church was burnt down by a bushfire some twenty-five years ago and another devastating fire burnt out the rest of the prison buildings some years later ... We sailed and rowed across a mile of blue, clear water to the 'Isle of the Dead' ... Free men and convicts were buried here together ...

It is an island covered, (according to an Australian newspaper) with scrub and native flowers with here and there a geranium run wild from the grave in which it was originally planted and on it may be seen the ruins of the grave-digger's hut, a desperate character, who lived here alone among the dead and whose office was meant as a punishment.

He must often have looked across the water under the bright southern moon and seen the lights twinkling about the settlement ... By daylight he would see the long line of tall, white buildings, the barracks, the penitentiary, the hospital, fronting the blue water, backed and flanked by the dark grove of trees. The governor's fine house still stands on the edge of the bay, with its large garden sloping down to the water. He would have seen behind it the semaphore station, and if he could have read its signals he would sometimes have seen them telling the news of men who had broken their bonds and got away, perhaps to be captured by the bloodhounds on the narrow Eagle's Neck, perhaps to escape that danger and perish in the bush, but very, very seldom to win their forfeited liberty.

And another visitor to the scene of the story concludes his description of the prison and its surroundings with the remark:

The scenes depicted in *For the Term of His Natural Life* had their types in sober fact. All the incidents of that remarkable book were founded on authoritative documents. It is the moral history of a modern equivalent of Dante's *Inferno*.

To conclude: if, as has been said of Charles Reade, that he will always be remembered for having given to the world *The Cloister and the Hearth*, one may also cherish the hope that as long as interest survives in the early history of the Australian Commonwealth – a period when the harshness of our criminal code entailed on those under sentence of transportation 'across the seas' the maximum of suffering – so long will the name of Marcus Clarke also be remembered, even if all his other work sink into oblivion, as the author of the remarkable story we have been considering, *For the Term of His Natural Life.*

Marcus Clarke aged 20, before he left Ledcourt Station. SLV H81.204/2 : mp013422

Gerard Manley Hopkins about age 18 and the time he left for Oxford and Clarke, aged sixteen, went to Australia.

Cyril Hopkins (no age or date given).

Marian Dunn, Marcus Clarke's wife.
SLV H2007.44/8 : PIC LTA 2236

Marcus Clarke, aged 28, (photograph by Batchelder & Co.), three years after he had written *His Natural Life*.

Hall's Gap (Clarke called it Hell's Gap), from Mount Difficult, Grampians, Victoria.

The Argus office, 76 Collins Street East, Melbourne 1867.

F W Haddon (editor of the *Argus*), Aubrey Brown and Marcus Clarke, 1868.

'Dialogue between an Old and New Chum', by Nicholas Chevalier, *Melbourne Punch*, 1855.

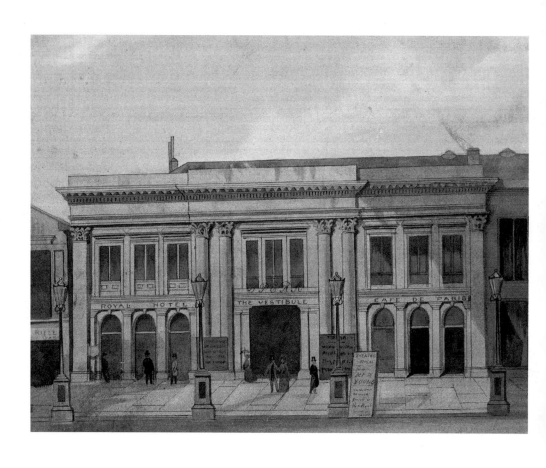

A large tinted print of the Theatre Royal and Café de Paris – focal points of Marcus's Melbourne life, 75 Bourke Street, Melbourne, c. 1861. SLV H4990 : b28366

No 36.

Application for the post of Librarian to the Public library.

28th October 1880

To the Trustees of the Public Library.

Gentlemen,

I have the honor to reply to your advertisement calling for applications for the office of Librarian to the Public Library from persons — 1. well acquainted with ancient literatures and the chief modern languages 2. having experience in the control of a staff of subordinates, 3. and possessing a knowledge of bibliography.

I have 1. a thorough knowledge — without of course making pretence to "scholarship" in its highest sense — of the Latin and Greek languages and literatures, having read all the books prescribed by the Universities and being familiar with many others not read in the schools; French is as familiar to me as English. I have read the Spanish and Italian classics and translated for the press both from the French and German. 2. I have for 7 years occupied the position of Sublibrarian at the Public Library my duty being to control the staff. I am happy to say that during the time I have held that responsible position I have never had occasion to call in the aid of the Librarian to support my authority though the admitted efficacy of the staff — the largest of its kind in Australia — vouches for the quality of the discipline maintained. 3. For knowledge of bibliography I may claim special consideration. My personal tastes and public circumstances have alike led me to make that branch of information my peculiar study. Privately I have collected largely while it has been my good fortune to have been entrusted with the compilation of the Bibliographical Catalogue of the Public Library, which in my holograph — has been used in stock taking since 1874, and I have also collated every book and pamphlet which has come into the library for the last 7 years.

In addition to these qualifications I beg respectfully to urge the special claim of my present position, & ask to point out — that I am next in rank to the present Librarian and on his retirement reasonably expect promotion; that I have refused the place of Parliamentary Librarian in the hope of ultimately getting a step in the Institution with which I have been connected for 10 years, and that although indeed the President fairly told me when I informed him of the offer of the Government that I must not consider myself as possessing a

Marcus Clarke's ms application for the Melbourne Librarianship. SLV

an indisputable right to office now to be vacant, he did not ignore
the spirit of the resolution passed by the Trustees in April 1873, when
my post of Secretary was filled on my promotion, by the gentlemen now
holding it, that — vacancies should be filled whenever possible by members
of the existing staff according to seniority.

I have the honor to be

Gentlemen

Your most obedient Servant

Marcus Clarke

Melbourne Public Library in Marcus's day. SLV H93.64/21 : pi005677

Queen's Hall Reading Room, Melbourne Public Library. 1859. SLV H17860 : b22080

The cover of *Humbug*, Marcus Clarke's short-lived, comic–satiric magazine, for 27 September 1869. SLV

KING NOBBLER;
OR, THE CURSE OF THE COUNTRY.

Satiric engraving, 'King Nobbler, or the Curse of the Country' from *Humbug*, 15 September 1869
– a nobbler of brandy was common drink, brandy and water. SLV

John Dunn (Clarke's father-in law) as 'Pauline' in the burlesque, Lady of Lyons. SLV H9453 : mp009451

'IN HIS HABIT AS HE LIVED'

'In his Habit as He Lived' (Sir Redmond Barry), c.1880, painting by Frank Goldstraw. SLV H4710 : a15214

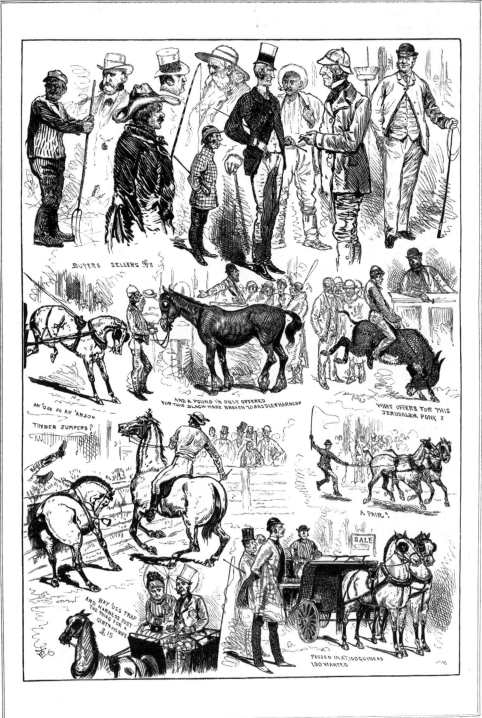

Horse Yards, Kirk's Bazaar, *Australasian Sketcher*, 1882. SLV A/S03/06/82/164 : mp008936

Tombstone, broken column, from Marcus's grave, Melbourne cemetery.

THE COSTUME FOOTBALL MATCH.

Costume football charity match, organised for Clarke's family by Melbourne actors, *Australasian Sketcher*, 1881.

Chapter 23 (i)

First literary ventures. – Light, humorous and satirical articles contributed to Humbug *and other comic papers. – Extracts from 'Our Glorious Climate,' being the experiences of a newcomer of that of the state of Victoria. – Mention of the titles of others, and references to and extracts from those on 'Business Men', 'Relationships', 'Charity Bazaars', 'Borrowing Money', 'In a Bark Hut', and 'A Pawnbroker's Shop on Saturday Night'.*

Marcus Clarke, in the early days of his literary career, first attracted notice by his clever satires on local topics and amusing skits on miscellaneous subjects, some of them couched in a vein of pure burlesque but it was burlesque nevertheless containing a substratum of truth. He threw off these productions with amazing ease and rapidity and they appeared in the pages of *Humbug* and other publications of the day, producing an effect not unlike that of 'Happy Thoughts' in the London *Punch* at a subsequent period.

One of these amusing outbursts, 'Our Glorious Climate', was doubtless suggested, like 'The Puff Conclusive', by the rather extravagant eulogies of the Australian climate that he frequently met with in print. The following extracts make it clear that the author's object was to convey to native born Australians (certainly in an absurdly exaggerated manner) a newcomer's impressions of a climate whose praises he had, previously to his arrival, heard so sedulously sounded:

5 a.m. – Awoke to find the window open, wind blowing in like a truant tornado, looking-glass broken, and cold in my left ear. Shut the casement; tra-la-la. Glorious climate!

6 a.m. – I must have been asleep 'lulled by sweet zephyrs through the broken pane.' Hem, Pope! 'Tis as hot as a furnace. Pooh! open the window. The wind has changed.

7 a.m. – I should say it had. Dust! I believe you. Ugh! It's a north wind now, and floor of my chamber is an inch deep in sand …

7.30. – Doors and windows hermetically sealed. I sneak to my bath like the first robber … All is ready … I will lave my limbs in the pellucid. Dorothea at the fountain … how I long for the refreshing … – *What!* No water --- ? … A thin pipe-stem of the cooling stream only flows. 'Was it thus, thou didst deceive me, waterman?' …

9 a. m … Where are my boots? Choked with sand. The wash-hand basin full of gravel, and my writing-table a drifted ruin like the Sphinx in the desert. *Glorious* climate!

9. 30. – Breakfast … 'The milk has turned sour, and couldn't be used. It's the heat.' Whack-fol-ther-riddle-iddle-li-do!

9.49. – The morning papers. 'Fearful iceberg at the South Pole!' … 'But who could hold a fire in his hand by thinking on the frosted Caucasus?' … Swallowed a blow-fly. Think of Abernethy, and catch a spider. Tarantula. 'Oh, then I see Queen Mab hath been with you!'

10 a.m. – Hail a cab. The back seat like a gridiron. St. Lawrence must have been an Australian: –
   'Oh, turn me over, the old man cried,
   For I am quite done brown on the other side.'
Wonderful these old ballads.

10.30. – Dust storm. Nose, ears, mouth, eyes stopped up. I think of the Pelican of the Wilderness, who buries his beak in the sand to feed his young. Just like me …

12 noon. – Drinks. The cooling brandy-smash of commerce. Query, 'Did David kill Goliath with a gin-sling?' Mem. – Ask mamma by Shirley Brooks.

12.10. – Drinks. The healing cocktail. Why cocktail?
   'And he cocked his tail at a ten foot rail,

And over it he sprang.'

Oh for an Arab steed, and the merry, merry sunshine! ... A bumper of burgundy
bring, bring to me. Let those who prefer it pale ale. But give me the lass with the
bonny black eye that carries the milking-pail. Thermometer at 108 ... I would
I were a bird – I mean a fish. 'I'd be a butterfly.' No, the grub's the thing. *Mem.
for joke*. – Why is Old Tom on a monument like an insect? Something about
caterpillar ...

7 p.m. – Can't have dinner for an hour, for the boiler has burst, the oven is full of
sand, and the meat has turned bad. Never mind. 'My bark is on the sea, and my
bier is on the shore, and I drain a cup of tea for the good-bye at the door.'

7.10 – Stroll out in white flannel and cigar! Cool as a cucumber. This *is* a glorious
climate.

7.11. – Looks dark in the south. Sou'west atmospherically interested cabman says,
'We'll get some rain!' I hope so.

7.15. – We do. Buckets full of it. It's come down with savage persistency.
Gutters run over. Half-crowns hopping up on the pavement. Omnibuses full,
and my flannel soaked to the skin – *my* skin. Oh, then, we'll merry, merry be
...

8 p.m. – Home again. Everything burst. Bathroom flooded! Kitchen like a
watercourse, and the dinner floating down the back yard. The pipe in my bedroom *had* burst, but Biddy 'shtuffed it with some ould papers.'
My tragedy of 'Slooman' in nineteen acts! 'When the heart of man is oppressed
with cares the mist is dispelled when a woman appears!' Bless her!

8.30 p.m. – Message from Jack. My uncle, Rumbelow, who promised to leave me
£20,000, had a sunstroke when going to his solicitors to make his will, and is
dead. Just my luck. Fancy *black*, too, in weather like this.

9 p.m. – Drank.

10 p.m. – Drunk!

11 p.m. – Come to conclush'on s'was a *glor-i-oshus* climate.

But as such extravagant nonsense, however amusing at first, is apt after a time to
pall, I shall pass briefly over the remaining skits of a somewhat similar though
generally less exuberant nature, in some cases merely mentioning their titles, as for
instance, 'On Borrowing Money', 'Teetotalism', 'The Roaring of Colonial Lions',

'Business Men', 'Loafing Round', 'Bazaars', 'Friendship', 'Relationships', 'The Diary of a Drunkard', and others. The last named is conceived in a slightly different vein, being in fact rather tragedy in disguise than broad farce or comedy.

The reference in 'Business Men' to his schoolboy experiences is a rather highly coloured account of an actual case of the kind, but of which he was not himself the victim (as he leads his readers to suppose) for he would never have tolerated such imposition:

> When I was at school, I suffered. Young MacMammon used to lend me his pocket money at about 700 per cent interest for the quarter, so that the loan of half-a-crown in September amounted to a new sovereign, a five-bladed pocket knife, a cricket-bat, a case of silkworms, the chrysalis of the Death's Head Moth, (very rare), *The Boy's Own Book*, a pair of clubbed skates,[70] and a crib to *Arnold's Greek Prose* in February.

In the same vein of humorous exaggeration he goes on to relate some (supposed) later experiences of his in the state of Victoria:

> If I made a 'proper representation' to the Government, they never took any notice of it, while Palmoil, my neighbour, seemed to be able to do anything he liked with them. I asked him how it was done one day, when he was going into the Land Office with a roll of notes in his hand and he said, 'My dear boy, the fact is' – here he shook the notes playfully – 'these matters want *working*, and – and – you're not a Business Man.'

In the article 'On Relationships' there is a rather pathetic allusion to his motherless childhood when any touch of feminine kindness was keenly appreciated by him. 'Aunts are good. I like the gold-spectacled maiden ones best, the dear old ladies who have white hair and ask you, "Which would you rather do, sing a hymn or have an orange?" and when you say, "Sing a hymn, Aunt", give you two oranges.' Nor can the opening sentence of that on charity bazaars be considered very far from the truth – 'A bazaar is a place where you buy things you don't want, for the benefit of people you don't care about and pay ten times more for them than you would do anywhere else' – for this seems to be a rather generally accepted opinion. I remember hearing

---

70   These were quite a novelty at the date in question.

a popular entertainer whilst personating a rural vicar say with a clever imitation of the clerical voice and manner, 'Well, ladies and gentlemen, we've tried every *honest* means of raising the money in my parish and failed, and now, (here he paused, gave a sad smile and gasped) *now*, we're going to have a bazaar!' The actor's expression seemed to convey a hint that the step contemplated was of doubtful rectitude, an impression confirmed by the laughter of the audience.

One wonders, on the other hand, how, in view of his own notorious weakness in money matters, Marcus Clarke could have brought himself to write, even in fun, in the article 'On Borrowing Money', the passage 'I am rather good at it. I have been always borrowing. If I can borrow nothing else, I borrow ideas,' because this was the very charge occasionally brought against him by unfriendly contemporaries. Perhaps, however, he was aiming at the latter when he penned the paragraph in question, for referring to 'new ideas,' he asserts shortly afterwards, 'They' (i.e. the ideas) 'are scarce here, however, and that is why these papers are so stupid,' thus scoring off his critics whilst apparently deprecating his own work.

But other miscellaneous articles of his were of quite a different nature. Nothing could well be more graphic or devoid of exaggeration than 'A Bush Fire', nor one more touched with natural feeling than 'In a Bark Hut', at the conclusion of which he admits that whilst living in one he had frequently grumbled at the conditions of a life that in retrospect appeared delightful, a not uncommon idiosyncrasy of human nature. For, as he tells his readers in that lively and picturesque article, 'Thither':

> Never came the trader, never waved a European flag, a glorious barbarism was thine; a jovial freedom from the cares of the morrow was the charter of thy liberties. I disliked thee once, and grumblingly did abuse thy hospitable shelter; but I have since found other roofs less pleasant than thine; have since – pent within stucco and immured in marble mockery of grandeur – yearned for the careless fortune of thy uncultured surroundings, cried often in vain amid the uncomfortable comfort of a city,
>
> > Give me again my hollow tree,
> > My crust of bread and liberty!

His descriptions of up-country life are generally far superior to those of Melbourne street-life. The latter, though frequently bright and witty are marred, to my mind, by a hackneyed strain of adulation of 'Bohemianism' (so-called) by no means convincing to the discriminating reader, or are pen-and-ink sketches of self-seeking politicians and other types of that day, many of which have probably passed away.

An exception, however, is 'A Pawnbroker's Shop on a Saturday Night', which, though differing little from similar articles in the London press, (as, for instance, those that appeared *seriatim* by a writer who signed himself 'One of the Crowd') nevertheless, has an originality of its own and suggests in certain passages the personality of the author.

Concertinas, violins, and cornets-à-piston speak the distress of the musical profession; and some twenty rapiers, broadswords, and daggers testify to the smallness of theatrical salaries, or the improvidence of theatrical people. Kemble is reported to have said that 'scarcely one actor in a hundred could boast of having never visited a pawnshop,' and the truth of his remark appears to be confirmed here. Crowns, sceptres and embroidered cloaks are all visible. Here hangs the dagger – there the bowl. 'Properties' of all kinds are in pledge; and the lute of the Troubadour rests lovingly against the suit of 'complete steel' in which the ghost of Elsinore 'revisited the glimpses of the moon'.

Were we inclined for sentimental meditation, we could find ample food for fancy in the incongruous articles around us, each of which has its little history. Here is a collection of gorgeously-bound prayer books, and on opening one, we read:
'B---, Somerset,
15th May, '51.
'Presented to Mary ---
on her seventeenth birthday with the best wishes and prayers of her affectionate mother.'

The poor soul who owned this volume must have seen many troubles since she left B---, Somerset.

Chapter 23 (ii)

Failure of Marcus Clarke to follow up his first great literary success. – Some of the reasons for this failure. – Literary hack work. – Appointed his cousin, Lieutenant-General Sir Andrew Clarke's agent with full powers to manage the latter's property in Victoria. – Becomes involved in speculative schemes in connection with that property and mismanages it. – Signs of failing health. – His essay on 'The money-lenders of Barataria' and correspondence on this and cognate subjects in the Sydney Bulletin. *– Retrenchment and removal to St. Kilda, Melbourne. – Fits of depression. – Alleged attempt at suicide. – Incapacity in business matters and tendency to give offence in his articles and writings. – Mr. H. G. Turner's estimate of his talents and character in the* Melbourne Review.

The generous appreciation of the merits of his tragic story *For the Term of his Natural Life* by many literary authorities (some of which I have quoted), and its steadily increasing popularity during the years immediately succeeding its first appearance (a popularity and a recognition that have not waned but rather grown since the death of the author and its publication in a cheap form), naturally suggest the question so frequently asked in his lifetime: why did not Marcus Clarke follow up the success he had achieved by other novels of equal power? Francis Adams, for instance, refers to this point and appears to be reflecting a widespread criticism by the following unfavourable comments on the failure of Marcus to do this:

He never did anything concentrated and sustained before this book: he never did anything at all in the same style afterwards.

It is true that circumstances were unfavourable, but power of this calibre, if it is an organic part of a man, and not a mere phase of his development, cannot be suppressed by, at any rate, such toil and trouble as Clarke had to endure.

And Mr. A. B. Paterson, after some generous and at the same time discriminating eulogy of the same novel, concludes with the rather astonishing assertion, 'So far as the rest of his work is concerned, his talents were practically wasted. He who might have written a high-class tragedy had to adapt pantomimes and write paragraphs for a living …' an estimate of Marcus Clarke's work which quite omits the many interesting short stories and fine essays he composed. But to the question referred to above I am afraid that there is a very simple reply although the latter cannot easily be given in an equally concise form. I have seen it stated that the worst mistake a novelist can make is to write an exceptionally clever book, unless, indeed, he is certain that he can write another equally clever. Possibly had Marcus lived to complete *Felix and Felicitas* he might have achieved this feat. The truth is that owing to circumstances he had to turn his hand to any literary work that promised a quick return in cash. For although he had not to rely upon literature for a livelihood owing to his official position at the Public Library, nevertheless with a wife and eventually six young children dependent on him he was obliged to supplement his salary with any literary work that offered and which he could execute in the time that could be spared from his public duties.

The latter were not, it would seem, of a very arduous character, but neither was the salary very abundant. His wife had brought him 'no fortune beyond a sweet temper,' as he had himself put it in his letter to me on the subject of his marriage and his own ideas on the management of money (into which I had some insight in early life) were apparently akin to those of Robert Buchanan, who, (his biographer states) was 'never able to learn the art of compound addition, was an incurable dreamer who saw the realities of life and especially of money in no rigid lines of accuracy but in the confused limning of his imagination. And thus it was,' she adds, 'that he spent his life in struggle – much of it ignoble; that he was embittered … and condemned to much ignoble pot-boiling.'[71]

---

71   *Robert Buchanan: Some account of his life, his life's work and his literary friendships*, by Harriet Jay.

All this might have been written of Marcus Clarke. For as is pointed out by Mr. Mackenzie Bell in his interesting memoir of Charles Whitehead, the contemporary and early friend of Dickens, and himself a writer of great promise who eventually emigrated to Australia and died in obscurity in a Melbourne hospital,[72] those who live by their pen must devote much of their time to the drudgery of literature. Outsiders frequently overlook this. 'Who shall say,' asks Whitehead's biographer, 'how many noble and immortal works have been lost to the world, owing to the men who had the power to produce them being compelled to devote themselves almost exclusively to anonymous routine journalism, or to the well-nigh equally barren labour of mere compilation?'

Apart from all this, moreover, in the case we are considering there were other and special reasons. Marcus had been appointed agent and manager of his cousin Lieut.-General Sir Andrew Clarke's landed estate at Cheltenham (Victoria). It will be remembered that this cousin, when a young engineer officer, had been a great favourite and *protégé* of Marcus Clarke's father and that, after the death of the latter, he had been one of the first to come forward and assist his son, when stunned by the sudden blow of his parental loss and the discovery of his own embarrassed circumstances, in his resolution of emigrating to Australia. But the consequences (which are well summed up in the following passage from Mackinnon's biography) were almost disastrous:

> Paradoxical as this statement may appear, it is nevertheless too true that the confidence placed by Sir Andrew Clarke in his cousin's ability to act as his sole and unchecked agent in business matters, was one of the most fatal though amiable errors ever committed, both for the principal and the agent. For the former it meant heavy pecuniary loss, for the latter neglect of all literary work and being 'got at,' to use a vulgar phrase, while playing the *rôle* of the landed proprietor. In other words, a ridiculously large amount of money was expended upon the land in question, taking into consideration its intrinsic value, and, moreover, was expended in a most foolish way as regarded results. That Marcus Clarke was altogether to blame for the 'mixed' condition into which the business affairs of Sir Andrew Clarke got is simply absurd. All that can be urged against him in the matter is that he was negligent and

---

72   *Charles Whitehead: A Forgotten Genius*, by Mackenzie Bell.

thoughtless in connection with them, as he had always been with his own, and, what is not generally known, as easily misled through an excess of foolish vanity which imagined itself capable of understanding and accomplishing all things … it was the greatest misfortune to Marcus Clarke that he had anything to do with this business, as it not only led him to abandon for a time his proper duties, but led him, also, deeper into the clutches of usurers, who eventually wrought him to death before his time.

In short, endless anxiety and keen disappointment were the fruits of poor Marcus's attempts to benefit his cousin and himself by speculative schemes and experiments with Sir Andrew's landed property in Victoria.

He had informed me in a letter written at the time when he first became involved in these schemes that a 'certain speculation in connection with coal' was afoot which would demand his constant attention and of course his presence on the spot for some time to come and would prevent his 'coming home' for certainly another five years. It was the first serious intimation I had received that he had really been contemplating a return to the 'old country' (although, as I have shown, he had at times expressed a hazy sort of desire of revisiting it) and he had concluded with the words, 'If this speculation fail, I shall never tempt fortune again.' From the date of this letter, it would seem, that the tide of fortune turned against Marcus Clarke who did not, I suppose, possess, despite his great abilities, 'the strenuous character to overcome difficulties', alluded to by Mr. Hall Caine, as the best university for the novelist. Outside the domain of literature, at least in matters of business and finance (excepting perhaps in his judgement and knowledge of horseflesh) he was neither alert nor able, and this 'coal speculation' evidently ended in disaster. His health too had gradually become unsatisfactory reacting of course disadvantageously on his mental powers:

> The once-active brain (to quote Mackinnon's words) became by degrees more lethargic and the work which at one time could be executed with rapidity and force, became a task too vast to be undertaken without great effort. The vivid, humorous imagination of the Peripatetic Philosopher assumed a more sombre hue, yielding itself up to the unravelling of psychological puzzles. The keen vein of playful satire, which was so marked a feature of his mental calibre, turned into a bitterness that but reflected the disappointed mind of this son of genius; and hence … (he is referring to the last year of Marcus Clarke's life) … no literary work of consequence was done.

Some time towards the end of his life and at a time when the bitterness of spirit abovementioned must have become the medium through which poor Marcus generally viewed the weaknesses of his fellows, it is understood that he wrote a story or an essay entitled 'The Money-lenders of Barataria.' It was sent to the Sydney *Bulletin* and is said to have been 'the most brilliantly cynical sketch that ever came from his pen.' But whatever its merits or demerits, it was never published, having mysteriously disappeared from the office of the newspaper in question. It may possibly have been removed by someone who had access to the M.S. department and who wished to suppress it. A correspondent, signing himself M. B., informed the readers of the Sydney *Bulletin*, in a letter addressed to that paper a few years ago, that Marcus had also aired his views about the money-lenders in the columns of provincial journals for whom he acted as Melbourne correspondent. 'M. B.' proceeded to contribute certain reminiscences of his own on the subject of Marcus's habits at this period of his life with the object, we may charitably suppose, of throwing further light upon an interesting and but slightly known phase of the author's career:

> Cheltenham (he explained) was then 'in the bush,' as the railway terminus was at Brighton. Clarke, of course had to be in town daily, and in a very short time his old habits seized upon him. Waxman, the money-lender, was carrying on business in Swanston-street, opposite the Library, and if Clarke was able to borrow ten pounds from the good-natured Waxman, who had a very high regard for clever literary men, Clarke would have dinner in town. On such an occasion it meant 'a night out,' as there was no possibility of getting a cab for a reasonable fare to Cheltenham after midnight ...
>
> He (Clarke) was certainly very bitter as a paragraphist, and indiscreetly attacked Melbourne money-lenders in a letter which he wrote for several provincial papers ... His quarrel with the money-lenders brought about Clarke's downfall. He struggled on for a few years but was ultimately compelled to file his schedule. He left the Library and in 1881 I stood at his grave in the Melbourne Cemetery ... We buried him at the age of thirty five.
>
> Another critic prefaces an admirable though brief review of Marcus's literary work in the same newspaper with a biographical summary. After enumerating the leading events of his earlier life (to which, however, the dates he affixes are not always correct) he mentions Marcus's appointment to an official post in the Public Library and concludes by saying that he 'for ten years wrote articles, plays, stories, sketches for half-a-dozen newspapers and theatres and was known as Melbourne's brightest, most improvident Bohemian; became insolvent and lost his place in the Library; lost also health, spirits, capacity and dribbled to death at the age of thirty-five.'

Soon after the appearance of these two letters, another correspondent, 'Dip', pointed out to the readers of the Sydney *Bulletin* that Marcus Clarke had never lost his billet in the Public Library but that what had happened was that when the chance of promotion to the position of Chief Librarian came (which he naturally expected to fill when a vacancy occurred) he was passed over; whilst yet another correspondent, 'Old Adullamite,' enquired how it was that as Marcus Clarke was 'a young man who had but few real friends and a host of acquaintances; and the circle of his intimates was narrow indeed', these reputed friends of his had really nothing to tell that was either 'pleasant or creditable?'

'Old Adullamite' might well put this question seeing that one of them had also written as follows: 'Clarke never impressed me as a serious student of literature, or as a man who was in love with his art. He was merely a lover of the good things of life; fond of good clothes, an elegant home, and plenty of leisure.' Those who have done me the honour of reading these reminiscences will not, I venture to think, dispute the soundness of the very different opinion I hold, based on my intimate knowledge of him in early life, that few authors of modern times, not excepting R. L. Stevenson himself, were more earnest students of their country's literature in youth, or more single minded and devoted aspirants for literary fame. For the rest, like his own favourite novelist, Honoré de Balzac, Marcus Clarke was undoubtedly very careful about his personal appearance and his dainty, somewhat fastidious nature could not be satisfied with a coarse or common environment.

Like that industrious and (in her day) popular novelist, the late Mrs. Oliphant, he required the best of everything. Even if it were only a question of toys for his children, destined to be speedily broken or discarded, expense was never allowed to be a bar, scarcely a consideration. Had cheap toys, for instance, been suggested as sufficient for the purpose, he would have refused to adopt the suggestion; would have regarded them, as he would any other low priced article, as being probably what is known in familiar phraseology as 'cheap and nasty.'

I have read that in Australia, 'If you are poor, there is no place where poverty so little cuts you off from social pleasures; whilst those who have to economise do not seem to find it the same dreary series of privations that it is apt to be in England.'[73] However that may be, Marcus was compelled by his growing pecuniary embarrassments to give up his pleasant country home and remove to a cheaper and (as regards situation) more

---

73   See an article on Australia in the *Cornhill Magazine*.

convenient residence in Inkermann Street, St. Kilda, a suburb of Melbourne, where his last years were passed. These were not, it is to be feared, very happy ones. Men of genius are not, as a rule, the best tempered or most contented people in the world. They feel (as has been well said by a modern writer) 'the deceptions with which life is strewn too keenly for their prevailing mood to be a cheerful one. More often than not men and women of genius are, when compared with ordinary mortals, like wild beasts caged. There is a pitiful resemblance in their life-stories. Until the heart of them is broken, they never cease to beat against the cruel wires.' Harassed by debt and anxiety which, although thrown off at intervals, returned with added force, Marcus was subject to fits of moody depression.

A companion of his on a country walk noticed him to be gazing intently over the edge of a deep declivity or ravine that abruptly terminated the high ground they had just been traversing and suddenly came to the conclusion that Marcus was contemplating a leap into the space yawning beneath. Fearing that he might actually carry out this intention, the witness of the incident dragged him away from the spot, for Marcus's movements had a deliberate appearance and did not seem caused by momentary dizziness or the strange sensation that often accompanies the act of looking down from a great altitude. My informant, however, added that he had himself when engaged in mining operations, prospecting for minerals in a certain mountainous and terribly rugged region of Northern Queensland, been occasionally nearly overcome by a frantic desire or momentary impulse to leap into the abyss below him, not from any conscious or – far less – deliberate intention of taking his own life but simply from an almost overpowering longing to leap into space, an inclination referred to (I believe) by Lombroso in his work on *The Man of Genius*.

For Marcus in his school days was not only agile but cool and collected in similar circumstances. I remember him, when still almost a small boy, walking along the narrow stone coping of the arched viaduct spanning the reservoir in the Highgate fields where a false step would have meant a fall of many feet into the water beneath, without the least fear or hesitation. Not by any means an extraordinary feat and one that some of his companions also performed; but still one that would not have been attempted by a nervous boy or one not possessed of some presence of mind. It is therefore possible that he may have been really contemplating suicide when his friend observed him but more probable I think that he was merely yielding to the impulse I have alluded to than deliberately planning an act of self destruction.

I cannot perhaps do better, in referring to the circumstances that conspired to mar the literary activity of Marcus Clarke towards the end of his life, than quote the concluding paragraph of Mr. H. G. Turner's article in the *Melbourne Review*, published some months after the former's death, in January 1882. He had described Marcus as a 'notable pioneer in the fiction fields of Australia and one of the most promising *littérateurs* ever developed under exclusively Australian surroundings' and closed with the following well chosen and thoughtful words:

> Marcus Clarke undoubtedly possessed genius of a high order; and, in connection with literary work, he rarely touched anything that he did not adorn by the epigrammatic brightness of his style and the naturalness of his diction … But take the pen out of his hand, and he at once became conspicuous from his utter inability to adapt himself to the practical affairs of everyday life; as is common with the possessors of a brilliant imagination, he was essentially a creature of impulse, and did whatever seemed the pleasantest and most desirable thing at the moment. This incapacity to give any weight to prudential considerations surrounded him with perpetual difficulties and carping cares, from which he lacked the energy, though he often expressed the earnest wish, to free himself. He might have formed the subject of an additional chapter for the elder Disraeli's *Calamities and Quarrels of Authors*; for, while he possessed much of the kindly generosity of Oliver Goldsmith, it was of the same irresponsible kind, and he was generally involved in as many bitter feuds as that inveterate quarreller, Walter Savage Landor. He had an unhappy talent for alienating friends, and generally rendered the first breach irreparable by the caustic cynicism of his pen. Nevertheless, he retained some strong friendships to the day of his death, and in his impulsive way he gave his whole heart where it evoked a responsive feeling of regard …
>
> Had he possessed, even in a moderate degree, a sense of the importance of prudential considerations, his life would have been a happier one for himself and for those he has left. The ability to control his expenditure within Mr. Micawber's well defined lines would have given him equal strength to husband his intellectual powers, and have enabled him to leave some more enduring evidences of his talent than the evanescent contributions which he scattered so freely. But, alas! while always a worker, and wearing out his powers under high pressure, he was as prodigal of his intellect as of its more prosaic results, and fell by the wayside in the harness which he donned in hope and pride, but which, ere the end came, galled him sorely.

Chapter 24 (i)

Marcus Clarke's humour and its similarity in character with that of Lord Rosebery. – His first book, The Peripatetic Philosopher. *– Some extracts from his preface to it and the imaginary comments of the Press. – His opinion, when a boy, of Charles Lever's novels and their worthlessness as true pictures of Irish life. – Striking confirmation of his views by the well known Irish novelist, Miss Ella MacMahon, and by other modern writers on Ireland. – The charm of Marcus Clarke's literary conversation.*

A good classical scholar and a humorist born, Marcus Clarke was skilful in the manipulation of that vein of graceful, easy satire which one associates with the speeches of Lord Rosebery in his lighter moods. Such as that one, for instance, in which he warned his audience that it would be impossible for the late Duke of Argyll to act up to the advice he had been giving his followers 'to forget party', because the Duke of Argyll's party consisted of himself; adding, 'whatever may be your wishes … when you have a party in that compact and singular, I might almost say that portable form, it is one of which you cannot divest yourself and it is one of which, I think, the Duke, on reflection, would be unwilling to divest himself.'

A similar stream of light banter flows from the pen of *The Peripatetic Philosopher*, a little work written, to adopt the words of a contemporary critic, in 'a style of singular lightness, ease and flexibility – a style which many a veteran might have envied him.'[74] *The Peripatetic Philosopher* is a collection of light essays originally published in the *Australasian* and some of the titles of which remind the reader occasionally of similar amusing compositions by Mr. Israel Zangwill; although the latter may possibly never have heard of Marcus Clarke or heard of him only as the author of the well known novel, *For the Term of his Natural Life*. There is nevertheless a certain similarity of thought to be noticed in the selection of their subjects. For whereas our Melbourne philosopher deals with such topics as 'Art Criticism in the Colonies', 'Sharebroking', 'Election Meetings', 'Gaslight and Daylight', 'Modern Boys', and 'Business Men', the following figure *inter alia*, among Mr. Zangwill's *Philosophic Excursions*: 'Art in England', 'In Defence of Gambling', 'Concerning General Elections', 'Moonshine', 'The Small Boy' and 'Credit'; whilst a certain passage recording Mr. Zangwill's impressions of Glasgow might have been penned by the Peripatetic Philosopher of Melbourne himself, for it breathes the same air of humorous reflection:

> An awesome air of wealth hung over the men and the place, a crushing suggestion of vast enterprises – of engineering and railway building and the running of steamers, a subtle aroma of colossal fortunes, wrested from the world by the leverage of an initial half-crown. I have often gone to places with only half a crown in my pocket, but it never seemed to lead to anything.

Marcus Clarke added a preface to his volume of peripatetic philosophy which ran as follows:

> Dear PUBLIC,
>
> Everybody owes you something. You are a universal creditor, and if you could only get in your outstanding debts, would be rich to fifty-Rothschild power. 'It is a duty which I owe the Public!' cries the venomous journalist, who for private pique gibbets one friend in the newspaper of another. 'It is a duty which I owe to the Public!' simpers Werdespynner, the author, when he sends an account of his own birth, parentage and education to 'Men of the Time,' and thinks that he has made himself famous ... Always the Public, on any pretence! What is not owed to Public

---

74   Francis Adams.

Morality, Public Decency, Public Welfare? Now I owe you something, also; I owe you an EXPLANATION.

How comes it, you not unnaturally ask, that this fellow thrusts himself into Print, and publishes a preposterous book, full of stale jokes, and borrowed metaphors, and stolen thoughts, and hashed-up ideas of other people? How comes it that this miserable decoction of Thackeray and Dickens and Balzac, and George Sala, and Douglas Jerrold, and anybody else whose works are obtainable to be plagiarised, is shaken up in a half-crown bottle, with a gaudy label on it, and sold to me as 'Philosophy'? … Was it not bad enough, you say, to have read his balderdash *once*? Why should I have it thrust upon me in a collated and a collected form? Why am I to be Humbugged any more by this vagabond?

I will tell you, my most esteemed public. I do not publish this volume because I have a 'high moral purpose in view;' I do not publish it at the 'request of a few of my friends;' I do not publish it 'merely for private circulation;' I do not even publish it because I 'feel that it will supply a long-felt social want;' I publish it because I think it will SELL!

I am,

Dear Public,

Your obedient servant,

THE PERIPATETIC PHILOSOPHER

And then ensues an imaginary summary of press notices, of which the following are specimens:

We have seen many stupid books, but this is incomparably the worst.
– *Times*.

Atheistical and infamous; a disgrace alike to printer, publisher, and writer.
– *Record*.

An admirable book for the use of schools. – *Daily News*.

The author conceals a profound knowledge of human nature beneath a
mask of indifference and scorn. – *Pall Mall Gazette*.

Written probably by some impertinent schoolboy. – *Globe*.

Clever and amusing. He tells us some sad, sad truths. – *Herald*.

Worth, we should say, about half-a-guinea per column. – *Australasian*.

Left us in tears. – *Evening Star*.

Thackeray without the sarcasm. – *Ballarat Courier*.

Douglas Jerrold without the wit. – *Ballarat Star*.

The cover seems pretty – we will refer to it more fully on some future
   occasion. – *Daily Telegraph*.

The name of the *Peripatetic Philosopher* will live when Milton, Shakespeare,
   and Ben Jonson are forgotten. – *Nashville Mercury*.

The foregoing clever nonsense, so characteristic of the author in his earlier and
brighter moods, enables one to understand and appreciate the force of the remark
of a contemporary and fellow journalist on the pleasure to be derived from social
intercourse with Marcus Clarke:

> His literary conversation was delightful and as artistic as his writings; he was essentially
> a man of wit. An hour of his society was a bright relief to the dreary platitudes of
> everyday life and as refreshing as it would be to light on a verse of Herrick in a volume
> of Tucker's *Proverbial Philosophy*.

In connection with the subject of humour, a vague but persistent recollection of a
certain conversation at school on the subject of Lever's novels haunts my memory,
in which Marcus took a leading part. Lever's characters and pictures of Irish life were
denounced by him as stagy and conventional. He had accompanied his father on
short visits to his relatives in the North of Ireland and had compared, in his crude and
boyish but observant manner, the people he had seen and met with the types depicted
by the novelist, and regarded by the ordinary, untravelled English reader of that day as
truthful portraits of the average Irishman, and had found them wanting.

Remembering this conversation, I was much interested in an article by the gifted
Irish novelist Miss Ella MacMahon, from which I select the following passage as
proving the accuracy of his youthful observations:

> The decay of humour in Ireland is a favourite lamentation … So far as I can gather it
> is based upon the fact that Ireland, as we know it today, is not Ireland as Lever knew
> it. Certainly it is not; but I very much doubt if Ireland was ever what he represented
> it, and for this reason: Lever's conception of humour was burlesque, pure and simple,
> and I do not think it is too harsh to call him a literary buffoon. He met with amusing
> persons and incidents during his lifetime, as we all do, but if we all took the trouble to
> note them down as he did, I believe we should run him very close in the number and

humour of them even today. And if we had his ability and strung them all together and labelled them Ireland, we should certainly make a volume, or many volumes, with a good deal of amusement in them, but we would not show Ireland as it is. Even in Ireland, life is not, and never could have been, a continuous succession of humorous incidents, any more than it is a continuous succession of pathetic incidents.

In his letters to me, Marcus Clarke occasionally referred to the subject of Ireland and the Irish. He felt that he had Irish blood in his veins, even if his father's family was settled in the North of Ireland, and he was of course far too broad-minded and enlightened not to regard the Irish masses with sympathy and interest. These references of his were chiefly directed to the myth of the stage-Irishman, in fact, to what a literary critic in the *Times* recently described as the delusion which English people are only now abandoning, the delusion that the Irishman of real life really at all resembled the caricature of him that formerly did duty on the stage.

The *Times* reviewer spoke of the value of three recent works on Ireland 'in setting a period for the ludicrous notion of the stage Irishman which John Bull has nursed to his fancy for so long ... The life of Ireland has been hidden from knowledge by the myth of the Irishman whose only business was to cry "Slainte and slainte and slainte agin", and to make bulls and jokes.' That Marcus Clarke should have penetrated this delusion in early life from personal experience of the real Ireland was certainly in so observant a youth by no means remarkable; but it strikes one as a little curious that he should have, some few years later, first made his mark in the literary world as a writer of humorous satire and that some of his earliest productions in that line, such as 'The Puff Conclusive' and 'Our Glorious Climate', might perhaps have deserved to be designated, in Miss Ella MacMahon's words, as 'burlesque, pure and simple.'

Chapter 24 (ii)

Clarke's reticence on the subject of his own work. – His capricious literary tastes. – He despatches a number of stories to me for publication in London, and states his reasons for not sending them to a literary friend there (Mrs. Cashel Hoey). – Name of the novel he was at work upon. – Alleged reasons for not proceeding with it. – Mismanagement of his cousin's property in Victoria with which he had been entrusted, and consequent neglect of literary work in general and especially of this novel.

The postscript to the letter quoted in the last chapter appears to me significant, because a writer in the Sydney *Bulletin*, describing his impressions of Marcus Clarke, says of him:

> Clarke would not talk of his own work … Of books he talked curiously. The larger lights of the world, even as the wider horizon of Australia, seemed in some mysterious way beyond his ken. He would talk Theodore Hook, Leigh Hunt, Praed, Clough, Pater, Hamerton; but Browning was 'a weariness to body and soul', and if one spoke of Spenser as a gold mine, he retorted 'Dig him, then, if you will, I myself prefer the minted coin.' A very little intercourse served to clinch the conviction that he held everything save the joy of life in utter contempt. If a true pathos seized and compelled him at times as in 'Holiday Peak' and 'Pretty Dick', he held it as a hateful obsession. Of his great book he said, 'It is a chamber of real horrors indifferently assorted, and confound it! It doesn't draw.'

I was equally delighted and disillusioned on that trip. Never was there a merrier, kinder, less exigent companion. Take him as such, as those who knew and loved him best did, and all was very well. But regard him as the bulk whence samples had been given to the world, in all his fragmentary work, and the disappointment was keen. He regarded or affected to regard those fragments as shed scales of a foul disease. As is very well known he took this view seriously in his writings. Whether there was any hidden regard for them I had no opportunity for discovering. It seems impossible that such fairy children as 'Holiday Peak' and 'Pretty Dick' should not have a permanent abiding-place in some close-walled chamber of their creator's mind.

The fact is, I take it, that Marcus Clarke was intensely reserved and never wore his heart upon his sleeve in regard to such matters. But I venture to think that the light I have been able to throw on his character in early life and certain references, in some of his letters, to his literary ambitions are fair evidence that, deep down in his heart, he cherished a very different conception of the literary and artistic merits of his work to the one he chose to exhibit to chance acquaintances. I think that some of his later essays will convince the impartial reader that he took himself more seriously in fact than the writer in the *Bulletin* supposes. He could not but be aware of his latent powers.

Six months after the receipt of the letter quoted in the previous chapter he forwarded to me a number of stories in manuscript, for publication, if possible, in London. Although by this time he must have been in his chronic state of pecuniary embarrassment again, he wrote with characteristic disregard of anything like bargaining; or perhaps from natural delicacy at bothering a friend, to make terms for him:

> I do not want any coin for them, though of course if the publisher pays, so much the better; but I am preparing another novel and I want to keep my name up, as actors say, in the meantime. I offered the stories to Bentley but he refused them saying that he did not care for stories but would publish the novel. I fancy Sampson Low would do it. However use your own judgement; I leave all things in your hands. You can, if you like, select some of the stories and try a magazine with them, though the fact of their having appeared in an Australian paper may – I think *will* – be a bar to that. I am not particular as to the titles either so you can change *them* if you like. I think that 'La Béguine' is the best story, but, however, do what you like with them *ad majorem*

Clerici gloriam! I want the dedication to appear as Mrs. Cashel Hoey took some pains to correct proofs of *His Natural Life* ...

Excuse the trouble I am giving you about the book but I know nobody in a literary way in London who would bother themselves about me except Mrs. Cashel Hoey and I want to surprise her with the dedication.

Always truly yours,
Marcus Clarke.

It will be noticed that in this letter he alludes to the novel he was preparing and adds that Bentley had promised to publish it. The novel in question was to have been called *Felix and Felicitas*. Mr. Patchett Martin, in his brief memoir, speaks of Clarke's want of energy in working at this novel (of which, at his death, he had only left a fragment), in the following terms:

> The revised version of *His Natural Life* was published in London and Melbourne in 1874, when the author was only in his twenty-seventh year, but that date marks ... the decline of his literary career ... He had been appointed ... at first Secretary to the Trustees of the Public Library of Melbourne, and afterwards ... Assistant Librarian at a salary of some £400 a year – 'just a sufficient sum,' as he used to say, 'to keep one's pen idle'. Whether it was the benumbing influence of this easy berth – as he himself used to fancy – or that his vitality was steadily declining, certain it is that, though never idle, he accomplished no great literary work during the seven years of life that remained to him, unless we reckon the fragment of a novel which hung on his hands for many a weary month.

The writer in the Sydney *Bulletin* previously mentioned, also records how, from the time he made Clarke's acquaintance in 1876 until his death (1881), he waited in vain for the appearance of another novel from Clarke's pen but experienced no great surprise, as the years slipped by and none such ever came. On the other hand, Mr. Hamilton Mackinnon, who knew more of the facts, ascribes the abandonment of the attempts to complete *Felix and Felicitas* to 'the unfortunate pecuniary and other complications' in which Marcus became involved in connection with his management (or mismanagement) of his cousin's property. He says:

> That Marcus Clarke was altogether to blame for the 'mixed' condition into which the business affairs of Sir Andrew Clarke got is simply absurd. All that can be urged

against him in the matter is that he was negligent and thoughtless in connection with them, as he had always been with his own, and, what is not generally known, as easily misled, through an excess of foolish vanity which imagined itself capable of understanding and accomplishing all things …

It may safely be assumed that it was owing to this unfortunate business craze, which, apparently seized hold of our author, that there has been left behind, in an unfinished state, a novel which began so brilliantly as *Felix and Felicitas*. Commenced years before, it was allowed to lie by during his 'landlord' days, and until a few months previous to his demise, when it was recommenced, but alas! too late, for the hand of death was already upon him.

Chapter 25

Miscellaneous Work

The 'Noah's Ark' papers. – Mrs. Robert P. Whitworth on the character of Marcus Clarke. – His love of the Puritan period and English rural scenery as pictured in the poetry of Milton. – Secular and religious education in Victoria. – Mrs. Aphra Behn, the pioneer of English novelists. – The Bacon–Shakespeare controversy. – Magic and the Supernatural. – Erewhon and In a Glass Darkly. – A boyish panic. – Love of study of early medical science and medieval philosophy. – 'Regiomontanus' and The Second Deluge. – Edgar Allan Poe and plagiarists. – 'The Haunted Author' and the 'Typical Digger.' – Mr. Hornung's confirmation in his novel. – The Unbidden Guest. – 'A Christmas Eve Watch.' – 'The Poor Artist.'

After the publication of the well known story of convict life reviewed in the previous two chapters, Marcus Clarke returned to the composition of those less ambitious but sparkling and amusing essays, short stories, and verses in which he had previously excelled. With the exception of one historical romance, *Chidiock Tichbourne*, and the opening chapters of a novel that was to have been a special study of character and temperament – the fragment *Felix and Felicitas* – his literary output consisted of essays, some serious, some light and amusing, short stories of various descriptions, verses and plays. It must also be remembered that he contributed numerous articles to the press, some of them so good from a literary point of view as to be well worth the trouble of perusal even at the present day.

As several of his short stories and verses first saw the light in the columns of a weekly newspaper under the heading of the 'Noah's Ark' papers, I begin with this miscellaneous series, afterwards republished in volume form in 1873. They purport to be a record of the conversations of a group of intimate friends who meet at frequent intervals at the house of one of their number. And because it thus becomes a *rendezvous* for airing the views of thinkers of different opinions on various subjects and for the display of differing types of intellect in amicable controversy, he calls it 'Noah's Ark'; for it is an ark of refuge for them all. If the conversation flags, someone is always ready with an anecdote or a fresh and interesting topic.

One of the characters, 'Mrs. Sweetwinter,' was drawn from the life, and was intended for Mrs. Robert P. Whitworth, the wife of a fellow journalist, who had collaborated with Marcus in the adaptation of stories for the stage and to whom the latter had been a kind friend. This lady has frequently referred to Marcus Clarke as one whom to know was to love and admire, adding significantly, 'He had troubles of which people at the time had no idea. His life is in his short stories. I am astonished to think how dull we were in not seeing it before.' He had confided to her his intention of returning to England and, if possible, bringing up his family there, just as he had done in his earlier letters to me. It was possibly of her he was thinking, although more probably of his own wife, when he penned the soliloquy 'On Female Education', in these papers commencing, 'Nothing is a more melancholy subject of contemplation than a too well educated woman. In the soul of every true woman, there should be cool breadths of shadeful ignorance,' a sentiment that, however out of date and distasteful it may appear to some in these days of sex equality and often sex antagonism, will not appeal in vain to others – and they are still numerous – who in their hearts at least would be found to share it.

There are many scattered allusions of an autobiographical character. For instance, just as in his sketch of 'Bullocktown' (Glenorchy) he had referred to 'those intelligent land surveyors that mark "agricultural areas" on the top of lofty mountains,' so in these 'Noah's Ark' papers, one of the circle in the course of a chat on the physical characteristics of Australia acclaims, '"Pure the air and light the soil." You know what Milton says,' to which another replies, 'I have some soil on an agricultural area that is very light … I took it up under the 42nd clause, and when I went to look at it, lo, it was on the top of the Grampians (the mountain chain visible from Ledcourt Station). It was marked "arable land" on the map, but I am convinced Glaisher, the aeronaut, is the only man who could get a plough there.'

And then comes another reference to his favourite poet, Milton, and to the Puritan period in England:

> What charming pictures of quiet, country life do the poets of that broad-hatted, broad-belted age give us. How purely beautiful a limning of English rural life is 'L'Allegro,' for instance. The single distich,
>> Mountains on whose barren breast
>> The labouring clouds do often rest
> is a veritable Ruysdael for quite coolness of sentiment.

Interesting allusions to the topics of the day and some amusing anecdotes are scattered about these pages. Here is one on the subject of secular or religious education, recalling Thackeray in its quiet and good-humoured but effective sarcasm. A Church of England Dean had invited a liberal-minded Roman Catholic priest to examine the children at a school in Victoria where the system was purely secular. The priest

> asked a scholar if any remarkable event occurred in England during the reign of Henry VIII? The lad replied at once. 'The Reformation, sir.' 'And pray what was *that*?' asked the priest. There was a moment's silence, and then a sharp girl of nine years, stretching out a skinny finger, squeaked in the satisfactory words of the text-book, *'It was a protest by all intelligent minds, sir, against the damnable errors of Popery!'* The Dean turned as red as Latimer at the stake.

Presently there occurs a reference to the novels of Mrs. Aphra Behn, of whose name and fame the ordinary reader has probably never so much as heard. Whilst wondering who she might have been, I saw, shortly after reading the passage concerning her, a review of a book dealing with her works, and learned from it that she was not only the first Englishwoman who made her living by her pen but might fairly be considered the earliest English novelist. The reviewer, however, added that her stories could scarcely be considered 'novels' in the modern sense of the word.

The study of so quaint an author was precisely of the kind that would commend itself to Marcus Clarke, as the whole tenour of the 'Noah's Ark' dialogues testifies. Again, bearing in mind the fact that so many years have passed since his death, and a considerably longer period since the appearance of the said 'Noah's Ark' papers, it is enlightening to read a conversation upon the merits of the great Bacon–Shakespeare controversy so prominently before the public in recent years.

More interesting however from a biographical point of view is the account of a discussion on early beliefs in Magic and the Supernatural. After a reference to *Erewhon* by Samuel Butler, one speaker remarks, 'The creepiest book I have for a long time seen is by Sheridan Le Fanu and is called, *In a Glass Darkly*. Later on the same individual bids his audience read 'Green Tea' in a lonely house at midnight and tell him how they feel, to which his host replies, 'I shall play no such tricks with myself. He who artificially excites his imagination often rouses a devil he cannot lay,' and then recalls the old formula recited by those desirous of testing its efficiency in front of a looking-glass at midnight, whilst repeating aloud their own names.

Whether, when a boy, Marcus himself had ever practised this antiquated, superstitious ceremony I do not know, but that he occasionally indulged in the practice he here condemns, that of deliberately exciting his own imagination, I remember well. I recall at least two instances.

The first may perhaps be dismissed as trivial – a mere childish escapade which eventually alarmed him as much as his companions. One Saturday half holiday of his first or second year at Highgate school, his father had come over to see him and taken him and a couple of his schoolfellows out for a walk to Hampstead. He concluded by giving them a meal at the well known tavern on Hampstead Heath of 'Jack Straw's Castle.' After dinner his father parted with the boys and returned direct from Hampstead to his home at Kensington, leaving them to make their way back across the Heath and past the equally well-known 'Spaniards' tavern down the long and winding country lane leading thence alongside Ken Wood to the small town of Highgate. This lane was in those days dark and lonely at night and during the first part of the walk Marcus had been entertaining his companions with ghost stories. Suddenly, as it appeared to them, after plunging into the shadows of the lane, they heard peculiar-sounding footsteps behind them, and half in a spirit of fun, half in panic, took to their heels, never drawing breath until they had reached the sheltering lights of Highgate. Marcus insisted that it was not from fear of tramps or garrotters (of whom there were then or were supposed to be many about) that they had taken fright, but because he, for his part, had felt like the wayfarer in Coleridge's 'Ancient Mariner,'

Like one that on a lonesome road

Doth walk in fear and dread,

And having once turned round walks on,

And turns no more his head;

Because he knows a frightful fiend

Doth close behind him tread.

The other instance that I remember is that of Marcus telling me some two or three years after this incident, and when older and more developed, how he frequently sat up at home during the holidays, reading, and how once when engrossed in some tale of mystery or witchcraft, the lamp burned low and flickered out, leaving him to make his way to his bed.room in the dark with his imagination wrought up to a pitch of excitement of which he was afterwards ashamed. In this connection I may mention that on one occasion he proposed that when we two had reached man's estate we should share apartments in some old world continental city (such as we had read of) for a time, and institute experiments of a psychological character, of the kind we conceived the lover in Poe's well known poem of 'The Raven' to have been engaged upon, when his strange visitor intruded on his nocturnal musings.

The fact is, Marcus Clarke's boyish imagination was always running on the supernatural, on magic and mystery; not the vulgar blood-curdling *Mystery of a Hansom Cab* order, (that of the penny novelette) but that of the strange beliefs and superstitions of the past. In fact, like the hero of the ballad referred to above, Marcus loved to ponder 'over many a quaint and curious volume of forgotten lore,' particularly on those dealing with astrology and the strange ideas and theories of the earlier exponents of medical science and philosophy. Thus in these papers he cites the prophecies of Albunazar and Arnaud de Villeneuve concerning the end of the world, and those of Regiomontanus as to the date of the second deluge.

The latter, inserted by Savonarola in his *Liber Mirabilis* had such an effect on a certain Toulouse professor as to induce him to keep a small ship always ready to transport him to safety. 'He died in his intelligent bed, however, in 1540, and the deluge hasn't come yet,' is the drily humorous comment with which Marcus dismisses the professor and his hallucinations. But there have been many instances since the professor in question, as Marcus must have known, of public men, popular divines amongst them, who have been almost as credulous in such matters even in comparatively recent times.

Other topics of literary interest besides that of the Bacon–Shakespeare controversy are dealt with in the 'Noah's Ark' papers, amongst them one that I saw recently raised in a London literary weekly, under the heading, 'Was Poe a plagiarist?' This very question forms the subject of one of the discussions of the 'Noah's Ark' circle, a by no means astonishing coincidence, however, considering how steeped in Poe's stories and verses Marcus Clarke had been since early childhood.

Then there are amusing compositions of a nondescript character, some of which, although apparently merely short stories, are found, on closer inspection, even when cast in that form, to be rather the vehicle for the author's humorous reflections or the play of his fancy, than short stories in the ordinary sense of the term. They are therefore best noticed here, when dealing with his miscellaneous writings. Of this description is 'The Haunted Author,' whose various characters meet him in corporeal form and load him with threats and reproaches. The reference to the goldminers of the early days of Australian gold discoveries recalls passages of his first letters to me wherein he essayed to describe their peculiarities, as have done so many Australian authors:

> All at once a man clad in a red shirt jumped from behind a bush and seized the head of the mare.
>
> 'Who are you?' I cried.
>
> 'The most abused of all,' said he, 'I am the Typical Digger! I am the man whom you and others of your tribe have made eat bank notes as sandwiches. I have shod my horse with gold, and swilled champagne – which I detest – out of stable buckets. Frank Fowler has maligned me, Orion Horne has sneered at me, Kingsley has mocked me, Howitt has slandered me, Thatcher has made ballads on me. Do y' think a man is never to change his shirt? Why should I always be compelled to appear in this sanguinary garment? Am I to pass my life in finding repeatedly gigantic nuggets, and being perpetually robbed of the same? Am I to be considered for ever such an ass as to give handfuls of gold-dust for a glass of brandy? Must I never shave? Shall the tyranny of the fictionmonger compel me to sleep in boots?'
>
> 'Calm yourself, my friend,' I said, 'There is not much harm done. I know of some poor fellows whom the fictionmongers have treated much more rudely.'
>
> At that instant the demoniac howls of my pursuers were borne upon the blast.
>
> 'That may be,' roared the Digger of Romance, 'but I will be avenged on *thee*. Come!'
>
> The cabriolet disappeared in the distance – there was never a cabriolet that did not

do so under such circumstances – and my captor led me away.

He paused at the door of the usual bush inn (how well I knew it), and striking three loud blows upon the door (they invariably struck three loud blows), we were admitted into a long apartment. I beheld with astonishment that all the personages whom I had imagined the creatures of my own too fertile brain were there.

'Wretch!' cried the fair Madeleine, 'why did you not unite me to the Duke? You know you only changed your mind at the last moment.'

'Monster,' cried the lovely Violet, 'you made me pass three nights of horror in the Red Farm, when one stroke of your pen would have freed me.'

'Miserable man,' cried Jabez Jamrack, 'the blood of the Earl be upon your head. You knew that I had no intention of killing his lordship until the base lack of a "sensation" for your last chapter impelled me to the bloody deed!'

'Christian dog!' roared Mordecai the Jew, 'I was born with charitable impulses, and should have lent in peace the humble shilling upon the ragged coat of honest poverty, had not your felon soul plunged me into crime to gratify the tastes of a blood-and-thunder loving public!'

'And I,' remarked Henry Mortimer, with that cynical smile that I had so often depicted curling his proud lip, 'did I wish to throw my elder brother down a well in order to succeed to his name and heritage? No! I loved him fondly, madly, as you took pains to state in your earlier chapters. I should have loved him still, had not Cora the Gipsy wound her spells about my heart. Who brought her to me? Did I of my own accord, I, a proud scion of Britain's aristocracy, demean myself to such a love? No, minion, 'twas thy brain contrived the meeting, thy hand that hurled my elder brother into the abyss, and stamped the brand of Cain upon my brow.'

'Away with him!' hissed Lady Millicent, the Poisoner, 'I knew not of the deadly power of strychnine until he told me. A lovely child, I roamed the lordly gardens of my father's princely mansion, and chased the butterfly from flower to flower. 'Twas he that set on the smugglers to seize me, and under his vile tuition I acquired in ten short chapters all the hideous knowledge of the Borgias! Away with him!'

''Twas he dishonored my bills,' cried Lord Augustus Plantagenet.

''Twas he that let me linger in consumption for forty pages folio!' cried Coralie de Belleisle, the planter's daughter.

''Twas he that blighted my voluptuous contours with an entirely unnecessary railway accident!' wept the lovely Geraldine.

'Away with him!'

'Mercy!' I cried, gazing in terror on the well-known lineaments, 'mercy!'

'Mercy!' cried the Lost Heiress, Isabella Beaumanoir, 'when for two long hours you deliberated whether my sainted mother or the poacher's wife should give me birth! Mercy for *thee*! Oh, no, no, no!'

It was terrible to hear my own impassioned language thus turned against me.

'Ladies and Gentlemen,' cried I in despair, 'consider the exigencies of fiction.'

'Fiction be blowed!' roared the digger. 'This way, boys!'

A deserted drive was before me – how many luckless wretches had not I thrown down it? – and I made one supreme effort.

'Ladies and gentlemen,' I shouted, 'consider dramatic unity! You could not all be happy.'

'Dramatic unity be d----d!' snarled Jabez Jamrack, 'that is the last thing you thought of.'

I trembled over the abyss …

I was going, going, – gone, when – the alarm-bell sounded, and the door was burst open and –

* * *

Bridget entered.

'It is the boy from the printers' for the proofs,' said she.

'Tell him to wait,' said I; and wiping the sweat from my intellectual brow, I seized my pen, and in ten lines had got my Villain comfortably in irons at Norfolk Island.

The 'typical digger,' the 'the most abused of all' the haunted author's types, whom he and 'others of his tribe' had made eat bank-notes as sandwiches and commit other extravagancies, is of course a prominent figure in the pages of Australian authors when they are dealing with the period of the first gold discoveries – a period of great excitement, bewilderment and sudden changes of fortune in the lives both of immigrants and residents.

A graphic picture is drawn, for instance, of those times in Mr. E. W. Hornung's novel, *The Unbidden Guest*:

'Now his watch,' continued Mr. Teesdale, 'has hardly ever left my pocket – but to go under my pillow – since he put it in my hands on July 3, 1851. Here's the date and our initials inside the case; but you've seen them before. Ay, but there are few who came out in '51 – and stopped out – who have done as poorly as me. The day after we dropped anchor in Hobson's Bay there wasn't a living soul aboard our ship; captain, Mates, passengers and crew, all gone to the diggings. Every man Jack but me! It was just before you were born, John William, and I wasn't going. It may have been a mistake, but the Lord knows best. To be sure, we had our hard times when the diggers were coming into Melbourne and shoeing their horses with gold, and filling buckets with champagne, and standing by with a pannikin to make everybody drink that passed; if you wouldn't, you'd got to take off your coat and show why. I remember one of them offering me a hundred pounds for this very watch, and precious hard up I was, but I wouldn't take it, not I, though I didn't refuse a sovereign for telling him the time. Ay, sovereigns were the pennies of those days.

With the facility of the born humorist, Marcus Clarke follows up the story of 'The Haunted Author' and its atmosphere of burlesque with one on an entirely different vein, 'A Christmas Eve Watch', wherein he voices the reflections of a successful but worldly-wise husband as he sits by the bedside of his dying wife. He had married her when both of them were young, poor and obscure, and having risen in life since then, had become rather ashamed of her. Now remorse assails him and he would give much to have it in his power to reverse the past and to atone for his selfish and heartless conduct towards her; for he knows that she has never wavered in her love for him. He resolves for her sake and as an act of atonement for his neglect of her that for the remainder of his life he will be considerate and helpful to all members of her sex. But his conscience tells him that although such a line of conduct may be the right one to pursue it will not buy him immunity from anguish. He knows that one face will haunt him still. Finally he prays that when his own summons comes and his fainting spirit glides from its mortal thrall, 'A glad presence shall meet him, and blend him with her celestial light, and buoy him up in her encircling arms, and plead for him, nor plead in vain – "O, Lord of Pity and of Love, I loved him once, and did pity him, and dying, gave him my forgiveness. I do beseech Thee, give him Thine!"' The pathos is not strained and the line of thought throughout is elevating and sincere.

I will close this chapter with an autobiographical anecdote that appears in the pages of the 'Noah's Ark' papers in the guise of a short story entitled 'The Poor Artist': an anecdote that illustrates the generous and sympathetic nature of the outwardly reserved and flippant and sarcastic Marcus Clarke. He has been commissioned by the editor of the *Peacock*,[75] (the newspaper to the staff of which he is attached) to go to a certain address in Bourke Street to inspect a picture on view there and write a

---

75 Melbourne *Argus*.

report on it for the journal in question. On arriving at the address indicated he finds that the studio of Mr. Bell, whose picture he is to examine, is situated on the fourth floor of a building, the remaining floors of which are used as a sewing-machine shop, a hairdresser's, and a tobacconist's, respectively. He tries the handle of the door on which is painted the word 'studio,' only to find it locked, so enters an adjoining apartment reeking of collodion, and evidently the operating room of a photographer. Seating himself upon a chair he awaits the advent of someone connected with the establishment. Meanwhile he becomes conscious that his movements are under observation by some invisible eye and presently there enters a middle-aged woman in a shabby, black-stuff dress, whose demeanour and the fact that she emits certain sucking noises give the impression that he has disturbed her at dinner.

A certain heartiness of manner that had marked her entrance seems to evaporate when she perceives that he is alone and not a 'group' come to be photographed. Marcus explains the nature of his errand, and on learning it, she plunges into a glowing eulogy of her son's talents, at the same time expressing her regret at his absence, for, she explains, he is out giving a drawing-lesson to a pupil at Hawthorn.[76] Eventually she shows Marcus into the studio, an apartment which, as he had suspected, is also used 'for the noble art of dining,' for, with a cloth thrown over it, is a tray containing the dinner. Here upon an easel he finds the picture that is the object of his visit. The subject is the meeting of Cortez and Montezuma, King of Mexico.

The artist's mother dilates upon its merits in her garrulous and ignorant fashion. She deplores the absence of 'Tom,' who knows, it appears, all that there is to know about art, has been a pupil 'at a school of design and that,' and concludes by summoning her daughter-in-law, Polly, to assist in doing the honours.

Polly accordingly enters, a slim, dark-haired girl, with a camels-hair brush stuck behind her ear, which she blushingly removes, an action that elicits the explanation that Polly was accustomed to colour the photographs. The latter is able to explain the intentions of the artist in a more intelligent manner than her mother-in-law, but after doing so, joins with her in an appeal to Marcus to use his influence with the Trustees to induce them to purchase the picture for the Melbourne National Gallery. He replies guardedly that they might possibly do so, but adds significantly that of course they have their own buyer in London.

---

76   A suburb of Melbourne.

There is a palpable slip here. Marcus had forgotten that when relating an actual occurrence in the form of fiction, he had set out by describing himself as a journalist sent to make a report for his paper and not (as was actually the case, I believe) an official of the Public Library and Picture Gallery with some influence in the matter of advising as to purchases for that gallery. He should of course either have so described himself at the commencement of the story or adhered to the role of journalist all through. This by the way. His narrative continues: 'The picture was thoroughly bad. The figures were out of drawing; the landscape was out of perspective. The sacrificial tower resembled the ruins of a windmill.' Had he come across it in a gallery or indeed under any other circumstances he would have turned upon his heel at once and either have condemned it as a preposterous or been altogether silent about it. But the evident anxiety and devotion of the young wife and the middle-aged mother appeal to his better nature. Upon his return to the office of the *Peacock* he tells the editor something of the truth, but pleads for the artist, explaining that he is a 'poor devil; struggling, don't you know?' The editor replies with a genial smile, 'Oh! D—n him, yes! Let him down easily.' So Marcus writes a paragraph of a 'non-commital' character for which Mr. Bell himself comes to thank him a few days afterwards. He expresses his regret, however, that the strong points of the picture had not been more enlarged upon and concludes by a personal appeal for his aid in finding a purchaser for it.

The artist, who wears a red beard and has dirty fingernails, proves to be the most hopeless of mediocrities. But partly from sheer compassion, partly because he perceives that the man is really making a brave struggle to earn a livelihood for himself and those dependent on him, Marcus does his utmost to induce one or other of his wealthier acquaintances to buy the painting. Incidentally, he allows us to surmise that his sympathy for the plucky Polly, who coloured the photographs, may count for something in these efforts of his to assist the Bell family. But alas! All in vain. The more publicity that is gained for the artist's work, the lower does it sink in the public estimation. The artist himself, who is consumptive, steadily deteriorates in health, and although he still continues to cherish the delusion that he has genius, exclaiming, 'It's in me, sir, and, by God, it shall come out!' the vigour of the sentiment is alas! its only recommendation, for the poor fellow dies in the course of a few months and Marcus attends his funeral at Carlton Cemetery. 'He is happy now! He will be appreciated now!' say the faithful women mourners. 'But,' concludes the anecdotist, glancing at one of his audience, 'Mrs. Sweetwinter, you are crying!'

Chapter 26

Miscellaneous Work continued

Letterpress to the illustrated catalogue of the pictures in the National Gallery, Melbourne.
– Preface to A. L. Gordon's bush ballads, generally regarded as an essay on the character of
Australian scenery.

R. L. Stevenson has pointed out that every book is, in an intimate sense, a circular letter to the friends of the writer, a dictum particularly applicable to the miscellaneous lighter work of Marcus Clarke. And an excellent example of his lighter work is furnished by the letterpress he contributed to the illustrated catalogue of the pictures in the Melbourne National Gallery, displaying as it does his appreciation of Art, wide reading, and delicate play of fancy in dealing with the subject in question.

Commencing with a painting by Hillemacher, entitled 'Psyche aux Enfers', he awakens our interest in the artist's choice of subject by referring to the legend of Cupid and Psyche of which it forms part:

The reader of the 'Golden Ass of Apuleius' will remember that when the amiable maiden, 'Charité', was captured by the band of robbers in whose service was the metamorphosed Lucius, an old woman related, to cheer the captivity of the imprisoned damsel, the story of Cupid and Psyche ...

This charming fable is not the invention of Apuleius; it is alluded to by Plato, Plotinus and Synesius ... It is not desirable to here discuss too minutely the meaning of those myths of sin, suffering, death and subsequent resurrection and happiness which have formed the basis of religious teaching in all ages ... The story of Psyche represents the lapse of the human soul from the divine and its struggle in search of intellectual, as opposed to sensual love; the trials imposed by Venus (*Venus Dione*) being typical of the purifications which human nature must undergo to fit it for a union with Divinity.

And, continuing this causerie in the same entertaining manner, he finds much more to say before he passes on to the next picture. The latter is Mr. Edwin Long's 'Dancing Girl, or A Question of Propriety', the excuse for such congenial topics as the Inquisition in Spain, the 'Ballos de Zingaras' and similar 'Cosas de España' of a bygone period enlivened by quotations from the pages of Victor Hugo. In Marcus Clarke's opinion, the picture might well be a representation of the scene in Longfellow's *Spanish Student* where Preciosa, the gipsy, dances the cachuca before the Archbishop of Toledo:

> the motif of the painting appears to reflect so nearly the incident of the play as to induce the belief that the artist had but designed to re-echo his Grace's sentiment,
>
> > 'Now shall your eyes behold
> >
> > In what angelic yet voluptuous shape,
> >
> > The Devil came to tempt Saint Anthony'
>
> and reproduced the humorous scene in the Episcopal Palace referred to. This however is not the case. A replica of the picture was exhibited at the Royal Academy Exhibition in London in the year 1871 under the title of 'A Question of Propriety,' and a note in the catalogue refers the spectator to *The Annals of the Inquisition in Seville, 1627; Francisco Patcheco.* There seemed to be some error in the matter of this note, for the subject of the picture is evidently a sitting of that celebrated Board, known as Censores y Vedadores, which, in the seventeenth century, was attached to the Holy Office.
>
> The 'Censores y Vedadores' – literally the Censurers and Seers – travelled the country in the interests of morality ... They reviewed the Ballos de Zingaras, or gipsy dances,

and inspected, with not unkindly severity, the 'Zarzuelas', or musical farces which set a-gaping the honest wine-sellers of Andalusia. Any sentiment which smacked of heresy was excised, any attitude which prompted to aught but respectability of manners was forbidden … Some Esmeralda, Dolores or Maritana has been dancing a dance which, though entertaining enough in the twinkling eyes of the market-place crowd, has been reported by a modest Familiar … as eminently unsuited for the calming of that Spanish blood which at all times beats with sufficient fierceness … attention may be called to the expression on the face of the Friar who holds the torch, as finely contrasted in its tender, fatherly pity for the handsome and ignorant gipsy with the carelessly insolent stare of the Officer who, – a Spanish Captain Phoebus – has, doubtless seen enough and to spare of the brown skinned beauties of the Alcazar.

The next picture, described in the catalogue as 'River, Mill, and Farm,' by F. R. Lee, R.A. is, in the opinion of the author of the letterpress, 'a charming illustration of the cool and tranquil scenery which inspired the healthful memories of country-loving Milton. The blue range of hills, the tanned haycock in the mead, the old thatched mill and the brawling mill stream could exist nowhere but in a country of

>   Russet lawns and fallows grey
>   Where the nibbling flocks do stray,'

and he comes to the conclusion that 'when studying Mr. Lee's picture, the imagination transports us without difficulty to England. We recall the green foliage sparkling with sharp-broken lights, we see again the leaf-shadows dancing on the brilliant turf, catch the laughter of the haymakers, and flinging ourselves down beneath the moss-grown mill, fall a day-dreaming upon country pleasures, our thoughts attuned to the soothing monotone of the ever-rippling river.' These recollections of his may have been to some extent steeped in the *couleur de rose* lent by time and distance to every mental retrospect but they are interesting and enlightening as evidence of the impressions he had gathered in early life.

'Checkmate,' by C. M. Webb, a cottage interior in a French provincial town with two old fellows seated beside a chess-board is analysed at some length, but I shall content myself with one characteristic quotation:

> This charming little cabinet picture is just exactly one of those works which Mr.
> Michael Angelo Titmarsh – better known, by the way, to readers of this generation by

his family name of William Makepeace Thackeray – would have rejoiced in reviewing for the pages of *Fraser*. There is an Hogarthian neatness of composition about it which is quite in the Titmarsh manner …

The story is told in words scarcely less simple than those chosen by the historical knife-grinder of Mr. Canning.

The artist may have merited these compliments but the author of the letterpress elaborates them with his usual charm of style; but perhaps at unnecessary length. Finally Mr Bough's picture, 'The Weald of Kent,' elicits a second eulogy of English rural scenery, concluding with the following fine passage:

The white cliffs of Dover we may see no more, and in view of his increased prosperity, the successful Australian colonist may be content to lose them, but he who has once trod Kentish soil must be indeed satisfied with his lot if, amid the shadowless glare of our fierce southern summer, he has not sometimes thought with regret of the cool boughs of apple-bearing orchards, the sweet smell of English turf, the rush of reddened leaves, the magnificence of sinking suns, the chastened splendour of autumn in the 'Garden of England.'

And now by a quite natural transition I pass from Marcus Clarke's memories of the scenery of the land of his birth to his impressions of that of the country of his adoption. These are to be found in scattered passages throughout his works, but nowhere in such striking form as in his well known introduction to Adam Lindsay Gordon's volume of bush ballads, so much so, that it has come to be regarded less as an essay on their poetical merits than as one on his own impressions of Australian scenery. Be that as it may, however, this introduction or preface to Gordon's verses was regarded by Lord Lytton and other eminent literary men as the finest piece of work that ever came from the pen of Marcus Clarke.

After a brief sketch of Gordon's career he proceeds to quote from 'The Sick Stockrider' the passage commencing with the lines,

'Twas merry in the glowing morn, among the gleaming grass,
To wander as we've wander'd many a mile,

and terminating,

> And the golden-tinted fern leaves, how they rustled underneath!
> And the honeysuckle osiers, how they crash'd!

and pays the following tribute to his poetic abilities:

> This is genuine. There is no 'poetic evolution from the depths of internal consciousness'
> here. The writer has ridden his ride as well as written it.
>
> The student of these unpretending volumes will be repaid for his labour. He will
> find in them something very like the beginnings of a national school of Australian
> poetry. In historic Europe … the least imaginative can find food for sad and sweet
> reflection. When strolling at noon down an English country lane, lounging at sunset
> by some ruined chapel on the margin of an Irish lake, or watching the mists of
> morning unveil Ben Lomond, we feel all the charm which springs from association
> with the past … But this our native or adopted land has no past, no story. No poet
> speaks to us. Do we need a poet to interpret Nature's teachings, we must look into
> our own hearts, if perchance we may find a poet there.

So far there is nothing to challenge criticism. It is what follows that has been the
subject of such heated controversy. And yet if proof were needed of the poetical
temperament, artistic perception and literary ability of the author, the concluding
paragraph of this preface would be quite sufficient to vindicate his claim to those
qualities, for they breathe the very spirit of poetry. They are of its essence, although
not cast in the form of lyrics or blank verse. Immaterial whether every allusion to the
animal and vegetable life of the region he is describing – his version of its fauna and
flora – be or be not strictly accurate. He is merely striving to reproduce, in striking
and brilliant language, the mental impressions acquired during his sojourn in its
midst, impressions of a wild nature which had awed and yet partly captivated his
easily excited imagination and which continued to haunt it long after he had left the
scenes where it is present, and was living amidst quite other surroundings, just as the
refrain of some melody, learnt in childhood, haunts us at intervals throughout our
after-life, forgotten for long periods at a time but suddenly recurring to our memory
and never entirely losing its potency and charm.

In short, he is aiming at drawing a vivid picture of certain phenomena which he
had studied at close quarters and of thus conveying to his readers some idea of that
'subtle charm' attributed by himself and by others to the nature of the wild Australian
bush. And the following is a summary of his impressions and ideas of it:

What is the dominant note of Australian scenery? That which is the dominant note of Edgar Allan Poe's poetry – Weird Melancholy. A poem like 'L'Allegro' could never be written by an Australian. It is too airy, too sweet, too freshly happy. The Australian mountain forests are funereal, secret, stern. Their solitude is desolation. They seem to stifle, in their black gorges, a story of sullen despair. No tender sentiment is nourished in their shade. In other lands the dying year is mourned, the falling leaves drop lightly on his bier. In the Australian forests no leaves fall. The savage winds shout among the rock clefts. From the melancholy gums strips of white bark hang and rustle. The very animal life of these frowning hills is either grotesque or ghostly. Great grey kangaroos hop noiselessly over the coarse grass. Flights of white cockatoos stream out, shrieking like evil souls. The sun suddenly sinks, and the mopokes burst out into horrible peals of semi-human laughter. The natives aver that, when night comes, from out the bottomless depth of some lagoon the Bunyip rises, and, in form like a monstrous sea-calf, drags his loathsome length from out the ooze. From a corner of the silent forest rises a dismal chant, and around a fire dance natives painted like skeletons. All is fear-inspiring and gloomy. No bright fancies are linked with the memories of the mountains. Hopeless explorers have named them out of their sufferings – Mount Misery, Mount Dreadful, Mount Despair. As when among sylvan scenes in places

>Made green with the running of rivers,

>And gracious with temperate air,

the soul is soothed and satisfied, so, placed before the frightful grandeur of these barren hills, it drinks in their sentiment of defiant ferocity, and is steeped in bitterness.

Australia has rightly been named the Land of the Dawning. Wrapped in the mists of early morning, her history looms vague and gigantic …

There is a poem in every form of tree or flower, but the poetry which lives in the trees and flowers of Australia differs from those of other countries … In Australia alone is to be found the Grotesque, the Weird, the strange scribblings of Nature learning how to write. Some see no beauty in our trees without shade, our flowers without perfume, our birds who cannot fly, and our beasts who have not yet learned to walk on all fours. But the dweller in the wilderness acknowledges the subtle charm of this fantastic land of monstrosities. He becomes familiar with the beauty of loneliness. Whispered to by the myriad tongues of the wilderness, he learns the language of the barren and the uncouth, and can read the hieroglyphs of haggard gum-trees, blown into odd shapes, distorted with fierce hot winds, or cramped with cold nights, when the Southern Cross freezes in a cloudless sky of icy blue. The phantasmagoria of that wild dream-land termed the Bush interprets itself, and the Poet of our desolation begins to comprehend why free Esau loved his heritage of desert sand better than all the bountiful richness of Egypt.

These vivid paragraphs have been subjected to the most searching criticism, as if Marcus Clarke's impressions of the scenery of a certain locality should be weighed with the judicial severity which would be properly meted out to the assertions of a government Emigration Agent. Thus the author of *The New Nation* considers them 'impressive writing,' but is careful to add that the 'impression conveyed is radically false,' for, he contends, to 'the normal Australian, the gum is not "melancholy", but the most beautiful tree in the world. To him there is nothing in the least "grotesque" or "ghostly" about a kangaroo; and the mountains, far from raising in his soul ... a sentiment of defiant ferocity, soothe him with their exquisite harmonies of gold and indigo.'

Mr. Wallace Nelson again, after pointing out the contrast between the ideal delights of a drover's life as pictured in Paterson's verses, and the reverse of the picture as drawn in Lawson's reply, writes,

> Marcus Clarke has painted in prose as gruesome a picture of the Australian forest as Lawson has of her sun-dried plains. In his famous introduction to the works of Adam Lindsay Gordon, he writes, 'The Australian forests are funereal, secret, stern,'

and after quoting the entire passage continues,

> Now, all this is absurdly gruesome and false. The mopoke does not laugh. Australian forests are no more funereal than other forests. They are less so, for they are bathed in perpetual sunshine. Nor is it quite clear what there is about their solitude that makes it desolation. Why they should seem to stifle in their black gorges a silent story of despair, I cannot for the life of me suppose. I have been in many Australian forests and have experienced no such impression. Some of the forest country is very magnificent, and the only feeling it ever inspired in me was that of awe and admiration.

Another critic considers that the 'dominant note of Australian scenery' is rather that of 'weird expectancy' than of the 'weird melancholy' attributed to it by Marcus Clarke. From what follows in his article, however, it is clear that this very critic is in substantial agreement with the latter on the subject of the Bush scenery and the sense of awe which it inspires.

So far we have given the views of hostile critics or one or two representative examples, for, although numerous, their comments are more or less identical. Let us therefore summon witnesses for the defence, and review the evidence in support of Marcus Clarke's assertion that a sense of depression or melancholy is engendered by the nature of the scenery, even if we concede that, in all probability, like others of a highly strung and imaginative temperament he unconsciously exaggerated and read into his environment what was partly the creation of his own morbid fancy. I will begin with the impressions of a recent visitor, Mr John Foster Fraser, who writes in his well known book *Australia: the Making of a Nation*:

> The 'sadness of the landscape' is a worn commonplace in Australia. The 'native born' is tired of being told about it. He does not notice it.
>
> Yet, no one with a touch of imagination can fail to be depressed by the sombreness of the land. I shall never forget my first weeks in Australia. It looked a weary land – conscious of its own shortcomings. It looked as though the Almighty had started to make a fine continent of it and left it half-made ... The birds were made beautiful – how delicious it was to see them, with their gorgeous rainbow plumages, flitting amongst the trees – but it was forgotten to provide most of them with song. Trees grew, but mostly of the eucalyptus family – the 'eternal blue gum' as it is called – and you can journey days, weeks, and see nothing but the dark bluish foliage of the gums. The wood is hard, and most of the trees are gnarled. Some of them seem to shed their bark in despair, and stand miserable. Few flowers have been given to Australia. Suddenly, however, you come across a blaze of wattle, ribbons of flaming gold, and the delight of the Australian, the rhapsody in which he or she indulges, at this splash of beauty in the sad landscape, is almost pathetic in its enthusiasm.

The author of *The Record of an Adventurous Life*, Mr. H. M. Hyndman, is another witness in support of Marcus Clarke's views for he writes in the following strain upon the subject:

> I can imagine nothing more depressing than a long ride through the Australian bush. The climate of New South Wales and Victoria is as a whole bright and cheerful and healthy. Wherever also European trees have been cultivated, the appearance of the country is delightful ... But to this day I never look upon a blue gum tree without a mournful feeling coming over me. I see again the long rows of those forbidding trees which I passed through at the stock-horse canter ... the intolerable weariness of those

> woeful gums oppressed me. They are the most dissipated looking trees I ever beheld.
> Dante could well have represented them in his Inferno, in the shape of drunken men,
> as trees, standing around in sempiternal penitence for their orgies of the past … We
> read much in Australian books … about the charms of the Australian climate and the
> delights of Australian scenery. The exquisite fern-tree gullies of Tasmania and certain
> Australian districts are rightly paraded as of almost unrivalled beauty; but the tree of
> trees in New South Wales, Victoria, and South Australia, is the blue gum, and whereas
> I cherish most pleasing memories of Melbourne, Sydney and some of the planted and
> semi-tropical regions, the nightmare of the gum-tree forests weighs upon me still.

And with regard to Marcus Clarke's allusions to the songless birds and scentless
flowers which have also been characterized as false and misleading, the evidence
of the author just quoted confirms their approximate accuracy for he points out
that, 'In birds there have been special types like the cassowary and the emu and
bowerbird of gorgeous plumage but not many birds rich in song' and referring
to the second, he remarks, 'Some similarity has been noticed between the flora
of Australia and that of South Africa. The flowers are bright but most of them
are scentless. There is the brilliant waratah and the golden wattle, but there is
neither the variety nor the delicacy of blooms which is to be found in other
countries of the world.'

As a third witness, let us summon a native-born Australian, the well known
novelist, Mrs. Campbell Praed, and quote her evidence, for it seems to me that
her impressions of the scenery amidst which she grew up are almost identical with
those of Marcus Clarke.

> Words fail for painting the loneliness of the Australian bush. Mile after mile of
> primeval forest, interminable vistas of melancholy gum-trees,

whilst in the description she gives of her early home occurs the following passage:

> It sounds idyllic, this bush garden. Below it lay a fearsome lagoon – fearsome because
> of the Bunyip tradition that clung to it – and gloomy with melancholy she-oaks and
> flooded gums. This Bunyip tradition was fairly well authenticated. A girl wandering
> in maiden reverie by the lagoon's banks, saw the monster, flew and told a graphic tale.
> She described it as an immense, slimy creature with a calf-like head and the body of a
> great serpent. I can myself testify that the Blacks held Bungroopim waterhole in direst

awe. They said, 'Debbil-debbil sat down like-it that place,' and not one of them could ever be persuaded to swim from bank to bank.

There must have been some foundation for the many Bunyip legends. No doubt, a creature unclassified by naturalists did once exist in the creeks and lagoons till, scared by civilized intruders, it hid itself and pined, dying out at length like the dodo and great auk … The Bunyip, perhaps, was the last survival of Lemurian mythology … How that may be I know not, but I can well imagine that only monsters could have inhabited those gruesome pools locked in the grotesque arms of hoary gums and shadowed by she-oaks – the most dismal of trees, with their straight, black stems and thin, dropping foliage, which whispers mysteriously in a light breeze and gives piteous moans when the wind swells into a blast.

Finally her graphic description of a native corroboree which she witnessed when a child, recalls the passage in Marcus Clarke's preface, 'From a corner of the silent forest rises a dismal chant, and around a fire dance natives painted like skeletons,' for she depicts the scene in the following language:

> The chiefs in the front seem to direct the performance. Some of them are painted to represent skeletons, others in spiral stripes as though huge snakes were coiled round their bodies.

They were rehearsing an attack on a white man's station and some 'effigies of women' ('saplings … draped with blankets') were

> dragged in to the circus and stood upright. They are saluted with screams of horrible laughter, and the warriors, painted like skeletons, mock them with gestures of derision.[77]

At a meeting of the Australian Literary Society held in Melbourne some years ago[78] a paper was read by a member, Mr. William Moore, on the subject of 'local colour,' in connection with an exhibition of the work of Victorian artists then open. An interesting discussion followed and it was subsequently continued in the columns

---

77   *My Australian Girlhood. Sketches and Impressions of Bush Life* by Mrs. Campbell Praed.
78   October 11, 1911.

of the Melbourne *Herald*, the theme being, as before, 'The Australian landscape – sunshine and shadow.' Naturally, stress was laid on Marcus Clarke's assertion that the dominant note of Australian scenery was 'Weird Melancholy,' for Mr. Moore had contended that as sunshine was one of the best assets of the Commonwealth, Australia could hardly be the gloomy wilderness Clarke, and other writers also, had represented. But another speaker, Mr. Bernard O'Dowd, pointed out that behind the thin fringe of purple land along the coast, Australia was and would remain a desert until humanised. The true note of all nature was desolation, and writers, describing what they saw, fell into a melancholy strain in spite of themselves. But a painter must depict sunlight on his canvas, for the Australian sun wrote on the air in a way differing from that of any other country. Another member, Mr. McClintock, thought that the art exhibition should settle the question, for they would there find Australia painted as she was, with sunlit air and blue skies, there not being a dull landscape in the show.

The opening writer in the correspondence that ensued in the *Herald* (Mr. Rosenbaum), however, thought that there had been too apparent a desire amongst those present at the meeting to insist on this aspect of the scenery of their country to the exclusion of any other, except in the case of Mr. O'Dowd, 'We all know of these things re sunshine and blue skies,' he continued:

> but it is another matter for our writers and painters, who live in comfortable city or suburban homes, to face the true Australia, that the bush-dweller knows and that Marcus Clarke wrote of. In all the world where is there a more tragic place than the untrodden Australian bush by night? For those writers and painters who only know the bush as the result of various annual picnics, perchance, 'sun-lit air and blue skies' are the dominant memories. Let the optimistic enthusiast sleep out for a night or two, far from the possibility of immediate return to home and comfort. Let him listen to the weird voices of the wild, as they join in a more fantastic symphonic poem than ever Richard Strauss imagined in his strangest flights of fancy – the mopoke's minor chord, the long-drawn portamento of the plover by the marsh-side, the monotonous complaining of the native bear on the distant range – *then* let him write a sonnet to the Australian sunlight, or paint a picture in green and gold. It seems to me that there is something particularly insincere, or wanting in right knowledge, in this cheap desire to boom in our art and literature a 'sunny Australia.' Let us leave that to the Commonwealth advertising agents and to other unimportant people. The only true note in art is the personal one. Temperament is everything, and surely the attempt

to encourage only one point of view from which to see our country is against the interests of all true artistic development. So far as Australia is concerned, there is gloom as well as sunlight. May the shadows only serve to heighten the light!

Mr. Rosenbaum's letter was followed by one from Mr. Ernest H. Clarke, a son of Marcus Clarke, and himself possessed of personal experience of life in the bush. His letter ran as follows:

> Marcus Clarke wrote of the Australian bush as he knew it. He lived in the bush for some years. The 'Weird' is probably an English youth's exaggeration, but 'melancholy' *is* the dominant note, as all dwellers in the bush must know. I mean the Australian bush, not the bush of the fringe of city and township, with its imported trees and tilled soil. Take the vast majority of our land, the 'outback' of all the states and you will find the bush in its primeval state with its dominant note of melancholy.
>
> It is to our bushmen and women that we must look for an opinion, not to the town dweller with his ideas formed after a few hours' sojourn near a railhead and within 'cooee' of a bush 'pub' … Note the demeanour of our bush dwellers, even of those near to the 'shining roads of steel' – a tone of 'greyness' is in their speech; they look 'grey' and move with the melancholy depression of their surroundings …
>
> Critics of my father and other writers should remember that the Wimmera country, where my father lived as a youth, is a very different country now, with its towns and farms and railroads … To these critics I say, 'Roll the bluey and make for the outback' … Live the life our pioneers lived and the bushman lives today; get at the heart of the bush and suffer as they did! Take the bush tales of my father, Lawson, Paterson, the songs of Boake, Gordon, Kendall, men who lived in the bush, lived near the 'heart of things' – they knew. Is there not a melancholy note throughout their works? We have 'sunlit air and blue skies,' granted; but let us face the other side also.
>
> I have lived ten years of my life in the bush, … and the note I struck was one of melancholy. I would not have it otherwise. The South African bush, the Canadian forests, or the 'green lanes of England' cannot erase the memories that linger.

Ernest Clarke's ideas elicited the following comment from T. K. whose letter seems to be that of a man of broad views and common sense, one with a grasp of the subject:

The interesting question raised by Mr. Clarke has, on many occasions occupied the thoughts of Australian people … As Mr. Clarke truly says, the bush of today cannot be compared with the bush in the time of his father and A. L. Gordon, on account of the ever advancing influence of civilisation, which is spreading over the continent. To the true nature-lover the bush, in all its aspects, is always beautiful, but it is undeniable that the sameness and monotony of our primeval forests seems to have a saddening effect on those who reside constantly within their shades, and the glories of the forest which ravish the soul of the city man are altogether lost on the bush dweller. Byron found some of his loftiest inspiration listening to the roar of the ocean on some desolate, awe-inspiring shore; and Wordsworth wrote some of his masterpieces within the shade of dense woods. Each of these gifted authors could immediately return from his retreat to a cultured circle amid refining influences. How different has been the lot of many of our most gifted Australian authors whose surroundings were often cast amid fires, drought and floods, away from the comforts and ease of advancing civilisation; and cut off from all cultured associates.

Alexander Selkirk on the island of Juan Fernandez, amid glorious scenery by sea and land, is made to exclaim,

O Solitude! where are the charms

That sages have seen in thy face?

Better dwell in the midst of alarms,

Than reign in this horrible place.

The solitude was driving him mad; and it is the solitude of the bush that causes the 'grey' note among our Australian authors and the bush dwellers that Mr. Clarke complains about.

The electric telegraph, the railway, telephone, cheap literature, and the comforts of life are rapidly killing the monotony of the bush, and the overshadowing note of pessimism to be found in most of our Australian literature in the past is rapidly disappearing in our present day authors. With the advance of decentralisation, an influx of the right sort of immigrants, and an increased standard of education throughout Australia, the bush will soon be robbed of its monotony. Education alone will largely help to kill it, for a well-stored mind is never lonely. Our future poets will sing of a bright and happy land amid smiling plenty instead of our 'sun-cursed regions.'

The following reference in the *Spectator* to the contrasts presented in its natural features by the Australian continent in certain districts, seems to throw considerable light on the vexed question of the accuracy of Marcus Clarke's description:

Most of those who trouble to think about Australia at all, picture to themselves a flat, sandy country, monotonous in its scenery and comparatively uninteresting in its 'fauna' and 'flora.' It may be news to some that the vast island-continent possesses some of the finest hill scenery imaginable, some of the most beautiful forests, and some of the boldest cliffs in the world.

Just so. It would have been more accurate perhaps had Marcus Clarke, when he wrote his description of Australian mountain scenery, made it clearer that he had in mind the district where he had lived for a time and where its character was as he described it.

But thinking probably of the effect such a landscape would have upon a temperament like that of the poet Gordon (an immigrant like himself) in this preface of his to Gordon's bush ballads, he was led into dealing in generalities and to some extent perhaps into the language of exaggeration. But such negative criticism as that of Mr. Wallace Nelson, 'I have been in many Australian forests and experienced no such impression,' is surely the most futile and unconvincing.

A friend, whose opinion I sought, and who before he settled in New Zealand, had travelled extensively, replied that much depended on individual temperament with regard either to natural scenery or music. He remembered certain districts in Great Britain, for instance a deer forest in Argyllshire that he considered more dreary 'on a day of rain and mist and when the raven's croak was audible than anything of the kind likely to be encountered in Australia,' and which would probably have depressed Clarke to a greater extent than the desolate hills of the Wimmera, but he added that he had no personal knowledge of the bush in Australia, although he had of that in Tasmania, and the effect of which upon himself had been rather exhilarating.

Some of the forest scenery in New Zealand and particularly the beauty and variety of the ferns to be found there had seemed to him like a glimpse of fairyland.

No one was more susceptible to the attractive side of Australian country life than Marcus Clarke himself, for in his earlier letters to me from the Wimmera district he had expressed himself with regard to the beauty of the dawn in language very similar to that of another Australian author: 'Coming out at early dawn into that miraculously fresh, sweet-scented air which makes of each rising in the Australian bush a renewed delight,' but in this preface of his to Gordon's verses, he endeavours to bring home to his readers the feeling of insignificance, helplessness and solitude conveyed by the rugged grandeur of the mountain ranges, and the illimitable plains beyond, to the spectator as he gazes at them in awe-struck admiration. It is the feeling voiced by the Russian author, Grigorovitch, in his novel, *The Peasant*, in a striking passage:

> But in the country a totally different impression is made on us by the vast spaces which surround us from morn to eve. In the streets among the houses you are an object to be remarked, but here you are but a speck in the universe … The mind, struck by the endless superiority of the works of nature, … is everywhere awed by the greatness, and silently acknowledges its childish impotence.[79]

---

79   *The Peasant*, by Demetrius Gregorovich. Translated from the Russian by Beatrix L. Tollemache.

Chapter 27

Pecuniary results of Clarke's work. – Money troubles. 'A fortunate man.' – Insolvency. – Providing for his family. – Possible result of a meeting between youthful friends. – Continuance of his pecuniary troubles. – A gallant struggle to provide for those dependent on him. – His kindness of heart taken advantage of by unscrupulous acquaintances. – The impression he made on a stranger in 1876. – Offer from the editor of the London Daily Telegraph. *– His reply to it. – His domestic establishment. – The manner in which he would prefer a meeting to take place between us. – A reminiscence of school life. – A significant postscript.*

Those who measure an author's success by his pecuniary rewards would have to place Marcus Clarke far down on the list. Mr. Andrew Lang, for instance, writing of R. L. Stevenson, says: 'His period of recognition was very brief,' and goes on to express his doubts as to whether he ever received twenty-five thousand pounds for a single story, nor does he remember, he remarks, having seen any stationer's advertisement like this: 'Yes, you may say that I used your patent, ameliorated blotting-pad when I wrote *The Wrecker* etc. R. L. S.'

What would Clarke have thought of any such sum as twenty five thousand pounds for all his literary work put together?

At all events his first successful novel cannot have gained an early recognition in England, for in a letter dated June 1874, he thus refers to it and to the pecuniary misfortunes that had overtaken him in a characteristic manner:

Dear C.

I write this in a dirty little newspaper office in a place called Gisborne. There is nothing but 'flimsy' to write upon and the ink is like mud. But your letter, which was forwarded to me here, has made me write, despite kerosene lamp, two drunken diggers, a bad pen and an Italian concert all at once.

Then comes a recapitulation of the leading events of his life and the following account of his circumstances at the time of inditing this letter, for a considerable gap had elapsed in our correspondence:

I am librarian to the Public Library here, a good place secured by parliamentary vote; two hundred thousand volumes and five hundred a year. I make some five hundred more by scribbling 'Our Melbourne Correspondence' or some twaddle in a local journal (i.e. as Melbourne correspondent of a country paper). I have written for the press and written two novels. I send you one which I had hoped might meet with notice in London, but which – up to this time – hasn't …

Everybody says that I am a most fortunate man. Last year I became insolvent – but insolvency is here a matter of no moment, especially to a *fortunate* man …

My wife was an actress and had no fortune of her own except a good temper, and something of originality which pleases me better than money. We get on very well and have three children. I have taken the precaution to settle on my family a little farm of eight hundred acres and orchard situated some fifteen miles from the town which I became 'enfeoffed' of, and I can regard their ultimate fortune with calmness. For myself it is just impossible to say what I might do or where I might go. A cousin of mine – one Sir Andrew Clarke – being Governor of the Straits Settlements, has been waging war against the piratical chiefs of that peninsula. He has asked me to visit him. I have never been to China and that soft, insensate ass 'X' must have blundered as usual in swallowing news from his informant. I have had no such fortune as to travel 'all over the world.' I wish I had had …

Do I remember W? and the post-chaise and his dead mama in a winding-sheet and his wife with two black eyes? Don't I? (An allusion to a ghost story I had told him when we were at school together.) Do *you* remember half as well as I do – you dear old vegetable running to pecuniary seed in Cornhill? Do you remember – and the walks with me in Highgate Woods and the story-telling? …

Ah, my dear old boy, you and I shall never live those days over again but I should like to rise up some night, spectre-like, in High Holborn and come into your chambers for a smoke and then *vanish*! Wouldn't Mrs. C. say 'Where *have* you been, my dear'? It is doubtful if I shall return to London and, as you say, more than doubtful if you would care about me, or I about you, if we met. How can we control these things? 'Marriage and Death and Division make barren our lives' – as sings my Algernon! …

Your Petshorin comparison is a simple fact in all but the end (This in allusion to my comparison of him to the hero of Lermontoff's story in a recent letter of mine). Write me a line if business or domesticity permit to the Public Library, Melbourne, which address will find me, however far I may stray, and remember that if somebody comes up your office-stairs, three at a time, and says, 'Why *don't* ye be a cobbler?' it will be,

Always yours truly,
Marcus Clarke.

This was a favourite enquiry the headmaster of Highgate School in our time had of addressing to a pupil in difficulties with his lesson, and was intended to convey, with gentle irony, to the unhappy youth his unfitness for any walk in life superior to that of the humble calling in question.

Alluding to Clarke's insolvency, Mr. Hamilton Mackinnon writes as follows:

Though long expected, and known to be inevitable, the thoughtless writer of thoughtful literature put off the evil day by every means in his power, thereby sinking deeper and deeper into the mire, till, at last, his doom had to be sealed, and his name appeared in the bankruptcy list. What those who had led him into living beyond his means felt when the disagreeable fact became known can only be conjectured, but, at any rate, their foolish dupe felt the position more acutely than any acquaintance of his could possibly imagine, judging by the light-hearted manner in which he discussed the subject with one and all. Only those who knew Marcus Clarke intimately – and they were few – realised how keenly he suffered …

But he goes on to say that Marcus's insolvency was not followed by a reformation, 'for no sooner was one difficulty overcome than another commenced, ending only when life was no more,' whilst Mr. A. B. Paterson, in his short memoir of Clarke, touches more nearly the heart of the matter, when he writes:

The profession of letters has never been very highly remunerated in Australia, and Marcus Clarke, with expensive tastes, with a reputation as a *bon viveur* to keep up, and without any of the self-denial necessary for the occasion, was sure to find himself sooner or later in financial troubles. In these troubles he lived and died.

I have read in a biography of Bret Harte that the latter 'was utterly destitute of what is sometimes called the '"money sense".' Apparently the same might well have been said of Marcus Clarke. Mr. A. B. Paterson, however, remarks with discrimination:

> While unable to keep himself out of debt, he took on his shoulders the task of providing for a young wife; and cheerfully and pluckily he struggled to fulfil the task. His character was free from those vices and infidelities that so often haunt the ways of genius, and all through his career of debt, doubt and disappointment he did his best for those dependent on him.

This may have been so, but alas! from the date of the letter to me quoted above to the end of his life, his family cares and pecuniary troubles increased; and there were left as his survivors without any resources a widow and six children (four sons and two daughters). Not only this but unscrupulous acquaintances were not wanting who took advantage of his foolish good nature and weakness to borrow money of him.

Mrs. Clarke, sitting up awaiting his return from some press dinner or other entertainment one moonlight night, watched him approach the house with a companion at his side, who appeared to be addressing Marcus in a confidential manner. Guessing the nature of the subject under discussion she listened until some stray words reached her ear which placed the matter beyond reasonable doubt. Throwing up the window sash rather noisily she greeted the two friends in her naturally cordial manner but so as to intimate that she was aware of what was passing.

The effect was instantaneous. The would-be borrower, greeting Mrs. Clarke with an embarrassed laugh, beat a hasty retreat – his design on this occasion frustrated. But probably only for a time. In one of his later letters to me Marcus mentions the names of several old school-fellows whom, at one time or another, he had met in Australia.

Amongst them he described one who had imposed on his good nature in the following fashion:

> The wretched 'O' made his appearance. Said he was studying for the church under the Anglican Bishop and borrowed seventy pounds of me. Like an ass I lent it to him on his acceptance at three months. Of course he never paid and I never saw him again.

But to resume the dropped thread of our correspondence. His next letter (intended to convey to me that I had been remiss in writing) was of the following dimensions:

The Public Library, Melbourne.

Dear Cyril,
    Are you yet alive?

Yours always,
Marcus Clarke.

And it was followed by one containing a photograph of himself (identical with that prefixed to Mr. Hamilton Mackinnon's memoir) and couched in the following terms:

The Public Library, Melbourne,
May 12, 1876

Dear Cyril,
Do you know whom this represents? You never write to me now, so until I hear from you, I shall not tell you a lot of good news which I have to tell. Have you read my novel *His Natural Life* published by Bentley? It has been fairly reviewed in the press. Write-Write-Write!

Thine as always,
Marcus Clarke.

And I did write in consequence, but receiving no reply, after an interval of several months, I sent him another letter, reminding him of his promise and the terms of his last communication. Before appending his reply, I cannot refrain from reproducing a description of him by a recent writer in the Sydney *Bulletin* as he struck an outsider in this very year, 1876:

> He was nice. It is not a flattering term in masculine association but it fitted him like a glove. And his niceness was a velvet cushion whereon to display the few facets – not one of them is a perfect jewel – of his genius. Nice as his surroundings he seemed when I met him in the year 1876. It was late January and fiercely hot, but within the National Gallery there was coolness and rest, and in the room with the pleasant outlook off the Library just such surroundings as a literary man might desire! I had a bundle

of manuscript and no other introduction whatever. Nevertheless the 'lips of laughter' moved pleasantly and the 'eyes of light' shone in a little while, and I got a glimpse of the most charming personality that has so far graced the literary world of Australia. He had only the old familiar counsel as to the literary life. 'If you want to prove that life is not worth living, persist!' It was discordant with himself as with his surroundings.

My last appeal elicited the following response, most of which I give verbatim:

The Public Library, Melbourne,
January 11th 1877

Dear Cyril,

Your reproachful note has just arrived and galvanized me into writing. The 'good news' that I had to tell you was merely that the *Daily Telegraph* people wrote to ask me what terms I would take to join their staff in London. I did not care to go – having interests here; but said I should require a free passage to London and an engagement of one thousand a year for five years. They have not replied to my letter so I suppose that they found the terms too high. Perhaps they were; but my income here is not less from all sources and I am beginning to look at the securing of a crust for old age. When one is thirty-one and has five children, two of whom are girls, one begins to think seriously of the duties of life.

Now for some news about myself. I am Assistant Librarian at the Public Library. Duties: sit in the office and direct other people; order books etc. from 4 p.m. until 10 every day except Saturday, when I work from 10 a.m. until 9 p.m. thus getting from 9 p.m. on Saturday to 4 p.m. on Monday as holiday. That time I spend usually at a little property belonging to my cousin (Sir Andrew Clarke) for whom I act as agent. He owns fifteen hundred acres near Melbourne on which I built a shooting-box of six rooms. There is a fine orchard and plenty of game at the place. Two or three people go with me and we spend the time pleasantly. I live at a place called Brighton – because, I suppose, it is on the sea beach, and have a reasonably comfortable house and garden running to the beach, a boat etc. The principal expense here is labour. I give my cook forty pounds a year, my nurse thirty-six, and my housemaid thirty pounds a year. My groom demands no less than fifty. All these people have to be fed.

There follow various other particulars of his domestic expenditure, none of which, I have been assured, however, on the highest authority in such matters, were quite correct or reliable, although true in a general way. He disposed of this subject by saying in conclusion, 'I am considered well off, am always in debt and contrive to live pleasantly.' It is useless to enlarge on this subject. He did *not* contrive to live pleasantly for his debts and worries eventually killed him. His letter continues:

> There is no society in Melbourne. Bankers, merchants and rich men of the 'shoddy' class form the only society which can afford to entertain. The really nice people – the retired officers, stray doctors or barristers are not rich enough to return hospitalities and the squatters or sheep farmers live away on their stations. The city is hateful but I want to put in another ten years. By that time I ought to have been for at least five in receipt of eight hundred a year from my promotion to my chief's place, and to be able to sell my land for increased value. It is quite possible I may never return home at all. I have so many luxuries here, pony-carriage for my wife, saddle-horses, small cutter etc. which I could never hope to have in England that I fear lest I should be discontented when I reached home.
>
> My cousin (Sir Andrew Clarke), now Minister for Public Works in India, offered me a billet in that service but I declined it for somewhat the same reasons. In fact, my dear Cyril, I am growing lazy. *Ich habe gewonnen* etc. I have tasted most things and am not so eager for violent emotions as of old.
>
> I should much like to see you again. Not with mutual wives and children because that would be embarrassing and restraining but to meet you – say by accident – in a solitary railway carriage between London and Carlisle – have our fill of talk and then get out and each go our separate ways. Ah me, dear boy; that vanished youth of ours in the Highgate fields – we can never recall it!
>
> Always yours,
> Marcus Clarke.

A few days later he added a couple of sheets of a more intimate character, one passage of which however I shall cite as affording an additional proof of the strong hold the associations of early life had retained on his memory:

> I bought at a bookshop the other day a complete set of *Once a Week*, and as I turned over the leaves, I recalled how we used to look for the weekly issues and devour the thrilling stories in them such as *The Pythagorean*, etc.

Finally came a postscript; a significant one:

> 'How did you like *His Un-Natural Life*? I mean *really* you know?' (The word 'really' strongly underlined.) 'Tell me in thy reply!'

Chapter 28

Marcus Clarke's friendship with Dr. Patrick Moloney. – Their amusement at overhearing a
conversation between two 'digging mates' on St. Patrick's day in which the nature and extent of
the saint's blessing on Ireland was defined. – The charm of Marcus's laughter and the spell of his
personality. – His adventure with a bailiff and its fortunate issue. – The indulgences accorded
Marcus by his superiors at the Public Library. – Popular exaggeration of his eccentricities. –
Points of resemblance in his character and mental outlook with that of R. L. Stevenson. –
Charm of Marcus Clarke's lighter literary work. – His freedom from jealousy and readiness to
assist any rising writer of merit of his day in Australia to the extent of his ability.

In the obituary notice of Marcus Clarke contributed by Mr. H. G. Turner to the
Melbourne Review (an extract from which I gave in a preceding chapter) he stated that
the former had 'retained some strong friendships to the day of his death'. One of these
friendships was that of Dr. Patrick Moloney who shared with Marcus his capacity for
the enjoyment of a joke and his love of the observation of human nature.

These two, on the evening of a certain St. Patrick's day (March 17th) were in the
private bar of Garton's Hotel overlooking the public bar with its separate entrance from
the street (a feature of all large Australian hotels) when there entered two men, splendid
physical specimens of manhood, evidently 'digging mates' (a sacred relationship in
Australia) and drank together, each, according to the proper etiquette, standing treat in
turn. One of them, obviously an Irishman, wanting a third drink, his friend objected.

'It's St. Patrick's day', urged the Irishman, 'the saint who banished the snakes from Ireland.' 'Well', replied the other, 'there are no snakes in New Zealand, as you and I found out when we were working at the Thames River and you can't say St. Patrick ever came there.' The Irishman was moving away nonplussed, when he returned suddenly with a gleam of fun in his eyes. 'Look here, Jim', said he, 'Do you think, when St. Patrick put down his foot to banish the snakes and bless Ireland, he gave it a twopenny-halfpenny, six-inch blessing? No Sir! It went right through the worruld and came out at the Antipodes!' They drank and as (adds Dr. Moloney) immediately afterwards I saw Clarke off to his train, his laugh, the most musical I ever heard, lighting up his handsome face, is a treasured memory.

I have myself, earlier in these reminiscences, alluded to this silvery laugh of his, so musical in its cadence and in youth so easily provoked, as an individual characteristic impossible for anyone who had once known him intimately ever to entirely forget. There must have been a potent spell in it and in his whole personality, for when, many years after he had sped to that 'undiscovered country / From whose bourn no traveller returns,' I began to re-read the letters I had received from him, written chiefly from Swinton and Ledcourt Stations, I found myself once more in spirit under its sway. My mood, in fact, resembled that of the man depicted by Marcus himself, 'middle-aged and world-worn,' but who, 'when turning over some old drawer with much comminatory muttering' lights upon a packet of letters, yellow with age and who, recognising the handwriting, experiences a sudden revulsion of feeling. For these letters recall to him in a flash of memory the personality of the writer and summon early associations connected with them, so that he goes down to dinner mournfully repeating, 'Gilliam's dead – God rest her soul! How I loved her twenty years syne!'

A proof that even during the last few troubled years of his life, Marcus Clarke could upon occasion throw off depression and conquer untoward circumstances by sheer force of character and the infectious spirit of natural gaiety of temperament was supplied me by a member of his family. The incident actually occurred within some months of his death and was brought about, primarily, of course by his own pecuniary embarrassments.

A bailiff had been sent to his house to take possession of his goods and chattels on behalf of his creditors. It was not, alas! the first visit of its kind. Mrs. Clarke, returning home from a walk in the course of a certain afternoon, found to her surprise on re-entering her house, a stranger entertaining the children. He rose and greeted her politely but – as it seemed to her – with considerable embarrassment and proceeded to explain the meaning of his presence speaking in a low tone of voice and in such a manner as not to rouse the suspicions of the children. In possession of this unwelcome intelligence she naturally took the first opportunity that offered of asking Marcus how it was that he had again allowed matters to come to such a pass? Her distress was great and it was with downright astonishment that even she (despite her knowledge of the surprises of Marcus's character) heard him reply, with a ringing laugh, and in the very language of his school days, 'Where is my festive Cuss? I'll settle him!' She implored him to be discreet but on learning that the bailiff was in the kitchen, he immediately rushed in and before the astonished functionary had time to recover from his surprise and collect his scattered wits, had slapped him with gentle familiarity on the back and greeted him with the following extraordinary words of welcome, 'Hallo, John, how are you, my boy! Didn't expect to see you so soon – how's the family?' a greeting followed-up by a rapid glance and gesture of explanation to the servant-maid and the announcement in a matter-of-fact tone to the children (as if affording information unwittingly forgotten by him) that the stranger was their 'Uncle John, from – the East' (he added vaguely) whose visit (as they would probably surmise from his manner) was not quite unexpected by their parents but of the date of whose arrival they had doubtless been uncertain.

The maid looked suspicious, and Mrs. Clarke rather aghast, as her husband hurriedly escorted this newly discovered relative of his into the dining-room insisting that he must give him the pleasure of his society at dinner. During the progress of the meal Marcus, who had taken the measure of his man, aided by the effect of the viands and the wine with which he plied him, had succeeded in effecting such a change in the demeanour of his strange guest by his conversation and personal charm that at a later period of the evening Mrs. Clarke overheard snatches of conversation and peals of laughter issuing from Marcus's study to which they had adjourned for coffee and cigars. Thus encouraged, she entered to find the two men on the friendliest possible terms: the bailiff convulsed with laughter and somewhat excited by the wine with which he had been liberally regaled, expressing in rather unparliamentary language his appreciation of some anecdote with which Marcus had just entertained him, for he proved to be a man of some little education, at least of sufficient to be able to appreciate Marcus Clarke's humorous sallies.

The result of all these manoeuvres was that the immediate difficulties occasioned by the bailiff's presence in the house were for the time being surmounted and that for the next few days 'Uncle John from the East' chopped wood and did odd jobs about the house – in short played up to the part of the hardly expected but welcome guest so strangely thrust upon him until, for some reason I am unable to give, but which is comparatively immaterial, he saw fit to take his departure confiding to a friend (as it afterwards transpired) that sooner than see Marcus Clarke suffer, he would prefer to go to prison himself.

Marcus had thus completely succeeded in fairly fascinating a hostile intruder out of his duty but, in spite of its comic aspects, the ignominy of the situation was not really lost upon him and in his heart of hearts, he felt it keenly. In any case the incident seems to prove the truth of the Chief of the Melbourne Public Library, Mr. E. La Touche Armstrong's contention when in allusion to Marcus Clarke, he wrote:

> If his services to the institution were not what they might have been, he at least gained the admiration and affection of his colleagues, and pardonable pride may be felt in the fact that one who was so auspiciously connected with the early literature of Australia was also closely associated with the Public Library … Sir Redmond Barry and his fellow Trustees, and, indeed, most people who knew him, were very merciful to Marcus Clarke. Faults that would have gone far to ruin another man were overlooked in him. Genius has an imperialism of its own, and save perhaps by his creditors, Marcus Clarke was generally regarded as *Legibus solutus*.

Francis Adams, writing a few years after Marcus's death during a visit to Australia, touched lightly on these faults and it is indeed certain that as in the very analogous case of the American poet Poe, they were weaknesses of which far too much has been made. For he generously says about Marcus in this connection, 'His reckless Bohemianism still furnishes endless, more or less disparaging and apocryphal anecdotes to the good Philistines of Melbourne; but the pathos of his life, the charm of his lighter work and the power of his solitary novel (sic) attract one to him with a deep, personal interest and affection,' whilst Mr. Walter Murdoch, writing comparatively recently, remarks in allusion to these 'more or less disparaging and apocryphal anecdotes,' that it is not for him to rake among them with their 'ancient and fish-like smell,' adding

> it is abundantly clear that Clarke's doings were not, on the whole, such as Dr. Smiles would have loved to chronicle. It is clear that he did not invariably act wisely, and that he spoke at times even less wisely than he acted. What then? Whose biography can

afford to dispense with some reticence in the writing and some charity in the reading? Not yours, nor mine, I fear. 'His faults', says a recent critic writing of Henry Fielding, 'were those which spring from too easy a temper and too mercurial a disposition.' That, after all, is the worst that will be said of Marcus Clarke, when the verdict of posterity comes to be uttered.

Sir Leslie Stephen was of opinion that the secret of R. L. Stevenson's exalted position in literature during the later years of his life was to be found in his personal charm. 'He had the good fortune' says Sir Leslie, 'to number some of the leading critics among his personal friends and under the spell of his individuality they lifted him to a pinnacle of fame which has already become a little shaky and is scarcely likely to be upheld by posterity.' With Marcus Clarke it was far otherwise; for although possessed of great personal charm, he was too apt to give offence by his plain speaking and by the keen invective of his controversial methods, not to mention his occasional eccentricities, to escape making some enemies. He was, in fact, in these respects more like his American prototype, Edgar Allan Poe, (to whom I have so frequently referred in these pages) misunderstood by his contemporaries and thus it came about perhaps that less than justice was done him occasionally during his life and even for some years after his death.

In some respects he resembled R. L. Stevenson, both in the nature of his genius and in disposition. At all events the so called Bohemianism of both appears to have been of the same stamp. A critic of Stevenson's writes with considerable penetration on the subject of this idiosyncrasy in my opinion:

> The Bohemian, taking Stevenson's version of the character, the man who looks from the outside upon the ordinary, humdrum citizen, may be a very fascinating personage, but he really lacks something. Delighted with the exceptional and the picturesque, he has less insight into the more ordinary and after all, most important springs of action.

Secondly he resembled Stevenson in the conscientious thoroughness of his work and the artistic finish of his style. Francis Adams in his careful summary and comparison of the merits and the limitations of the two representative Australian writers, Marcus Clarke and Adam Lindsay Gordon (the steeple-chase rider and ballad-writer) says of the former that a certain classical sense saved him from Balzac's pedantry, if he was unable to fathom Balzac's profundity, adding in reference to the novel *For the Term of his Natural Life* what is, of course, sufficiently obvious, 'None of his other works, assuredly, could have given him his European fame; but his minor work as a whole forms an important adminicle of his fame.'

I have endeavoured in the foregoing pages to give a general idea of the nature and scope of this 'minor work.' Some readers may well indeed prefer the picturesque sketches of Australian scenery, the light banter of the 'Peripatetic Philosopher', and the intensely interesting narratives of the early days of settlement in the island-continent, or the poetic imagery of some of his essays and verses, even the skilful touch in his one historical romance *Chidiock Tichbourne* and some of his plays to the theme of that powerful but gloomy and hopelessly depressing story *For the Term of his Natural Life*.

'Brilliant,' continues Francis Adams, 'is a word we do not use in speaking of the greatest names in literature; it is hard to speak of Marcus Clarke without using it again and again … From beginning to end it was the same. Such was his unfailing literary tact that, whatever else he might be, he could never be dull.'

Thirdly he resembled Stevenson in the absence of jealousy he exhibited towards his contemporaries. The late Mr. Patchett Martin (a fellow journalist but by no means an indiscriminate admirer) in an article contributed by him to the (London) *Temple Bar Magazine*[80] not very long after the death of Marcus Clarke, dwells on this trait in the latter's character:

> there was a worthy side to our author's character, which seems strangely to have escaped the notice even of his local panegyrists. I allude to that entire absence of that bane of literary life so aptly called by the Laureate, 'narrowing envy.' … It was this absence of jealousy, as much as his recognised literary talents, that placed Marcus Clarke, despite his want of earnestness of purpose, at the head of the rising literature of Australia …
>
> He was the friend of any Australian writer of talent, and I can well remember his generous commendations of the gifted colonial lady who writes under the *nom de plume* of 'Tasma,' though he had not her personal acquaintance.
>
> He was always glad to use his press influence to bring into prominence the merits of any rising writer, and his advice to such was more kindly than might have been expected from one of his temperament.

FINIS.

---

80   See *Temple Bar Magazine*.

Abbreviations

ADB	*Australian Dictionary of Biography*
AE	*The Austral Edition of the Selected Works of Marcus Clarke*, ed. Hamilton Mackinnon, Fergusson and Mitchell, Melbourne, 1890
ALS	*Australian Literary Studies*
AT	*Australian Tales* (A. W. Bruce, Melbourne, 1896), reprinted as *Australian Tales of the Bush* (George Robertson, Melbourne, 1897), both reissues of Mackinnon's *AE*, part II, 'Australian Tales and Sketches'
BE	Brian Elliott, *Marcus Clarke*, Clarendon Press, Oxford, 1958
BW	Bill Wannan, ed., *A Marcus Clarke Reader*, Lansdowne Press, Melbourne, 1963
CC	*A Colonial City: High and Low Life; Selected Journalism of Marcus Clarke*, ed. L. T. Hergenhan, University of Queensland Press, St Lucia, 1972
CH	Cyril Hopkins
GMH	Gerard Manley Hopkins
HNL	Marcus Clarke, *His Natural Life*, George Robertson, Melbourne, 1874; Richard Bentley, London, 1875; serialised in the *Australian Journal*, March 1870 – June 1872
LMC	*The Well-Selected Library of Mr Marcus Clarke*, May & Company, Melbourne, [1874]; reprinted in facsimile in McL
LO	Marcus Clarke, *Long Odds*, Clarson, Massina, Melbourne, 1869
MC	*Marcus Clarke* ed. Michael Wilding, University of Queensland Press, St Lucia, 1976 (Portable Australian Authors series), 2nd edn 1988 (Australian Authors series)
McL	Ian F. McLaren, *Marcus Clarke: An Annotated Bibliography*, Library Council of Victoria, Melbourne, 1982
ML	Mitchell Library, State Library of New South Wales
MV	*The Marcus Clarke Memorial Volume*, ed. Hamilton Mackinnon, Cameron, Laing & Co, Melbourne, 1884
OT	Marcus Clarke, *Old Tales of a Young Country*, Mason, Firth & McCutcheon, Melbourne, 1871; facsimile reprint, introduced by Joan Poole, Sydney University Press, Sydney, 1972
PP	*The Peripatetic Philosopher by 'Q'* (George Robertson, Melbourne, 1869) (a selection from Clarke's column in the *Australasian*, 23 November 1867 – 17 April 1869; the column continued until 11 June 1870)
SLV	State Library of Victoria
ST	Marcus Clarke, *Stories*, introduction by Michael Wilding, Hale & Iremonger, Sydney, 1983; reissue of Mackinnon *AE* part II, 'Australian Tales and Sketches' (*AT*) and *AE* part III 'Stories – Imaginative and Fanciful'

Notes

Author's Preface

p. 003   No complete biography: the first – and so far, only – full length biography is *Marcus Clarke*, by Brian Elliott (1958); it is now in need of updating and expanding in the light of later Clarke research. Cyril's MS is one of the two main sources for BE, the other was Hamilton Mackinnon (BE 268), see note below.

p. 003   Forty-three years ago: Cyril originally wrote 'a quarter of a century ago'. From this we can deduce that the manuscript was written originally around 1906, and was revised in 1924, with some minor revisions made between these two dates; cf. note to Ch. 9.

p. 003   A well-known Melbourne journalist: Walter Murdoch, in 'Marcus Clarke', *Argus*, 22 October 1904, 4, collected in Murdoch, *Loose Leaves* (George Robertson, Melbourne, 1910) 50–5.

p. 004   Henry Gyles Turner wrote on 'Marcus Clarke' in the *Melbourne Review*, 7, 25, January 1882, 1–15, and in *Once a Month* (London) 3, 4, October 1885, 241–6. The two essays were absorbed into the collaborative volume he wrote with Alexander Sutherland, *The Development of Australian Literature* (1898), which deals with Clarke (300–43).

p. 004   Hamilton Nisbet Crawfurd Mackinnon (1846–97) was born in India to a Scots family from the Isle of Skye, and emigrated to Australia c. 1867, where he variously worked on the *Wagga Wagga Advertiser*, as a stock and station agent, in a bank, and as a literary agent. His uncle, Lachlan Mackinnon, was one of the proprietors of the *Argus* newspaper in Melbourne, 'but there was no cordiality between the uncle and the nephew' (BE 78–9). He separated from his wife and family c. 1881, and became a lodger in the house of Marcus Clarke's widow, where he died from a gunshot wound after 'fooling about with revolvers' with a friend, Matthew Aikman. Mackinnon's 'Biography' of Clarke first appeared in *The Marcus Clarke Memorial Volume* (1884), which he edited; McLaren (1982) notes that 'large sections were deleted as they were considered libellous, leaving asterisked sections in the book' (133). The amended biography, with further deletions and changes, was later printed in *The Austral Edition of the Selected Works of Marcus Clarke* (1890) and reprinted in Clarke's *Australian Tales* (1896), *Australian Tales of the Bush* (1897) and *Stories of Australia in the Early Days* (1897).

p. 004   Opening sentence: *MV*, 13.

p. 004   Bret Harte (1836–1902) was born in Albany, New York, and taken to California
           when he was eighteen. He achieved international fame with his stories of Western life,
           collected in *The Luck of Roaring Camp* (1870) which Clarke reviewed in the *Australian
           Journal*, March 1871, 389–90; Clarke reviewed Harte's poems in the *Australian Journal*,
           July 1871, 645. He mentions Harte in 'The Traveller of the Period', *Argus*, 13 April
           1872, 6. On Harte's influence on Clarke, see Michael Wilding, 'Weird Melancholy:
           Inner and Outer Landscapes in Marcus Clarke's Stories', in Wilding, *Studies in
           Classic Australian Fiction* (1997) 14–16. Clarke admired and was influenced by many
           American writers. The protagonist of *HNL* takes the name of an American poet,
           Rufus Dawes. Clarke at various times refers to the works of Poe, Melville, Whitman,
           Longfellow, Emerson, Washington Irving, Fennimore Cooper, Nathaniel Hawthorne
           (from whose *Twice Told Tales* (1837) he derived the title of his 'Old Tales Retold' series
           in the weekly *Australasian*, 19 February 1870 – 24 June 1871, collected as *Old Tales
           of a Young Country*) and Oliver Wendell Holmes, to whom he dedicated *Holiday Peak
           and Other Stories* (1873). He refers to Melville's novels in 'Henry Kendall', *Leader*
           supplement, 19 March 1881. See further in Clarke's discussion of American literature
           in his 'Noah's Ark' column, *Australasian*, 25 May 1872, where he refers to Whitman,
           Twain, Harte, Longfellow, Poe, Hawthorne, Holmes. He refers to *The Scarlet Letter* in
           'Taking Mine Ease in Mine Inn', *Australasian*, 3 July 1869, 8; to Fennimore Cooper in
           'In Outer Darkness', *Australasian*, 21 August 1869, 232. *LMC* lists Bret Harte's *Poetry
           and Prose*, Hawthorne's *Twice-Told Tales*, *The House with the Seven Gables* and *The
           Scarlet Letter*, Herman Melville's *Mardi, Omoo, and Typee*, Holmes' *The Professor at the
           Breakfast Table*, *The Works of Edgar Allan Poe*, and Artemus Ward's *Lecture*.

p. 004   Robert Louis Stevenson (1850–94), Scots novelist, author of *New Arabian Nights*
           (1882), *Treasure Island* (1883), *The Strange Case of Dr Jekyll and Mr Hyde* (1886),
           Kidnapped (1886), *Island Nights' Entertainments* (1893), etc. Stevenson settled in Samoa
           in October 1890. Hopkins draws on a letter of Stevenson's from Samoa in Ch. 6, and
           frequently cites him in discussing Clarke.

p. 004   Rudyard Kipling (1865–1936), English novelist and poet, born in Bombay, whose
           books include *The Jungle Book* (1894), *Just So Stories* (1902) and *Kim* (1901).

p. 004   *For the Term of His Natural Life*: the title given to Clarke's novel posthumously when
           it was reissued the year following his death (Richard Bentley, London, 1882; George
           Robertson, Melbourne, 1882) (McL 42). Clarke's title was *His Natural Life* for both the
           serial and the book version.

p. 004   Lord Lytton: 'the present Lord Lytton declared that it so fascinated him that he could
           not lay it down until he had finished it', Arthur Patchett Martin, 'An Australian
           Novelist', *Temple Bar*, 71, May 1884, 103. Lord Lytton (1831–91) was the son of the
           novelist Bulwer Lytton (1803–73); a poet (publishing initially as 'Owen Meredith'), he
           was Viceroy of India, 1876–80; Marcus's cousin Sir Andrew Clarke was a member of
           the Viceroy's Council at that time.

p. 004   Desmond Byrne, *Australian Writers* (1896) 29.

p. 004   William Makepeace Thackeray (1811–63), English novelist. Clarke was familiar with
           his work and refers to him in *LO*, in his essay 'Charles Dickens', *Argus*, 8 July 1870, 7,
           and in 'Of French Novels', *Argus*, 2 February 1872, 6. Thackeray's *Dennis Duval* (1864)
           and *Vanity Fair* (1847–48) are referred to in Clarke's story 'Holiday Peak', *Australasian*,
           18 January 1873, 72; 25 January, 104. *Vanity Fair* is referred to in Ch. 17 below, and
           with *Barry Lyndon* (1852) in *Old Tales of a Young Country* (1871). Thackeray's early
           journalism is referred to in Clarke's text to the *Photographs of Pictures in the National
           Gallery, Melbourne*, quoted in Ch. 26. Clarke acknowledges Thackeray's influence on
           his journalism in the preface to *The Peripatetic Philosopher* (1869) quoted in Ch. 24,
           and he wrote on Thackeray in the *Leader* supplement, 30 October 1880. Thackeray
           is cited as an influence on his novel *Long Odds* (1869) by H. M. Hyndman in his
           review in the *Argus*, 2 July 1869, 5–6. Thackeray was the first editor of the *Cornhill
           Magazine*, to which Manley Hopkins (the father of Cyril and Gerard) contributed,

along with Trollope, Mrs Gaskell, Charles Reade, George Eliot, Tennyson, Browning, and Swinburne amongst others. *LMC* lists Thackeray's *Vanity Fair*, *The Newcomes*, *Pendennis*, *The Virginians*, *Catherine*, *Little Travels*, *The Fitz-Boodle Papers*, *Barry Lyndon*, *Titmarsh*, and *Paris Sketch Book*.

p. 005   Marcus Clarke, *The Future Australian Race* (1877).

p. 005   Clarke seems to foretell the federation: the last verse of Clarke's poem 'An Australian Paean – 1876', 'written to commemorate the achievement by Australian workers of an eight-hour working day' (BW 55–7). MS has 'If England gave us birth'.

p. 005   Adam Lindsay Gordon (1833–70), born in the Azores of English and Scottish parents and educated at the Royal Military Academy, Woolwich, at Cheltenham College, and at the Royal Grammar School, Worcester, before emigrating to Australia at the age of twenty in 1853, where he served the South Australian Mounted Police for two years. After various ventures in horse breaking and horse racing, Gordon published two volumes of poetry at his own expense in 1867, *Ashtaroth* (Clarson, Massina, Melbourne) and *Sea Spray and Smoke Drift* (George Robertson, Melbourne). In 1868 he came to Victoria where he met Clarke and became a member of the Yorick Club – see note to Ch. 17. Clarke's *Colonial Monthly*, December 1868, 262–5, hailed Gordon as 'the most Australian of our literary aspirants … We look forward, with some pride and much hope, to the day when it will be a boast to have discovered his genius in 1868.' Clarke's parody of Gordon's verse, 'Mark Clancy's Leap', appeared in *Humbug*, 22 December 1869, 11, reprinted in the *Australian Journal*, January 1870, 309–10. Gordon shot himself on 24 June 1870, the day after his *Bush Ballads and Galloping Rhymes* was published, in debt and unable to pay the printer. Clarke contributed a preface to the posthumous reprint of *Sea Spray and Smoke Drift* (Clarson, Massina, Melbourne, 1876), which was reprinted in the collected *Poems of the Late Adam Lindsay Gordon* (A. H. Massina, Melbourne, 1880) and in successive editions. McLaren collected some eighty-eight different printings and issues of the preface (McL 92). It is reprinted in BW and *MC*. Shorn of the specific references to Gordon, it is reprinted as 'Australian Scenery' in *MV*, *AE*, *AT* and *ST*, and in various anthologies subsequently. It incorporated in its concluding two-fifths material Clarke had previously written to accompany the photographic reproduction of Louis Buvelot's *Waterpool near Coleraine* and Nicholas Chevalier's *The Buffalo Ranges* in *Photographs of Pictures in the National Gallery, Melbourne*, ed. Marcus Clarke (1874), reprinted in *CC*. See S. R. Simmons, *A Problem and a Solution: Marcus Clarke and the Writing of* Long Odds (1946); L. T. Hergenhan, 'Marcus Clarke and the Colonial Landscape', *Quadrant*, 13, 1969, 31–51; Leonie Kramer, 'The Literary Reputation of Adam Lindsay Gordon', *ALS*, 1, 1963, 43–4; Brian Kiernan, *Criticism* (1974) 7–12; and Laurel Clark, 'Marcus Clarke and F. F. Baillière', *Margin*, 40, November 1996, 27–8. Clarke took a line from Gordon's poem 'A Dedication' from *Sea Spray and Smoke Drift* for the title of his novel *'Twixt Shadow and Shine* (1875; 1893). He wrote on Gordon in the *Leader* supplement, 30 October 1880, and refers to him in his piece on Kendall in the *Leader* supplement, 19 March 1881, reprinted *CC*. ML holds a letter from Gordon to Clarke quoted in the Introduction and by Mackinnon in *MV*, *AE*. *LMC* lists Gordon's *Ashtaroth*, *Bush Ballads and Galloping Rhymes* and *Seaspray and Smoke Drift*, special edition, on toned paper.

p. 005   *My Brilliant Career*: UK edition, Blackwood, Edinburgh and London, 1904, 187; the first novel of Miles Franklin (1879–1954), Australian novelist, published with an introduction by Henry Lawson, 1901. CH is not necessarily correct to infer that Clarke's bush stories were unknown to Franklin: Gordon's legend had grown, and had been heightened by the success of the contemporary balladists Paterson and Lawson. Clarke wrote of the bush, and presciently, but not in ballad form, or in ways that would ignite the bush legend so noticeably; and he was of course renowned for his treatment of the convict 'legend'. The passage of twenty years since Clarke's death, and the relative inaccessibility of his writings on the bush, might as credibly explain

Franklin's omission of Clarke from her list. Other references to bush writers and writing in Franklin's novel occur, for example, on pp. 43–4, 71 and 118.

p. 005 Henry Lawson (1867–1922), Australian short story writer and poet. He expresses his admiration for *HNL* in 'A Fragment of Autobiography', in *Henry Lawson, Autobiographical and Other Writings 1887–1922*, ed. Colin Roderick, two volumes (Angus & Robertson, Sydney, 1972) vol. 2, 193, and in brief comments in the preliminaries to Hilary Lofting's edition of the serial version of *HNL* (Angus & Robertson, Sydney, 1929).

p. 005 Henry Kendall (1839–82), Australian poet. He lived in Melbourne April 1869 – October 1870 and was a fellow member of the Yorick Club with Clarke, and contributor to the *Humbug* under Clarke's editorship. Clarke's parody of Kendall's verse, 'Glycera', appeared in *Humbug*, 22 December 1869, 6, reprinted in the *Australian Journal*, January 1870, 309–10. Clarke wrote on Kendall in the *Leader* supplement, 19 March 1881, 3, reprinted *CC*. Kendall wrote an obituary of Clarke in the *Sydney Mail*, 13 August 1881, 277. His elegy 'In Memoriam – Marcus Clarke', *Bulletin*, 3 September 1881, 1, is reprinted in *MV* and *AE*, and together with his comments on Clarke's work in 'Notes upon Men and Books no. 8 – Men of Letters in New South Wales and Victoria', *The Freeman's Journal*, 2 March 1872, in *Henry Kendall*, ed. Leonie Kramer and A. D. Hope (1973) 81–3. On Kendall's often fraught relationship with Clarke, see Ken Stewart, '"A Careworn Writer for the Press": Henry Kendall in Melbourne', in R. McDougall, ed., *Henry Kendall, The Muse of Australia* (Centre for Australian Language and Literature Studies, University of New England, Armidale, 1991), reprinted in Ken Stewart, *Investigations in Australian Literature* (2000) 47–88. *LMC* lists Kendall's *Leaves from Australian Forests*.

p. 005 twelve best novels: *Argus*, 22 August 1927, 15.

p. 005 Sir Walter Scott (1771–1832), Scots novelist and poet. Clarke's espousal of the 'romance of reality' of Charles Dickens against the 'medieval romance' of Scott is expressed in his essay 'Charles Dickens' in the *Argus*, 8 July 1870. Clarke mentions Scott in *HNL*. *LMC* lists Walter Scott's *Woodstock* and the Poetical Works.

p. 005 Charles Dickens (1812–70), English novelist, author of *Oliver Twist* (1837–38), *Dombey and Son* (1848), *David Copperfield* (1849–50), *Our Mutual Friend* (1864–65), etc. Clarke wrote an obituary tribute, 'Charles Dickens', in the *Argus*, 8 July 1870, 7. He acknowledges his influence in the preface to *The Peripatetic Philosopher*, quoted Ch. 24. Clarke refers to him in *LO*, in his review of Bret Harte's *The Luck of Roaring Camp*, *Australian Journal*, March 1871, 389–90, in the 'Peripatetic Philosopher' column, *Australasian*, 9 February 1868, 177, 19 March 1870, 358, 26 March 1870, 401, in 'A Cheap Lodging-House', *Australasian*, 31 July 1869, 136. Dickens is cited as an influence on Clarke's novel *Long Odds* by H. M. Hyndman in his review in the *Argus*, Melbourne, 2 July 1869, 5–6. According to Hopkins, Ch. 2, *Barnaby Rudge* (1841) was 'a story that Marcus admired when at school and which, it appears, in after life he preferred to any other of Dickens' novels'. Clarke's story 'A Mining Township', his only story ever sold to a magazine in Britain, appeared in *All the Year Round, incorporating Household Words*, the journal founded and edited by Charles Dickens, as 'An Australian Mining Township', 22 February 1873, 352–7; letter of acceptance is in the Marcus Clarke papers, Mitchell Library MSS ZA819, State Library of New South Wales. *LMC* lists Dickens' *Nicholas Nickleby*, with Cruikshank's original plates, *Master Humphrey's Clock*, containing *The Old Curiosity Shop* and *Barnaby Rudge*, two volumes in one, with illustrations by Cattermole, *Little Dorrit*, *A Tale of Two Cities*, *The Night Mail*, *Bleak House*, *Dombey and Son*, *Edwin Drood*, *David Copperfield*, *Our Mutual Friend*, *Sketches by Boz* and Sala's *Life of Dickens*.

p. 006 George Eliot, pseudonym of Mary Ann Evans (1819–90), English novelist, author of *Adam Bede* (1859), *Middlemarch* (1871–72), etc. MC refers to her in 'Noah's Ark' *Australasian*, 25 May 1872, and 'The Buncle Correspondence', *Argus*, 2 February 1872, reprinted *CC*. *Middlemarch* was serialised in the *Australasian* in 1872.

p. 006   R. D. Blackmore (1825–1900), English novelist, author of *Lorna Doone* (1869).

p. 006   Charles Kingsley (1819–75), English novelist and poet, author of *Westward Ho!* (1855),
             The Water Babies (1863), etc. Kingsley's *The Roman and the Teuton* is listed in *LMC*.

p. 006   Alexandre Dumas (1802–70), French novelist and dramatist. Clarke refers to him in
             his essay 'Balzac and Modern French Literature', *Australasian*, 3 August 1867, in *LO*,
             and in 'Of French Novels', *Argus*, 2 February 1872, 6. He alludes to his *The Count of
             Monte Cristo* (1844–45) in *HNL*, in 'Holiday Peak', *Australasian*, 18 January 1873, 72;
             25 January, 104, and in 'Gypsies of the Sea: or the Island of Gold', Melbourne *Herald*,
             24–31 December, 4, 1874, reprinted in *Sensational Tales*, *AE* and *ST* as 'A Modern
             Eldorado'. Its account of Edmond Dantès' imprisonment on a false charge provided
             one of the models for *HNL*. A copy is listed in *LMC*. *MC* discusses Dumas in 'Of
             French Novels', *Argus*, 2 February 1872. He refers to Dumas' *The Three Musketeers*
             (1844–45) in Ch. 11 below, and in 'In a Bark Hut', *Australasian*, 17 May 1873.
             Clarke's adaptation of Dumas' novel *Le Vicomte de Bragelonne* (1848–50) as *Plot!* was
             performed in Melbourne in August 1872. *LMC* lists Dumas' *The Count of Monte
             Cristo*, *Chicôt the Jester*, *Dr Basilius*, *The Conspirators*, *Nanon*, *The Two Dianas*, *The Three
             Musketeers*, *Twenty Years After*, *The Vicomte de Bragelonne*, *Forty-five Guardsmen*, *Taking
             the Bastille*, *The Queen's Necklace*, *The Countess de Charny*, *The Memoirs of a Physician*,
             Le Chevalier de Maison Rouge, *La Reine Margot* and *Glacier Land*.

p. 006   Charlotte Bronte (1816–55), English novelist. Clarke refers to her *Jane Eyre* (1847) in
             his review of Bret Harte's *The Luck of Roaring Camp*, *Australian Journal*, March 1871,
             389–90, reprinted in *CC* and *MC*.

p. 006   Mrs Craik (1826–87), English novelist, author of *John Halifax, Gentleman* (1856).

p. 006   Henry Kingsley (1830–76), English novelist. The younger brother of Charles Kingsley,
             he lived in Australia from 1853 to 1858. Of his twenty-one books, *The Recollections
             of Geoffry Hamlyn* (1859) and *The Hillyars and the Burtons* (1865) are both set in
             Australia. The conservative stance of *Geoffry Hamlyn* annoyed many Australian writers,
             notably Joseph Furphy; Kingsley's comment that Australia was the 'workingman's
             paradise' provided the title, sardonically applied, for William Lane's novel *The
             Workingman's Paradise* (1890). Clarke's admiration for *Geoffry Hamlyn* – the 'best
             Australian novel that has been, and probably will be written' – is expressed in the
             preface to his novel *Long Odds* (1869). Clarke refers to *Geoffry Hamlyn* in a letter to
             Hopkins printed in Ch. 8, and in his story 'Hunted Down', *Australasian*, 6 May 1871,
             quoted in Ch. 25. Kingsley turns up in person in 'The Café Lutetia', *Weekly Times*, 28
             February 1874, 9, and in 'Holiday Peak', *Australasian*, 18 January 1873, 72; 25 January,
             104. See further, notes to Ch. 16. *LMC* lists Kingsley's *Ravenshoe*.

p. 006   *Felix and Felicitas*: Clarke's unfinished novel. Page proofs of the opening chapters are
             preserved in the Mitchell Library, State Library of New South Wales. Clarke negotiated
             with the London publisher Richard Bentley for publication, without success (BE 188,
             335–6). See Wendy Abbott-Young, 'The Felix and Felicitas Papers of Marcus Clarke:
             An Annotated Edition with an Introduction' (1987). Cyril's comment that 'in the
             following pages will be found the full text of *Felix and Felicitas*' suggests that at some
             point he intended to include in his biography such material of the novel as existed, but
             it does not appear in the MS.

p. 006   Isle of Wight: the Hopkins family regularly holidayed there. It became a popular
             holiday spot after Queen Victoria acquired Osborne House there in 1845. R. B. Martin
             in his biography of GMH reproduces two of Gerard's drawings of Shanklin on the Isle
             of Wight from 1863 and 1866 (plates 9a, 9b). (Robert Bernard Martin, *Gerard Manley
             Hopkins: A Very Private Life*, 1991, 12–13)

p. 006   a brother: this is the first reference to Gerard Manley Hopkins (1844–89). He was the
             eldest of eight surviving children of Manley Hopkins (1818–97) and his wife Kate
             (1821–1920). Cyril was next in age to Gerard. According to R. B. Martin, 'The two
             brothers got along well enough but seem never to have been close; when they were

young, Gerard tended to make fun of Cyril and to be a touch patronizing to him, as befitted his age'. (9)

p. 006   bodily weakness: the disease was anchylosis treated by an operation early in life, leaving the length of the left arm 'several inches short'. This did not impede Clarke's activities, indeed it may have spurred him on, as in his life at school where he was fond of diving, and later in Australia where he enjoyed riding, but he was sensitive about displaying it and 'habitually kept his left hand in his pocket;' see BE who quotes Cyril (254) and adds his own comment 6–7. This first meeting with the Hopkins brothers has been tentatively dated as June or July 1850, shortly after the father had been widowed (BE 6). Clarke would have been four at this time, Cyril the same and Gerard two years older; this seems early for such a vivid memory. Norman White, *Hopkins: A Literary Biography* (1992), dates the meeting as 1854, which seems more likely.

p. 006   Patrick Moloney (1843–1904), born Ireland, migrated to Australia 1862, where he was one of the first two students to graduate in medicine from Melbourne University. Editor of the *Australian Medical Journal* and contributor to Melbourne *Punch* and the *Australasian*. A member of the Yorick Club and a friend of Clarke's, whom he attended in his last illness. Moloney's memoir of Clarke has not been traced. His brother James, a solicitor, was a friend of Adam Lindsay Gordon's; his anecdote of a day spent with Clarke, Gordon and Walter Montgomery is given in *The Poems of Adam Lindsay Gordon*, ed. Frank Maldon Robb, xxi–xxii; MS of James on MC, Barr Smith Library, University of Adelaide (McLaren 3243). On Patrick Moloney see Hugh McCrae, *My Father and My Father's Friends*, 56–9; G. G. McCrae, '"The Golden Age of Australian Literature" 1860–1870,' *Southerly*, 5, 1944, 39–46, and Harold Love, *James Edward Neild: Victorian Virtuoso* (1989) passim.

p. 007   *La Peau de Chagrin* (*The Wild Ass's Skin*) (1831), by the French novelist Honoré de Balzac (1799–1850). Clarke refers to it in 'Melbourne Streets at Midnight', *Argus*, 28 February 1868. Clarke's love and admiration of the fiction of Balzac is testified in his essay 'Balzac and Modern French Literature', *Australasian*, 3 August 1867, 136. Clarke wrote about him and other French novelists in 'Of French Novels' in 'The Buncle Correspondence', *Argus*, 2 February 1872, 6. He refers to him in *LO*, *OT* and in his obituary of Dickens, *Argus*, 18 July 1870. The Rev North reads Balzac's *La Fausse Maîtresse* (1841) in *HNL*. The journalist Bland sighs 'with lost illusions' in *LO*. Doré's illustrations to Balzac's *Le Succube* are referred to in the first of Clarke's 'Lower Bohemia' articles, 'A Night at the Immigrants' Home', *Australasian*, 12 June 1869, 762–3, and 'Taking Mine Ease in Mine Inn', *Australasian*, 3 July 1869, 8. In letters to Hopkins Clarke wrote of reading *Eugénie Grandet* (1833), *Gobseck* (1830), *La recherche de l'absolu* (1834) and *Le père Goriot* (1834); see Ch. 17. *LMC* lists the forty-volume collected edition of Balzac's *Comédie humaine* (1842–48), and *Les Contes Drolatiques*, illustrated with 2,000 engravings by Gustave Doré.

Chapter 1

p. 009   Marcus's birth certificate records: Birth of Marcus Clarke – Date: 24 April 1846 – Place: 11 Leonard Place, Kensington. The family later moved. His mother's death certificate records: Amelia Elizabeth Clarke died aged 26 years, 13 March 1850 at 23 Notting Hill Terrace, Kensington. The SLV holds a copy of Dryden's *Virgil* with the inscription 'ex libris Marci Clerici free fly: Marcus Clarke 49 Gloucester Place London' (McL 2865).

p. 009   Holland House: a Jacobean mansion, built 1605–07 for Sir Walter Cope. In the mid-eighteenth century, it was bought by the Fox family. Henry Richard Vassall Fox, the third Lord Holland (1773–1840), had literary tastes and during the first four decades of the nineteenth century he entertained many writers there, including Sir Walter Scott, Wordsworth, Bulwer Lytton, Thomas Campbell, Thomas Moore, Washington

Irving, James Fennimore Cooper, Sydney Smith, Samuel Rogers, Hookham Frere, Mme de Staël, and Ugo Foscolo and artists such as C. R. Leslie, Wilkie and Canova. Under the fourth Lord Holland there was some revival of the salon in the 1850s, with such visitors as Macaulay, George Frederick Watts, and Alexandre Dumas, who wrote an account of driving through Holland Park, full of lowing herds and countless deer, to the ancient castle. See William Gaunt, *Kensington* (1958) 267, 32–3.

p. 010 John Thurloe (1616–68), was Oliver Cromwell's Secretary of State and ran the secret service. His portfolio of responsibilities did not include Ireland, but in his role as fine-grained enforcer of Cromwellianism, he remained closely in touch with the chief English representatives there, and especially with Fleetwood and Henry Cromwell, who were successively Lord Deputies in the 1650s. To have a claim expedited, going through Thurloe to get to Henry Cromwell or Fleetwood would have been a good route. On Thurloe's close dealings with the Lord Deputies, see Philip Aubrey, *Mr Secretary Thurloe: Cromwell's Secretary of State, 1652–1660* (1990) 131. Granting soldiers confiscated land in lieu of pay was a practice followed when parliament failed to allocate pay for the army that Oliver Cromwell used to put down the ten-year long Irish rebellion in 1649. Only a tiny minority of the New Model Army actually got any land, and preference went to higher ranks; as a colonel, Clarke's ancestor was well placed. The key work on the Cromwellian settlement in Ireland is Karl Bottigheimer, *English Money and Irish Land* (1971). BE does not include the Thurloe and Cromwell information.

p. 010 life of Lieutenant-General Sir Andrew Clarke: R. H. Vetch, *General Sir Andrew Clarke* (John Murray, London, 1905).

p. 010 Duc de Feltre: see MC, 'Duc de Feltre and the Clarke family', *Notes and Queries*, 26 July 1879, 67. BE, 232, claims that Cyril is in error about the Duc de Feltre connection – 'a private joke among Clarke's friends. It appears in several letters.' The nature of the joke is suggested by Cyril's note on Feltre ('His [Feltre's] special weakness was a taste for genealogy. He traced his descent from … so many illustrious families that Napoleon once rallied him …' It seems that Clarke may have used this allusion to the Feltre connection in playful self-irony amongst his close friends, though it would be a recondite joke. Perhaps, too, Clarke's affiliation with French culture, and a feeling of having lost caste in the colonies, led him to fantasise, even if in fun, a genealogical French connection of high birth. Hopkins apparently recognises the doubtfulness of the evidence about Feltre, even though he spends some time upon it (also including a long footnote) when he continues: 'However this may be it is better to adopt the account given in "The Life of L-G Sir Andrew Clarke".' Hopkins is skimpy about the family of the Scots/Irish male Clarkes, omitting information which Elliott gives about the important positions the Clarke relatives held in colonial Australia (BE 1–3). Hopkins states here and earlier in his MS that Sir Andrew Clarke's biographer was his source of information about the Clarke family history and Marcus's father, without naming him. He was R. H. Vetch, author of *General Sir Andrew Clarke* (John Murray, London, 1905). But later on in this chapter, Hopkins states that his information about Marcus's mother came directly from Sir Andrew Clarke.

p. 011 Sir Andrew Clarke (1824–1902), cousin of Marcus Clarke, son of Sir Andrew Clarke (1793–1847) who had been appointed Governor of Western Australia in 1846 and died there the following year. Andrew Jr was brought up by his paternal grandfather and two uncles (one of whom was Marcus Clarke's father) at the family home of Belmont, near Lifford, Ireland. A military engineer and public servant, he was private secretary to Sir William Denison, Governor of Van Diemen's Land, in 1846, and a superintendent of convict labour in Hobart. In 1853 he became surveyor-general of Victoria; he ensured that Melbourne should have a pure water supply, was responsible for much of the planning of Victoria's first railways, and installed the first electric telegraph from Melbourne to Williamstown. In 1853 he entered the Victorian Legislative Council as an official representative and later held the seat for South Melbourne in the

Legislative Assembly. He was grand master of the Melbourne freemasons. He initiated the Melbourne Museum of Natural History and was president of the Philosophical Institute (later the Royal Society of Victoria) in 1855. After visiting Italy, he urged the Victorian government to found the National Gallery of Victoria. He left Australia in 1862. From 1873 to 1875 he was governor of the Straits Settlements, and from 1875 to 1880 he had a seat on the Council of the Viceroy of India; the Viceroy was Lord Lytton, Bulwer Lytton's son. Sir Andrew is described as 'a great man, popular and sympathetic, to whom belongs the fame of being the first founder of the Federated Malay States. His features, as preserved in the splendid bust in the entrance hall of the Singapore Club, are a mirror of courage and determination' (*One Hundred Years of Singapore*, ed. Walter Makepeace, Gilbert E. Brooke and Roland St J. Braddell [John Murray, London, 1921] vol. 1, 101–2; new edition, [Oxford, 1991], introduction by C. M. Turnbull). The club no longer exists and the whereabouts of the bust are unknown. Clarke Quay in Singapore is named after him (www.clarkequay.com.sg). He was commandant of the School of Military Engineering, 1881–82, and from 1882 to 1886, inspector-general of fortifications in England. After Marcus's father's collapse, Sir Andrew, then in London, arranged to send Marcus to Melbourne where another uncle, James Langton Clarke, a County Court judge at Ararat, could perhaps keep an eye on him – though Ararat was 150 miles from Melbourne. Clarke may have stayed with James on first arriving in Australia (BE 29).

p. 012 'The Peripatetic Philosopher': a humorous column by Clarke about Melbourne life and general news published in the weekly *Australasian*, 23 November 1867 – 11 June 1870, under this title and signed 'Q' though his authorship was an open secret. He collected some of them in volume form in *The Peripatetic Philosopher by 'Q'* (1869), describing them in the preface as 'this miserable decoction of Thackeray, and Dickens, and Balzac, and George Sala, and Douglas Jerrold …' A selection is reprinted in *MV*, *AE* and *CC*. 'Q' was the brand of the stock station at Swinton near Glenorchy where Clarke had worked 1865–67. 'Q' was also used as a pseudonym by the English writers Douglas Jerrold (1803–57), and Sir Arthur Quiller-Couch (1863–1944). In his memoir of his early days in Melbourne, 'Austin Friars', *Australian Monthly Magazine*, May 1866, reprinted *MV*, *CC*, Clarke writes of how he and his friends 'would indulge in what we termed "peripatetic philosophy", which consisted in making conjectures as to everybody's business, as to where the man with the electrical machine at the top of Bourke street lived, and what became of all the orange-peel left in the pit of the theatres'. The term 'peripatetic' comes from the habit of philosophers who were followers of Aristotle of delivering their teachings in public while walking back and forth in the *peripatoi*, the colonnade, of the Lyceum gymnasium in classical Athens. Clarke may also be implying a vagrant itinerary quality to his life, perhaps recalling Matthew Arnold's poem 'The Scholar Gypsy' (1853), 'who came as most men thought to little good,/ But came to Oxford and his friends no more'. The idea of a peripatetic philosopher journalistic column may have been partly prompted by 'Le Flâneur' columns which were popular in nineteenth-century journalism.

p. 012 'A West Indian Anecdote': 'The Peripatetic Philosopher', *Australasian*, 8 February 1868, 177, reprinted *PP*, 74–5.

p. 012 Lord Rosebery: Archibald Philip Primrose, fifth Earl of Rosebery (1847–1929), English statesman, under-secretary at the Home Office 1881–83; Foreign Secretary in the Gladstone administration in 1886 and 1892; Prime Minister 1894–95, married to the heiress Hannah de Rothschild. He visited Australia in 1883–84. On 16 January 1884, Rosebery wrote a letter to Clarke's widow accepting at her request the dedication of Mackinnon's *Marcus Clarke Memorial Volume* (1884). In it he gives the novel high praise. 'To me, I confess, it is the most terrible of all novels, more terrible than *Oliver Twist*, or Victor Hugo's most startling effects, for the simple reason that it is more real. It has all the solemn ghastliness of truth.' The letter was printed in *MV*, *AE* and elsewhere and was widely quoted in the posthumous promotion of editions of

Clarke's work (McL 199–201, 1230, 1363, 2816 and other items, including newspaper references listed in his index). Rosebery's correspondence with Mrs Marian Clarke and Hamilton Mackinnon is in the SLV (McL 2816–23). See Thomas F. G. Coates, *Lord Rosebery: His Life and Speeches*, 2 vols (Hutchinson, London, 1900) 388–91. Leo McKinstry, *Rosebery: Statesman in Turmoil* (John Murray, London, 2005).

p. 012   Emily Brontë (1818–48), English novelist, author of *Wuthering Heights* (1847). Cyril is following Lord Rosebery here and in subsequent comparisons. Rosebery wrote: 'Long ago I fell upon *His Natural Life* by accident, and read it not once or twice but many times, at different periods. Since then I have frequently given away copies to men whose opinions I valued, and have always received from them the same opinion as to the extraordinary power of the book … I fancy that your husband's works are not sufficiently appreciated in Australia. I am sure that they are insufficiently appreciated in Great Britain … It is rare, I think, that so young a country has produced so great a literary force. I cannot believe but that the time will come when Australians will feel a melancholy pride in this true son of genius, and Australian genius … And in England you may find that like another power in the world of letters, not dissimilar in genius, I mean Emily Brontë, he may have made up to him in posthumous honor what was lacking in his lifetime.'

p. 012   Marcus Clarke's mother: her surname is given as Matthews on its first mention and on its second as Mathews by Cyril Hopkins, and as Matthew by Patchett Martin, *Temple Bar*, May 1884, 96; what little is described of her in BE is taken from Cyril's brief second-hand memories here of what Clarke himself had picked up or pieced together, also at second-hand, and also directly from Sir Andrew Clarke, Marcus Clarke's cousin, see above. Patchett Martin claims 'she had been on the stage herself'. According to A. G. Stephens, she was an actress of Jewish descent: *Bookfellow*, 15 January 1920, reprinted in Leon Cantrell, ed., *A. G. Stephens: Selected Writings* (1977); the grounds for this claim are unknown. Her death certificate records: Death of Amelia Elizabeth Clarke – Age: 26 years – Date: 13 March 1850 – Place: 23 Notting Hill Terrace, Kensington – Cause of Death: Phthisis Certified.

p. 012   Benjamin Lumley (1811/12–75), born in Canada he came to London, trained as a solicitor, then became manager of His Majesty's Theatre's Royal Italian Opera Company.

p. 014   'Holiday Peak': *Australasian*, 18 January 1873, 72; 25 January, 104, reprinted in *Holiday Peak and Other Tales* (1873); Mackinnon's text in *MV* is slightly different from Hopkins' MS.

p. 014   one of the characters: oddly, Cyril does not point out that this is an imagined alternative version of GMH.

p. 014   Gerard: GMH.

p. 015   *Dennis Duval*, serialised in the *Cornhill Magazine*, was unfinished when Thackeray died suddenly on Christmas Eve, 1863.

p. 015   'Human Repetends': Hopkins' text differs slightly from that in Clarke's 'Noah's Ark' in the *Australasian*, 14 September 1872, 326, reprinted in *MC*. Clarke never collected the story in his lifetime. It appeared posthumously in Marcus Clarke, *The Mystery of Major Molineux and Human Repetends* (1881) and, as 'A Mysterious Coincidence', in *Sensational Tales*, *AE* and *ST*. It is Clarke at his most Borgesian, before Borges.

p. 015   another passage referring to this period of his life: in Clarke's story 'La Béguine', *Australasian*, 8 February 1873, 166, reprinted by Clarke in *Four Stories High* (1877) but not collected by Mackinnon in *MV* or *AE*, presumably because of the story's sexual theme, or in deference to Clarke's widow. It is reprinted in *MC*. Hopkins' MS text, given here, differs in some details from the *Four Stories High* version, and may draw on a MS sent to him by Clarke. In the printed text, 'Rev. Gammon's' is 'Rev Crammer's', and 'Little Master' is 'little Marston'.

p. 015   of cousin Tom from Woolwich, of cousin Dick from Sandhurst, of cousin Harry from Aldershot: the text in *Four Stories High* has 'of cousin Tom from Woolwich, of cousin

Dick from from Addiscombe, of cousin Harry from Colchester or Knightsbridge'. Woolwich, Sandhurst and Aldershot are all military academies. Adam Lindsay Gordon was briefly at Woolwich.

p. 015   The Earl of Cinqbars' son, the Honourable Tom Ringwood, is a swindler in 'A Caution to Travellers' in W. M. Thackeray, *The Paris Notebook* (1840).

p. 015   Algernon Deucedere: there is an Hon. A. P. Deucease, a card-sharper, in W. M. Thackeray's *The Great Hoggarty Diamond* (1841).

p. 015   Cremorne Gardens in Chelsea, mentioned in 'La Béguine', were a popular entertainment site in nineteenth-century London. They became notorious for their provision of sexual opportunities and were closed down in 1877.

p. 016   Australian writer and friend of Marcus: Charles Bright, 'Marcus Clarke', *Cosmos*, 30, April 1895, 419. He was 'closely associated with Clarke in one of his literary enterprises', *Humbug* (*ibid.*, 422). Bright (1832–1903), English-born writer, and spiritualist, came to Australia during the gold rush, and then joined the *Argus* as parliamentary journalist. Edited the *Melbourne Punch* (1863–66), wrote for the *Examiner and Melbourne Weekly News* (1859–64) and contributed to the *Herald*, and *Age*.

p. 016   James Payn (1830–98), English popular novelist and journalist, a regular contributor to *Household Words*, editor of *Chambers' Journal* (1859–74) and the *Cornhill Magazine* (1882–96). *Richard Arbour, or The Family Scapegrace* (Edinburgh, 1861), reissued as *The Family Scapegrace, or Richard Arbour* (London, 1869), is one of the hundred of novels he wrote. Clarke refers to him in an article for the London *Daily Telegraph*, quoted in Ch. 12.

p. 00   'Human Repetends' and 'La Béguine': all those commenting on Clarke's early years rely, like Cyril, upon the two stories 'Human Repetends' and 'La Béguine'. It is commonly agreed they draw indirectly and ambiguously on Clarke's life, though there is disagreement among critics about their biographical significance. Cyril, here, as elsewhere, is apologetic and defensive out of loyalty and propriety about both father and son, while Elliott as an academic biographer is perhaps over-cautious. Both critics realise that here Clarke is typically drawing on literature as well as on life. Elliott points to the context of French literature which Clarke got to know early, while Hopkins finds a source closer to home in the romance novelist James Payn. This is an example where Cyril's English background and contemporaneity with Clarke enables him to recuperate aspects of the latter's reading hitherto lost or overlooked by later critics in Australia.

p. 016   Hamilton Mackinnon has done well: Hopkins sometimes defers to this first biographer but BE questions Mackinnon's reliability, see later note.

p. 016   amassing a competence or a fortune for the benefit of his son: there is no evidence for this. Hopkins is being apologetic when he says the father would probably have realised this aim if 'his fatal breakdown' had not occurred. As BE suggests, the father may have been physically ill for some time. No one has suggested, as far as we know, however, that the father's 'reclusiveness' and financial disorganisation may have been partly due to depression setting in after his widowhood, a disability or disease common at the time but much misunderstood. This raises the question, hitherto unexplored, of how far Clarke's notoriously 'mercurial' moments may have alternated with depression, something Cyril would have avoided, as does Elliott. Cyril does (as does BE), however, mention Clarke's swings of mood. In the next chapter he refers to the bent of Clarke's mind, 'which in contradistinction to his boyish high spirits and genial manners, was always of a morbidly imaginative character'. The father had to be removed to an asylum for the insane, dying a year later from 'softening of the brain several years certified' (BE 20).

Chapter 2

p. 017   William Cowper (1731–1800), English poet. Clarke refers to his *Olney Hymns* (1779) in *HNL* and to 'The Solitude of Alexander Selkirk', Ch. 16. 'The rose had been washed …' is from his poem 'The Rose'.

p. 018   grammar school at Highgate: Sir Roger Cholmeley's School at Highgate, founded
1565; sometimes spelled Cholmondeley (pronounced Chumley); before 1871
referred to as The Free Grammar School at Highgate or as the Cholmeley School, but
from the later nineteenth century usually called Highgate School. See further *www.
highgateschool.org.uk* and Thomas Hinde, *Highgate School: A History* (James and James,
London, 1993). There were eighty day boys and fifty boarders in Clarke's time. Fees for
day boys were just over £18 p.a., which was considered expensive (R. B. Martin, 12–3).
Gerard was at the school from 1854 until 1863, a boarder except for his last year. Cyril
was there from 1856 to 1861 (Martin 14). Clarke started there in 1858, aged twelve.
He was forced to leave by his father's illness, five years later. Cyril was in Clarke's year,
Gerard was two years older (BE, 14, 26) but was nevertheless among what Cyril later
calls in this chapter 'intimate friends', their literary interests and abilities drawing them
together. Ruggles in *Gerard Manley Hopkins* describes them as best friends. Gerard
wrote years later, 'The truth is I had no love for my school days, and wished to banish
the remembrance of them, even, I am ashamed to say, to the degree of neglecting some
people who had been very kind to me' (*The Correspondence of Gerard Manley Hopkins
and Richard Watson Dixon*, ed. C. C. Abbott, 1970, 12). Clarke seems to have been
one of those he neglected: there is no record of any correspondence between them. BE
(222) cites Clarke in the *Australasian*, on school speech days (28 December 1867), on
being flogged by Dyne, with possible disguised references to Gerard and Cyril (24 July
1869), and on fare-welling a schoolmaster which may echo GMH's account elsewhere
(12 December 1868). Another contemporary of Clarke's was Frederick Campbell, 'the
father of Australian rugby', born in 1846 at 'Duntroon' in southern NSW (now in
ACT), the grazing property of his grandfather Robert Campbell, Sydney's first major
shipping merchant (after whom Campbell's Cove at Circular Quay was named). Fred
was taken to England and enrolled at the school 1854–63, where he played in the
rugby team. There is no record of Clarke's being on the team.

p. 018   George du Maurier (1834–96), English novelist and illustrator, author of *Trilby* (1894).
His last novel *The Martian* (1897) is a story based on school life.

p. 018   the senior Clarke a brisk, well set-up man: this is a more vigorous picture of Clarke's
father, five years before he died, than the one drawn by Cyril when they first met.

p. 018   Albert Smith (1816–60), English author, lecturer and entertainer. Clarke refers to him
in 'Charles Dickens', *Argus*, 8 July 1870, 7, and 'Balzac and Modern French Literature',
Australasian, 3 August 1867, 136. See further, note to Ch. 8.

p. 018   Alfred, Lord Tennyson (1809–92), English poet laureate, author of *Maud, and other
Poems* (1855) and *Idylls of the King* (the first four of which appeared 1859, the complete
sequence in 1891). Clarke refers to him in 'The Peripatetic Philosopher', 26 September
1868, 26 March 1870, in his review of Bret Harte's *The Luck of Roaring Camp*,
Australian Journal, March 1871, 389–90, and to his 'Locksley Hall' in *LO*, and in a
report on the Melbourne Cup, *Argus*, 1 November 1867 and, to the *Northern Farmer*
in 'Noah's Ark' on American literature, 25 May 1872, and to *Enoch Arden* (1864) in
OT. In *HNL*, Tennyson is Mrs Frere's favourite poet, the Rev. North writes a critical
essay on him and Tennyson's *Locksley Hall* (1842) is quoted. Cyril's father, Manley
Hopkins, reviewed Tennyson's 'The Princess' and 'In Memoriam' in the *Times*, 28
November 1851. The influence of Tennyson's 'The Palace of Art' has been detected on
GMH's school prize poem of 1860 (Martin 20). Robb discusses Tennyson's influence
on Gordon, *Poems*, xciii–xcv. Henry Kendall contributed 'Stray Thoughts on Tennyson'
to Clarke's *Colonial Monthly*, June 1869, and reviewed Tennyson's *The Holy Grail* in the
Australasian, 30 April 1870. *LMC* lists Tennyson's *Princess*, and *Enoch Arden*.

p. 019   mathematics: both Clarke and Gerard detested mathematics, though Cyril did well
at it. The emphasis of the curriculum at Highgate School was on classics and on
the writing of English, and in the latter Gerard and Marcus both shone. Clarke also
excelled in French whereas Gerard did not do well in German, the other foreign

language taught. The headmaster, Dyne, despised foreign languages and countries (Norman White, *Hopkins: A Literary Biography*, 1992, 24–6).

p. 019   *Ripple and Flood*: a novel by James Prior, pseudonym of James Prior Kirk (1850–1922) (London, 1897). Hopkins has *By Ripple and Flood*.

p. 020   Horace (Quintus Horatius Flaccus) (65–68 BC), Latin poet. Clarke's story 'A Night with Horace' appeared in the *Australasian*, 22 July 1871, 101, and was collected in his *Holiday Peak* (1873). Horace is quoted and cited in *HNL*, and in 'The Peripatetic Philosopher', *Australasian*, 3 October 1868, 20 February 1869, *Argus*, 13 April 1872, *Daily Telegraph*, 6 September 1877, all reprinted *CC*, and 'An Up-country Township', *Australasian*, 6 August 1870. Horace's poems were a basic element of the English public school curriculum. A knowledge of the classics was regarded as *de rigueur* and the mark of a true gentleman by Dyne, headmaster of Highgate School. According to Father Julian Tenison Woods, who knew Adam Lindsay Gordon when the poet was an itinerant horse-breaker in South Australia, 'the book Gordon loved best was a Horace to carry about in his lonely rides', Douglas Sladen, ed., *The Poems of Adam Lindsay Gordon* (1913) xvii; see Julian E. Tenison Woods, 'Personal Reminiscences of Adam Lindsay Gordon', *Melbourne Review*, 9, 1884, 131–5.

p. 020   Irish blood: according to Cyril's introduction, the male Clarke line is said to derive from Scottish Protestants who had settled in northern Ireland. However, Hopkins records, Ch. 24, 'He felt that he had Irish blood in his veins, even if his father's family was settled in the North of Ireland'. Gerard, incidentally, had a 'lifelong dislike of the Irish' (Martin 6, 63, passim).

p. 020   Sir Arthur Conan Doyle (1859–1930), Scots writer, author of the Sherlock Holmes stories, historical novels and works on spiritualism. He was a schoolboy at Stonyhurst when Gerard was at St Mary's Hall seminary there (Martin 201). His autobiographical *Memories and Adventures* was published in 1924.

p. 020   S. R. Crockett (1816–1914), Scots novelist, author of *The Raiders* (1894).

p. 021   Charles Bright, 'Marcus Clarke', *Cosmos*, 30 April 1895, 421. The passage Bright quotes is from Clarke's 'In A Bark Hut', *Australasian*, 17 May 1873, 616.

p. 021   McAlister: Hopkins identifies him in a note as 'the late Hon. John Mackenzie, afterwards well-known in political circles in New Zealand'. Sir John McKenzie (1838–1901), born in Scotland, emigrated to New Zealand, where he was a farmer, station manager and member of parliament. Minister of Lands and Agriculture, 1890. Chief of the Gaelic Society for some years. Bright spells his name M'Allister.

p. 021   Sheherezade: the story-teller in the *Arabian Nights Entertainments, or, The Thousand and One Nights*. They were translated from the Arabic into French by Antoine Galland between 1704 and 1717. English translations appeared in 1705–08, and, by E. W. Lane, in 1838–40. Clarke refers to the *Arabian Nights* again in 'The Gypsies of the Sea, or the Island of Gold', Melbourne *Herald*, 24–31 December 1874, reprinted as 'A Modern Eldorado'.

p. 021   unfettered access to the library of a man who owned few prejudices for moral fig-leaves: the writers and works Clarke goes on to itemise were, with the exception of Bede, famous for their dealing with sexual themes and for their critical attitudes towards religion and society.

p. 021   Pierre de Bourdeilles, seigneur de Brantome (c. 1534–1614), French army officer and courtier whose *Vie des dames galantes* (1665) and other memoirs record court scandals and intrigues.

p. 021   William Wycherley (1641–1715), English Restoration playwright, whose works include *Love in a Wood, or, St James's Park* (1672) and *The Country Wife* (1675), etc. His work has been both admired for its acute social criticism of sexual morality and condemned as licentious. Clarke refers to him in 'The Traveller of the Period', *Argus*, 13 April 1872. *LMC* lists *The Complete Works of Wycherley and Congreve*, edited by Dyce.

p. 021   Philip Massinger (1583–1640), English playwright, whose works include the social comedies *A New Way to Pay Old Debts* (1633) and *The City Madam* (1658).

p. 021   George Farquhar (c. 1677–1707), Irish playwright, whose works include *The Recruiting Officer* (1706) and *The Beaux' Stratagem* (1707).

p. 021   George Gordon, Lord Byron (1788–1824), British poet. Clarke refers to Byron in *LO*, and in 'Holiday Peak', *Australasian*, 18 January 1873, 72; 25 January, 104. He quotes him in 'The Brief Experience of Mr Thomas Twopenny', *Weekly Times*, 14 March 1874, cites him in the *Leader*, 24 January 1880, both reprinted *CC*, refers to Byron's *Childe Harold's Pilgrimage* (1812–18) in *OT* and to his 'Prisoner of Chillon' in *HNL*. Robb discusses his influence on Gordon, in Gordon, *The Poems of Adam Lindsay Gordon* (1912), lxxv–xci. *LMC* lists Byron's *Don Juan*.

p. 021   *Gil Blas* (1715–35), novel by the French writer Alain-René Lesage (1668–1747), translated into English in 1749 by the Scots novelist Tobias Smollett (1721–71). Clarke refers to it in *LO*, in his account of Jorgenson in *OT* and in 'Of French Novels', *Argus*, 2 February 1872.

p. 021   the Alchemists: Clarke had a lifelong interest and reading in alchemy. His first contribution to the *Australian Monthly Magazine*, 2, March 1866, 51–6, was a story 'The Mantuan Apothecary: A Picture in Two Panels', which greatly embellishes the alchemical motifs from Shakespeare's *Romeo and Juliet*. For one of Clarke's writings as a schoolboy, GMH provided a drawing called 'The Alchemist in the City' that shows the theme of 'variations on arcane knowledge' (White (1992) 31). He writes of the 'Alchemist experience' 'Tout l'or pour toi, mais rends moi mes beaux jours!' in 'La Béguine', *Australasian*, 8 February 1873. The complex and extensive alchemical structure and symbolism of *HNL* have been analysed in Lyndy Abraham, 'The Australian Crucible: Alchemy in Marcus Clarke's *His Natural Life*', *ALS*, 15, 1991–92, 38–55. However, the sources of his extensive knowledge of alchemical processes are generally unknown. Hopkins' recording in Ch. 17 of Clarke's reading *La recherche de l'absolu* is important in this context. Balzac's novel concerns the life of an alchemist, Balthazar Claes, and his attempt to crystallise carbon to produce diamonds, a process referred to in the original serial version *HNL* (ed. Murray-Smith, 906). Claes is also referred to in Clarke's story 'Holiday Peak', *Australasian*, 18 January 1873, 72; 25 January, 104. The same alchemical process is a preoccupation of the alchemist-priest Claude Frollo in Victor Hugo's *Notre Dame de Paris* (1831), a novel Clarke refers to in his story 'Poor Jo', *Australasian*, 15 April 1871, 453, reprinted in *Holiday Peak* (see Michael Wilding, *Studies in Classic Australian Fiction*, 1997, 16, 22). A third novel with an alchemical theme, *Elective Affinities* (*Die Wahlverwandtschaften*, 1809) by J. W. von Goethe (1749–1832) seems to be alluded to by Sylvia Vickers in *HNL*: '"There are persons," says Sylvia, "who have no Affinity for each other. I read about it in a book Papa had, and I suppose that's what it is. I have no Affinity for you"' (*MC* 145). A translation of the novel, titled *Sexual Affinity*, is listed in *LMC*, together with Goethe's *Faust* and *Poems*. Also listed in *LMC* is *Extraordinary Popular Delusions* by Charles Mackay, which deals with the alchemists.

p. 021   Horace: see note above.

p. 021   The Venerable Bede (673–735), English churchman, author of the *History of the English Church* and Biblical commentaries. Clarke refers to him in 'Noah's Ark', *Australasian*, 18 May 1872.

p. 021   *Candide* (1759), satiric novel by the French philosopher Voltaire, pseudonym of François-Marie Arouet (1694–1778). Clarke refers to it in *LO*, in his account of Jorgenson in *OT*, and to Voltaire in 'New Chums', *Australasian*, 10 October 1869, in 'Balzac and Modern French Literature', *Australasian*, 3 August 1867, in 'Noah's Ark', *Australasian*, 18 May 1872, reprinted *CC*, and in the *Age*, 23 March 1880, reprinted *CC*. *LMC* lists *L'Esprit de Voltaire*, *Le Théâtre de Voltaire*, 3 vols, and Voltaire's *Philosophical Dictionary*, 2 vols, American edition.

p. 021   Dr. Lardner's *Encyclopaedia*: Dionysius Lardner (1793–1859), a populariser of science and technology, whose many books include the 133 volumes of *The Cabinet*

Cyclopaedia (London, 1830–49) and *Dr. Lardner's Cabinet Library* (London, 1830–32). *LMC* lists *Lardner's Handbook of Natural Philosophy*.

p. 022   Hogarth: William Hogarth (1697–1764), English painter and social and political caricaturist. Clarke refers to him in 'Taking Mine Ease in Mine Inn', *Australasian*, 3 July 1869, 8, and in 'Noah's Ark', *Australasian*, 25 May 1872, reprinted *CC*.

p. 022   Thomas Paine (1737–1809), English radical, author of *The Rights of Man* (1791–92) and *The Age of Reason* (1793). Clarke refers to him in 'The Settler in Tasmania' in *OT*. *LMC* lists Thomas Paine's *Age of Reason*.

p. 022   Moll Flanders, heroine of the eponymous novel (1722) by the English novelist Daniel Defoe (1660–1731). Clarke refers to *Moll Flanders* again in Ch. 17, and to Defoe's *Colonel Jack* (1722) in his essay 'Charles Dickens', *Argus*, 8 July 1870. Defoe's *Robinson Crusoe* (1719) is referred to in Clarke's 'Peripatetic Philosopher' column, *Australasian*, 6 June 1868, reprinted *PP*, in 'William Buckley' and 'An Australian Crusoe' in *OT*, and in 'In Outer Darkness', *Australasian*, 21 August 1869, 232. It is one of the books read by Sylvia Vickers in *HNL*; see Ken Stewart, 'Sylvia's Books' in *Investigations in Australian Literature* (2000), 99–102. The significance of *Robinson Crusoe* to Clarke's novel is discussed in L. T. Hergenhan, 'The Redemptive Theme in *His Natural Life*', *ALS*, 2, 1965, 32–49. *LMC* lists *The Complete Works* of Daniel Defoe.

p. 022   'Blow, blow, thou winter wind': *As You Like It* (2.7.175), by William Shakespeare (1564–1616). Clarke refers to Shakespeare frequently in *LO*, and in his obituary of Dickens, *Argus*, 18 July 1870; to *The Winter's Tale* in 'A Cheap Lodging House', *Australasian*, 31 July 1869; to Falstaff in 'In Outer Darkness', *Argus*, 21 August 1869; to *King Lear* in 'What Shall We Do with Our Girls?', *Humbug*, 17 November 1869, and 'Of French Novels', *Argus*, 2 February 1872; to *Macbeth*, *LO* and *Weekly Times*, 24 January 1874, and to Johnson's textual emendations to *Macbeth* in 'Noah's Ark', 18 May 1872, all reprinted *CC*. *LMC* lists a two-volume edition of Shakespeare's Works.

p. 022   the scriptural outburst: *Acts* 26:24. 'And as he thus spake for himself, Festus said with a loud voice, Paul, thou art beside thyself; much learning doth make thee mad.'

p. 023   The late Andrew Lang said: CH originally wrote 'Mr. Andrew Lang said' but emended the manuscript after Lang's death. Andrew Lang (1844–1912), Scots man of letters, author of *Books and Bookmen* (1886), *Letters on Literature* (1889), *History of English Literature* (1912), etc.

p. 023   Stephen Phillips (1864–1915), actor, poet and dramatist. *Aylmer's Secret* (1905).

p. 024   The author of an article in the *Melbourne Review*: Henry Gyles Turner, 'Marcus Clarke', *The Melbourne Review*, 7, 25 (January 1882), 14.

p. 024   *Frankenstein, or the Modern Prometheus* (1818) by the English novelist Mary Shelley (1797–1851). She was married to Percy Bysshe Shelley (1792–1822), the English poet, whose collected poems are listed in *LMC*; Clarke refers to him in *LO* and quotes him in 'Noah's Ark', *Australasian*, 17 May 1873, reprinted *CC*. She was the daughter of the English writer William Godwin (1756–1836), whose novel *Things As They Are: or The Adventures of Caleb Williams* (1794) is referred to by Clarke in his essay 'Charles Dickens', *Argus*, 8 July 1870, reprinted in *CC*, *MC*. Robb discusses Shelley's influence on Gordon, in Gordon, *The Poems of Adam Lindsay Gordon* (1912) lxxxliii–lxxxv.

p. 024   'The Mantuan Apothecary: A Picture in Two Panels', *Australian Monthly Magazine*, 2, 1866, 51–6. An early version of this story, written before Clarke left Britain, is contained in a notebook from his school days held at the ML.

p. 024   Clarke's ballad 'The Lady of Lynn' was published in the first issue of the *Colonial Monthly* he edited, March 1868, 15–17, reprinted *MV* (but without the introductory prose context). White (1992) discusses 'The Lady of Lynn' in detail (31) and GMH's frontispiece drawing to it, which he called 'The Alchemist in the City'. GMH wrote to his school-friend E. H. Coleridge, 'Clarke writes v g poetry. He and I compare notes and ideas. I think I shewed you his "Lady of Lynn" …' (Claude Colleer Abbott, ed., *Further Letters of Gerard Manley Hopkins including his correspondence with Coventry Patmore*, 1956, 14).

p. 024   'The Mystery of Major Molineux': *Campbelltown Herald* (Victoria), July 1881 (McL
          190); collected posthumously in Marcus Clarke, *The Mystery of Major Molineux and
          Human Repetends* (1881), with an introduction by R. P. Whitworth. A facsimile reprint
          of 'Major Molineux' alone was published by Mulini Press, Canberra, 1996. See Andrew
          McCann, 'Colonial Gothic: Morbid Anatomy, Commodification and Critique in
          Marcus Clarke's *The Mystery of Major Molineux*', *ALS*, 19, 2000, 399–412 and Ch. 5
          of McCann, *Marcus Clarke's Bohemia: Literature and Modernity in Colonial Melbourne*
          (2004).

p. 024   Edgar Allan Poe (1809–49), American poet and short story writer. Clarke quotes
          Poe's phrase 'weird melancholy' to describe 'the dominant note of Australian scenery'
          in his introduction to Adam Lindsay Gordon's poems *Sea Spray and Smoke Drift*
          (1876), which was frequently reprinted in successive editions of Gordon's collected
          Poems (1880). It is reprinted in BW and *MC*. Shorn of the specific references to
          Gordon, it is reprinted as 'Australian Scenery' in *MV, AE, AT* and *ST*. See note to
          preface on Gordon. Poe's detective stories are an undoubted influence on Clarke's
          'The Doppelgänger', *Australian Monthly Magazine*, July and August 1866, 363–74,
          433–40, reprinted as 'The Dual Existence' in *Sensational Tales, AE* and *ST*. On Poe's
          influence on Clarke's stories, see Michael Wilding, 'Weird Melancholy', *Studies in*
          Classic Australian Fiction (1997), 30–1. Clarke quotes Poe in letters reproduced by
          CH in Ch. 21 and Ch. 25, and refers to him in *LO*, and (reprinted in *CC*) 'Charles
          Dickens', *Argus*, 8 July 1870, 'Noah's Ark', *Australasian*, 25 May 1872, and 'The Buncle
          Correspondence', *Argus*, 2 February 1872. He cites Poe's 'Arthur Gordon Pym' in *OT*.
          Clarke reprinted passages from Poe's stories in 'The Library Table' feature when editing
          the *Australian Journal* (see McCann, 2004, 158). Clarke gave Gerard a copy of Poe's
          poems which the latter passed on to Cyril when he joined the Jesuits (White (1992)
          30). *LMC* lists Poe's *Tales of Mystery*, and *The Works of Edgar Allan Poe*, American
          edition, three volumes.

p. 027   frontispiece, supplied by my brother Gerard: (White (1992) 31) refers to another
          illustration by Gerard called 'The Alchemist in the City'. The MSS of stories by Clarke
          and drawings by GMH have not survived, though Cyril obviously had some in his
          possession. The note Cyril supplies on Gerard – 'Father Gerard M. Hopkins, S.J. died
          1889' – written long before he became famous as a poet, is the first and only explicit
          reference to GMH, though 'Gerard' appears in Ch. 1. Gerard was received into the
          Roman Catholic Church, 21 October 1866 and took his final vows 15 August 1882;
          he became a novitiate of the Society of Jesus at Manresa, in Roehampton, in 1868,
          and entered the Jesuit seminary of St Mary's Hall, Stonyhurst in Lancashire, in 1870,
          studying there until August 1873, after which he returned to Manresa as Professor
          of Rhetoric (Martin 274–6). He was at Stonyhurst when Clarke published his story
          'Holiday Peak', where he writes of 'Gerard my boy friend, who fled from Oxford to
          Stonyhurst, and embraced the discipline of Loyola', *Australasian*, 18 and 25 January
          1873. On Stonyhurst, see further: Gerald Roberts, 'The Jaded Muse: Hopkins at
          Stonyhurst', *Hopkins Quarterly*, Spring 1979, 6, 1, 35–47, and Thomas Zaniello, 'The
          Stonyhurst Philosophers', *Hopkins Quarterly*, Winter 1983, 9, 133–59. BE (226–7)
          cites Clarke on Jesuits in *Australasian*, 20 December 1867. Clarke wrote a 'Peripatetic
          Philosopher' column, *Australasian*, 21 December 1867, on 'The Jesuit of Fiction',
          reprinted *PP*.

p. 027   *Barnaby Rudge* (1841). The Gordon anti-popery riots occurred in 1780.

p. 027   *The Ingoldsby Legends: or Mirth and Marvels by Thomas Ingoldsby Esq* (1840) by
          the English writer R. H. Barham (1788–1845). Clarke's copy is held by the Royal
          Historical Society of Victoria (McL 3068).

p. 028   Clement King Shorter (1857–1926), English man of letters, author of *Charlotte Brontë*
          and Her Circle (Hodder & Stoughton, London, 1896) and *The Brontës: Life and Letters:*
          Being an Attempt to Present a Full and Final Record of the Lives of the Three Sisters
          Charlotte, Emily and Ann Brontë, two volumes (Hodder & Stoughton, London, 1908).

Chapter 3

p. 029   Bulwer Lytton: Edward Bulwer-Lytton, first Earl of Lytton (1804–73), English novelist and statesman, author of *Pelham* (1828), *The Last Days of Pompeii* (1834), *Zanoni* (1842), *The Last of the Barons* (1843), *The Coming Race* (1871) etc. Clarke refers to him in *LO*, reprinted his story 'The Haunted and the Haunters' in 'The Library Table' feature in the *Australian Journal*, June 1871 (see Andrew McCann, *Marcus Clarke's Bohemia: Literature and Modernity in Colonial Melbourne*, 2004, 158–62), and refers to his *The Caxtons* (1849) in 'A Mining Township', *Australasian*, 5 November 1870, 582. *LMC* lists Lytton's *Kenelm Chillingley* (1873). As Secretary of State for the Colonies, 1858–59, he was responsible for granting Queensland statehood. His son was Viceroy of India, 1876–80, the period Marcus's uncle Sir Andrew Clarke had a seat on the council of the viceroy.

p. 029   Charles Lever (1806–72), Irish born novelist who later settled in Europe. His *The Dodd Family Abroad* (1852–4) describes an English family's experiences in Europe. Clarke refers to his novel *The O'Donoghue* in his essay 'George Barrington' in *OT*. On Clarke's assessment of Lever, see Ch. 24.

p. 029   Charles Reade (1814–84), English dramatist and novelist. Clarke refers to Reade's *It is Never too Late to Mend* (1856), a novel of Australian life, in his dedication to Sir Charles Gavan Duffy of the first book edition of *HNL*: 'Charles Reade has drawn the interior of a house of correction in England'. Reade never visited Australia, though Clarke playfully refers to him in 'The Café Lutetia' as having 'broken bread there', *Weekly Times*, 28 February 1874. Clarke's dramatisation of Reade's novel *Foul Play* (serialised in *Once a Week* in 1868 and published in book form in 1869; itself adapted from Reade's play *Gold!*) ran for a week in Melbourne in 1868 (BE 131). Clarke refers to *Foul Play* in his account of Jorgenson in *OT*, to reading Reade's novel *Griffith Gaunt* (1866) in Ch. 22, and to *Peg Woffington* in 'Galen Square', 'The Wicked World', *Weekly Times*, 24 January 1874, reprinted *CC*, and 'The Café Lutetia', *Weekly Times*, 28 February 1874. *LMC* lists Reade's *Foul Play* (in two editions), *The Course of True Love, Love Me Little Love Me Long, Christy Johnston, It is Never too Late to Mend, Peg Woffington, Double Marriage, Griffith Gaunt*. Mitchell Library, State Library of New South Wales, holds a letter from Reade to Clarke. See Ian Henderson, '"There Are French Novels and There Are French Novels": Charles Reade and the "Other Sources" of Marcus Clarke's *His Natural Life*', *JASAL*, 1, 2002, 51–66. Hopkins has 'Read'.

p. 029   Captain Frederic Marryat (1792–1848), English novelist, author of *Mr. Midshipman Easy* (1836), *The Children of the New Forest* (1847) and *Masterman Ready* (1841). Clarke refers to him in 'Le Roi s'amuse', *Australasian*, 19 June 1869, reprinted *CC*.

p. 029   James Fenimore Cooper (1789–1851), American novelist, author of the *Leather-Stocking* saga (1823 ff). Hopkins has 'Fennimore'.

p. 029   William Harrison Ainsworth (1805–82), English novelist, author of *Rookwood* (1824), *Old St Paul's* (1841), *The Lancashire Witches* (1848) etc. and poems under the name 'Cheviot Ticheborne' (1822). Clarke refers to him in his essay 'Charles Dickens', *Argus*, 8 July 1870, 7.

p. 029   James Grant (1822–87), Scottish writer, author of novels and memoirs on military and historical topics.

p. 029   Dickens: see note to Preface.

p. 029   Thackeray: see note to Preface.

p. 029   George Augustus Sala (1828–95), English journalist and novelist, on the staff of the London *Daily Telegraph*. Clarke acknowledges his influence in the preface to *The Peripatetic Philosopher*, quoted Ch. 24, and refers to him in his 'Charles Dickens', *Argus*, 8 July 1870, 7, and in 'The Traveller of the Period', *Argus*, 13 April 1872, 6. Sala introduced 'a new journalism, a new verve and dash, a witty audacity and freedom, which made Clarke his disciple' (BE 84). 'Bottle of Hay' is Ch. 11 of Sala's *Gaslight and Daylight: With Some London Scenes They Shine Upon* (London, 1859), a series of descriptive essays on London streets and people, originally published in *All the Year Round* and *Household Words* between 1851–58 – remarked on by Cyril in Ch. 7 below. Sala was a protégé of Dickens; see P. D. Edwards, *Dickens' 'Young Men': George Augustus Sala, Edmund Yates and the World of Victorian Journalism* (Ashgate, Aldershot, 1997). *LMC* lists Sala's *Twice Round the Clock: or, Life in London* and his *Life of Dickens*.

p. 029   George Eliot: see note to Preface. Hopkins has 'Elliot'.

p. 029   Scott: see note to Preface.

p. 030   admiration for Marcus's novel: Sala wrote to Mackinnon (21 August 1885) that he had read 'every line' of Mackinnon's *MV* biography and expressed regret that someone 'who could produce a book of such extraordinary genius as *His Natural Life* did not avail himself of the splendid opportunity [writing for the *Daily Telegraph*] awaiting him in London', quoted in Robert Dingley, *The Land of the Golden Fleece: George Augustus Sala in Australia* (Mulini Press, Canberra, 1995) xiii. Sala's *The Land of the Golden Fleece* (1885) is an account of his travels in Australia. Elliott quotes Sala as writing '"Charles Reade never wrote so powerful a romance as *His Natural Life*", praise Clarke would have savoured' (BE 162). 'If you have ever chanced to read Marcus Clarke's *For the Term of His Natural Life*, you will come across horrors not much less harrowing than those I set down in the little halfpenny paper. There may be a reason for this. Marcus Clarke, who was many years my junior, seems to have gone to the very same sources that I resorted to in 1848.' *The Life and Adventures of G. A. Sala, written by himself* (Cassell, London, 1895), quoted BE 259. Sala's *The Australian Nights Entertainments*, 'supposed to have been related by convicts at the Antipodes while lying in their hammocks after sunset' appeared in *Chat* in 1848 (BE 143).

p. 030   Algernon Charles Swinburne (1837–1909), English poet. 'Lady of Pain' is one of the epithets applied to the eponymous subject of the poem 'Dolores' in *Poems and Ballads* (1866). It can be related to the pleasure he derived from flagellation. He spent much of his childhood on the Isle of Wight – where Clarke first encountered the Hopkins family. Clarke refers to Dolores in 'The Peripatetic Philosopher', *Australasian*, 22 January 1870, reprinted *CC*, and 'A Night at the Immigrants' Home', *Australasian*, 12 June 1869, 762–3, discusses his poetry further in Ch. 22, refers to his influence on Adam Lindsay Gordon in his preface to Gordon's poems (1876), and mentions him in 'Noah's Ark', 7 July 1872, and in 'The Café Lutetia', *Weekly Times*, 28 February 1874, and in 'Of French Novels' *Argus*, 2 February 1872. He turns up as a character in Clarke's story 'Holiday Peak', *Australasian*, 18 January 1873, 72; 25 January, 104. Gerard met Swinburne on at least two occasions, in 1864 and 1868 (R. B. Martin, 73, 177–8). Adam Lindsay Gordon in one of his letters writes, 'A. C. Swinburne has sent him [Henry Kendall] a most complimentary letter upon a work of his which went home; indeed it is a sort of rhapsody' (Gordon, *The Poems of Adam Lindsay Gordon*, ed. Frank Maldon Robb, lxxii). Robb discusses Swinburne's influence on Gordon's poetry, xci–xciii.

p. 030   John Ruskin (1819–1900), English writer on art and society, author of *The Seven Lamps of Architecture* (1849), *The Stones of Venice* (1851–53), etc. On Ruskin's early and lasting influence on Clarke's writing, see BE 24–6. Clarke refers to the 'pre-Rafaelite pruriency of the Ruskinian Reynolds' in 'A Night at the Immigrants' Home', *Australasian*, 12 June 1869.

p. 030   Alexandre Dumas: see note to Preface.

p. 030   *Lady with the Camellias*: *La dame aux Camélias* (1852) a novel by Alexandre Dumas *fils* (1824–95): Marguerite Gautier is the former courtesan heroine. Clarke discusses it in 'Of French Novels', *Argus*, 2 February 1872. Clarke refers to Dumas *fils* in 'A Night at the Immigrants' Home', *Australasian*, 12 June 1869. A young courtesan is the subject of Clarke's story 'La Béguine', *Australasian*, 8 February 1873, 166, collected in *Four Stories High. LMC* lists *Antonine*, par Dumas *fils*. Hopkins has 'Camelias'

p. 030   *Valentine Vox* (1840), a novel by Henry Cockton (1807–52).

p. 030   John Poole (1786-1872), English novelist, author of *Little Pedlington and the Pedlingtonians* (1839). Clarke refers to it in 'The Peripatetic Philosopher', *Australasian*, 19 September 1868, reprinted *PP* and *CC*.

p. 030   *Don Quixote de la Mancha* (part 1, 1605, part 2, 1615), satirical romance by the Spanish novelist Miguel de Cervantes Saavedra (1547–1616). *LMC* lists *The Life and Adventures of Don Quixote*, profusely illustrated by Tony Johannot.

p. 031   Benjamin Elliott Nicholls, *Help to Reading of the Bible* (1838).

p. 031   W. H. Hudson (1841–1922), born in Argentina of American parents, settled in London in 1874. His tales of life in Argentina, *The Purple Land That England Lost*, appeared in 1885.

p. 031   Sir Roger Cholmeley's school at Highgate: see Introduction.

p. 031   Delille's *Repertoire des Prosateurs Français: Selections in Prose from the Best French Authors* (Whittaker, London, 1867) and many subsequent editions.

p. 031   *Gobseck* (1830), novel by Balzac.

p. 031   Joseph-Étienne Jouy (1764–1846), French author of vaudevilles, *opéras-comiques* and satiric sketches. *L'Hermite de la Chaussée d'Antin* (1812–14).

p. 032   *Long Odds*: (1869) 80; Clarke's first novel, originally serialised in the *Colonial Monthly*, March 1868 – July 1869; the unrevised serial text was reissued as *Heavy Odds* (Hutchinson, London; J. B. Lippincott, Philadelphia, 1896).

p. 032   Molière, pseudonym of Jean-Baptiste Poquelin (1622–73), French playwright. His play *Le Bourgeois Gentilhomme* (1660) was adapted by Clarke as *Peacock's Feathers*, September 1871. Clarke refers to Molière in his essay 'Balzac and Modern French Literature', *Australasian*, 3 August 1867. *LMC* lists *Oeuvres Complètes de Molière*.

p. 032   The use of the personal pronoun 'I', written with a capital, was a striking proof of the intense egotism of the British nation: this is quoted by GMH's biographer (White (1992) 31), from a letter from GMH, possibly 'originating in a joke contrived by him and Clarke', about the German master at Highgate, Professor Müncke. It is interesting to see the reference turning up late in Cyril's MS, apparently as a recondite allusion back to school days. 'Clarke thought of Müncke as a worthy disciple of Baron Münchausen' (White).

p. 032   Émile Zola (1840–1902), French novelist, author of the novels *Thérèse Raquin* (1867), *Germinal* (1885) etc, and of a letter to the newspaper *L'Aurore*, 'J'Accuse' in the Dreyfus case, 1898.

p. 032   Vizetelly: Zola's publisher in Britain.

p. 032   Norwood: a suburb of London. Zola spent eleven months in exile in Britain, 1898–99, to avoid imprisonment for libel after publishing 'J'Accuse'.

p. 033   Baron Münchausen (1720–97), officer in the Russian army whose exaggerated accounts of his experiences were recorded in a narrative (1785) by Rudolph Erich Raspe (1737–94).

p. 033   whilst at school Marcus kept an album: its whereabouts are no longer known but a notebook from this period survives, see note Ch. 5.

p. 033   Kaleidoscopic etc: this much-quoted description was first ascribed to GMH by Mackinnon (*MV* 16). No such entry is to be found in surviving notebooks (BE, 16, n. 2).

p. 033   Thaumatropic: adjective from the thaumatrope, a nineteenth-century scientific toy consisting of a disc with a different picture on each side, these appearing to combine into one when the disc is rapidly rotated. From Greek *thauma*, 'marvel' and *tropos*, 'turning'.

p. 033   epitaphs in Latin doggerel: discussed together with one on Cyril, BE 18–19. Epitaph on Clarke, *MV*, 16.

p. 033   Robert Louis Stevenson: see note to Preface. *Selected Letters*, ed. Sidney Colvin, 2 vols 1899, 4 vols 1911. Letter of November 1883. La Solitude was the name of Stevenson's house at Hyères.

p. 034   natural tendency to Bohemianism: Clarke was to maintain a lifelong interest, as reader, writer and *bon viveur* in the life of the streets, those outside respectable society and down-and-outs, or as he put it, Upper and Lower Bohemia. See *CC*, Michael Wilding,

'Marcus Clarke, Bohemian', *Hemisphere*, 26, 1981, 148–51 and introduction to *ST*, and Andrew McCann, *Marcus Clarke's Bohemia* (2004). Upper and Lower Bohemia and its derivation via Balzac and representation in popular Victorian writers is discussed in P. D. Edwards, *Dickens's Young Men: George Augustus Sala, Edmund Yates and the World of Victorian Journalism.*

p. 035   On Clarke's relations with the school authorities, including the headmaster Dr Dyne, see Introduction, and BE 15.

p. 035   Julius Caesar, bar-maid Cleopatra etc: *Bulletin* 13 August 1881, 1–2.

p. 035   Anna Kingsford (1846–88), English doctor of medicine and religious writer, vegetarian and anti-vivisectionist; president of the Theosophical Society 1883, founder of the Hermetic Society 1884. She wrote stories for the *Penny Post* (1868–72) and in 1872 became editor and proprietor of *The Lady's Own Paper*. Quotation from Edward Maitland, *Anna Kingsford, Her Life Letters Diaries and Work,* ed. Samuel Hopgood Hart, 3rd edn, (Watkins, London, 1913).

p. 036   Gustave Doré (1832–83), French artist. He illustrated the Bible (1866), and the works of many writers including Cervantes' *Don Quixote*, Tennyson's *Idylls of the King*, Coleridge's *Rime of the Ancient Mariner* and Milton's *Paradise Lost*. Clarke's essay 'Popular Art and Gustave Doré' appeared in the *Australasian*, 28 September 1867, 392. It is discussed in McCann (2004). Doré's illustrated Dante is mentioned as lying on the table when Clarke experimented with hashish in 'Cannabis Indica (a Psychological Experiment)', *Colonial Monthly*, February 1868, and his illustrated Balzac is referred to in 'A Night at the Immigrants' Home', *Australasian*, 12 June 1869. He is a subject of discussion in 'The Café Lutetia', *Weekly Times*, 28 February 1874, and mentioned in 'Of French Novels', *Argus*, 2 February 1872, and 'Nasturtium Villas', *Weekly Times*, 14 February 1874, all reprinted *CC*. *LMC* lists the following volumes with illustrations by Gustave Doré: Balzac's *Les Contes Drolatiques*, *Historical Cartoons*, Dante's *Inferno*, *The History of Croque Mitaine, or the Chivalric Times of Charlemagne*, translated from the French of L'Epine by Tom Hood, and *The Fables of La Fontaine*, translated into English verse by Walter Thornbury.

p. 036   pictures in the National Gallery in Melbourne: see note to Preface on Adam Lindsay Gordon, to Ch. 2 on Poe, and on Nicholas Chevalier, below.

p. 036   Leslie's 'Little Brigand': a painting by Charles Robert Leslie (1794–1859), English genre and history painter, illustrator of Cervantes, Shakespeare and Molière. He is represented in the National Gallery of Victoria. He was a regular visitor to Holland House, near Clarke's birthplace, and has a painting of the library there, reproduced in William Gaunt, *Kensington* (1958).

p. 036   Nicholas Chevalier (1828–1902), born in St Petersburg, Russia, of a Russian mother and Swiss father, settled in Melbourne in 1855. Painter and illustrator. Introduced chromo-lithography to Australia. His *The Buffalo Ranges*, the first Australian painting purchased for the National Gallery of Victoria, is one of the paintings described by Clarke in the text accompanying the *Photographs of the Pictures in the National Gallery Melbourne* (1874). Excerpts from Clarke's commentary on Chevalier's painting and on Louis Buvelot's *Waterpool at Coleraine* were adapted with slight changes for the well-known passage on Australian scenery in Clarke's preface to Adam Lindsay Gordon's *Sea Spray and Smoke Drift* (1876) and much reprinted and quoted thereafter. It is reprinted in BW and *MC*. Shorn of the specific references to Gordon, it is reprinted as 'Australian Scenery' in *MV*, *AE*, *AT* and *ST*. The original commentary on the paintings is reprinted in *CC*.

p. 036   Myles Birket Foster (1825–99), English painter of idyllic rural scenes. 'Birket Foster, with his golden-haired rustics, eternally meditating in gowns of coloured cotton with his impossible hedgerows, his marvellous clouds, his perpetual briar hedges …' Clarke wrote in 'Nasturtium Villas', *Weekly Times*, 14 February 1874, reprinted *CC*. He is one of the artists (together with Gustave Doré, John Martin, Cattermole, and Holbein) whose work adorns the room described in Clarke's 'Cannabis Indica', *Colonial Monthly*, 6 February 1868. His work is represented in the Art Gallery of New South Wales.

p. 036   Julius Olssen (1864–1942), painter of coastal scenes, exhibited at the Royal Academy. Hopkins has 'Olsen'.

p. 036   George Sutherland (1855–1905), *Australia, or England in the South* (1886), 118. Born in Scotland, he migrated to Sydney in 1864, moved to Melbourne in 1870 and later to Adelaide. Journalist and author of *Tales of the Goldfields* (1880) and co-author with his brother Alexander Sutherland of *The History of Australia* (1877).

Chapter 4

p. 037   Mrs. Gamp: a character in Charles Dickens' novel *Martin Chuzzlewit* (1843–44).

p. 038   'Ken Wood as I have seen it written': 'as I have seen it written' later deleted by CH. The park of Ken Wood, Lord Mansfield's home, contained a pool in which Highgate Grammar School boys used to swim.

p. 038   Virgil (Publius Vergilius Maro) (70–19 BC), Roman poet, author of *Aeneid* etc. *LMC* lists *Specimens of Translations of Catullus and Virgil.*

p. 038   'At length, above a door of ivory': the quotation is from Clarke's story 'Holiday Peak', *Australasian*, 18 January 1873, 72; 25 January, 104. Hopkins' use of this published piece to illustrate Clarke's schoolboy conversation is misleading and puzzling here and may show him conflating memories from different periods.

p. 038   Lenore: the name may derive from Lenora d'Este, the legendary subject of the passion of Tasso, the Italian epic poet, referred to by Clarke in Ch. 9; or from the popular ballad 'Lenore' (1774) by the German poet Gottfried August Bürger (1747–94), translated into English by William Taylor (1765–1836); or, most likely, from Poe's ballads 'The Raven' and 'Lenore'.

p. 038   Dante Alighieri (1265–1321), Florentine poet, whose love for Beatrice is celebrated in his *Vita nuova* and the *Divina Commedia*. Clarke refers to Beatrice in *LO*, and to Dante in 'The Peripatetic Philosopher', *Australasian*, 5 March 1870, reprinted *CC*, in 'A Night at the Immigrants' Home', *Australasian*, 12 June 1869, and *HNL*. Doré's illustrated Dante is mentioned as lying on the table when Clarke experimented with hashish in 'Cannabis Indica', *Colonial Monthly*, February 1868. A copy of the *Inferno*, translated by Henry Cary (1772–1844) is listed in *LMC*.

p. 038   Petrarch (Francesco Petrarca) (1304–74), Italian poet.

p. 038   Robert Burns (1759–96), Scots poet, whose poems include 'Mary Morison' and 'To Mary in Heaven'. *LMC* lists The Songs of Burns.

p. 038   Byron: see note to Ch. 2.

p. 038   The Raven possibly derives from Edgar Allen Poe's ballad (1845), referred to in Ch. 5.

p. 040   'Cigars and Cognac': a familiar soldiers' song from, though possibly predating, the American Civil War. It is referred to in *Gardner's Photographic Sketchbook of the War* (1866), plate 50, 'The Halt', and in *Scribner's Monthly* (December 1878). Clarke cites it in *LO*.

p. 040   Agnes Beckwith: billed as 'the greatest lady swimmer in the world' at the Royal Aquarium, Westminster: in 1875 as a teenager she swam from London Bridge to Greenwich, a distance of six miles.

p. 040   Lord Mansfield's meadow: the park of Ken Wood, Lord Mansfield's home, contained a pool in which Highgate boys used to swim. Clarke found these the most enjoyable times of his school days and swimming later became Gerard's favourite physical recreation. They customarily swam naked, hence there was 'an undercurrent of sensuality about it' (R. B. Martin, 13–14). Frederick Walker's painting *Bathers* (1867), featuring a group of naked boys, was a favourite of GMH's (Martin plate 16).

p. 040   A friend of his father's: Rev. Edward Penny and his sister Mrs Zwilchenbart, named as Clarke's guardians in his father's will. Clarke recalled his farewell visit to them in 'Sunday at Farnham Rectory', *Leader* supplement, 24 April 1880 (BE 23). An incomplete draft of a letter from Clarke to Mrs Zwilchenbart survives in SLV (McL 2892; see Ian F. McLaren, 'Marcus Clarke Writes "Home" to Mrs Zwilchenbart', *Margin*, 7, August 1981, 14–19).

p. 040   Popular airs from operas: *Il trovatore* (1853) and *La traviata* (1853) by Giuseppe Verdi (1813–1901); *L'elisir d'amore* (1832) by Gaetano Donizetti (1797–1848); *Dinorah (Le pardon de Ploërmel)* (1859) by Giacomo Meyerbeer (1791–1864). Clarke refers to Verdi in *LO*.

p. 040   of whom he gossiped afterwards to his readers: apparently Clarke wrote to the Hopkins boys from home when not at school and Cyril draws on these letters for Clarke's experiences before he went to Australia.

p. 040   'Life is vanity we know': from Clarke's essay 'The Pursuit of Pleasure', *Australasian*, 18 April 1868, reprinted in *The Peripatetic Philosopher*, 44, and in *CC* as 'Colonial Holiday Making'.

p. 041   Robert Herrick (1591–1674), English poet, author of *Hesperides and Noble Numbers* (1647). The quoted lines express the *carpe diem* theme characteristic of Herrick's work, but do not seem to be written by him. 'Be happy while we may' echoes, however faintly, Herrick's 'Gather ye rosebuds while ye may'.

p. 041   middle aged Mephistopheles: from 'Humans Repetends', *Australasian*, 14 September 1872, 326. Although this is unusually colourful language for Clarke to have used, the tone of the passage suggests that it should be taken seriously and that although again Cyril omits parts of Clarke's letter, probably censoring it, Clarke was genuinely bitter and disappointed about being exposed too early in life to the rakish or hawkish behaviour of his older military cousins, whether or not this was due to his father's supposed indifference or his withdrawal from the world. Clarke was inclined to boast boyishly to his friends of the freedom he was allowed, especially in observing sexual adventures, if not participating, as in the following reference to an episode at Como. While BE is cautious and sees no reason to believe that Clarke's own 'dissipation' was 'excessive', there is also no reason to disbelieve that, while no Victorian moralist, he may have been revolted by the sexual exploitation of young girls shown in a veiled way in the autobiographical story 'La Béguine', possibly seeing in it something of what he saw in his own case as a lack of care (see note to Ch. 1 on this story and 'Human Repetends').

p. 041   Lord Dundreary is a character in the play *Our American Cousin* (1858) by Tom Taylor (1817–80), English dramatist, author of more than seventy plays, professor of English, and editor of *Punch*. This was the play that Abraham Lincoln was attending when he was assassinated, 14 April 1865. GMH wrote to E. H. Coleridge, 3 September 1862, 'I *have* seen Lord Dundreary. It is truly admirable. I wish you could have seen it' (C. C. Abbott, ed., *Further Letters of Gerard Manley Hopkins*, 8).

p. 041   'Raindeer – a deer with large horns, which, in the northern regions draws sledges through the snow', Samuel Johnson (1709–84), *A Dictionary of the English Language* (London, 1775). Clarke refers to Johnson and Boswell in *LO* and to Johnson's textual emendations to *Macbeth* in 'Noah's Ark', 18 May 1872, reprinted *CC*. *LMC* lists *The Works of Samuel Johnson*, edited by Arthur Murphy and Boswell's *Life of Johnson*.

p. 041   'Speech Days and School Days': in 'The Peripatetic Philosopher' column, *Australasian*, 28 December 1867, 817, reprinted *PP* 86. See Brian Elliott, 'Gerard Hopkins and Marcus Clarke', *Southerly*, 8, 1947, 221–23.

p. 042   Tommy Tug: *Tommy Tagg: A Collection of Pretty Poems for the Amusement of Children Three Foot High*, by John Newbery (1713–67), London, 1756.

p. 042   oppidan: of or pertaining to a town; formerly, pertaining to a university town as opposed to the university itself; at Eton college, a student who is not on the foundation and who boards with a housemaster.

p. 042   Lilliputian: miniaturised. From *Gulliver's Travels* (1726), by the Irish writer Jonathan Swift (1667–1745). Clarke uses 'Lilliputian' and 'Brobdignagian' in *LO* and refers to

Swift in 'Of French Novels', *Argus*, 2 February 1872. *LMC* lists *The Complete Works of Swift* in two volumes.

p. 042   Thomas Traddles and David Copperfield, characters in *David Copperfield* (1849–50); Paul Dombey, character in *Dombey and Son* (1848), novels by Charles Dickens.

p. 042   Coventry Patmore (1823–96), English poet who, upon his father's financial crash, became assistant in the printed book department of the British Museum. He converted to Roman Catholicism and in 1883 became a friend of GMH. See Claude Colleer Abbott, ed., *Further Letters of Gerard Manley Hopkins including his correspondence with Coventry Patmore* (1956). His brother was an editor of the Melbourne *Argus* (Sir Charles Gavan Duffy, *My Life in Two Hemispheres*, 1898, 2, 237n).

Chapter 5

p. 043   Hamilton Mackinnon: *The Marcus Clarke Memorial Volume*, ed. Hamilton Mackinnon (1884) 19. Mackinnon condenses and paraphrases the concluding lines of the passage.

p. 044   The death certificate of Clarke's father reads: Death of William Hislop Clarke – Age: 56 years – Profession: Barrister at Law – Date: 1 December 1863 – Place: Northumberland House Lunatic Asylum – Cause of Death: Softening of the Brain – Several years Certified. – District: Stoke Newington, County of Middlesex.

p. 045   enabled to sail for Melbourne: according to Judge Langton Clarke, Marcus arrived in Australia with £300 (McL, item 3072, 252). This is markedly less than the £800 Hugh Pontifex inherits in the story 'Human Repetends'.

p. 046   'The Lady of Lynn': a copy of this poem is contained in Clarke's Notebook held in the ML. It is reprinted in *MV*. The whereabouts of GMH's illustration are not known.

p. 046   Lord John Russell, first Earl Russell (1792–73), English politician, Prime Minister 1846–52, 1865, Foreign Secretary 1852–53, 1859–65. *The Official Correspondence on the Claims of the United States in respect to the* Alabama, preface by Earl Russell (1867).

p. 046   Alexander William Kinglake (1809–91), author of *Eothen: or Traces of Travel Brought Home from the East* (1844), referred to by Clarke in Ch. 8. Kinglake accompanied the British troops to the Crimea in 1854 and wrote a history of the war, *The Invasion of the Crimea: Its Origin, and an Account of Its Progress down to the Death of Lord Raglan* (1863–87). Kinglake's *History of the Crimean War* is listed in *LMC*.

p. 046   Elizabeth Gaskell (1810–65), English novelist, author of *North and South* (1855).

p. 046   *Once a Week*: 'we three had jointly taken it school' i.e. GMH, Clarke and Cyril. Manley Hopkins contributed regularly to it. One of GMH's earliest poems, 'Winter with the Gulf Stream', one of the few published in his lifetime, appeared in *Once a Week* in 1863, probably through his father's association with the magazine (R. B. Martin, 21). It seems that Clarke continued to read *Once a Week* in Australia. In 1874 he bought a complete set of the journal, see Ch. 27. Charles Reade's novel *Foul Play* was serialised in *Once a Week* in 1868 before book publication the following year; Clarke's adaptation of it for the stage was performed at the Duke of Edinburgh Theatre, Melbourne, 7 December 1868.

Clarke's unsuccessful attempts to get his poetry into print can be paralleled with GMH's unsuccessful attempts to publish 'The Wreck of the *Deutschland*' and 'The Loss of the Eurydice' in *The Month* in 1875 and 1879 (Martin 249, 313–14). Of Clarke's attempt to place his writing in England, 'A Mining Township' was the only story he ever sold to a magazine there – to *All the Year Round, incorporating Household Words*, the journal founded and edited by Charles Dickens. The story appeared as 'An Australian Mining Township', 22 February 1873, 352–7. Publication had been arranged not by Cyril Hopkins but by Mrs Cashel Hoey; letter of acceptance in ML, MSS ZA819, State Library of New South Wales. Clarke later contributed a number of articles to the London *Daily Telegraph* (see Ch. 12) and a dozen scholarly items to *Notes and Queries*

(see Michael Wilding and Joan Poole, 'Marcus Clarke's Contributions to *Notes &*
Queries', *ALS*, 6, 1973, 186–9).

p. 046   George Meredith (1828–1909), English novelist and poet, author of *Beauchamp's*
Career (1876), *The Egoist* (1879) etc. *Evan Harrington* was serialised in *Once a Week*,
11 February – 13 October 1860; published in book form by Harper, New York, 1 vol.,
1860, and Bradbury & Evans, London, 3 vols, 1861. He also published 'A Storytelling
Party' in *Once a Week*, 24 December 1859, and poems there in 1859 and 1864.

p. 046   *The Silver Chord*: a novel (1861) by Shirley Brookes (1816–74), the editor of *Punch*.
LMC lists *Sooner or Later* by Shirley Brookes, 2 volumes.

p. 046   *Ready Money Mortiboy*: a popular novel (1872) by Sir Walter Besant (1836–1901) and
James Rice (1843–82).

p. 046   Tennyson: see note to Ch. 2.

p. 046   Swinburne: see note to Ch. 3.

p. 046   Dante Gabriel Rossetti (1828–82), English poet and painter, co-founder of the Pre-
Raphaelite Brotherhood. Christina Rossetti (1830–94) was his sister. GMH met them
both in 1864. *LMC* lists Rossetti's Poems.

p. 046   F. L. Lampson: F. Locker-Lampson (1821–95), English poet.

p. 046   Austin Dobson (1840–1921), English poet, essayist and biographer.

p. 046   John Everett Millais (1829–96), English painter. His painting *A Huguenot* (1851–52),
depicting lovers parted by historical events, was immensely popular; to the end of his
life, Clarke treasured an engraving of it inherited from his father, mentioned in Ch. 5
– a painting which GMH was still using as an illustration, in an 1881 argument with
Bridges (White (1992) 24–6, 29–30). White states that it was under Marcus's influence
that GMH developed his liking for Millais and Frederick Walker. Clarke refers to
Millais in *LO*. See further in Introduction.

p. 046   Frederick Walker (1840–75), English painter of rustic scenes and illustrator. He
was one of the illustrators of Manley Hopkins' verse in *Once a Week*, and he also
contributed to *Cornhill Magazine*. Walker was Gerard's favourite Victorian painter
(Martin 230–2).

p. 046   John Leech (1817–64), English artist and *Punch* caricaturist.

p. 046   Hablot Knight Browne (1815–82), illustrator of Dickens' novels under the pseudonym
'Phiz'. Clarke refers to him in his essay 'Charles Dickens', *Argus*, 8 July 1870, reprinted
in *CC, MC*.

p. 046   Du Maurier, see note to Ch. 2.

p. 046   Edward Walford (1823–97), English writer. From 1859 to 1897 he was sub-editor and
afterwards editor of *Once a Week*.

p. 046   *Richard Savage* (1842), a novel by Charles Whitehead (1804–62), English novelist
and dramatist, who emigrated to Australia and died in poverty. See Clive Turnbull,
Mulberry Leaves: The Story of Charles Whitehead (Hawthorn Press, Melbourne, 1945).
Clarke's friend J. E. Neild tried to help Whitehead in his last years. Whitehead's
novel is based on the tragic life of the English writer Richard Savage (c. 1697–1743),
commemorated in a biography (1744) by Samuel Johnson. Clarke refers to Savage in
LO and uses the name Savage to describe his friend Alfred Telo, with whom he had
shared rooms, in his memoir of his own literary Bohemian years, 'The Café Lutetia',
Weekly Times, 28 February 1874. Clarke wrote an obituary of Telo in the *Leader*, 11
October 1879, reprinted in *CC*.

p. 046   'The Haunted House' by Thomas Hood (1799–1845), English poet. Clarke refers
to 'genial Tom Hood' in his essay 'Charles Dickens', *Argus*, 8 July 1870, 7. *LMC* lists
Hood's *Whims and Oddities*, and *The History of Croque-Mitaine, or the Chivalric Times*
of Charlemagne, translated by Tom Hood.

p. 046   I took a copy of the original MS of Marcus's verses: the text of the 'Lady of Lynn'
quoted by Hopkins here differs somewhat from that in *MV*; it is presumably taken
from the MS sent to him by Clarke.

p. 048   Samuel Taylor Coleridge (1772–1834), English poet. His 'Christabel' was published in *Christabel and Other Poems* (1816). Clarke refers to his *The Rime of the Ancient Mariner* (1798) in Ch. 25 below, in 'An Australian Crusoe' in *OT*, in his comments on Rabelais in 'Balzac and Modern French Literature', *Australasian*, 3 August 1867, and in 'Noah's Ark', 18 May 1872, reprinted *CC*. Coleridge was buried in the Highgate School chapel, his grandson, a friend of GMH, being an Old Cholmeleian. The body was disinterred in 1961 following a dispute with the local council. *LMC* lists a copy of 'Faust translated by Hayward' with the annotation '*Author's presentation copy to S. T. Coleridge*'.

p. 048   'Human Repetends': see note to Ch. 1 and Ch. 4.

p. 048   Millais, 'The Huguenots': see note above. The correct title of the painting is *A Huguenot*.

p. 048   The photograph we selected: originally CH wrote 'The portrait selected'.

p. 049   'weird melancholy': in Clarke's preface to Adam Lindsay Gordon's *Sea Spray and Smoke Drift* (1876) and *Poems* (1880), reprinted in BW and *MC*. Shorn of the specific references to Gordon, it is reprinted as 'Australian Scenery' in *MV*, *AE*, *AT* and *ST*. See further in notes to Preface on A. L. Gordon and to Ch. 2 on Poe.

p. 049   'wearing his heart upon his sleeve for daws to peck at': 'But I will wear my heart upon my sleeve/ For daws to peck at', Shakespeare, *Othello*, 1, 1, 64–5. A favourite maxim of Clarke's; quoted in *LO* and in 'Noah's Ark', *Australasian*, 7 December 1872, reprinted *CC*. Daws are jackdaws, a bird obsessed with snapping up trifles, and also a carrion eater. Cf. Rufus Dawes in *HNL*.

p. 049   James Hannay (1827–73), Scottish novelist and critic; quotation from his *The Poetical Works of Edgar Allan Poe with a Notice of his Life and Genius by J. H.* (Addey & Co., London, 1853) xiv. The verses quoted are from William Wordsworth's poem 'Ruth'.

Chapter 6

p. 050   Clarke left for Australia on 16 March 1863; the following month, Gerard left his parents' house at 9 Oak Hill Park, Hampstead, to take up residence at Balliol College, Oxford. GMH wrote to E. T. Coleridge, 22 March 1863: 'Poor Clarke is on the voyage out to Australia, his father having met with a paralysis of the brain' (Claude Colleer Abbott, ed., *Further Letters of Gerard Manley Hopkins including his correspondence with Coventry Patmore,*, 1956, 14). Clarke's father lingered on; he died 1 December 1863.

p. 050   The first letter I received: cf. Clarke's 'Peripatetic Philosopher' essay, 'Letters from Home', *Australasian*, 28 November 1868, 689, reprinted *PP*. 'Do we not remember the glowing letters we were wont – for the first six months – to send home? How we described the voyage, and the captain, and the passengers, and the crew – how we gave our experience of the tropics, and our impressions of the Southern Cross – how we revelled in accounts of Melbourne, and talked about "lucky diggers" and buck-jumping horses – how we found out that "society here is not very different from society at home" … By and bye we get less communicative …'.

p. 050   tension of nature: MS has 'tenison'.

p. 051   Mark Twain, pseudonym of Samuel Langhorne Clemens (1835–1910), American writer, author of *The Adventures of Huckleberry Finn* (1884) etc. He writes about his travels in Australia in Part 3 of *Following the Equator: A Journey Around the World* (1897), quoted Chapters 13, 15, 18. A fuller text was published in England under the title *More Tramps Abroad*. Clarke refers to him in 'The Peripatetic Philosopher', *Australasian*, 3 October 1868, and 'Noah's Ark', *Australasian*, 25 May 1872, both reprinted *CC*. ML holds a letter from Twain to Clarke. Twain's *Innocents Abroad* is listed in *LMC*.

p. 051   crossed the Equator: Mark Twain, *More Tramps Abroad*, Ch. IV, 32.

p. 052   Mark Twain's commendation of Clarke: see Miriam Shillingsburg, *At Home Abroad: Mark Twain in Australia* (University of Mississippi Press, Jackson and London, 1988) and 'From Ballarat to Bendigo with Mark Twain', *ALS*, 12, 1985, 116–19; see also, Francis Madigan, *Mark Twain's Passage to India* (Microfilms International, Ann Arbor Michigan, 1977), and Laurie Hergenhan, 'Beautiful Lies, Ugly Truths', *Overland* 187, 2007, 42–6. McL cites several references (under Samuel Clemens): 186–87, 199–201, 1687, 3125, 3330. Another American writer, Jack London, who visited Australia in 1908, also singled out *HNL* as one of the country's best and 'classic' novels. See Laurie Hergenhan, 'Jack London and the Never Never', *Overland*, 4, 2004, 58.

p. 052   'a sunset that much impressed him': for discussion of this and its similarity to GMH, see introduction, Norman White, *Hopkins: A Literary Biography* (1992) and BE 24–5. CH copies a diagram from Clarke's letter.

p. 052   R. L. Stevenson, *Vailima Letters: being correspondence addressed by R. L. S. to Sidney Colvin* (Methuen, London, 1895) 158–60; letter of 1 May 1892.

p. 054   Ludovic de Beauvoir (1846–1929), *Australie. Voyage autour du monde* (Henri Plon, Paris, 5th edn 1871. English translation 3 vols, 1869–72, London, John Murray). An account of a voyage around the world, 1866–68, including travels in Victoria, Tasmania and New South Wales.

p. 056   'He landed at Melbourne': 'Eighty-one days after leaving Plymouth, on 6 June 1863, Cape Otway was sighted. It was the first land seen since the Cape of Good Hope. The morning was stormy and the ship ran before an erratic north to north-west gale. She passed Port Phillip Heads during the following night and berthed next day at the Melbourne and Hobson's Bay Railway pier at Port Melbourne, then known as Sandridge' (BE 26). Hyndman's voyage out in 1869 took 104 days (H. M. Hyndman, *The Record of an Adventurous Life*, 1911, 89).

p. 056   Howitt: Alfred Howitt (1830–1908), Australian naturalist, son of English authors William Howitt (1792–1879 and Mary Howitt (1799–1888), led one of the parties to find ill-fated explorers Burke and Wills.

p. 056   in the words of Hamilton Mackinnon: *MV* 19.

Chapter 7

p. 057   James Langton Clarke (1800–86), Marcus's uncle, was educated at Sandhurst but left the army for the law, taking his MA at Cambridge and being called to the bar at the Middle Temple at the age of forty-two. Ten years later he married a Miss Harrison, who predeceased him. He emigrated to Melbourne about 1855, setting up as a barrister at 40 Temple Court, Little Collins Street West. In July 1858 he was appointed Judge of Mines and of the County Court at Mount Ararat, a flourishing gold mining town 150 miles from Melbourne. His last appointments were to conduct the General Sessions at Maryborough in 1868 and Inglewood in 1869. He left Australia in 1870 and settled at Nice and afterwards at Mentone (BE 2–3).

The uncle's responsibilities began immediately when Marcus seemed to disappear on arrival. James Langton Clarke sent from Ararat, 10 June 1863, an 'urgent electric telegram for Capt. Standish, Chief Commissioner of Police: Marcus Andrew Clarke my nephew aged seventeen arrived by *Wellesley* from London on Sunday. Mr. Lamoile, Criterion Hotel, St. Kilda promised to go on board for him. Have heard nothing from either of them though I telegraphed Mr. Lamoile yesterday. As he had three hundred pounds (300) something may have happened to him. I am anxious to know if he is safe. Langton Clarke, Judge.' The Chief Commissioner took it seriously and put out a memo to Supt. Nicolson the same day: 'For immediate inquiry. Shd any information be procured this evening, I wish it to be sent to my private residence. Frank Standish, C. C. P.' The following day C. H. Nicholson sent a Memo for immediate delivery: 'The young man Marcus Andrew Clarke arrived at the Criterion Hotel last night with his luggage, and a letter to that effect was forwarded to Judge Clarke from the landlord by last night's post. M. A. Clarke left the hotel about noon today, having been invited out to dine.' The documents are preserved in the Melbourne Savage Club (McL 3072).

Judge Clarke later arranged Clarke's brief experience on a sheep station near Ararat in which he had an interest. BE suggests 'there was a tutelary relationship between them for some years, tenuous as at times it must have been' (BE 29) and Clarke eventually made his own way into journalism and authorship against family traditions of careers in the army, law and the civil service.

p. 057	Hamilton Mackinnon observes: *MV* 19.
p. 058	Leveresque: from the novelist Charles Lever; see note to Ch. 3. On Clarke's assessment of Lever, see Ch. 24.
p. 058	G. A. Sala, *Gaslight and Daylight: with some London Scenes They Shine Upon* (Chapman and Hall, London, 1859). On Sala, see note to Ch. 3.
p. 058	*In Her Earliest Youth* (1890) by Tasma, pseudonym of Jessie Couvreur (1848–97), Australian novelist, author of *Uncle Piper of Piper's Hill* (1889). Born at Highgate, London, she came to Australia as a child; travelled in Europe, settling in Brussels with her second husband, Auguste Couvreur, journalist and politician.
p. 058	Francis Adams … *Fortnightly*: the passage Hopkins quotes is not from Adams' 'Two Australian Writers', *Fortnightly Review*, 1 September 1892, but from his 'Melbourne and Her Civilization' in Francis W. L. Adams, *Australian Essays* (Inglis, Melbourne, 1886) 1–10.
p. 058	*Daily Telegraph*: on Clarke's contributions to the London *Daily Telegraph*, see notes to Ch. 27.
p. 059	New Chum: the jocular term indicated a condescending superiority of the experienced colonial to newly arrived British migrants. New Chums were a stock topic and target in colonial journalism (extending beyond Henry Lawson's times), like Christmas in Australia and Melbourne cabs and cabbies, as well as in cartoons. The first issue of the Melbourne *Punch*, 1, 1855, 50, contained a cartoon by Nicholas Chevalier of a 'Dialogue between an Old and New Chum;' 'A New Chum's Experience', *Illustrated Australian News*, 11 June 1884, is reprinted *CC* 43.
p. 059	article by Marcus in the *Australasian*: 'New Chums', *Australasian*, 10 October 1868, 465, reprinted in *PP, MV, AE, CC*.
p. 059	glasses: i.e. looking-glasses.
p. 059	they begin life at the Port Phillip or Scott's: Clarke writes of these two hotels in Ch. 8: 'the Port Phillip Club Hotel, patronised by "New Chums," being opposite the Railway-Station … Scott's, the great resting-place of squatters'. For a description see *CC*, notes, 414, and Clarke's essay on Melbourne Hotels, 'Taking Mine Ease in Mine Inn', *Australasian*, 3 July 1869, 8. Dudley Smooth stays at Scott's in 'Arcades Ambo', *Australasian*, 26 February 1870, reprinted as 'Squatters Old and New' in *Holiday Peak*. The narrator Pontifex lives at Scott's in Clarke's story 'Human Repetends', *Australasian*, 14 September 1872, 326.
p. 060	The Peripatetic Philosopher: Clarke used this pseudonym for a series of articles in the *Australasian*, 23 November 1867 – 11 June 1870. He collected some of them in volume form: *The Peripatetic Philosopher by 'Q'* (1869). A selection is reprinted in *MV, AE* and *CC*.
p. 060	Brummagem: term used for counterfeit or shoddy products made in the English light industrial city of Birmingham, from the local dialect form of the city's name. So called after the counterfeit coins made there in the 1670s, and cheap, consumer products through the nineteenth century.
p. 060	'The youth who arrives in Australia from the old country for the purpose of being broken into the life of the Bush': George Sutherland, *Australia, or England in the South* (1886) 72–3. On Sutherland, see note to Ch. 3.
p. 061	A writer on life at Johannesburg: Sutherland 7.

Chapter 8

p. 062   'A Day in Melbourne': this piece is dated by Hopkins, January 1865 (the date of Clarke's letter from which it is taken). BE (49) comments that it was written at the end of Clarke's first sojourn in Melbourne, which Mackinnon dates as January 1865. Harold Love describes it as 'one of Clarke's finest sketches of Melbourne life' in *James Edward Neild* (1989) 68. Some of the details appear in *LO*, the opening paragraphs of Ch. XI. It is loosely based on Clarke's own experiences as a New Chum in Melbourne, as are the following pieces published later with which it may be compared: 'The Brief Experiences of Thomas Twopenny', *Weekly Times*, 14 March 1874; and 'Austin Friars', *Australian Monthly Magazine*, May 1866, reprinted *MV, CC*.

p. 062   'The travelling Briton … is a being quite unknown at the Antipodes': Hopkins exaggerates and is speaking comparatively. The gold rush and later times saw a number of visitors who wrote of their travels (as in the source books which H. H. Richardson drew upon for *Richard Mahony*) and subsequently there were some notable travellers, including Froude and Anthony Trollope.

p. 062   go-ahead Yankees: Hopkins' note suggests this may refer to R. H. Dana (1815–82), American author of *Two Years Before the Mast* (1840). Manley Hopkins quotes him in his *Hawaii: The Past, Present, and Future of Its Island-Kingdom* (1862).

p. 063   *It is Never too Late to Mend* (1856) by Charles Reade, see note to Ch. 3. The MS omits *It Is* from the title. Clarke refers to Reade's novel in his dedication to Sir Charles Gavan Duffy of the first book edition of *HNL*.

p. 063   *The Recollections of Geoffry Hamlyn* (1859) by Henry Kingsley; see note to Preface. The MS misspells the title as 'Geoffrey'.

p. 063   'Derry Boys': possibly the Londonderry Apprentice Boys.

p. 065   Port Phillip Club Hotel, Criterion, Scott's: see notes to Clarke's essay on 'New Chums' in Ch. 7 and notes in *CC* 44.

p. 065   do thee utterly brown: so in MS.

p. 065   nobbler: 'a glass of liquor, usually spirits and water' (G. A. Wilkes, *A Dictionary of Australian Colloquialisms*, 1985, 290). In Clarke's work, it is usually brandy and water.

p. 065   coon: derogatory term for an Afro-American. Wilkes records first use for an Aborigine as 1921.

p. 00   do thee utterly down: MS has 'utterly brown'.

p. 066   Barry Sullivan as Hamlet: Barry Sullivan (1821–91), actor, born in Birmingham, England, of Irish parents, arrived in Melbourne 1862, made his début as Hamlet in Melbourne's Theatre Royal, 1862, and became manager of the Theatre Royal, 1866. Clarke refers to him in 'Austin Friars', *Australian Monthly Magazine*, May 1866, and in 'Noah's Ark', *Australasian*, 7 July 1872, reprinted *CC*.

p. 066   Joseph Jefferson (1829–1905), American actor. He visited Melbourne and Sydney in 1862, playing in theatres there. He left for London in April 1865 (Love 93–4, 201).

p. 066   Albert Smith: see note to Ch. 2. He performed his sketches and entertainments in London from 1850 at Willis's Rooms and, from 1858, at the Egyptian Hall.

p. 066   Kirk's Horse Bazaar: built in 1840 by James Bowie Kirk, this was situated in Kirk's Lane, now Hardware Lane, between Swanston and Queen streets. It was a horse and livery trading centre. Clarke refers to it in 'Austin Friars', *Australian Monthly Magazine*, May 1866, and in *LO*.

p. 067   Sir John Tenniel (1820–1914), English artist, cartoonist for *Punch*, and illustrator of *Alice's Adventures in Wonderland* (1865) and *Through the Looking Glass* (1871). Clarke refers to him in *LO*.

p. 067   the *Argus* has a gorgeous palace: in his journalism, Clarke sometimes referred to the *Argus* newspaper as the *Peacock* and the *Age* as the *Screechowl*; see note below on the Café de Paris.

p. 067   *Telegraph* office: CH footnotes this as an allusion to the London *Daily Telegraph* office – but was that familiar to Clarke? Possibly he is referring to a posts and telegraph office.

p. 069	*Eothen: or traces of travel brought home from the East* by Alexander William Kinglake (1844); see note to Ch. 5.
p. 069	Gilbert Burnet (1643–1715), Scots latitudinarian churchman, author of *Some Passages in the Life and Death of the Right Honourable John Wilmot Earl of Rochester* (1680) and *The History of My Own Times* (2 vols, 1724, 1734).
p. 069	Sir Harry Bedmont: Sir Redmond Barry (1813–80), born Ireland, admitted to the Irish Bar 1838; arrived in Australia 1839. First Solicitor-General of Victoria, 1851, elevated to the bench of the Supreme Court 1852. He played a major part in founding the University of Melbourne, becoming its first Chancellor. He was a judge of the Supreme Court and chair of the trustees of the Melbourne Public Library. He was a friend of Clarke's uncles, Andrew Clarke and James Langton Clarke, and both BE and Mackinnon suggest that Barry was helpful to their nephew, perhaps encouraging him to apply for a position in the Library in 1870 (BE 168–9). Barry was presiding judge at the sentencing of Ned Kelly and died two weeks later. The relationship of Clarke and Barry is the subject of a play, *The Future Australian Race*, by Sue Gore and Bill Garner, first performed in the Queen's Hall, State Library of Victoria, on 5 May 2008.
p. 069	Buffins the Librarian: the founding librarian in 1856 was Augustus Tulk (1810–73); upon his death, he was succeeded by Henry Sheffield.
p. 069	*Bell's Life in Melbourne*: one of Melbourne's thirteen newspapers. It was absorbed by the *Australasian*. Adam Lindsay Gordon was a contributor.
p. 069	Allsop or Bass, Perkins or Barclay? Meux or Guinness: proprietary brands of beer. Allsop and Bass are English; Guinness is Irish stout.
p. 070	'from morn till dewy eve': 'from morn / To noon he fell, from noon to dewy eve', Milton, *Paradise Lost*, 1, 742–3.
p. 071	Robinson, Manager of the Bank of Australasia: MS has Bank of Australia in the text, and Bank of Australasia in the footnote, which identifies Robinson as Henry Gyles Turner [MS incorrectly has 'Giles']. Turner (1831–1920) was not manager, but had become 'chief accountant' in the Bank of Australasia in 1864. He appears in Clarke's novel '*Twixt Shadow and Shine* as 'Mr. Thomas Turnover Scrimminger' (BE 212). His essays on Clarke are cited by Hopkins, see note to Preface.
p. 071	A. Spendall, the Editor of Melbourne *Punch*: Butler Cole Aspinall (1830–75), barrister, journalist, politician. Aspinall was one of several solicitors who defended the Eureka rebels free of charge. Celebrated as a wit, he became 'the most sought after dinner guest in Melbourne' but 'led a life of gay dissipation' (*Australian Dictionary of Biography*) and was, as Clarke's punning soubriquet suggests, notoriously extravagant. He died almost penniless. The Melbourne *Punch*, modelled on the English humorous magazine, ran from August 1855 to December 1925. The first editor was Frederick Sinnett, followed by James Smith (1857–63) and Charles Bright (1863–66). Aspinall was never editor, but had an 'informal association with the magazine during Bright's editorship' (Love 111). 'The Conservative Party were effectually served by a satirical journal named *Melbourne Punch*', Sir Charles Gavan Duffy, *My Life in Two Hemispheres* (1898) 2, 177n.
p. 071	Dr Smiles: Samuel Smiles (1812–1904), English writer, author of *Self-help* (1859).
p. 071	Money Moulinet: Henry Miller (1809–1888), Melbourne financier, insurance broker and politician, known as 'Money' Miller.
p. 072	Thomas Blowhard Bellows: probably refers, in part at least, to Justice Sir Redmond Barry (see note above), formerly a barrister in Sydney, known and painted as a sprightly and portly equestrian. His companion, Mrs Louisa Barrow, who customarily accompanied him on social occasions, bore him four children who were given Barry's surname.
p. 072	Edward Gibson: Edward Wilson. Gavan Duffy recalls 'a bold *coup* struck at this time by Edward Wilson, the proprietor of the *Argus*. As England continued to send her convicts to Australia, he proposed to collect some of the worst of them whose sentences had expired, and send them back to their native country. A committee was formed of men willing to aid this project … The passages of about a dozen of them were paid, and an order given to each of them for a small sum to be handed to him

on landing. The expense of returning one of these seasoned ruffians to London or Liverpool amounted to about £15, and Mr. Wilson was persuaded that there would be funds forthcoming for the passage of a thousand. But before a dozen of these prodigal children had returned to their country, transportation was abandoned, this bold stroke being, I am persuaded, the chief factor in our deliverance' (Duffy 2, 248–9).

p. 072   carmen: cab drivers. Clarke wrote on them in the 'Peripatetic Philosopher' column, *Australasian*, 20 February 1869, reprinted *PP, MV, AE, CC*.

p. 073   Café Royal: Café de Paris, the upstairs luncheon and supper rooms with a private bar-lounge, attached to the Theatre Royal in Bourke Street; 'sometimes referred to as the Theatre Royal Café though this was never its official name' (*CC* 463–4). Clarke later wrote it up nostalgically as 'The Café Lutetia', *Weekly Times*, 28 February 1874, 9. See further next note.

p. 074   Theatre Royal: opened in July 1855 with a capacity of 3,300. 'Erected at a cost of £95000, the building measured 91 feet by 313, covering an area of upwards of half an acre. The interior, with its three magnificent tiers, was brilliantly lit by 600 burners that were fuelled by the theatre's own 7000 cubic feet gasworks.' The original owner was John Black. In 1856, the Royal was taken over by the entrepreneur George Coppin and his partner Gustavus Brooke. As part of their efforts to rebuild the theatre's reputation and profitability, they installed Felix Spiers and George Hennelle as licensees of the hotel. However, in 1858, Hennelle was replaced by the more experienced hotelier Christopher Pond, and on the eastern side of the theatre, Spiers and Pond launched their Café de Paris, a lavish upstairs restaurant boasting facilities for billiards, coffee drinking and reading newspapers. (*The Yorker*, 35, Summer 2002–03)

p. 074   Charles Young: Charles Frederick Horace Frisby Young (1819–74), an acclaimed comedian and supporting actor, was in 1863 playing at Melbourne's Theatre Royal with star tragedian Barry Sullivan, actor-manager of the 'Royal Company' (as Clarke calls it). Young quarrelled with Sullivan, and later performed in Sydney with Charles Matthews. A son of a successful London theatre manager, he had gained recognition for his role as Noah Claypole in his father's production of *Oliver Twist*. He migrated and performed in Hobart and Launceston under George Coppin, became manager of Melbourne's Queen's Theatre in 1849, and joined G. V. Brooke's company during the gold rushes.

p. 074   Jesse Rural: a character (a clergyman) in Dion Boucicault's comedy *Old Heads and Young Hearts*, first performed at Haymarket Theatre, London, 1844. Clarke mentions him in 'Nasturtium Villas', *Weekly Times*, 14 February 1874, reprinted *CC*.

p. 074   Ambrose Hawke: Ambrose Kyte (1822–68), owner of the Melbourne Theatre Royal during the period in question. Clarke refers to 'dens' in Melbourne's Chinese quarter as owned by this shady entrepreneur, 'The Chinese Quarter', *Argus*, 9 March 1868, 5–6.

p. 075   Dundreary, a character in the play *Our American Cousin* by Tom Taylor. See note to Ch. 4. Taylor also wrote the melodrama *The Ticket-of-Leave Man* (1863), featuring a wrongly transported convict, Bob Brierly, released on ticket-of-leave.

p. 075   *The Vicar of Wakefield* (1766), a novel by Oliver Goldsmith (1730–74), Anglo-Irish writer. Clarke refers to him in *LO* and 'Charles Dickens', *Argus*, 8 July 1870, 7.

p. 075   Sothern: Edward Askew Sothern (1826–81), English-born actor whose performance as Lord Dundreary in an 1858 New York production of *Our American Cousin* brought to that character enduring theatrical fame.

p. 076   the Vestibule: the Vestibule of the Theatre Royal, 'where *the most depraved characters* gathered in *beastly abominable crowds*. No doubt their presence was encouraged by the doors on the western side which led into the Royal Hotel where, at a 150-foot bar, drinkers were served by girls in tights. From this area, known as "The Saddling Paddock", women of ill repute departed with their clients' (*The Yorker*, 35, Summer 2002–03).

p. 076   The Saddling Paddock: a pick-up place for prostitutes; see *CC* 463.

p. 077   Clelia Howson, actress and singer, was born in Hobart in 1845, a daughter of Frank Howson, the first significant impresario of opera in Australia. She was a celebrated performer in pantomime and 'extravaganza', as well as opera, in the colonies. After her marriage to Hosmer Pearson in 1870, she lived in New York. See Nicole Anae, 'The New Prima Donnas: "Homegrown" Tasmanian "Stars" of the 1860s, Emma and Clelia Howson', in *Journal of Australasian Studies*, January 2005, 173–85.

p. 078   the great haunt of Chinamen: Clarke wrote up 'The Chinese Quarter' of Little Bourke Street, concentrating on vice and drugs, as the third of a series of 'Night Scenes in Melbourne', *Argus*, 9 March 1868, 5–6.

p. 078   Mohier's wax works: Sohier's Waxwork Exhibition, an imitation of Madame Tussaud's in London, see Love 67–9.

p. 078   The Bushranger Gardiner: Francis Gardiner (1830–1904), bushranger, also known as Francis Christie and Francis Clarke. Sentenced to thirty-two years hard labour on two non-capital charges, he was released in 1874 after a petition organised by his defending lawyer, W. B. Dalley, on condition that he went into exile. He went to San Francisco where he opened a successful bar. See Alec Morrisson, *Frank Gardiner: Bushranger to Businessman 1830–1904* (John Wiley, Brisbane, 2003).

p. 079   Captain Price: for discussion of Price as a model for Maurice Frere in *HNL*, see H. J. Boehm, '*His Natural Life* and its Sources', *ALS*, 5, 1971, 42–64 and J. V. Barry, *The Life and Death of John Price* (Melbourne University Press, Melbourne, 1964).

p. 081   Cockamaroo: 'Russian' bagatelle.

p. 081   blind hookey: a card game in which no one looks at his cards, but each makes his stake purely on speculation.

p. 081   Jews, Turks, infidels and heretics: from the 3rd Collect for Good Friday, *Book of Common Prayer* (1662): 'have mercy upon all Jews, Turks, Infidels and Hereticks'. Cf. Adam Lindsay Gordon, 'De Te':

> No man may shirk the allotted work,
> > The deed to do, the death to die;
> At least I think so, – neither Turk,
> > Nor Jew, nor infidel am I.

On nineteenth-century racial attitudes in Australia, see *Who Are Our Enemies? Racism and the Australian Working Class*, ed. Anne Curthoys and Andrew Markus (Hale & Iremonger, Sydney, 1978).

Chapter 9

p. 084   of more than 50 years ago: in his MS Hopkins has changed this from 'of forty five years ago'. This suggests that, given the date of Clarke's 'A Day in Melbourne' (1865) in the previous chapter, Hopkins originally wrote his biography circa 1910 and made minor changes in the ensuing years, such as the change here circa 1915, and in 1924 in the preface; see note to Preface, and Introduction on the provenance of the text.

p. 084   Bank of Australasia: Clarke's uncle, the judge, had not agreed with the idea of a career in writing and journalism. When the judge advised him to take a job in the bank, Clarke was appointed on a probationary basis to a junior position. 'The Brief Experiences of Thomas Twopenny', *Weekly Times*, 14 March 1874, draws satirically upon Clarke's experiences in the bank. Clarke did not like the work, leaving it after a year or less to go up-country to a station near where the judge lived. Clarke wrote satirically about the bank in 'In a Bark Hut' (see note to Ch. 11). P. G. Wodehouse had a similar lack of enthusiasm for his early job in a bank, 1900–02 – see Robert McCrum, *Wodehouse: A Life* (Viking, London, 2004) Ch. 3. Both he and Clarke far preferred journalism, fiction and the theatre.

p. 084   Booroondara, Kew: today situated on a hill on the perimeter of the inner suburbs, and regarded comparatively as one itself, Kew remains a prestigious suburb whose famous residents have included John Wren, model for the protagonist of Frank Hardy's novel *Power Without Glory*, and Archbishop Mannix in his palace of Raheen.

p. 084 entrée into some pleasant houses: Clarke had influential connections, such as his uncle and Judge Barry, but in 1946 a lady in her nineties told Elliott that Clarke had not been '*crème de la crème*' (BE 256), though she may have been thinking about his later years.

p. 084 I am told: possibly by Clarke's wife or children, with whom Hopkins was in contact before and after he wrote his biography. See editorial note on the provenance of the text.

p. 085 Thomas De Quincey (1785–1859), English author of *Confessions of an English Opium Eater* (1822), cited by Clarke in his account of an experiment with hashish, 'Cannabis Indica', *Colonial Monthly*, February 1868, 454–68. De Quincey's account of his involvement with the young prostitute Ann has possible echoes in Clarke's stories 'Holiday Peak', *Australasian*, 18 January 1873, 72; 25 January, 104 and 'La Béguine', *Australasian*, 8 February 1873, 166.

p. 085 Jacques Callot (1592/93–1635), French engraver, who specialised in depicting beggars and grotesques. Clarke refers to him in *HNL*, and in 'A Cheap Lodging-House', *Australasian*, 31 July 1869, and 'Of French Novels', *Argus*, 2 February 1872.

p. 085 'The Puff Conclusive': *Melbourne Punch*, 19 November 1863, 162.

p. 085 Charles Kean (1811–68), English actor, son of the actor Edmund Kean (1787–1833).

p. 086 The actors cited by Clarke, English unless otherwise specified, are: Mrs Elizabeth Barry (1653–1713), the first great tragedienne of the English stage; John Philip Kemble (1757–1823), brother of Sarah Siddons; William Charles Macready (1793–1873), considered by William Hazlitt 'the best tragic actor of my remembrance, except Kean;' George Davies Harley (d. 1811); Edward Kynaston (1640–1706); James William Dodd (1734–96); Thomas Betterton (1635–1710), the most famous English actor of the Restoration; Thomas Doggett (1670–1721), known for comic roles; Barton Booth (1681–1721); Sarah Siddons (1755–1831) leading English tragedienne; Eliza Farren, Countess of Derby (1778–1848); Powell, American actor, who founded the New Exhibition Room in Boston in 1792; Jordan – Dorothea Jordan (1772–1816), English actor, mistress of the Duke of Clarence; Dowton – William Dowton (1763–1851) or William Payton Dowton (1795–1883); Robert William Elliston (1774–1831), who developed the 'burletta'; Richard Suett (1755–1805); Robert Wilks (1665–1732); David Garrick (1717–79), the great eighteenth-century actor-manager (referred to in *LO*); Susannah Cibber (1714–66), sister of the composer Thomas Arne and wife of Colley Cibber's son, Theophilus: Handel is said to have arranged contralto parts for her in his *Messiah*; Henry Mossop (1729/30–1773/74); James Quin (1694–1766), who headed the Covent Garden Theatre Company; and Charles Bannister (d. 1804). Amongst titles listed in *LMC* is Morley's *Journal of a London Playgoer*, with the annotation 'Mr. Morley was for many years the critic for the *Advertiser*, and his observations comprise notices of Brooke, Kean, Sullivan, and others, when these actors first appeared upon the stage'.

p. 086 Préville, Clairon, Mademoiselle Mars: famous French actresses in eighteenth-century Paris.

p. 086 Torquato Tasso (1544–95), Italian epic poet, author of *Gerusalemme liberata*, whose father Bernardo Tasso was also a poet.

p. 086 Raffaelo Sanzio (Raphael) (1483–1520), Italian painter, son of the painter Giovanni Santi.

p. 086 'Natura lo fece e ruppe la stampa': Nature made him and [then] broke the mould [used to make him].

p. 087 'What May Happen to a Man in Victoria': McL lists this as a farce, played at the Theatre Royal, c. 1864, text unseen. 'A play called "What a Man May Suffer in Victoria", by an unknown author was twice performed at the Melbourne Theatre Royal in 1857 (six years before Clarke arrived in Australia) … In 1878 E. C. Martin's drama, "What May Happen to a Man in Victoria", was given three performances at the Princess Theatre in Melbourne, but this, far from being a farce dealt with the possibility of circumstantial evidence sending a man to the gallows.' Eric Irvin, 'Marcus Clarke and the Theatre', *ALS*, 7, 1, May 1975, 3.

p. 087 The Lady of the Lake [Moustique]: listed by McL (text unseen) as 'a burlesque, a parody from W. Scott, played Theatre Royal'. McL (1166) cites conflicting information about this play: Irvin (3) states: 'It is not possible to find any evidence that a version of 'The Lady of the Lake' by Clarke was ever produced. The play of that name known to Melbourne audiences during his lifetime was one of six versions of the story written by English playwrights between 1810 and 1873.' Then McL also goes on to cite John Spring, *A Frequency List of Dramatic Performances* (1977) as 'listing 8 performances', presumably of the Clarke.

p. 087 some time late in 1864: evidently a mistake for 1867, since 'The Peripatetic Philosopher' did not begin publication until 23 November 1867.

p. 087 Peripatetic Philosophy: Clarke's *Australasian* column under the name of 'The Peripatetic Philosopher', using Sala's journalism as one model, and the basis of his first book. It ran from 23 November 1867 to 11 June 1870.

p. 088 G. A. Sala, *Twice Round the Clock* (Maxwell, London, 1859); listed in *LMC*.

p. 088 the 'Noah's Ark' papers: this regular column 'Noah's Ark. By Marcus Clarke' appeared in the weekly *Australasian* from 18 May 1872 to 13 September 1873. It included stories, poems, essays, sketches and dialogues. A selection is reprinted in *CC* 275–81. It may have been in part modelled on the essays of the American writer Oliver Wendell Holmes (1809–94), Professor of Anatomy and Physiology at Harvard University from 1847 to 1882, whose *Autocrat at the Breakfast Table* appeared in the *Atlantic Monthly* 1857–58, followed by *The Professor at the Breakfast Table* (1860) and *The Poet at the Breakfast Table*, begun four months previously to 'Noah's Ark' in 1872 (mentioned by Clarke in the series). Clarke dedicated *Holiday Peak* (1873) to Holmes. Some of its stories – including the title story – first appeared in 'Noah's Ark'. There are five MS letters from Holmes to Clarke in the ML (McL 3137–41); Mackinnon prints one about 'Pretty Dick' and excerpts another about *HNL* (*MV* 44, 40–1). *LMC* lists Holmes' *The Professor at the Breakfast Table* and *Guardian Angel*.

p. 088 my mercurial temperament: this recalls GMH's famous description of him when at school, as a 'Kaleidoscopic, Parti-colored, Harlequinesque, Thaumatropic' being, quoted by Cyril in Ch. 3. BE comments in a footnote (16 n. 2) 'the words are ascribed to Gerard Hopkins by Mackinnon, who says he found them written in Hopkins' hand in one of Marcus Clarke's notebooks; but no such entry is to be found in any of the notebooks which survive'.

p. 088 his letters: it is clear here and elsewhere that Hopkins is drawing on only a selection of letters.

p. 088 Ernest Renan (1823–92), French historian, author of *Vie de Jésus* (1863). Clarke refers to him in 'The Peripatetic Philosopher', 18 April 1868 and the *Age*, 23 March 1880, both reprinted *CC*. *LMC* lists *The Life of Jesus* (in the section of the catalogue comprising criminal trials).

p. 088 Ralph Waldo Emerson (1803–82), American poet and philosopher. 'Mr. Emerson's doctrine of compensation' is referred to in Clarke's sketch an 'An Up-country Township', *Australasian*, 6 August 1870, 170.

p. 088 Thomas Carlyle (1795–1881), Scots writer and historian, author of *History of the French Revolution* (1837), *Chartism* (1839), *Past and Present* (1843) etc. Clarke refers to him in 'New Chums' in 'The Peripatetic Philosopher', *Australasian*, 10 October, 1868, and in *LO*. Clarke reprinted his account of the siege of the Bastille in 'The Library Table' feature when editing the *Australian Journal* (see Andrew McCann, *Marcus Clarke's Bohemia: Literature and Modernity in Colonial Melbourne*, 158). Clarke's acquaintance Charles Gavan Duffy was author of *Conversations with Carlyle* (Cassell, London, 1892). *LMC* lists Carlyle's *French Revolution*. MS has 'Carlisle'.

p. 088 Ruskin; see note to Ch. 3.

p. 088 Robert Browning (1812–89), English poet. Clarke refers to him as an influence on Adam Lindsay Gordon's verse in his preface to Gordon's *Sea Spray and Smoke Drift* (1876), reprinted in BW and *MC*. Robb discusses extensively his influence on Gordon

(*Poems*, 1912, xcv–cxx). GMH met him in 1864, but in later life was unimpressed by his poetry (R. B. Martin, 72, 338–9). Clarke felt similarly. Clarke refers to his wife, Elizabeth Browning, in 'Noah's Ark', *Australasian*, 25 May 1872, reprinted *CC. LMC* lists Browning's *Fifine at the Fair.*

p. 088   Immanuel Kant (1724–1804), Prussian philosopher.

p. 088   Jacques Bénigne Bossuet (1627–1704), French preacher.

p. 088   volunteer for military service in New Zealand: between 1863 and 1872, over 2,000 Australian volunteers saw service in New Zealand as reinforcements to regular troops in the colonial wars against the Maori from 1820 until the late 1830s. Clarke considered enlisting, partly in the hope of a land grant in New Zealand, though he wrote in the 'Peripatetic Philosopher' column, *Australasian*, 14 August 1869, that he regarded the British occupation 'as a gross swindle from beginning to end'. He nevertheless continued that 'we' would be fools not to keep the land, that treaties should be stamped out and 'the Maoris must be exterminated!' 'To make treaties and talk bunkum is perfectly useless; they must be stamped out and utterly annihilated.' McCann remarks 'There are strains of Swift's *A Modest Proposal* here to be sure ... What is unclear here is whether or not Clarke intended to reveal the brutality and hypocrisy of colonial policy, or whether a quip about extermination (indeed a *bagatelle pour un massacre*) was simply another deliberately controversial statement like so many others that he made as a way of buoying up his career' (75–6). Clarke was similarly unsympathetic to the Australian Aborigines. He refers to the 'Maori wars' in *The Lady of the Lake* (BE 257).

p. 089   Gardiner: see note to Ch. 8. MS has 'Gardner' here.

Chapter 10

p. 091   Wood's Point in Gipp's Land: a mining township 120 kilometres from Melbourne at the headwaters of the Goulburn River where gold was discovered in 1861. Clarke refers to it in in his review of Bret Harte, *The Luck of Roaring Camp, Australian Journal*, March 1871, 389–90. MS has Gipp's Land; now Gippsland.

p. 092   The Seven Dials: infamous rookery of slums and vice in Covent Garden in Victorian times, often featured in literature, fictional and journalistic. Clarke describes an 'Antipodean Seven Dials' in 'A Melbourne Alsatia', *Colonial Monthly*, February 1869, 473–9.

p. 092   Benjamin Farjeon (1838–1903), English novelist of Jewish descent who came to Australia in 1854, went to New Zealand in 1861 and returned to England after Dickens responded kindly to his first book, *Shadows on the Snow* (1865). *Grif: A Story of Australian Life* was published in Dunedin, 1866, and by Tinsley, London, 2 vols, 1870. He wrote some fifty further novels. Father of the writer Eleanor Farjeon. There is a letter from Farjeon to Clarke in ML.

p. 093   Dunolly: a central, early goldfields town in Victoria famous for one of the largest nuggets discovered. This may have prompted Clarke's sketch, 'The Monster Nugget', see below.

p. 093   'The Monster Nugget': 'Peripatetic Philosopher' column, *Australasian*, 13 February 1869, reprinted *PP.*

p. 093   Hated methodical book-keeping: Mackinnon, *MV* 20, quoting from H. G. Turner, *Melbourne Review*, January 1882.

p. 094   anecdote has already been quoted: Mackinnon quotes from Clarke's 'On Business Men', *Humbug*, 3 November 1869. Text here follows that in *CC* rather than *MV*, which is slightly different.

p. 094   Arthur Patchett Martin, 'An Australian Novelist', *Temple Bar*, 71, May 1884, 97. Martin (1851–1902) emigrated when a baby to Melbourne, later taking an active part in its early literary life and editing the *Melbourne Review*, 1876–82. He then returned to England where he wrote *The Beginnings of an Australian Literature* (1898). Martin's correspondence with Mrs Marian Clarke and Hamilton Mackinnon is in SLV (McL 2804–10).

p. 095   Bank clerk: Charles Bright, *Cosmos*, 30 April 1895, 419.

p. 095   Judge Clarke … squatting station: Bright 420.

Chapter 11

p. 096   'Priestcraft and People': Clarke returned to this project in his essay 'Civilisation without Delusion', see note below.

p. 096   Ruskin; see note to Ch. 3. *The Stones of Venice* (1851–3).

p. 097   Grant Allen (1848–99), born in Canada and educated in the USA and England, writer on philosophical and scientific subjects and later a novelist, author of *The Woman Who Did* (1895).

p. 097   *The Lords of the Ghostland*: (1907), by Edgar Saltus (1855–1921), American writer of novels and philosophical works.

p. 097   Clarke's essay 'Civilisation without Delusion' appeared in the *Victorian Review*, I, 1, November 1879, 65–75, reprinted *MC*. Together with Bishop Moorhouse's reply and Clarke's rejoinder, the whole controversy was collected in book form as *Civilisation without Delusion* (1880) and reprinted with changes as *What Is Religion?* (1895).

p. 098   Swinton station: 'Judge Clarke had lately become interested in a property not far from Ararat, and it was arranged that Marcus should be placed there … The manager of the property, later its owner, was John Holt, a young man himself, well educated, and a booklover, whose background of English middle-class life with army associations very much resembled that of the Clarkes' (BE 46–7). 'Judge Clarke's interest may have been financial but not proprietary. Holt appears as a lessee later' (BE 49).

p. 098   River Wimmera: this becomes the Great Glimmera or Pollywog Creek in 'An Up-country Township', *Australasian*, 6 August 1870.

p. 098   acquire his colonial experience: the emigration to the Australian bush of young sons of *bon viveurs* and literary gentlemen was not completely unusual in the 1860s. Charles Dickens' son, Alfred D'Orsay Tennyson Dickens, was about a year older than Marcus when he migrated, also in 1863, and bought a partnership in a stock and station agency at Hamilton in western Victoria (about 60 km south of Glenorchy Station). Alfred's younger brother, Edward Bulwer Lytton Dickens, migrated to manage a station at Wilcannia in 1869, soon after Clarke's expedition to Fort Bourke, also in western New South Wales. Edward represented Wilcannia in the NSW Legislative Assembly, 1889–94. Anthony Trollope's son Frederick took up a sheep station near Grenfell, New South Wales: the novelist visited him there in 1871 and 1875. Various journalists are known to have met with Trollope in Melbourne, and to have attended his lectures, but there is no record that Clarke was one of them. Nevertheless the eponymous hero of Trollope's *Harry Heathcote of Gangoil* (1874), who is largely based on Fred Trollope, parallels Clarke in some respects. Harry, like Clarke, has been 'left an orphan, with a small fortune', and like Clarke emigrates at the age of sixteen. Trollope depicts station life similarly to that described by Clarke at Glenorchy, showing the squatter's need to 'control' the 'men' in an assertive display of caste; and includes episodes concerning the misdemeanors of station hands, fire-fighting, long horse rides, reading English literature and recent fiction by lamplight on the veranda, etc. The fictional Gangoil is situated in southern Queensland, where Clarke's second ill-fated expedition in search of a property took him immediately before his move to Melbourne.

p. 098   the essay previously mentioned: 'In A Bark Hut', *Australasian*, 17 May 1873.

p. 098   'Dinkledoodledum station': Hopkins goes on to quote from Clarke's sketch, 'In a Bark Hut', *Australasian*, 17 May 1873.

p. 101   write like a literary Ishmael: Clarke did not often write about his feelings as an exile, but he gave indirect expression to them, not only in his great novel but in his

journalism. In 'The Language of Bohemia', *Australasian*, 17 July 1869, and 'In Outer
Darkness', *Australasian*, 21 August 1869, he refers to Ishmael as a metaphor, and
to Esau at the climax of his famous description of Australian scenery reprinted in
his preface to Gordon's poems. Ishmael, eldest son of Abraham, was (together with
his mother, the concubine Hagar) 'cast out to the wilderness' through the influence
of Abraham's wife, Sarah, when he was about sixteen. Sarah, who had been unable
to conceive before Ishmael's birth, wanted her son Isaac to become Abraham's heir.
Ishmael's daughter Mahalath married Esau, eldest son of Isaac and Rebekah, twin
brother of Jacob, who sold his right of inheritance to Jacob in return for some lentil
soup (*Genesis*, Chapters 16–25). The allusions to Ishmael and Esau appear to relate
not only to exile but also perhaps to loss of an inheritance expected by right of birth.
As well, Ishmael is a character in Herman Melville's novel *Moby Dick* (1851), which
Clarke refers to in 'Noah's Ark', *Australasian*, 18 May 1872, reprinted *CC*.

p. 101   the above reflections ... early letters from Swinton: Hopkins' vagueness about
whether a diagram, not included by him, of the station appeared in 'that [letter] or
the following one' indicates that he sometimes relied on memory of various letters
instead of working carefully from MSS. Also as a result, or to condense, as BE suggests,
Hopkins sews together selections from different letters without indication.

p. 101   River Wimmera and 'Hell's Gap': BE points out (490) that the stream was really a
tributary of the Wimmera, and that 'Hell's gap' should have been 'Hall's Gap' [in the
Fyans' Valley], though the former term recurs in Clarke's letters (see Ch. 12). Accurate
or not, it is consistent with Clarke's fondness for using in his writings the grimmer
names of Australian places.

p. 101   'The Cornflower': *Girl with the Cornflowers*, c. 1820s, by the Russian painter Alexey
Venetsianov (1780–1847).

p. 101   hunting sketches: among popular nineteenth-century prints are those by John Leech
(1817–64), illustrating Surtees (see note to Ch. 13), and a series *The Young English Fox
Hunter* engraved by Charles Hunt.

p. 102   William Holman Hunt (1827–1910), English painter, founder member of the Pre-
Raphaelite Brotherhood. Gerard met him in 1864 (R. B. Martin, 72). His painting
I Stand at the Door and Knock, highly praised by Ruskin, is usually called *The Light
of the World*. It shows the redemptive Christ with a lantern knocking at a door in
a wilderness, signifying the wish to visit and comfort every solitary human heart.
The original is in Keble College, Oxford; a larger version of this immensely popular
painting toured Canada, Australia and New Zealand in 1906–07; in Sydney it was
seen by 302,183 visitors in twenty-five days. In *HNL*, the Rev. North fitfully plays
this redemptive role as wayward priest, an alcoholic and would-be adulterer. See L. T.
Hergenhan, 'The Corruption of Rufus Dawes', *Southerly*, 19, 1969, 50–63 and 'The
Redemptive Theme in *His Natural Life*', *ALS*, 2, 1965, 32–49.

p. 102   'scab act for 1865': scab is a disease in sheep.

p. 102   *The Three Musketeers*; historical novel by Alexandre Dumas, see note to Preface. Clarke
refers to it in *LO* and in 'Of French Novels', *Argus*, 2 February 1872, reprinted *CC*.
Listed in *LMC*.

Chapter 12

p. 104   Horace's ode 'Ad Barinem': Horace, Lib. II, Car. 8; MS has 'Ad Barimen' and 'To
Barime'. Hopkins' text, followed here, differs slightly from that published in the
Colonial Monthly, May 1868, 192–3 – e.g. 'saucy' for 'jocund' in stanza 4, and in
lineation. Hopkins may be drawing on a copy of the MS that Clarke sent to him.

p. 104   illustration by my brother, Gerard: GMH illustrated Clarke's writing during their
school days, see Ch. 5.

p. 104   'The Sphinx-Riddle': Clarke's version of the poem by the German Jewish poet Heinrich
         Heine (1797–1856) was published *Australasian*, 7 September 1872, 296, reprinted
         MV, AE. See Andrew McCann, Marcus Clarke's Bohemia: *Literature and Modernity
         in Colonial Melbourne*, 2004, 107. Clarke refers to Heine in *LO*, in 'Noah's Ark',
         Australasian, 18 May 1872, reprinted *CC*, and in the *Age*, 23 March 1880, reprinted
         CC. LMC lists Heine's Poems, translated by Sir E. A. Bowring.

p. 105   *Once a Week:* earlier Cyril had tried unsuccessfully to place Clarke's 'The Lady of Lynn'
         there, see Ch. 5.

p. 106   a skit in verse on the curator of the Botanical Gardens: the curator from 1857 to
         1873 was Baron Ferdinand von Mueller (1825–96). McL does not record any Clarke
         contribution to *Punch* concerning him.

p. 106   Salanesque: i.e. in the manner of G. A. Sala. See above, note to Ch. 3.

p. 107   Burns' lines, 'A chiel's amang you takin' notes': 'On the Late Captain Grose's
         Peregrinations thro' Scotland, collecting the Antiquities of that Kingdom' (1789) 1–6:
         > Hear, Land o' Cakes and brither Scots,
         > Frae Maidenkirk to Johnny Groat's,
         > If there 's a hole in a' your coats,
         >   I rede ye tent it;
         >   A chiel's amang ye takin' notes,
         >   An faith he'll prent it!

p. 107   *Daily Telegraph*: see note to Ch. 27.

p. 107   on sheep-shearing: presumably 'McMillan and Gippsland', *Daily Telegraph*, 10 June
         1879.

p. 107   Melibœus: an exiled shepherd in Virgil's 'First Eclogue'. There is also 'A Tale of
         Meliboeus' in Geoffrey Chaucer's *The Canterbury Tales*. Clarke refers to 'the Melibœus
         of the antipodes' in *LO*.

p. 107   James Payn: see note to Ch. 1.

p. 107   Desmond Byrne: *Australian Writers*, 1896, 34–5. Hopkins quotes the passage in full
         in Ch. 17. Hopkins may be right in suggesting that Byrne and others romanticised
         and made light of Clarke's up-country experience. Elliott comments that Clarke
         'always presented a mask to the world, and those who have attempted to describe his
         association with Swinton have been led to take it lightly because that was the attitude
         he later affected towards it. Mackinnon's Memoir is principally responsible for the
         legend that it was merely a kind of picnic. But Mackinnon did not know all the facts,
         and in any case was disposed to make out a comical case, as with Clarke's period in the
         bank. It may be very much doubted whether Mackinnon became closely acquainted
         with Clarke until many years later, and Cyril Hopkins, who already knew him well
         and corresponded with him through these years, is a more reliable witness ... What
         Mackinnon said therefore needs to be modified, because his was the only statement of
         any length published close to Clarke's death. As a result every other account since that
         time – even, it seems, Cyril Hopkins's when he was at a loss or remembered imperfectly
         – has been influenced by it, directly or indirectly' (BE 53).

p. 108   Bass: English brand of beer.

p. 108   a pugree: a silk or cotton scarf tied around a hat or sun-helmet, falling down behind
         and shielding the neck. Variant of 'puggaree'.

p. 108   Rolf Boldrewood: pseudonym of T. A. Browne (1826–1915), English born Australian
         novelist. His first novel, *The Squatter's Dream* (serialised 1875) was published as *Ups
         and Downs* (S. W. Silver, London; George Robertson, Melbourne, 1878). It was
         reissued as *The Squatter's Dream* (Macmillan, London, 1890). His *Robbery Under Arms*
         was serialised in the *Sydney Mail*, 1882–83, and published in London, 1888.

p. 108   bush fire: published in *MV*. McL lists no previous publication.

p. 109   Hell's Gap: actually Hall's Gap, see note to Ch. 11.

p. 110   Sir Wilfrid Lawson, second baronet (1829–1906), English politician and temperance
         campaigner.

Chapter 13

            unperfected Paige typesetting machine, Mark Twain made a lecture tour of the world
            to discharge his debts. See note to Ch. 6. His visit to the Stawell district is described in
            Part 3, Ch. 23, 227, of *Following the Equator* (1897), *More Tramps Abroad*, Ch. 25, 151.
            'From Horsham we went to Stawell. By rail. Still in the colony of Victoria. Stawell
            is in the gold-mining country. In the bank-safe was half a peck of surface-gold – gold
            dust, grain gold; rich; pure in fact, and pleasant to sift through one's fingers; and would
            be pleasanter if it would stick. And there were a couple of gold bricks, very heavy to
            handle, and worth $7,500 a piece. They were from a very valuable quartz mine; a lady
            owns two-thirds of it; she has an income of $75,000 a month from it, and is able to
            keep house.
            'The Stawell region is not productive of gold only; it has great vineyards, and
            produces exceptionally fine wines. One of these vineyards – the Great Western, owned
            by Mr. Irving – is regarded as a model. Its product has reputation abroad. It yields a
            choice champagne and a fine claret, and its hock took a prize in France two or three
            years ago. The champagne is kept in a maze of passages underground, cut in the
            rock, to secure it an even temperature during the three-year term required to perfect
            it. In those vaults I saw 120,000 bottles of champagne. The colony of Victoria has a
            population of 1,000,000, and those people are said to drink 25,000,000 bottles of
            champagne per year. The dryest community on the earth. The government has lately
            reduced the duty upon foreign wines. That is one of the unkindnesses of Protection.
            'A man invests years of work and a vast sum of money in a worthy enterprise, upon
            the faith of existing laws; then the law is changed, and the man is robbed by his own
            government.
            'On the way back to Stawell we had a chance to see a group of boulders called the
            Three Sisters – a curiosity oddly located; for it was upon high ground, with the land
            sloping away from it, and no height above it from whence the boulders could have
            rolled down. Relics of an early ice-drift, perhaps. They are noble boulders. One of them
            has the size and smoothness and plump sphericity of a balloon of the biggest pattern.'

            names of geographical places, along with the experiences recorded in these Hopkins
            chapters, for his later Gothic description of the Australian landscape used in his preface
            to Gordon's poems. This seminal description was 'in its own time the revelation of a
            new poetic faith in the landscape of Australia … [expressing] the kind of sensibility
            which had developed in Australia …' (BE 61); see also Brian Elliott, *The Landscape of
            Australian Poetry* (Cheshire, Melbourne, 1967).

p. 116 fellow pupil who was a Hungarian: Max Kabat, about whom little is known and who died on a disastrous journey with Clarke into New South Wales and Queensland (BE 50–1, 62, 70–1, 72, 73).

p. 116 photograph of himself: this may be the well-known photograph (copy in SLV) reproduced in BE and *ST* (frontispiece), and *MC* (cover). It resembles the one described in the note on squatters (see notes to Ch. 18).

p. 116 Leech's hunting men: John Leech (1817–64), English artist; a *Punch* caricaturist and illustrator of the fox-hunting novels of the English novelist R. H. Surtees (1805–64).

p. 117 Mackinnon's memoir: *MV* 24.

Chapter 14

p. 118 *Allusion to Carlyle*: MS has 'Carlisle'.

p. 119 Russo-Japanese war: this typifies Clarke's habit of keeping up with international news. Cyril was obviously a sounding board for what he read. Clarke's contacts with European emigrants to Australia, for instance Max Kabat (see note to Ch. 13) and Alfred Telo would have assisted in this, too. Clarke's reading of colonial romance, not just of the British empire, recalled again by Cyril in this chapter, also contributed to the wider context in which Clarke wrote in Australia.

p. 119 Captain Thomas Mayne Reid (1818–83), Irish born writer of boys' adventure stories. Clarke refers to him in 'In Outer Darkness', *Australasian*, 21 August 1869, 232. 'One of his early excitements was Mayne Reid's *The Boy Hunter on Hampstead Heath*, whose adventures were set in familiar ground' (BE 12).

p. 119 Gaucho: MS has 'guacho'.

p. 120 Mrs. Campbell Praed: *My Australian Girlhood: Sketches and Impressions of Bush Life* (T. Fisher Unwin, London, 1902) 165–6. Rosa Praed (1851–1935), Australian novelist. She married Arthur Campbell Praed in 1872. In 1875 they settled in England, where she became an immensely productive writer.

p. 120 George Sutherland: see note to Ch. 3.

p. 121 their Royal Highnesses: Hopkins is slightly astray here. It was the Duke and Duchess of Cornwall, the future King George V and Queen Mary, who visited Melbourne at the time, opening the first Commonwealth Parliament there. Clarke was to report satirically on the earlier visit of Prince Alfred, Duke of Edinburgh, in his 'Peripatetic Philosopher' column, *Australasian*, 30 November, 21 December 1867 and 11 January 1868, the first two pieces partially reprinted in *PP* and all in *CC*.

p. 121 one of Marcus Clarke's own sons saw service: his third son Rowley went to South Africa with the 2nd Commonwealth Contingent, taking with him the cabbage-tree hat made for Clarke at Pentridge (*Bulletin*, 1 March 1902, 15; McL 2128, 3003).

p. 121 Doré's engravings to the *Bible* were published in 1866, to *Don Quixote* in 1865. Clarke's essay 'Popular Art and Gustave Doré', concerning graphic art of the time, was published unsigned in the *Australasian*, 28 September 1867, 392, reprinted as 'Modern Art and Gustave Doré' in *MV*, *AE*. On Doré, see note to Ch. 3.

p. 121 ultra-pre-Raphaelite: MS has 'ultra-Prerafaelite'.

p. 121 Frederick Sandys (1832–1904), English artist and illustrator.

p. 121 Millais: on Clarke's appreciation of his work, see note to Ch. 5.

p. 121 Don't have my name put to them at full length: a number of Clarke's published writings were signed just with the initials M. C. See McL.

p. 122 the letter concludes with characteristic abruptness: this suggests that Clarke may have written his letters piecemeal, as with a diary.

p. 122 Thomas Carlyle (see note to Ch. 9) was invited to become Lord Rector of Edinburgh University in 1865, and delivered his inaugural speech 2 April 1866. MS has 'Carlisle'.

p. 122   Your affectionate chum: Cyril rarely gives such signings-off. This one suggests the
                schoolboy bond.

Chapter 15

p. 124   fierce heat: cf. the description of the debilitating effects of the sun on the boy
                protagonist in Clarke's story, 'Pretty Dick'.

p. 124   James Brunton Stephens (1835–1902), Australian poet, born in Scotland. His long
                narrative poem, in *Convict Once and other poems* (Macmillan, London, 1871), is about
                a former convict, now a governess, romantically involved with several men. Clarke
                wrote on his poems in the *Leader* supplement, 19 March 1881. *LMC* lists Brunton
                Stephens' *Godolphin Arabian*.

p. 125   'In A Bark Hut': *Australasian*, 17 May 1873, 616.

p. 125   northern territory: CH is misleading here. Fort Bourke, now Bourke, is in fact today
                980 km by road from Stawell. The Northern Territory did not exist under that name
                in Clarke's time; but the trip to Queensland described in Ch. 21 below may well have
                taken Clarke as far from the Victorian border as a trip from there to the Northern
                Territory today.

p. 125   the handbook for Australia: a book with this title and including New Zealand was
                published in 1874 by Silver in London and went into subsequent editions.

p. 125   excursion into unsettled country: this was an overland trip from Ballarat to Fort Bourke
                that Clarke undertook, searching for land to settle on (BE 58–9). Only one other brief
                account of this trip survives. As BE notes, Clarke's account is 'more emotional than
                informative'. The extent of the drought is indicated by the fact that at the time, 1865–
                67, the River Darling was closed to traffic.

p. 126   mallee scrub: eucalypts of many types with multiple trunks rising from a common base
                flourishing in arid areas.

p. 126   the 'bush', *par excellence*: this contains a highly impressionistic description. Clarke
                seems to have added a glimpse of rainforest to his account of the drought stricken
                plain, perhaps indicating that he was sometimes writing to impress or trying out
                literary effects of the 'grotesque' to be used later, as CH himself suggests below in his
                reference to 'Holiday Peak'. CH does not mention here or elsewhere that his brother
                Gerard appears in this story (see notes to Ch. 1 and 2), though he does elsewhere refer
                to Gerard.

p. 127   'Holiday Peak': *Australasian*, 18 January 1873, 72; 25 January, 104. CH has
                'shimmering reeds'; Clarke has 'shivering reeds' in *Holiday Peak* (1873).

p. 127   In another well-known passage: 'Holiday Peak', see above. This quoted passage is
                excerpted by Mackinnon as 'A Night in the Bush' in *MV*.

p. 127   bittern: a nocturnal heron.

p. 127   the influence of Marcus Clarke on all subsequent writers: CH's comment here has
                proved to be correct, even though he would have had limited access to Australian
                literature. Tasma was, as Hopkins says, probably influenced by Clarke's descriptions of
                the bush and the Gothic mode in which they are cast. Interestingly CH does not add
                to the examples of Tasma, Heney and Praed that of Henry Lawson who directly echoed
                Clarke's phrase of 'weird melancholy'. This may suggest that Lawson was less known to
                readers in England, though his work was published there. On Lawson's reception in the
                UK, see Michael Wilding, 'Henry Lawson's Radical Vision', in H. Gustav Klaus, ed.,
                The Rise of Socialist Fiction 1880–1914 (Harvester Press, Sussex: St Martin's Press, New
                York, 1987) 203–30, reprinted in *Studies in Classic Australian Fiction*, 1997.

p. 127   Mark Twain, *Following the Equator*, Part 3, Ch. 23, 252: 'The road led through a forest
                of great gum-trees, lean and scraggy and sorrowful. The road was cream-white – a
                clayey kind of earth, apparently. Along it toiled occasional freight wagons, drawn by
                long double files of oxen. Those wagons were going a journey of two hundred miles,

I was told, and were running a successful opposition to the railway! The railways are owned and run by the government.

'Those sad gums stood up out of the dry white clay, pictures of patience and resignation. It is a tree that can get along without water; still it is fond of it – ravenously so. It is a very intelligent tree and will detect the presence of hidden water at a distance of fifty feet, and send out slender long root-fibres to prospect it. They will find it; and will also get at it even through a cement wall six inches thick. Once a cement water-pipe underground at Stawell began to gradually reduce its output, and finally ceased altogether to deliver water. Upon examining into the matter it was found stopped up, wadded compactly with a mass of root-fibres, delicate and hair-like. How this stuff had gotten into the pipe was a puzzle for some little time; finally it was found that it had crept in through a crack that was almost invisible to the eye. A gum tree forty feet away had tapped the pipe and was drinking the water.'

Twain intended to quote from Clarke's description in the Gordon preface, with an introductory note saying: 'Let a master take the brush', but the passage was omitted. See Laurie Hergenhan, 'Beautiful Lies, Ugly Truths', *Overland*, 187, 2007, 42–6.

p. 128   Thomas Heney: (1862–1928), Australian journalist and novelist; the quotation is from *The Girl at Birrell's: a Pastoral of the Paroo: An Australian Story* (Ward Lock, London, 1896).

Chapter 16

p. 130   The late Francis Adams: *The Australians* (1893), 145–6, by Francis Adams (1862–93), English novelist and essayist, in Australia 1882–90, committed suicide in 1893 suffering from terminal tuberculosis.

p. 131   The minister of Lands: Sir James McCulloch (1829–93).

p. 131   mounted police: Adam Lindsay Gordon joined the South Australian Mounted Police shortly after his arrival in Adelaide in November 1853 and served for two years. He wrote to his friend Charley Walker in England shortly before leaving England: 'The Governor has got an offer of an appointment as officer in (what should you think?) the Mounted Police in Australia, devilish good pay, a horse, three suits of regimentals yearly and lots of grub, for me, of course, I don't mean for himself, and he wants me to take it', Edith Humphris and Douglas Sladen, *Adam Lindsay Gordon and His Friends in England and Australia* (Constable & Co., London, 1912) 404. In the event, Gordon enlisted as a trooper, not an officer. Henry Kingsley arrived in Australia in December 1853 and returned to England in 1857. In his biography of Kingsley, *The Passing Guest* (University of Queensland Press, St Lucia, 1983) 56–60, J. S. D. Mellick casts doubt on the frequent assertion that Kingsley was in the mounted police: 'the evidence shows that he was not'. 'Horne and Clarke's friend Walstab were members of this force, as well as Gordon' (BE 68). This occupation, for 'gentlemen' of little means, may have been an alternative to jackarooing but it had strict regulations surrounding it (BE 68).

p. 131   Arthur Patchett Martin, *The Beginnings of an Australian Literature* (1898) 25.

p. 132   'monarch of all one surveys': 'I am monarch of all I survey', opening line of 'The Solitude of Alexander Selkirk', by the English poet William Cowper (1731–1800), based on the life of Alexander Selkirk (1667–1721), Scots seaman on whom Defoe based *Robinson Crusoe*.

p. 132   needs must: needs must when the devil drives: *Oxford Dictionary of Proverbs* gives Lydgate, *Assembly of Gods*, c. 1420 as first use.

Chapter 17

p. 133   Desmond Byrne, *Australian Writers* (1896) 35.

p. 133   Mikhail Yurevich Lermontoff: Mikhail Yurevich Lermontov (1814–41), Russian
          novelist and poet. His novel *A Hero of Our Times* (1840) was translated into English
          in 1854. BE (120) suggests it was an influence on Clarke's story 'A Hero of Romance',
          Colonial Monthly, October 1868, 147–57, November 1868, 215–30. Lermontov was
          banished from the Guards Hussars after writing a poem attacking the Russian oligarchy
          for the death of Pushkin, and exiled to the Caucasus as a regular army officer, where he
          died in a duel at the age of twenty-six. MS has 'Mikhail Yurevich Lermontoff'.

p. 134   Maurice Baring (1874–1945), English writer. His *Landmarks in Russian Literature* was
          published in 1910.

p. 134   Pushkin: Alexander Sergeevich Pushkin (1799–1837), Russian poet, author of *Eugene
          Onegin* (1823–31), *Boris Godunov* (1825), *The Captain's Daughter* (1836) etc. MS has
          'Poushkin'.

p. 134   Nikolai Laurentievich Klado, *The Russian Navy in the Russo-Japanese War* (Hurst &
          Blackett, London, 1905).

p. 135   in one of the last letters he ever wrote me: Hopkins dates this as June 1874 in Ch. 27.
          BE comments that this 'seems too early for some of its details and too late for others.
          Two or three letters seem to have been inadvertently telescoped, but they belong pretty
          much about the same time ...' (BE 171–3). In the same letter Clarke wrote: 'Your
          Petshorin (Lermontov's main character in *A Hero*) comparison is a simple fact in all but
          the end' (BE 173). Clarke's story 'A Hero of Romance', *Colonial Monthly*, October–
          November 1868, includes a duelling scene which recalls the Lermontov story (McL
          859, BE 120).

p. 135   Lady Eastlake (1809–93), an influential writer and art critic, wrote *Letters of the Baltic*
          (1844) which includes travel in Russia.

p. 135   'The Bridal of Bela': in 'Noah's Ark', *Australasian*, 26 October 1872, 518–19. BE
          describes it as 'a consciously literary ballad ... derived from Lermontov' (185).

p. 135   'Playing with Fire': *Colonial Monthly*, November 1867, 168–84, reprinted in *Australian
          Journal*, February 1871, 326–30 (McL 676 and 844).

p. 135   tragedy ... farce: cf. Karl Marx (1818–83), *The Eighteenth Brumaire of Louis Bonaparte*
          (1852): 'Hegel says somewhere that all great events and personalities in world history
          reappear in one fashion or another. He forgot to add: the first time as tragedy, the
          second as farce.'

p. 136   *Maud, and other Poems* (1855) and *Idylls of the King* (the first four 1859, the complete
          sequence 1891) by Alfred, Lord Tennyson. See note to Ch. 2.

p. 136   Gronow: Rees Howell Gronow, *Reminiscences of Captain Gronow ... being Anecdotes
          of the Camp, the Court, and the Clubs, at the Close of the Last War with France*, London
          1862; second series, 1863; third series, 1865; *Anecdotes of Celebrities of London and Paris
          ... to which are added the Last Recollections of Captain Gronow* (Smith Elder, London,
          1870).

p. 136   Ernest Renan (1823–92), French historian, author of *Vie de Jésus* (1863). See note to
          Ch. 9.

p. 136   Jules Michelet (1798–1874), French historian, *La Sorcière* (1862). *LMC* lists Michelet's
          L'Amour, La Femme, and *Priests, Women and Families*.

p. 136   *The Improvisatore* (1845), a novel by Hans Christian Andersen (1805–75), Danish
          writer.

p. 136   *Charlie Thornhill*, by Charles Clarke (Chapman and Hall, London, 1863), an early
          detective story.

p. 136   *Ella Norman, or A Woman's Perils* by Elizabeth A. Murray (Hurst & Blackett, London,
          1864).

p. 136   *Guy Livingstone* (1857), by the English novelist George Alfred Lawrence (1827–76).
          It is referred to in Clarke's story 'Holiday Peak', *Australasian*, 18 January 1873, 72;
          25 January, 104. Its celebration of brute strength was parodied by Bret Harte in
          'Guy Heavystone'. Lawrence is cited as an influence on Clarke's novel *LO* by H. M.

Hyndman in his review in the *Argus*, 2 July 1869, 5–6. *LMC* lists *Maurice Dering*, by
the author of *Guy Livingstone*.

p. 136   *Armadale* (1866), a novel by Wilkie Collins (1824–89), English novelist, author of *The
Woman in White* (1860), *The Moonstone* (1868) etc. Contributor to *All the Year Round*
and *Household Words*, and associate of Charles Dickens. Clarke refers to *Armadale* in his
essay on Dickens in the *Argus*, 8 July 1870. Clarke adapted *The Moonstone* for the stage
(McL 1169, 2845, 3085–7, 3268). ML holds three letters from Collins to Clarke. *LMC*
lists Wilkie Collins' *No Name*.

p. 136   *Our Mutual Friend* (1864–65), novel by Charles Dickens.

p. 136   *Half a Million of Money* by Amelia B. Edwards (1831–92) (Bernard Tauchnitz, Leipzig,
1865; 3 vols, London, 1866).

p. 136   *Kestrels and Falcons*: George Alfred Lawrence, *Sans Merci, or Kestrels and Falcons*
(Tinsley Bros., London, 1866).

p. 136   *A Race for Wealth*: *The Race for Wealth* by Charlotte Eliza L. (Mrs. J. H.) Riddell [under
the name F. G. Trafford] (London, 1866). MS has 'Riddel'.

p. 136   *The Second Mrs. Tillotson* (Tinsley Bros., London, 1866) and *Never Forgotten* (Chapman
and Hall, London, 1865) by Percy Hetherington Fitzgerald (1834–1925), novelist.

p. 136   *The Village on the Cliff* (London, 1867) by Miss Thackeray [Anne Isabella Ritchie
(1837–1919), elder daughter of W. M. Thackeray].

p. 136   Arsène Houssaye, *L'amour comme il est* (Lévy, Paris, 1858). Clarke refers to his
'licentious fooleries' in 'Of French Novels', *Argus*, 2 February 1872.

p. 136   Victor Hugo (1802–85), French novelist, author of *Les Misérables* (1862) and *Les
travailleurs de la mer* (1866). Clarke alludes to Hugo's *Notre Dame de Paris* (1831) in
his story 'Poor Jo', *Australasian*, 15 April 1871, 453, reprinted in *Holiday Peak*, and
reprinted passage from it in 'The Library Table' when editing the *Australian Journal* (see
Michael Wilding, *Studies in Classic Australian Fiction* (1997), 16, 22; Andrew McCann,
Marcus Clarke's Bohemia: Literature and Modernity in Colonial Melbourne, 2004,
158). He discusses Hugo in 'Of French Novels', *Argus*, 2 February 1872, 6, 'Balzac
and Modern French Literature', *Australasian*, 3 August 1867, 136, 'A Night at the
Immigrants' Home', *Australasian*, 12 June 1869, 762–3, 'Le Roi s'amuse', *Australasian*,
19 June 1869, 776, his dedication to Sir Charles Gavan Duffy of the first book edition
of *HNL* ('Victor Hugo has shown how a French convict fares after the fulfilment of
his sentence'), 'Charles Dickens', *Argus*, 8 July 1870, 7, 'What to Do with Our Boys',
Australasian, 5 March 1870, 305, 'A Melbourne Alsatia', *Colonial Monthly*, February
1869, 473–9, and 'The Language of Bohemia', *Australasian*, 17 July 1869, 72. Walter
Murdoch compared *Les Misérables* with *HNL* in 'Marcus Clarke', *Argus*, 22 October
1904, 4, collected in Walter Murdoch, *Loose Leaves* (George Robertson, Melbourne,
1910) 50–5. Two of Hugo's works are listed in *LMC*, *L'Homme qui rit* (in French and
in English) and *Les Misérables*, the original French edition in ten volumes.

p. 136   *Le tourlourou* (1834) by Paul de Kock (1793–1871), French novelist and dramatist.
Clarke discusses him in 'Balzac and Modern French Literature', *Australasian*, 3 August
1867, in 'On the Pursuit of Pleasure', *Australasian*, 18 April 1868, 497, and in 'A
Night at the Immigrants' Home', *Australasian*, 12 June 1869, remarking in 'Of French
Novels', *Argus*, 2 February 1872, 'I do not recommend the cheerful Paul de Kock for
family consumption. Paul is more suited to the garret of Béranger than to the salons of
Madame Fichtaminel. Yet Paul has that knack of investing a flimsy story with interest
which is lost to many of our modern and more nice novelists.' MS has *Un tourlourou*.
LMC lists 'Soeur Anne, par Paul de Kock, La Femme de Trente Ans, etc, 1 vol.'

p. 136   George Sand (pseudonym of Amandine-Aurore Lucille Dupin, Baronne Dudevant,
1804–76), French novelist. Her *Adriani* was published in 1854. Clarke refers to her in
his essay 'Balzac and Modern French Literature', *Australasian*, 3 August 1867, and in
'Of French Novels', *Argus*, 2 February 1872. *LMC* lists Sand's *Jean de la Roche*, *Jeanne*,
and *Les beaux messieurs de bois d'orée*.

p. 136   *La peau de chagrin* (*The Wild Ass's Skin*) (1831), *Eugenie Grandet* (1833), *Gobseck*
           (1830), and *La recherche de l'absolu* (1834), novels by Balzac. Clarke recorded that
           he had been reading *Gobseck* in the afternoon before his experiment with hashish
           described in 'Cannabis Indica', *Colonial Monthly*, February 1868, 454–68. Cyril recalls
           Clarke's reading an excerpt from *Gobseck* in a school reader in Ch. 3. Clarke's mention
           of reading *La recherche de l'absolu* (translated as *The Quest of the Absolute*) is important
           in relation to his lifelong interest in alchemy, see note to Ch. 2.

p. 136   Lady Clara Vere de Vere: Lady Clara Vere de Vere is the eponymous subject of a poem
           by Tennyson first published in *Poems* (1842). It includes the lines 'The daughter of
           a hundred earls, / You are not one to be desired' and 'Kind hearts are more than
           coronets, / and simple faith than Norman blood', which indicate its moral theme. The
           De Vere family were the original owners of Kensington, the suburb in which Clarke
           was born.

p. 136   Moll Flagon: a partial allusion to Moll Flanders, heroine of the eponymous novel
           (1722) by Daniel Defoe.

p. 136   Doll Tearsheet: Falstaff's mistress in William Shakespeare's *Henry IV part two* (1600).
           Clarke refers to Falstaff in 'In Outer Darkness', *Australasian*, 21 August 1869, 232, and
           to Pistol and Mistress Quickly in 'La Béguine', *Australasian*, 8 February 1873, 166.
           Falstaff, Pistol and Mistress Quickly also appear in Shakespeare's *Henry IV part one*
           (1598) and *The Merry Wives of Windsor* (1602).

p. 136   Eugene Sue (1804–57), French novelist. Clarke refers to him in 'The Working Man
           from His Own Point of View', *Australasian*, 26 March 1870, 401, 'A Night at the
           Immigrants' Home', *Australasian*, 12 June 1869, 762–3, and in 'Of French Novels',
           Argus, 2 February 1872, 6. *LMC* lists Sue's *The Wandering Jew* (1842–43) (in French
           and English) and *The Mysteries of Paris* (1844–45).

p. 136   St Giles and Field Lane: slum areas of London.

p. 136   Lord Deucease: Hon. A. P. Deucease, a card-sharper in W. M. Thackeray's *The Great
           Hoggarty Diamond* (1841).

p. 136   Marquess of Steyne: a character in the novel *Vanity Fair* (1847–48) by W. M.
           Thackeray.

p. 136   The Hon. Rook: Captain Tom Rook, crook and blackguard in W. M. Thackeray,
           Character Sketches (1841).

p. 136   Tom Pigeon: probably Frederick Pigeon, gullible young gambler in *Vanity Fair*.

p. 136   Duchess of Quiverfull: the philoprogenitive Mrs. Quiverful is a character in Trollope's
           The Warden (1855), named after 'a quiver full of children', *Psalms* 127, 3–5.

p. 136   Nell Gwynne (1650–87), mistress of English monarch Charles II.

p. 136   verses of Charles Kingsley's: entitled 'Young and Old', these verses appeared in *The
           Water Babies* (London, 1863). GMH, writing to Bridges of Browning's poetry,
           remarked 'he has got a great deal of what came in with Kingsley and the Broad Church
           school, a way of talking (and making his people talk) with the air and spirit of a man
           bouncing up from the table with his mouth full of bread and cheese and saying that he
           meant to stand no blasted nonsense. There is a whole volume of Kingsley's essays which
           is all a kind of munch and a not standing of any blasted nonsense from cover to cover.'
           The Correspondence of Gerard Manley Hopkins to Robert Bridges, ed. C. C. Abbott, 1970,
           74; quoted in R. B. Martin, 1991, 338.

p. 137   Francis Adams, *The Australians* (1893), 114–15.

p. 138   *Le père Goriot* (1834), novel by Balzac.

p. 138   Vautrin, the master criminal, first appears in *Le père Goriot*, and later in a number
           of Balzac's novels including *Illusions perdues* (1837–43) and *Splendeurs et misères des
           courtisanes* (1839–47). Clarke refers to him in *OT*.

p. 138   I have been informed that Marcus: this suggests that Hopkins had indirect access to
           reports of personal accounts of Clarke at Ledcourt from the Clarke family or from
           essays such as Charles Bright's in *Cosmos*.

p. 138   Charlotte Brontë: her comments on Balzac are in a letter to G. H. Lewes, 17 October 1850: *The Letters of Charlotte Brontë*, ed. Margaret Smith (Clarendon Press, Oxford, 2000) vol. 2, 485. See note to Preface.

p. 138   Marcus Clarke, 'Balzac and Modern French Literature', *Australasian*, 3 August 1867, 136.

p. 139   Arthur Symons (1865–1945), English critic. The article appeared in the *Fortnightly Review*, May 1899, and is reprinted in Symons' *The Symbolist Movement in Literature* (1899).

p. 139   Clarke contributed a translation into French of the nursery rhyme 'Old King Cole' to the Melbourne *Punch*: not in McL or BE.

p. 139   'Le roi d'Yvetot': in his 'Imitations of Béranger' in *The Paris Sketchbook* (1840), Thackeray offered two versions of 'Le roi d'Yvetot' – 'The King of Yvetot' and 'The King of Brentford'. *LMC* lists *The Paris Sketchbook*.

p. 139   Marcus composed some verses: published in *MV* as 'Love and Wine', 297; listed by McL as taken from manuscript, now at ML, see McL 1230, 3081, 3194.

p. 139   George du Maurier, *The Martian* (1897).

p. 140   Walter Sichel (1885–1933), English critic, author of *Sterne: A Study; to which is added the Journal to Eliza* (Williams and Norgate, London, 1910).

p. 140   Sterne: Laurence Sterne (1713–68), English novelist, author *The Life and Opinions of Tristram Shandy* (1759–67), *A Sentimental Journey through France and Italy* (1767). Clarke refers to the latter, 'On the Pursuit of Pleasure', 18 April 1868, 497. According to BE (44) '*Tristram Shandy* remained one of his [Clarke's] favourite books', and he detects its influence on Clarke's essay 'Austin Friars', *Australian Monthly Magazine*, May 1866, 199–209. *LMC* lists *The Complete Works of Laurence Sterne*.

p. 140   Francois Rabelais (c. 1494 – c. 1553), French author of *Gargantua* (1534) and *Pantagruel* (1532/33). Clarke refers to him in *HNL*, and to Coleridge's comments on him in his essay 'Balzac and Modern French Literature', *Australasian*, 3 August 1867, 136. *LMC* lists a copy of 'Rabelais'.

p. 140   *Paul et Virginie* (1788) by Jacques-Henri Bernardin de Saint-Pierre, French philosopher and novelist. It is one of the books read by Sylvia Vickers in *HNL*; see Ken Stewart, 'Sylvia's Books' in *Investigations in Australian Literature*, 99–102 and McCann 195. Clarke may have adapted it as an operetta (BE 231); McL, 1192, lists it as a burlesque under 'Drama uncompleted' with manuscript in ML.

p. 140   Yorick Club: a Melbourne Bohemian club whose members included Clarke, Adam Lindsay Gordon, Henry Kendall, F. W. Haddon, J. J. Shillinglaw, G. A. Walstab, Alfred Telo, James Smith, J. E. Neild, R. P. Whitworth, Garnet Walch, George Gordon McCrae, Hamilton Mackinnon, Henry Gyles Turner and Patrick Moloney amongst others. Its name derives from Hamlet's 'Alas, poor Yorick' soliloquy in Shakespeare's *Hamlet* (5.1.180) and from Laurence Sterne's *Tristram Shandy*. The first meeting of the club was held 1 May 1868. A room was rented in the *Punch* office, 74 Collins Street. The *Argus* office was next door, Mueller's tavern below. 'In its early days Mueller catered for the club until two o'clock in the morning, after which it stayed open until four or five o'clock for members who were newspaper printers', Geoffrey Hutton, *Adam Lindsay Gordon: the Man and the Myth* (1978; 1996) 148. Clarke brought a skull to the club room given him by Dr Patrick Moloney, at the time an intern at Melbourne Hospital, placed it on the mantelshelf with a pipe under its jaw and suggested the club should be called the 'Golgotha' because it was 'the place of skulls'. (BE 102; Hutton 147). Despite Clarke's earnest advocacy, it was called the Yorick; but he refers to it as the Golgotha in a piece he wrote about it, 'A Quiet Club', in 'The Peripatetic Philosopher', *Australasian*, 9 May 1868, 593, reprinted *PP*. So does Henry Kendall in his account of the Yorick, 'A Colonial Literary Club', *Town and Country Journal*, 18 February 1871, reprinted in Michael Ackland, ed., *Henry Kendall: Poetry, Prose and Selected Correspondence* (1993) 160–6: Clarke features in it, not altogether positively, as Perks. The club's historians, F. T. D. Carrington and D. Watterson, record of Gordon that 'at times he was wildly jovial, and one evening pitched Clarke up to very near the ceiling and caught him again coming down', *The Yorick Club: Its Origin and Development, May 1868, to December 1910* (1911). The Yorick Club later merged with the Savage Club: see Joseph Johnson, *Laughter and the Love of Friends: A Centenary History of the Melbourne Savage Club 1894 to 1994 and a History of the Yorick Club 1868–1966* (Melbourne Savage Club, Melbourne, 1994). See further BE 94–106; L. E. Fredman, 'Melbourne Bohemia in the Nineteenth Century', *Southerly*, 18, 1957, 83–91. When the Yorick Club became too respectable, Clarke and others established the 'Cave of Adullam' (see 1 Samuel 22, 1). It is commemorated in his novel *'Twixt Shadow and Shine* (1875; 1893). See also Mark Finnane, ed., *The Difficulties of My Position: The Diaries of Prison Governor John Buckley Castieau 1855–1884* (National Library of Australia, Canberra, 2004).

p. 140   *The Village on the Cliff* (1867), by Miss Thackeray [Anne Isabella Ritchie (1837–1919), elder daughter of W. M. Thackeray].

p. 140   a novel of Trollope's appearing in serial form in the *Cornhill Magazine*: *The Claverings* (February 1866 – May 1867); Sophie Gordeloup is a foreign adventuress who befriended and had hopes of blackmailing the heroine, Lady Ongar.

p. 140   Anthony Trollope (1815–82), prolific English novelist; the Bishop of Barchester and his wife, the formidable Mrs. Proudie, are characters in his Barsetshire series: *The Warden* (1855), *Barchester Towers* (1857), *Dr Thorne* (1858), *Framley Parsonage* (1861), *The Small House at Allington* (1864) and *The Last Chronicle of Barset* (1867). His *Australia and New Zealand* (London, 1873) draws on his visit to Australia, where his son had emigrated. Clarke refers to him in *LO*, in 'American Literature', *Australasian*, 25 May 1872, 648, in 'Of French Novels', *Argus*, 2 February 1872, 6; as Mr. Cackleby Twaddle in 'The Traveller of the Period', *Argus*, 13 April 1872, 6: 'I am aware that Mr. Twaddle is an "eminent English author, well known to the trade," and that he manufactures an annual volume with ease, regularity and despatch;' and as Mr. Twitters in 'Mine Ease in Mine Inn', *Weekly Times*, 21 February 1874, and in 'Democracy in Australia 2', *Daily Telegraph* (London), 6 September 1877, all reprinted *CC*. In *Australia and New Zealand*, Trollope writes that Clarke's 'Australian tales are not only known familiarly by all colonists, but are almost as familiar to English readers' (I, 1873, 9). Clarke asked him to review *HNL* but Trollope refused; *Letters of Anthony Trollope*, ed. Bradford A. Booth (London, 1951) 313, *CC* 462. There is a letter from Trollope to Clarke in the ML, State Library of New South Wales.

p. 141   Not very long ago: amended by CH from, originally, 'only a short while ago'.

p. 141   Herbert Paul, 'The Victorian Novel', *Nineteenth Century*, May 1897, collected in Herbert Paul, *Men and Letters* (John Lane, London, 1901).

p. 141   Leslie Stephen, *Studies of a Biographer*, vol. 4 (Duckworth, London, 1902) 201. Sir Leslie Stephen (1832–1904), English writer, editor of the *Cornhill Magazine*, and the *Dictionary of National Biography*, father of Virginia Woolf.

Chapter 18

p. 144   Sutherland tells a story: George Sutherland, *Australia or England in the South* (1886), 90–1.

p. 144   Marcus Clarke, *The History of the Continent of Australia and the Island of Tasmania (1787–1870) compiled for the use of schools* (1877) 157.

p. 144   the small school history edited, but not written, by Marcus Clarke: *The History of the Continent of Australia and the Island of Tasmania* was commissioned by the Victorian Education Department and edited by Clarke: J. J. Shillinglaw and R. P. Whitworth assisted with the research. See Laurel Clark, 'Marcus Clarke and F. F. Baillière', *Margin*, 40, November 1996, 27–8: 'The publication was fraught with difficulties, reflected in the correspondence between Clarke, Baillière and Shillinglaw and its printers

McCarron Bird.' See Baillière to Shillinglaw, 30 May 1876, Shillinglaw papers Box 81/2, and Marcus Clarke papers MS 222 Box 455/2, La Trobe Australian Manuscripts Collection, SLV.

p. 144   Captain W. W. Hughes … Moonta copper mine: Sir Walter Watson Hughes (1803–87), born in Scotland, sailed as a whaler in the Arctic and opium trader in the Indian and China seas; he arrived Adelaide 1840, and went into sheep farming in northern Yorke Peninsula. Copper was discovered on his Moonta property; after court cases and paying off other claimants, Hughes secured the lease. The Moonta mine was phenomenally successful, the first in Australia to pay dividends in excess of £1,000,000.

p. 145   I don't like banks: see Clarke's essay 'On Business Men', *Humbug*, 3 November 1869, 6, 11, for his view of banks, based on his experience.

p. 145   'in a word I dread lest I become like others': this recalls Rufus Dawes' fear of brutalisation, of losing his inner self-respect, and gentlemanly characteristics and becoming like a 'common' convict, as he does. See L. T. Hergenhan, 'The corruption of Rufus Dawes', *Southerly*, 19, 1969, 211–21.

p. 146   Heraclitus of Ephesus (fl. c. 500 BC), Greek philosopher, who maintained that all creation is in a state of flux.

p. 146   Democritus (fl. c. 500 BC), Greek philosopher, who theorised that all creation was a concourse of atoms. Known as the 'laughing philosopher' in contrast to the melancholic Heraclitus.

p. 146   The slang is different: only three of the terms Clarke mentions are listed by Wilkes: 'Dover' (knife), 'humps his swag', 'knocks' down fifty notes. For 'Dover', Wilkes cites the serial version of *HNL*, quoting from a passage from the later goldfields section ('flash your Dover') as the earliest source. Wilkes comments that 'it is essentially colonial slang. The majority of clasp knives were imported in to the Australian colonies … made by one "Dover." Hence "flashing your Dover" is equivalent to "drawing your Toledo."' See G. A. Wilkes, *Dictionary of Australian Colloquialisms* (1985) 152. Of the mining terms that follow in this chapter only two are in Wilkes, four are not. Clarke's detailed interest in language suggests that in recording his observations of life while on the goldfields and up-country, he was even at this early stage thinking of using them as future copy (as he did in short stories and sketches) and that he was using his letters to Hopkins as a combination of notebook jotting and of literary exercise. When up-country he did, according to Mackinnon and as reported by Hopkins in this chapter, 'spend time in literary work. Probably in filling up notebooks with memoranda … as he had done at the gold-diggings …' Clarke's interest in specialised idioms can be seen further in his article 'The Language of Bohemia', *Australasian*, 17 July 1869, 72.

p. 147   a 'blower': Anthony Trollope's advice in *Australia and New Zealand* (London, 1873) was for Australians not to 'blow', i.e. not to blow their own trumpet.

p. 147   Edward E. Morris, *Austral English: A Dictionary of Australasian Words, Phrases and Usages* (Macmillan, London, 1898, reissued Sydney University Press, Sydney, 1972).

p. 147   Mark Twain, *More Tramps Abroad*, Ch. 24, 146–7; *Following the Equator*, Part 3, Ch. 22.

p. 147   he prides himself in being well-dressed: the following description of the squatter seems very like a much reproduced, studio photograph of the young Clarke, though sporting a swagger stick as well as a cigar and leg-boots, reproduced in the frontispiece of *BE* and *ST* and on the cover of *MC* and the present volume. Clarke wrote of the squatter as belonging to 'the aristocracy of Australia … [and comparable to] the southern planters of America', adding that he 'prides himself on being well-dressed' when he comes to Melbourne after sales ('Arcades Ambo', *Australasian*, 26 February, 1870, 273). Perhaps in his photograph Clarke was presenting himself as one of this 'aristocracy', and a young 'swell' to impress Hopkins back in London. See note to 'photograph of himself' to Ch. 13.

p. 148   reefer: miner.

p. 148   slabbing: keeping up the side of a shaft with timber slabs.

p. 148   driving: excavating horizontally.

p. 148   striking: discovering a rich vein of ore.

p. 148   bottoming: getting to the bed-rock or clay, below which it was useless to sink in gold-mining.

p. 148   quartz-crushing: crushing the veins or lodes of silica (quartz) to extract gold.

p. 148   tailings: the detritus carried off by water from a crushing machine or any gold-washing apparatus.

p. 148   general subservience to the almighty dollar: Washington Irving (1783–1859): 'the almighty dollar, that great object of universal devotion throughout our land' (1855). The phrase is used in Henry Kendall's essay, 'L. S. D. -ISM; Or, The Almighty Dollar', *Humbug*, 22 September 1869.

p. 148   'Squatters Past and Present': originally published as 'Arcades Ambo', *Australasian*, 26 February 1870, 273, reprinted *Holiday Peak* and *CC*, and as 'Squatters Past and Present', *MV, AE, AT, ST*.

p. 149   As some French author says: 'Si jeunesse savait; si viellesse pouvait.' Henri Estienne (1470–1520).

p. 149   *Australian Monthly Magazine:* see note to Ch. 22 part 1. MS has *Australian Magazine*.

p. 149   Marcus Scrivener: the nickname GMH used for Clarke at school and in writing a description of him in the latter's album, which does not survive; see Ch. 3. Later, Clarke used 'Mark Scrivener' as one of his pseudonyms to sign three of his early pieces in the *Australian Monthly Magazine*, including the autobiographical 'Austin Friars', July 1866 (McL 788, 791–2).

p. 149   'Q': Clarke used this as a pseudonym for his 'Peripatetic Philosopher' column (and in his first book, with the same title, of selections from it), though his authorship was an open secret. He had also used it twice before, in a notebook entry and for an article 'My Café and the People I Meet There', *Australian Monthly Magazine*, August 1867, 401–8.

Chapter 19

p. 150   There are two copies of Ch. 19 in the MS, slightly different from each other. One (marked 19A) has a typewritten note attached: 'THIS CHAPTER IS FAMILIAR TO ME AND I THINK I TYPED IT AND GAVE IT TO YOU WITH THE LAST LOT.' The text here follows the one marked 19.

p. 150   There are still some to be found who cherish his memory: here and below Hopkins apparently conflates reminiscences 'derived from accounts of Holt's neighbours at Swinton and Ledcourt' (as Hopkins states in Ch. 18) with his own school memories.

p. 151   writer in the *Cosmos* magazine: Charles Bright, *Cosmos*, 30 April 1895, 421.

p. 151   Dr Robert Lewins: amateur scientist and Comtean philosopher, author of *On the Identity of the Vital and Cosmical Principle* (George P. Bacon, Lewes, 1869). Staff surgeon to General Chute in the New Zealand colonial wars with the Maori, he returned to England via Australia in 1867. See Desmond Byrne, *Australian Writers* (1896) 35: 'Two years had thus been spent [at the Swinton Station] when a Dr Lewins, who was known as a "materialistic philosopher," visited the station and made the young Englishman's acquaintance. A warm mutual regard resulted, and soon Lewins succeeded in obtaining a small post for Clarke on the Melbourne *Argus*. This was the beginning of the most brilliant journalistic career established on the Australian press.' However, according to BE (78 ff.) who draws on correspondence from Lewins, now in the ML, both Byrne and Mackinnon, whom CH follows, are unreliable about Lewins' recommending Clarke's appointment to the *Argus*, about Lewins' intellectual standing and about how seriously Clarke took him. Lewins visited Holt at the beginning of 1867 and he renewed acquaintance with Clarke when the latter went to Melbourne. Lewins was a rationalist, 'author of a few provocative pamphlets and had some reputation as a controversialist'. He was not the learned thinker Mackinnon considered him with his references to Huxley and Tyndall. Lewins apparently patronised Clarke as a young man of talent and tried to convert him to his version of rationalism, encouraging him to write an essay (unpublished) on Comte, though Lewins was not a Comteist. Clarke could be controversial but he 'never went to the eccentric length of Lewins' iconoclasm'. BE believes Lewins' effect on Clarke was that 'the contact excited, stimulated and finally amused him … In a short while Lewins became a general joke …' and Clarke appears to have satirised him in a story called 'A Very Tough Subject', *Australian Monthly Magazine*, July 1867, 321–31, published under the pseudonym 'Mark Scrivener'. ML holds letters of Clarke to Lewins, 1867–68 MSS 55/1.

p. 151   Huxley: Thomas Henry Huxley (1825–95), English writer, friend of Charles Darwin, who coined the word 'agnostic'. Clarke refers to him in his essay 'Civilisation without Delusion' in the *Victorian Review*, see note below.

p. 151   my brother Gerard's adoption of the Roman Catholic faith: Gerard was received into the Church by Newman in 1866. See note to Ch. 2. Clarke's story 'Holiday Peak', *Australasian*, 18 and 25 January 1873, refers to Gerard as a Jesuit, but, drawing on his schoolboy memories of Gerard's artistic talents, imagines an alternate life for him as a painter. Clarke was never to know of Gerard's eventual success as a poet.

p. 152   Byrne 32.

p. 153   James Moorhouse (1826–1915), born in Sheffield, England, educated St John's, Cambridge, consecrated Bishop of Melbourne 1876 and installed at St James' Cathedral, William Street, 11 January 1877.

p. 153   A. W. Brazier, *Marcus Clarke: His Work and Genius* (Echo Publishing, Melbourne, 1902) 29.

p. 153   publication of his essay 'Civilisation without Delusion': *Victorian Review*, 1, 1, November 1879, 65–75, reprinted *MC*. The *Victorian Review* published a reply by the Bishop of Melbourne, Dr James Moorhouse, the following month, but refused Clarke's reply to the bishop, which then appeared in the *Melbourne Review*, January 1880, but all copies were withdrawn from sale almost immediately. The whole controversy was collected in book form as *Civilisation without Delusion* (1880), reprinted with changes as *What Is Religion?* (1895). See Joan Poole, 'Marcus Clarke: "Christianity is Dead,"' *ALS*, 6, 1973, 128–42.

p. 153   his favourite maxim: 'But I will wear my heart upon my sleeve/ For daws to peck at.' Shakespeare, *Othello*, I. 1. 64-65. Clarke quotes it in *LO* and in 'Noah's Ark', *Australasian*, 7 December 1872, reprinted *CC*.

p. 153   Walter Murdoch, 'Marcus Clarke', *Argus*, 22 October 1904, 4; collected in Walter Murdoch, *Loose Leaves* (George Robertson, Melbourne, 1910) 50–5.

p. 153   The essay in question: MS Ch. 19A adds '*Civilisation without Delusion*'.

p. 154   Ruskin's *The Stones of Venice* (1851–53), an epic work, with elaborate prose-poem descriptions, which includes his famous essay 'The Nature of Gothic'.

p. 154   Dr Frazer's *Golden Bough*: Sir James George Frazer (1854–1941), English anthropologist, author of *The Golden Bough* (1890–1915). The variant MS of this chapter (19A) cites another work by Frazer, *The Belief in Immortality and the Worship of the Dead*, 3 vols (1913–24).

p. 154   Alfred Ernest Crawley, *The Tree of Life: A Study of Religion* (Hutchinson, London, 1905).

p. 154   'Conceive my soul-felt joy': quoted in Arthur Patchett Martin, 'An Australian Novelist', *Temple Bar*, 71, May 1884, 106–7.

p. 155   The lonely horseman riding: from Clarke's preface to Adam Lindsay Gordon's *Sea Spray and Smoke Drift* (1876) and collected *Poems* (1880), slightly adapted from his earlier commentary on the painting *Waterpool near Coleraine* by Louis Buvelot; see note to Preface.

p. 155   however unorthodox?: The variant Chapter 19A ends at this point.

p. 155   'Noah's Ark' papers: the regular column, 'Noah's Ark. By Marcus Clarke', appeared in the weekly *Australasian*, 18 May 1872 – 13 September 1873. For possible real life sources of Clarke's conversationalists, see *CC* 449. The pieces that CH selects appear as part of two essays, 7 December 1872, 712, and 17 May 1873, 616, reprinted in *CC* under the title of 'Religious Controversy', 264–74. The quoted passages appear 272–4.

p. 155   James Clarence Mangan (1803–49), Irish poet. Clarke is quoting from his poem 'The
          One Mystery'. Clarke refers to him in 'Henry Kendall', *Leader* supplement, 19 March
          1881. CH ascribes to 'the wide ranging of Marcus Clarke's reading and culture' his
          familiarity with Mangan's work; but Mangan's friendship with Clarke's acquaintance
          Sir Charles Gavan Duffy may also be significant here – see Duffy, *My Life in Two
          Hemispheres* (1898), vol. 1, passim. Henry Kendall wrote on 'The Poems of Clarence
          Mangan' in *Freeman's Journal*, 7 September 1871.

p. 156   these same 'Noah's Ark' papers: *Australasian*, 17 May 1873, 616, reprinted *CC* 273–4.

Chapter 20

p. 159   fluky: infected with parasitic flukes, *fasciola hepatica*, flatworms which occur in the
          livers of affected sheep.

p. 160   Café Royal: see note above to Ch. 8.

p. 161   'Ah me! what injury has not "Commerce"': 'Noah's Ark', *Australasian*, 12 July 1873,
          43–4, reprinted *CC* 280. The excerpt echoes sentiments in Matthew Arnold's poem,
          'The Scholar-Gipsy' (1853), about a need to retreat from the hectic, commerce-driven
          life of Victorian times. Clarke refers to Arnold in *LO*.

Chapter 21

p. 162   There are two copies of this chapter in the MS, with a few minor variations. One
          of them, numbered as 'Chapter 20A', is marked 'Rough Copy', the inscription then
          crossed out. The text here follows the MS marked 'Chapter 21'.

p. 162   *The Lady of the Lake*: burlesque by Clarke, played at the Theatre Royal 1864; it survives
          in Mitchell Library, Clarke notebook, ML, MS C270; see McL 1165, 3194. Parody
          from Walter Scott. Music, Henry Kowalski. Also known as 'Moustique'. McL, 1166,
          and other references to later performances.

p. 163   'recapture the first, fine, careless rapture': Browning, 'Home-thoughts from Abroad'.
          See note to Browning, Ch. 9.

p. 163   apposite quotation from Lord Byron: *Don Juan,* Canto 1, line 136: 'Save thine
          "incomparable oil," Macassar.'

p. 163   macadam: road constructed of successive layers of consolidated broken stone of nearly
          uniform size, devised by John Loudon McAdam (1756–1836), British surveyor.

p. 163   112 in the shade: 112 degrees Fahrenheit, 44 Centigrade.

p. 163   165 all day: 74 degrees Centigrade.

p. 163   'police arrangement': Clarke's plan, now rejected, of joining the Mounted Police.

p. 163   letters from my cousins in England: cf. references to army cousins who led the narrator
          astray in 'Human Repetends', *Australasian*, 14 September 1872, 326.

p. 163   'Aston Hall': possibly the historic, Jacobean country house now situated in
          Birmingham, whose expansion overtook it. Washington Irving visited and wrote about
          it.

p. 163   Sevenoaks: town in Kent, now part of the London commuter belt.

p. 163   Debrett: *Debrett's Peerage and Baronetage*, English directory of aristocracy. Clarke refers
          to it in *LO*.

p. 163   'tenth transmitters of a foolish face': Richard Savage (1697?–1743), 'The Bastard': 'He
          lives to build, not boast, a generous race/ No tenth transmitter of a foolish face.'

p. 164   the writer in *Cosmos*: Charles Bright, 'Marcus Clarke', *Cosmos*, 30 April 1895, 41. On
          Clarke's beginning writing for the *Argus* in 1867, see BE 72ff. Hamilton Mackinnon
          writes that Lewins told the proprietor of the *Argus* (his uncle, Lachlan Mackinnon)
          about Clarke's abilities. The appointment would presumably have been made by
          the editor, F. W. Haddon (1839–1906). Born in England, Frederick Haddon was
          recruited in London by the proprietors of the *Argus*, Edward Wilson and Lachlan

Mackinnon, and arrived in Melbourne in December 1863, the same year as Clarke, and was appointed co-editor of the *Australasian*, the new weekly companion to the daily *Argus* launched on 1 October 1864, becoming editor in 1865; he became editor of the *Argus* in January 1867, continuing until 1898. The *Australasian* was then edited by T. L. Bright, who was replaced by James Smith in 1870. Haddon was sharing rooms with Clarke and Dr Aubrey Bowen in Collins Street, Melbourne, at the time they founded the Yorick Club, May 1868 (BE 94). The *Argus* was published from 1846 to 1957. There is a history, *The Argus: Life and Death of a Newspaper*, ed. Jim Usher (Australian Scholarly Publishing, Melbourne, 2007). The *Argus* was the daily paper of the conservative, squatters' interest; the *Age*, which Clarke wrote for later, was the more liberal daily.

p. 164   as Edgar Allan Poe says: 'What a prodigious influence must our thirteen times larger globe have exercised upon his satellite when an embryo in the womb of time the passive subject of chemical affinity!' ('The Unparalleled Adventures of One Hans Pfaal'): 'Tonight my heart is light, / Nor dirge will I upraise' ('Lenore').

p. 164   Mackinnon might have been led astray: this is a rare occasion when Hopkins questions Mackinnon instead of deferring to him, though the dating of Clarke's letters may be unreliable. BE comments that 'little is known about Mackinnon' and 'that his authority to speak [as a biographer] is never quite satisfactorily established' (99–100).

p. 164   Arthur Hopkins (1847–1930): graphic artist, brother of Cyril and Gerard Manley Hopkins. See Introduction.

p. 164   'under the shade of melancholy boughs': Shakespeare, *As You Like It*, 2.7.111–12.

p. 164   my uncle is going to England: Judge James Langton Clarke, see note to Ch. 7.

p. 164   I shall not go however: Clarke's decision, based on his feeling of failure, of having achieved nothing after choosing to come out to Australia, is, as BE points out (92), an important turning point. His self-styled 'mercurial' moods of his letters were also influenced by his disastrous overland trip. BE comments: 'Hopkins was his one remaining link with a life that might have been so different (cf. the theme of 'might have been' in 'Holiday Peak') ... Their correspondence was about to languish, and this ... rather than anything he [Clarke] actually said, shows his real state of mind ... He now wrote home only when his quicksilver was down ...' The beginning of Clarke's new, 'public' life as writer marked for Cyril the close of 'the private period of his life', meaning that for long afterwards he (Cyril) was not as close to his subject as he had been. Hence he has to rely more on second-hand Australian sources which can be unreliable, as BE shows.

p. 165   received your letters ... five in a bundle: this again shows the irregularity of the correspondence between Cyril and Clarke, which perhaps contributed to Cyril's apparently haphazard use of it.

p. 165   expedition to Queensland and Max Kabat: mentioned previously by Cyril, Kabat was Clarke's 'fellow-pupil' at Swinton. The trip was a 'catastrophic venture which cost Kabat his life', though his death 'is not officially recorded' (BE 70–1; 73).

p. 165   salary of three hundred a year: in his obituary of Alfred Telo, *Leader*, 11 October 1879, 18–19, Clarke writes that he was first employed as a 'reporter on a Melbourne daily at 30s. a week'; this is half the figure he quotes to Cyril. Possibly the position as theatrical critic involved a promotion and salary increase.

p. 166   'Lord, what fools these mortals be!': Shakespeare, *A Midsummer Night's Dream*, 3.2.115.

p. 166   the 'Balzac' and the 'Doré': 'Balzac and Modern French Literature', *Australasian*, 3 August 1867, 136; 'Popular Art and Gustave Doré', *Australasian*, 28 September 1867, 392. Both essays are unsigned: attribution is established by Clarke's letter quoted here by Hopkins. The *Australasian* was the weekly sister paper of the daily *Argus*.

p. 166   convict settlement in Tasmania: Clarke's January 1870 visit, with F. W. Haddon, to Hobart and Port Arthur together with his researches laid the foundation for *HNL*, serialised in the monthly *Australian Journal*, March 1870 – June 1872, and published in volume form by George Robertson, Melbourne, 1874. At the same time these

researches resulted in a series of fourteen articles, 'Old Tales Retold' published in the
weekly *Australasian* at irregular intervals between 19 February 1870 and 24 June 1871,
which Clarke collected with a fifteenth article ('The Rule of the Bushranger') in the
volume, *Old Tales of a Young Country* (Mason, Firth & McCutcheon, Melbourne, 1871;
facsimile reprint, introduced by Joan Poole, Sydney University Press, Sydney, 1972).
See Michael Wilding, 'Marcus Clarke's *Old Tales of a Young Country*', *Southerly*, 33,
1973, 394–408. Mackinnon reprinted the fifteen essays of the book together with five
additional historical essays as Part I of *The Austral Edition of the Selected Works of Marcus
Clarke* (1890); this section of *AE* was later published separately as *Stories of Australia in
the Early Days* (Hutchinson, London, 1897). Clarke wrote a recollection of his January
1870 visit to Hobart and Port Arthur in a three-part article, 'Port Arthur', *Argus*, 3, 12
and 26 July 1873, reprinted as 'A Visit to Port Arthur', *Australasian*, 26 July 1873, 102–
3 and 2 August 1873, 133–4; the first article attracted some controversy over Clarke's
comments on the Tasmanian Black war of 1830, and only the second and third articles
are reprinted in *AE*, *Stories of Australia in the Early Days* and BW. All three articles
together with the controversy from the letter columns of the *Argus* are reprinted in *MC*.

p. 166   writing for the stage: Clarke's stage writings are fully recorded in McL, with
supplementary information in Eric Irvin, *Australian Melodrama* (Sydney, 1981).

Chapter 22 (i)

p. 168   There are two copies of this chapter in the MS, one labelled 'Rough Copy', crossed out,
'Chapter 22', crossed out, replaced by '21'; a second one is labelled 'Chapter 22'. There
are some minor variants. The text followed is that labelled 'Chapter 22'. It is called here
Chapter 22 (i), because a further, different chapter, also labelled Chapter 22, follows in
the MS: that is here called Chapter 22 (ii).

p. 168   E. La Touche Armstrong (1864–1946), later Chief Librarian at the Melbourne
Public Library. The remarks are in Edmund La Touche Armstrong, *The Book of the
Public Library, Museums, and National Gallery of Victoria, 1856–1906* (Ford & Son,
Melbourne, 1906) 118–20, and in part quoted in McL (224), and in E. Morris
Miller, 'Some Public Library Memories', ed. Derek Drinkwater, *La Trobe Library
Journal*, 9, 35, 1985, 64. BE (171) questions Armstrong's opinion here, commenting
that 'estimates of Clarke's efficiency as a librarian vary and are not very reliable'.
Correspondence involving Clarke and the Library survives in SLV (McL 229).

p. 168   notice of a concert: Charles Bright, *Cosmos*, 30 April 1895, 421–2. Mackinnon also
tells this story adding that 'this carelessness led to Clarke's withdrawal from the *Argus*
reporting staff' (*MV* 27). BE (86–7) is sceptical of the story.

p. 169   Clarke severed his connection with the *Argus* and *Australasian* at the end of 1873, and
began writing for the *Weekly Times* in 1874, the *Leader* and the London *Daily Telegraph*
in 1877, and the *Age* in 1879 (BE 199–203, 215).

p. 169   Lord Rosebery: see note to Ch. 1. He visited Australia in 1883–84. He wrote in his
letter accepting the dedication of *MV*, 'Since I have been in Australia I have employed
some of the little time at my disposal in carefully examining the blue books on which
His Natural Life is founded, and during my recent visit to Tasmania I made some
personal enquiries on the same subject. The result has been to bring conviction to my
mind that the case is not one whit overstated – nay, that the fact in some particulars is
more frightful that the fiction. Perhaps the most appalling chapter in the book is that
which describes the escape and cannibalism of Gabbett, yet this is taken with almost
verbal accuracy from the narrative of the escape of Pearce and Cox from Macquarie
Harbour, in the appendix of the Transportation Report of 1837–38. That this should
be so only enhances, to my mind, the merit of the book.'

p. 169   want of industry: Mackinnon in *MV* sometimes (e.g. 37) gives this impression, which
Hopkins justifiably corrects.

p. 169 W. B. Dalley, *Sydney Morning Herald*: not in McL.

p. 169 William Bede Dalley (1831–88), son of convict parents, barrister, politician and contributor to the Sydney *Punch* and *Sydney Morning Herald*. There is a statue of him in Hyde Park, Sydney.

p. 170 A writer in the *National Review*: not in McL.

p. 170 Mr. Armstrong: Edmund La Touche Armstrong, *The Book of the Public Library*, 118–20.

p. 170 task of completing his story: the account of the delays in delivery of the instalments of *HNL* is based on statements in 'A Master Printer. Fifty Years in Business. Mr. A. H. Massina', *Herald* (Melbourne), 2 March 1909, 6. BE (154–6) refers to this as 'a legend too persistent to dismiss', adding 'once again Mackinnon's story may not be wrong, but needs to be regarded with caution [as with Massina's original account]'. In the *Australian Journal* for January 1871, only one chapter of *HNL* was provided, and the publishers included Clarke's story 'The Acclimatised Sparrow' to make up for the missing material; in the December 1871 issue there was no chapter of *HNL* at all (McL 326–7).

p. 170 the periodical that had first given to the world his bush stories (composed at Swinton and Ledcourt): Clarke's earliest stories appeared in the *Australian Monthly Magazine* in 1866; they may have been written in the bush but were not set in the bush. 'Pretty Dick', which has a bush setting, appeared in the *Colonial Monthly* in 1869. His sustained series of Bullocktown stories about the bush, set in Swinton and Ledcourt, began appearing in the *Australasian*, 6 August 1870 with 'An Up Country Township'.

p. 171 *Colonial Monthly*: the journal was founded by the printer W. H. Williams in September 1865 as the *Australian Monthly Magazine*. It is distinct from the monthly *Australian Journal*, founded by Clarson, Massina & Co., Melbourne, also in September 1865. In 1867, Clarson, Massina & Co. purchased the *Australian Monthly Magazine*, changing its name to the *Colonial Monthly*, and published it for a year. Then in March 1868, Clarke became editor and co-proprietor with J. J. Shillinglaw and others. In 'Alfred Telo: A Reminiscence' (*Leader*, 11 October 1879, 18–19) Clarke says that he took a 'sum of money which was to have proved my knowledge of the sheep-farming business' and 'started a magazine with it, and Telo helped me. For this magazine he translated Russian tales, and I wrote a novel – my first novel!' This 'first novel' was *LO*, which he serialised in the *Colonial Monthly*, March 1868 – July 1869. The magazine continued to lose money and Clarke relinquished the editorship in September 1869. Shillinglaw bought out the other proprietors and continued it until its final collapse in January 1870. Clarke's financial loss on the venture contributed to his later bankruptcy, 7 July 1874 – 27 February 1875; see BE 107–22, 176–7; Lurline Stuart, *Australian Periodicals: An Annotated Bibliography* (1979), and *Australian Periodicals with Literary Content 1821–1925* (2001).

p. 171 John Joseph Shillinglaw (1831–1905), born London, migrated to Australia in 1852; inspector of Water Police, secretary to Steam Navigation Board, Medical Board of Health, Police Superannuation Board and Board of Viticulture; associated with the Melbourne literary world and a fellow member with Clarke of the Yorick Club and the Cave of Adullam. He appears as Pennylex in Clarke's 'Noah's Ark' dialogues (BE 184) and also as a character in Clarke's novel '*Twixt Shadow and Shine*. He collaborated on research for the *History of the Continent of Australia and the Island of Tasmania*, edited by Clarke. The Shillinglaw papers in SLV contain correspondence with Clarke (McL 229, 236). See Hugh McCrae, *My Father and My Father's Friends* (1935) 17–22.

p. 171 Adam Lindsay Gordon: see note to Preface.

p. 171 Henry Kendall: see note to Preface.

p. 171 Richard Henry Horne (1802–84), English writer, author of the poem *Orion* (1843) which he sold at a farthing 'to mark the public contempt into which epic poetry had fallen'. He was in Australia from 1852 to 1869. Clarke refers to him (as 'Shakespeare's antipodes') in 'On the Pursuit of Pleasure', 18 April 1868, 497. Biography by Cyril Pearl, *Always Morning* (Cheshire, Melbourne, 1960) and Ann Blainey, *The Farthing Poet*

(Longmans, London, 1968). *LMC* lists *The Great Peacemaker* by Orion Horne, and two others. The McLaren Collection in the Baillieu Library, University of Melbourne, holds a copy of a letter from Clarke to Horne (McL 3024).

p. 171   George Gordon McCrae (1833–1927), born in Scotland, arrived in Victoria in 1841; employed in the Victorian government service 1854–93; poet and fellow member with Clarke of the Yorick Club. His son Hugh McCrae wrote of him in *My Father and My Father's Friends* (1935), reprinted in McCrae, *Story Book Only* (1948). G. G. McCrae's copy of *Holiday Peak* (1873) inscribed by Clarke is in Fisher Library, University of Sydney, RB1164.29, together with a copy of a letter from Clarke to McCrae about the cover art for the book, transcribed by his son.

p. 171   Marcus's first novel: *Long Odds,* serialised in the *Colonial Monthly*, March 1868 – July 1869, published in book form by Clarson, Massina, Melbourne, 1869; the unrevised serial text was reissued as *Heavy Odds* (Hutchinson, London, and J. B. Lippincott, Philadelphia, 1896). See S. R. Simmons, *A Problem and a Solution: Marcus Clarke and the Writing of* Long Odds (1946).

p. 171   severe accident: *MV* 30; the accident occurred sometime in June 1868. In his obituary of Alfred Telo, *Leader*, 11 October 1879, 18–19, Clarke writes: 'I was clever enough to fracture my skull, and was for some weeks senseless – for many weeks helpless. Alfred Telo nursed me like a woman through that long and tedious illness; when I was well enough to bear light and sound, he would read Russian or German novels to me, translating them into English as he read, without pause or hesitation …' There was no 'Peripatetic Philosopher' column on 13 June and the following five weeks. Clarke's friend Adam Lindsay Gordon suffered a number of severe riding accidents.

p. 171   George Arthur Walstab (1834–1909), born London, migrated to Victoria 1852 and became a cadet in the Mounted Police; sub-editor and editor of the Calcutta *Englishman* (1860–64); he returned to Australia in 1865 and was appointed the first editor of the monthly *Australian Journal* in September 1865, and was later editor of the *Australasian Monthly Review*, which failed and led to his bankruptcy in 1870 (BE 110). He became editor of the Melbourne *Herald* in 1882. He collaborated with Clarke in supplying news items to Victorian country papers, and in 1868 wrote Chapters 15–18 of Clarke's *LO* for the *Colonial Monthly* when Clarke suffered a riding accident. He was a fellow member of the Yorick Club with Clarke. He has a letter in *The Lone Hand*, August 1907, 418, disclaiming writing any of *HNL*. See further in Simmons.

p. 171   Walter Montgomery (1827–71), born in USA as Richard Tomlinson, grew up in England and acted in the provinces and, in 1863, in London. He toured Australian in 1867–69, opening at the Theatre Royal, Melbourne, on 21 July 1867 with a performance of Hamlet with a contentiously sane disposition; at the same time, James Anderson was performing a traditional melancholic Hamlet. The contrast gave rise to 'the Hamlet controversy', debated by J. E. Neild, James Smith and others and resulting in a book, *The Hamlet Controversy. Was Hamlet Mad? Or the Lucubrations of Messrs. Smith, Brown, Jones and Robinson*, ed. F. W. Haddon (Melbourne, 1867; London, 1871). Montgomery left Australia in January 1870 and shot himself in London in 1871, two days after his marriage. The following year, the new Theatre Royal in Melbourne featured a bust of Montgomery in its central dome, testifying to his impact on the city's theatrical life. See Philip Parsons ed., *Companion to Theatre in Australia* (Currency Press, Paddington NSW, 1995). BE (85) comments: 'Mackinnon [*MV*, 28] informs us provokingly that Clarke "wrote some admirable criticisms of the late Walter Montgomery's performances"', adding that 'perhaps these criticisms were his routine reports'. In 1869, Montgomery 'became involved in a press controversy with Marcus Clarke over the topic of the venality of critics' (Harold Love, *James Edward Neild: Victorian Virtuoso*, 1989, 233). Clarke refers to Montgomery in 'The Peripatetic Philosopher', *Australasian*, 10 April 1869, 465, and 'American Literature', *Australasian*, 25 May 1872, 648. On his feud with Clarke, see Ken Stewart, '"A Careworn Writer for the Press": Henry Kendall in Melbourne', in R. McDougall, ed., *Henry Kendall, The*

Muse of Australia (Centre for Australian Language and Literature Studies, University of New England, Armidale, 1991), reprinted in Ken Stewart, *Investigations in Australian Literature* (2000) 60–1.

p. 171   Max Nordau (1849–1923), Hungarian writer who lived in Paris most of his life. His *Degeneration* (1892, English translation 1895) was an attack on innovative or 'degenerative' art, the so-called 'decadent movement', including the work of Oscar Wilde.

p. 171   Cesare Lombroso (1835–1909): Italian professor of law and psychiatry, author of *L'Uomo di Genio in rapporto alla psichiatra, alla storia ed all'estetica* (Turin, 1888), translated as *The Man of Genius*, in which he writes 'Lesions of the head and brains are very frequent among men of genius. The celebrated Australian novelist, Marcus Clarke, when a child, received a blow from a horse's hoof, which crushed his skull' (quoted in Simmons 25), conflating Clarke's hunting accident with his childhood operation.

p. 172   hope shortly to see the *Colonial Monthly* a success: Clarke's hope was not to be fulfilled. The magazine was declining when Clarke and his associates bought it, and continued to lose money under his editorship. Clarke relinquished the editorship in September 1869, and then established the magazine *Humbug*, which ceased publication four months later, 13 January 1870. Selections from his contributions to *Humbug* are reprinted in *MV*, *AE* and *CC*. Clarke's affidavit of January 1875 in relation to his bankruptcy declares: 'In the year 1868 I in conjunction with some others started in Melbourne a magazine called the *Colonial Monthly*, and spent more than one thousand pounds in endeavouring to establish it; and in consequence of my partners not paying their share the whole of the expense fell upon me and I had to borrow at heavy interest to meet it. And I received no remuneration from the said publication ... In 1869 I endeavoured to establish a weekly comic journal called *Humbug* and spent considerable sums of money on it, but received no remuneration returns' (BE 122–3). In January 1870 he was appointed editor of the monthly *Australian Journal* and continued in that role until September 1871. The publishers of the *Australian Journal* noted that 'successful novelists, dramatists, poets or other writers of fiction, or imagination, have uniformly proved decided failures when they have tried their hands at the practical business of editing a journal' (*MC* xiv–xv).

p. 172   'I write leading articles for three dailies': 'His reference to three daily papers is a little puzzling ... Although a "contributor" to the *Argus*, he retained an informal "staff" status. He might have written for the *Age* without giving offence; but he could hardly have written for the *Herald*, between which paper and the *Argus* there was open hostility. But as he later wrote for the *Sydney Morning Herald* and the *Brisbane Courier*, perhaps he was already writing for newspapers in other cities' (BE 130). Bruce Page, in *The Murdoch Archipelago* (Simon & Schuster, London, 2003) writes that 'Australia was arguably the first country in which the press was authentically popular – that is, formed part of the life everybody led' (15); he quotes from Richard Twopeny, *Town Life in Australia* (1883), that Australia was 'essentially the land of newspapers' and that 'the proportion of the population who can afford to purchase and subscribe to newspapers is ten times as large as in England; hence the number of sheets issued is comparatively much greater'. Trollope remarked on Australia's newspaper culture in his *Australia and New Zealand* (1873). The liveliness and extent of the Australian press were no doubt factors that encouraged Clarke to remain in Australia and not take up the invitation to join the London *Daily Telegraph*. However, as Andrew McCann remarks, 'Clarke was caught up in the over-supply of periodical writing for a small and indifferent readership. With the growth of Melbourne in the wake of the gold rush, the prospects for writers may well have improved, yet as Michael Ackland points out, this expanding population base "in no way justified the massive annual increment of print, that was further swollen by the importation of standard British magazines such as *Household Words*, which were as popular in the Antipodes as in England". The offshoot of this situation was that virtually all the dedicated writers of any public prominence in this period also worked as journalists in order to make a living.' Andrew McCann, *Marcus*

Clarke's Bohemia: Literature and Modernity in Colonial Melbourne (2004) 24–5; Michael Ackland, *Henry Kendall: The Man and the Myths* (1995) 157–8.

p. 172   Berthold Auerbach (1812–82), German Jewish novelist and short story writer, born Moyses Baruch, author of *Auf der Höhe (On the Heights)* (1865).

p. 172   *Griffith Gaunt* (1866), scandalous at the time for its frank attitude to sexuality. Listed in *LMC*. It and *The Cloister and the Hearth* (1861) are the two novels by which Charles Reade is now remembered. On Reade, see note to Ch. 3.

p. 172   Dionysius Lardner Boucicault (1820–90), Irish dramatist, author and adaptor of some 200 plays. Walter Montgomery performed his works on his Australian tour. Boucicault visited Australia in 1885.

p. 172   *Chastelard* (1865), a verse play about Mary, Queen of Scots, by Swinburne. Adam Lindsay Gordon sent a copy of it to his friend E. G. Blackmore, the South Australia Parliamentary Librarian, in October 1868: see Hugh Anderson, ed., *The Last Letters, 1868–1870: Adam Lindsay Gordon to John Riddoch* (Hawthorn Press, Melbourne, 1970) 29.

p. 172   Edmund Yates (1831–94), English novelist, and editor of *The World*. He was educated at Highgate School and was a protégé of Dickens. He published a memoir in 1885, *Edmund Yates: His Recollections and his Experiences.* He is cited as an influence on Clarke's novel *Long Odds* (1869) by H. M. Hyndman in his review in the *Argus*, 2 July 1869, 5–6. Clarke refers to him in his essay 'Charles Dickens', *Argus*, 8 July 1870, 7. See P. D. Edwards, *Dickens' 'Young Men': George Augustus Sala, Edmund Yates and the World of Victorian Journalism* (Ashgate, Aldershot, 1997).

p. 172   Cholmleiian ... Sir Roger Chomley's school: Hopkins' spellings.

p. 172   Charles Bright, 'Marcus Clarke', *Cosmos*, 30 April 1895, 418–19. Bright was then on the parliamentary staff of the *Argus*. BE quotes a later allusion (a paragraph in the *Imperial Review*, Melbourne 1886), 'matching Bright's vignette', to 'a short, thin, handsome man, well described by his friends as a smaller edition of Alcibiades' (a handsome, talented Athenian politician) (BE 92–3) Clarke refers to Alcibiades in *LO*.

p. 173   Café de Paris, (Spiers and Pond's Melbourne success, before the firm migrated to London): Felix William Spiers (1832–1911), born in London, went to Australia in search of gold in 1851. There he met Christopher Pond (d. 1881), an Englishman, and together they established The Shakespeare Grill Room at the Melbourne National Hotel. Later they bought the Café de Paris. When they returned to London in March 1863, noting the poor food service at railway stations, they contracted to provide restaurants and cafés. They built the Criterion Restaurant and Theatre in Piccadilly Circus in 1874 and the Gaiety Theatre Restaurant in the Strand in 1894. (*The Daily Screw*, 8 March 2003; *The Yorker*, 35, Summer 2002–03.)

p. 173   Charles Lamb (1775–1834), English essayist. On his influence on Clarke's essay 'Austin Friars', *Australian Monthly Magazine*, May 1866, 199–209, see BE 44.

p. 173   absinthe: a liqueur with alcohol, wormwood (Greek *apsinthion*) and anise as essential ingredients. It has an alcohol level of up to seventy-five per cent, and hallucinogenic qualities resulting from the chemical thujone found in wormwood. It was used as a disinfectant and anti-malarial agent by French troops in North Africa and Indo-China and achieved cult status in mid- and late nineteenth- and early twentieth-century French literary and artistic culture. It is represented in the work of numerous artists, including Dégas, Gauguin and Van Gogh, and in Marie Corelli's novel *Wormwood* (1913). Recent studies of absinthe include Phil Baker, *The Dedalus Book of Absinthe* (2001), Marie-Claude Delahaye, *L'Absinthe, son histoire* (2001) and Jad Adams, *Hideous Absinthe: A History of the Devil in a Bottle* (2004). In the early twentieth century it was banned in France, Belgium, Switzerland and the USA, though not in Britain. Clarke refers to absinthe in *LO*, in 'Noah's Ark', *Australasian*, 27 July 1872, 104, and in 'Down Camomile Street', *Weekly Times*, 17 January 1874, 9, and to the Café d'Absinthe, in 'Taking a Drink', *Weekly Times*, 21 March 1874, 8, all reprinted *CC*.

     Opium, often taken in the form of laudanum, had its famous literary users, including Coleridge, De Quincey, Walter Scott, Bulwer Lytton, Wilkie Collins, Henry

Kendall and Adam Lindsay Gordon; see Alethea Hayter, *Opium and the Romantic Imagination* (1968). It was available in nineteenth-century Melbourne and features in Clarke's treatment of the Chinese community in Ch. 8, and in 'Night Scenes in Melbourne: No. III The Chinese Quarter', *Argus*, 9 March 1868, 5–6, and 'Noah's Ark', *Australasian*, 7 December 1872, 712, both reprinted *CC*, and to laudanum in *LO*. Charles Bright's anecdote of Clarke's use of opium and absinthe contributed to his Bohemian image. Clarke writes about Melbourne Bohemia in 'Austin Friars', *Australian Monthly Magazine*, May 1866, 199–209; in 'The Café Lutetia', *Weekly Times*, 28 February 1874, 9; and in 'A Quiet Club', *Australasian*, 9 May 1868, 593, reprinted *PP*. Further anecdotes are collected in Michael Wilding, 'Marcus Clarke, Bohemian', *Hemisphere*, 26, 1981, 148–51, reprinted as the first part of the introduction to Marcus Clarke, *ST*.

Clarke's experiment with hashish is recorded in his 'Cannabis Indica', *Colonial Monthly*, February 1868, 454–68. In 'Noah's Ark', *Australasian*, 7 December 1872, Marston remarks, 'I sometimes experiment upon myself, and after one has eaten hashish a depression of spirit follows', and in 'Noah's Ark', *Australasian*, 12 July 1873, 43–4, Clarke has a character called Dr Cannabis, both reprinted *CC*. The literary context of hashish experimentation is recorded in Wilding, 'Weird Melancholy: Inner and Outer Landscapes in Marcus Clarkes Stories', *Studies in Classic Australian Fiction* (1987), 24–31. An article 'Confessions of a French Haschisch Eater' in *Once A Week*, 1, 3, 18 April 1868, 340–51, appeared after Clarke's 'Cannabis Indica' was published.

p. 173   The likeness, accompanying this article: Cyril omits 'copied from a photograph kindly sent to me by Mrs. Clarke'. It is the photograph by Batchelder & Co., reproduced in this volume. Copies are in the SLV – accession number H4700, image number a15339, and H81.204/3, mp013432.

p. 174   Boanerges: a loud, vociferous preacher or orator.

p. 174   Melbourne Club: Clarke became a member of the establishment Melbourne Club in May 1868.

p. 174   H. M. Hyndman, *The Record of an Adventurous Life* (1911) 89–90, 91. CH does not repeat the famous anecdote about Melbourne with which Hyndman continues his praise of the city. 'Its only drawback was rather neatly expressed by the brother of Bernal Osborne, who held some British appointment in the metropolis of Victoria. Asked how he liked Melbourne he replied, with the drawl that was habitual to him, "Immensely. But don't you think it is a little far from town?"' (91).

p. 174   Henry Mayers Hyndman (1842–1921), English writer and editor, visited Australia in 1869. He reviewed Clarke's *LO* in the *Argus*, 2 July 1869, 5–6. The ML holds a letter from Hyndman to Clarke that 'introduces Clarke to Henty and Sala' (McL 3143).

Chapter 22 (ii)

p. 176   unable to discover in the numerous reviews: some are listed in *MV*, 38–40, and others in L. T. Hergenhan, 'The Contemporary Reception of *His Natural Life*', *Southerly*, 31, 1971, 50–63.

p. 176   Emily Bronte's novel: *Wuthering Heights* (1847). Hopkins is echoing Lord Rosebery who compared her novel to *HNL*, see notes to Ch. 1 and Ch. 22.

p. 177   *Treasure Island*: Robert Louis Stevenson's first book-length work of fiction, published 1883.

p. 177   much of the force of *His Natural Life* must have lain 'perdu': A. G. Stephens, 'Marcus Clarke's Minor Writings', *Bulletin*, 29 April 1899, red page; reprinted in Leon Cantrell, ed., *A. G. Stephens: Selected Writings* (1977) 172–5. Cantrell also reprints Stephens' two further essays on Clarke. In relation to Stephens' comment, cf. Lord Rosebery on *HNL*: 'The materials for great works of imagination lie all around us; but it is genius that selects and transposes them' (Letter accepting dedication of *MV*).

p. 177   H. M. Hyndman *The Record of an Adventurous Life* (1911) 97–8.

p. 178   Charles Bright: *Cosmos*, 30 April 1895, 422.

p. 178   his marriage with a charming actress of the day: Marcus Clarke married Marian Dunn
            (1846–1911) at St Peter's Church, Melbourne, 22 July 1869. They had six children. She
            was the 'daughter of the famous old comedian, John Dunn' (as Charles Bright describes
            him) (originally O'Donoghue), who was born in Ireland in 1816, and acted in London
            and America before settling in Melbourne where he died in 1876 (BE 132ff.). Clarke
            was involved with J. E. Neild, a forensic pathologist and drama critic, in revising John
            Dunn's autobiography, but family objections prevented its publication; see Harold
            Love, *James Edward Neild: Victorian Virtuoso* (1989) 235.

p. 179   *Humbug* was published from September 1869 to 13 January 1870; see BE 122–6.
            Selections in *MV, AE, CC*.

p. 179   Alfred Henry Massina (1834–1917), born London, apprenticed to the printer Sidney
            Waterlow and after emigrating to Australia in 1855 worked for W. H. Williams before
            founding his own company. See Ronald G. Campbell, *The First Ninety Years: The
            Printing House of Massina, Melbourne 1859 to 1949* (A. H. Massina & Co., Melbourne,
            [1949]).

p. 179   Finally we had to lock him in a room: BE (154–5) concedes that there may be some
            substance in this story but comments that this does not necessarily show dilatoriness,
            since in two and a half years there were only two lapses in instalments, neither due to
            negligence. BE (154) also argues that Mackinnon's similar stories of dilatoriness should
            be treated with caution. Moreover, stories of locking reluctant authors in rooms are
            often apocryphal.

p. 180   Cheap editions: *HNL*, re-titled *For the Term of His Natural Life* in 1885, was reprinted
            and reissued by numerous English publishers, including Macmillan (who took over
            Richard Bentley in 1897), Ward Lock, Collins in their Collins Classics series, Oxford
            University Press in their World's Classics series, and Penguin.

p. 180   dramatized: details can be found in Ian F. McLaren, *Marcus Clarke: An Annotated
            Bibliography* (1982), and in Elizabeth Webby, 'Stage, Screen and Other Versions of
            His Natural Life, 1886–1998', in Lurline Stuart, ed., Marcus Clarke, *His Natural Life*
            (2001) 591–605.

p. 180   review of the latest dramatic representation: *Australasian*, 13 March 1909.

p. 180   Until Lord Rosebery read and recognised its [*HNL*'s] merits: This view is supported by
            C. T. Clarke, who worked in George Robertson's Melbourne office and recalled that
            only when Rosebery visited Australia and praised the novel did the strong demand for
            the Australian edition set in (*All About Books*, 19 May 1930, 123).

p. 181   Edmund Yates, see note to Ch. 22 (i); *Nobody's Fortune. A Novel* (1872).

p. 181   Mahmoud II (1784–1839), Ottoman Sultan (1808-39), defeated the Greeks in the first
            war of independence and in 1826 ruthlessly purged the Turkish Janissary forces.

p. 181   Mehmet Ali (1769–1839), a viceroy of Egypt under the Ottomans, in 1811
            treacherously massacred the leaders of the Marmeluk [sic] Beys.

p. 181   Lord Ashley began his labours: Anthony Ashley Cooper (1801–85), seventh Earl of
            Shaftesbury, politician and reformer, including of the conditions of mill workers and
            miners, including women and children.

p. 181   Newgate Calendar: originally a bulletin of executions at Newgate Prison, London.
            Publishers used its name for chapbooks of biographies of notorious criminals, begun in
            the eighteenth century. The 1774 collected edition became standard.

p. 181   Edward Carpenter (1844–1929), English radical writer. *Prisons, Police and Punishment*
            (Fifield, London, 1905) 40–2.

p. 182   Desmond Byrne, *Australian Writers* (1896), 86.

p. 182   'But even as she turned, from under the shadow of the cuddy': *HNL*, Book 1, Ch. 1
            (*MC* 17).

p. 183   Sir Donald Wallace (1841–1919), journalist and author, in 1901 accompanied the
            Duke and Duchess of Cornwall, the future King George V and Queen Mary, on their

tour of the dominions, including Australia, which Wallace commemorated in *The Web of Empire* (1902). See note to Ch. 14 on royal visit.

p. 183   'Her little figure was as upright': *HNL*, Book 2, Ch. 5 (*MC* 96).

p. 184   'I wonder what book': *HNL*, Book 2, Ch. 6 (*MC* 105).

p. 184   Charles Bright, *Cosmos*, 30 April 1895, 419.

p. 184   Francis Adams, *The Australians* (1893), 115.

p. 184   'loading all the rifts of his subject with ore': 'load every rift' of your subject with ore, John Keats, letter to Shelley, August 1820.

p. 184   Walter Murdoch, 'Marcus Clarke', *Argus*, 22 October 1904, 4; collected in Walter Murdoch, *Loose Leaves* (George Robertson, Melbourne, 1910) 50–5.

p. 184   Æschylus (525–546 BC), Greek tragic dramatist, author of *Prometheus Bound*. Clarke's poem 'The Mystic' (from Æschylus) is reprinted in *MV* and *AE*.

p. 184   Gustave Flaubert (1821–80), French novelist, author of *Madame Bovary* (1857) and *L'Education Sentimental* (1869).

p. 184   Émile Zola: see note to Ch. 3.

p. 184   Victor Hugo, *Les Misérables* (1862): see note to Ch. 17. Listed in *LMC*.

p. 184   Daniel Defoe, *A Journal of the Plague Year* (1722).

p. 185   It is not a story with a moral, 'thrown externally over it', in Stevenson's phrase, 'like a carpet over a railing': Robert Louis Stevenson, *Familiar Studies of Men and Books* (1882) on Victor Hugo.

p. 185   sufferings of the British prisoners of war in Germany: that some readers drew a similar parallel with camps in World War II may be suggested by the fact that a condensed version of the novel was published by Penguin in 1944 as *Men in Chains*, reprinted from a serialisation in the London *Evening Standard* (McL gives no dates for serial).

p. 185   Moloney's memoir of Clarke has not been traced.

p. 185   translated into several foreign languages: Dutch, German, Russian, Swedish and Chinese; listed in McL 204–17.

p. 185   *Confessions of a Journalist*: possibly the book by Chris Healy (Chatto & Windus, London, 1904).

p. 186   Fyodor Mihailovich Dostoyevsky (1821–81), Russian novelist, author of *Crime and Punishment* (1866), *The Brothers Karamazov* (1880) etc. *Crime and Punishment* appeared eight years before *HNL*, but whether Clarke had heard of it is uncertain, though, as Hopkins shows, he was acquainted with other Russian fiction. MS has 'Dostoieffsky'.

p. 186   *In Steel and Scarlet*: *Scarlet and Steel. Some Modern Military Episodes* (1893) by E. Livingston Prescott.

p. 186   *Fettered for Life* (Chatto & Windus, London, 1889), a novel by Frank Barrett (b. 1848).

p. 186   *The Inimitable Mrs. Massingham: A Romance of Botany Bay* (Chatto & Windus, London, 1900), a novel by Herbert Compton (1853–1906).

p. 186   Archibald Marshall: pseudonym of Arthur Hammond Marshall (1866–1934). *Sunny Australia: Impressions of the Country and People* (Hodder & Stoughton, London, 1911) 223–4, 227–9.

p. 187   Eagle's Neck: i.e. Eaglehawk Neck.

Chapter 23 (i)

p. 189   experiences of a newcomer of that of the state of Victoria: that – i.e. the climate; state – Victoria was still a 'colony' when Clarke arrived.

p. 189   'Our Glorious Climate': *Humbug*, 12 January 1870, 5, reprinted *Australian Journal*, February 1870, 355, *MV* 65–8, *AE*.

p. 189   'The Puff Conclusive': *Melbourne Punch*, 19 November 1863, 162.

p. 190   Dorothea at the fountain: Cervantes, *Don Quixote*, 1, Ch. 35. Don Quixote, in
           attempting to rescue Dorothea, slashes pigskin sacks of red wine he mistakes for the
           body of a giant, and a fountain of wine issues from them.

p. 190   *Ask Mamma: Or the Richest Commoner in England* (Bradbury, Agnew and Co., London,
           1858) by Robert Surtees (1803–64).

p. 190   Shirley Brookes: (1816–74), novelist and editor of *Punch*.

p. 191   'When the heart of man is oppressed with cares the mist is dispelled when a woman
           appears!' *The Beggar's Opera* (1728), Act 2 scene 3, by John Gay (1685–1732). Clarke
           has 'oppressed', Gay's original has 'depressed'.

p. 191   'On Borrowing Money': *Humbug*, 29 September 1869, 8, 11, reprinted *MV*, *AE*, BW, *CC*.

p. 191   'On Teetotalism': *Humbug*, 20 October 1869, 8, 11, reprinted *MV*, *AE*, BW.

p. 191   'On the Roaring of Colonial Lions': *Humbug*, 27 October 1869, 8, 11, reprinted *MV*,
           CC. MS has 'The Roaring of Colonial Lions'.

p. 192   'On Business Men': *Humbug*, 3 November 1869, 6, 11, reprinted *MV*, *AE*, BW, *CC*.
           MS has 'Business Men'.

p. 192   'On Loafing Around': *Humbug*, 24 November 1869, 6, 11, reprinted *MV*, *AE*.

p. 192   'On Bazaars': *Humbug*, 15 December 1869, 6, 11, reprinted *MV*, *AE*.

p. 192   'On Friendship': *Humbug*, 10 November 1869, 6, reprinted *MV*, *AE*, BW.

p. 192   'On Relationships': *Humbug*, 17 November 1869, 6, 11, reprinted *MV*, *AE*.

p. 192   'The Diary of a Drunkard': *Humbug*, 22 September 1869, 11, reprinted *MV*.

p. 192   'A Bush Fire': in *MV*.

p. 193   'In a Bark Hut': *Australasian*, 17 May 1873, 616.

p. 193   'Thither': not in McL.

p. 194   'A Pawnbroker's Shop on a Saturday Night': *Argus*, 6 March 1868, 6, reprinted
           MV, *CC*. The second of three sketches under the general heading 'Night Scenes in
           Melbourne', unsigned.

p. 194   ghost of Elsinore: Shakespeare, *Hamlet*, 1, 4, 52–4: 'again in complete steel, / Revisits
           thus the glimpses of the moon, / Making night hideous.' Clarke refers to *Hamlet* again
           in *LO*, in 'Noah's Ark', 18 May and 7 December 1872, reprinted *CC* and 'The Curious
           Experience of Anthony Venn', *Australasian*, 27 September, 389, 18 October, 485, 1
           November 1873, 549, reprinted *AE*, *AT*, *ST* as 'The Mind Reader's Curse'.

Chapter 23 (ii)

p. 195   Francis Adams: *The Australians* (1893) 114.

p. 196   A. B. Paterson: (1864–1941), Australian poet, also wrote as 'the Banjo'; 'Introductory
           Memoir', *For the Term of His Natural Life* (Angus and Robertson, Sydney, 1899) xiv.
           Paterson's view reflects the general neglect of Clarke's other work.

p. 196   *Felix and Felicitas*: Clarke's uncompleted novel. Printer's proofs of the preliminary
           chapters, the only surviving, are in the ML. See note to Preface.

p. 196   Robert Buchanan (1841–1901), Scottish writer. He attacked Swinburne's work as
           immoral. *Robert Buchanan: Some Account of His Life, His Life's Work and His Literary
           Friendships*, by Harriet Jay (Unwin, London, 1903).

p. 197   Mackenzie Bell, *A Forgotten Genius: Charles Whitehead. A Critical Monograph* (Elliott
           Stock, London, 1884). See note to Ch. 5 on Whitehead's novel *Richard Savage*. On
           Whitehead, see also Clive Turnbull, *Mulberry Leaves* (Hawthorn Press, Melbourne,
           1965).

p. 197   agent and manager of his cousin: Hopkins follows Mackinnon (*MV* 57–8), whom he
           quotes, in tending to excuse Clarke's alleged mismanagement. BE gives a more critical
           account (177–8, 181–3).

p. 198   contemplating a return to the 'old country': this first 'serious intimation' to Cyril,
           unfortunately undated, nevertheless suggests that Clarke had been ambivalent about it
           for some time but did not want to admit it.

p. 198   Sir T. H. Hall Caine (1853–1931), English novelist. In 1881, R. W. Dixon sent him two of GMH's poems for an anthology he was editing; GMH sent another three. Caine rejected them all (R. B. Martin, 330).

p. 198   to quote Mackinnon's words: *MV* 61.

p. 199   'The Money-lenders of Baretaria': posthumously published in the *Bulletin*, 29 July 1893, 8.

p. 199   A correspondent, signing himself M. B.: A. G. Stephens, red page, *Bulletin*, 18 August 1904, quoting M. B.; cf. another contribution by the same hostile acquaintance, red page, 22 September 1904.

p. 199   Waxman: Aaron Waxman, a money-lender. BE (229) cites two anecdotes about Clarke and Waxman from the *Bulletin*, 25 September and 2 October 1880.

p. 200   'Dip': *Bulletin*, 8 September 1904, red page.

p. 200   'Old Adullamite': a pseudonym used by George Gordon McCrae, see note to Ch. 22 (i), referring to the Cave of Adullam Club, which Clarke and others established when the Yorick Club became too respectable. The article has not been located. Further commentators on Clarke in *Bulletin* include V. J. Daley, 24 September 1903, Frank Myers, 26 November 1903, and 'Old Penjostler', 21 January 1899, and 9 November 1903.

p. 200   my intimate knowledge of him in early life: Hopkins' view of Clarke as a 'literary' writer, extremely well read and allusive in his writings, based on his letters as well as on early acquaintance, is an unusual one for this time and for long after; cf. Wilding, *Marcus Clarke* (1977) and Ken Stewart, 'Sylvia's Books: Literature, Civilisation and *His Natural Life*', in Irmtraud Petersson and Martin Duwell, ed., *And What Books Do You Read?* 1–14, reprinted in Ken Stewart, *Investigations in Australian Literature*, 89–102.

p. 200   Mrs. Oliphant: Margaret Oliphant (1828–97), Scots novelist, prolific author of over 100 titles.

p. 200   an article on Australia in the *Cornhill Magazine*: Mrs B. R. Wise, 'Household Budgets Abroad – Australia', *Cornhill Magazine*, new series 17, 1904, 631–53.

p. 201   Inkermann Street, St Kilda: described by BE (252) as the 'poorest house in which he [Clarke] had ever lived'. BE does not give a street number. Death Certificate (46/674) gives address as 'Brighton Rd; Borough of S Kilda'. Earlier, according to Weston Bate, *A History of Brighton* (Melbourne University Press, Melbourne, 2nd edn, 1983) 289, 'Marcus Clarke lived in Outer Crescent [Brighton] from 1877 to 1879, hopeful of keeping up some sort of style'.

p. 201   contemplating a leap: Cyril Hopkins wrote to Rose Bradley, Clarke's grand-daughter, 27 July 1905: 'will your mother object to the mention of the incident you tell me of your father's [sic] strange behaviour during that walk? Because of course, although his impulse to leap over the edge of the cliff may have really arisen from mixed motives, the ordinary reader will regard it as simply an attempt at suicide … I have inserted the incident in [what he thought at the time was] the last chapter but followed it up by saying that his nature was far from morose and that he evidently enjoyed a joke to the last …' (MS ML). Cyril goes on: 'Further P.S. [sic] about that walk wd. [sic] greatly help me.' This again underlines Cyril's attempt in his MS description of this incident, and elsewhere, to represent Clarke in what he thought was, by Victorian standards, a positive light. BE comments on Clarke's attitude to suicide (145–6), citing Patrick Moloney, 'The Suicidal Stage of Existence', *Melbourne Review*, July 1877, and also Clarke's dispatch to the *Ballarat Star*, 26 July 1881, about the case of a man who hanged himself in the Treasury Gardens. BE adds (245 ff.) that 'more than one commentator has alleged that Marcus Clarke died by suicide. As a simple fact that is certainly untrue … Gloomy as was his mood [in 1877], it appears he looked on suicide with repugnance. In any case he had little time to change his mind. For when he wrote his dispatch he was already ill … and had only seven days of life remaining … But he had imprudently neglected his health, and begun too soon and continued too long "to elevate his outer rail".'

p. 202   Cesare Lombroso: see note to Ch. 22 (i).

p. 202   H. G. Turner, 'Marcus Clarke', *Melbourne Review*, 7, 25, January 1882. The first
            paragraph quoted is from early in the article, 4; the second paragraph is the close, 14–15.

p. 202   Isaac D'Israeli (1766–1848), English author of *Calamities of Authors* (1813) and
            Quarrels of Authors (1814). A copy of D'Israeli's *Curiosities of Literature* (1791) is listed
            in *LMC*. He was father of the novelist and politician Benjamin Disraeli, first earl of
            Beaconsfield (1804–81), on whose novels Clarke wrote in the *Daily Telegraph*, London,
            1 April 1879, and the *Leader*, 19 February 1881, reprinted *MV*. He refers to *Vivien
            Grey* in *LO*. *LMC* lists B. Disraeli's *Vivien Grey*.

p. 202   Oliver Goldsmith (1730–74), Anglo-Irish writer, author of *The Vicar of Wakefield*
            (1766). Clarke refers to him in his essay 'Charles Dickens', *Argus*, 8 July 1870, 7.

p. 202   Walter Savage Landor (1775–1864), English writer, known for his feuds.

p. 202   Mr. Micawber: character in Charles Dickens' novel *David Copperfield* (1849–50).

Chapter 24 (i)

p. 203   'Peripatetic Philosopher': see note to Ch. 1.

p. 204   Francis Adams, 'The Prose Works of Marcus Clarke', *Sydney Quarterly Magazine*, 4, 2,
            1887, 115–35.

p. 204   Israel Zangwill (1864–1926), English novelist and noted Jewish activist. His 'Philosophic
            Excursions' were journalistic pieces reprinted in his *Without Prejudice* (1896).

p. 204   our Melbourne philosopher deals with such topics: most of these from the 'Peripatetic
            Philosopher' column are reprinted in *MV, AE, CC*.

p. 205   Douglas Jerrold (1803–57), English dramatist and journalist. He contributed to *Punch*
            under the pseudonym 'Q' – a pseudonym Clarke used for the 'Peripatetic Philosopher'
            column. Clarke acknowledges his influence in the preface to *The Peripatetic Philosopher*
            (1869), and refers to him in 'On Advertising', *Humbug*, 1 December 1869, 6, 11, both
            reprinted *CC*. *LMC* lists Douglas Jerrold's *Men of Character, original complete edition, Punch's
            Letters to His Son, The Complete Letter-Writer, Sketches of the English, St Giles and St James, A
            Man made of Money, Clovernook, Douglas Jerrold's Caudle Lectures, original complete edition,
            The Story of a Feather, Comedies, Comedies and Dramas* and *Cakes and Ale*.

p. 206   Ben Jonson (1572/73–1637), English dramatist, author of *The Alchemist* (1610) etc.
            LMC lists *The Complete Works of Ben Jonson* edited by Gifford.

p. 206   Abraham Tucker (1705–74), English philosopher, author of *The Light of Nature
            Pursued*, 7 vols, 1765–74, a miscellany rather than a systematic treatise.

p. 206   Charles Lever: see note to Ch. 3.

p. 206   Ella MacMahon (b. Dublin?, d. 1956), Irish novelist.

p. 207   'The Puff Conclusive': *Melbourne Punch*, 19 November 1863, 162.

p. 207   'Our Glorious Climate': *Humbug*, 12 January 1870, 5.

Chapter 24 (ii)

p. 208   a writer in the Sydney *Bulletin*: F[rank] M[yers], 'Of Marcus Clarke (and some
            others)', *Bulletin*, 26 November 1903, red page.

p. 208   Theodore Hook (1788–1841), English wit and novelist of the fashionable world.
            Clarke refers to him in 'Noah's Ark', *Australasian*, 16 August 1873, 198–9, reprinted
            CC. *LMC* lists The *John Bull* Newspaper, edited by Theodore Hook, and containing
            the account of the trial of Queen Caroline, 17 December 1820 – 26 December 1824,
            complete, 4 vols.

p. 208   Leigh Hunt (1784–1859), English essayist and editor. He lived at 32 Edwardes Square, not
            far from Clarke's birthplace, from 1840 to 1851, and wrote an account of the Kensington

district, *The Old Court Suburb* (1855). *LMC* lists Leigh Hunt's *A Chimney Corner*. His son
Thornton Leigh Hunt (1810–73) was an editor of the London *Daily Telegraph*.

p. 208   Winthrop Mackworth Praed (1802–39), English writer of light verse. Clarke refers to
him in *LO*.

p. 208   Arthur Hugh Clough (1819–61), English poet, author of 'Amours de Voyage' (1858).

p. 208   Walter Pater (1839–94), English essayist, art historian and aesthete, author of *Studies
in the History of the Renaissance* (1873). A fellow of Brasenose College, Oxford, he was
GMH's tutor in 1866.

p. 208   Philip Gilbert Hamerton (1834–94), English artist, art critic and author whose works
included *The Intellectual Life* (1873).

p. 208   Browning: see note to Ch. 9.

p. 208   Edmund Spenser (c. 1552–99), English poet, author of *The Faerie Queene* (1590–96).

p. 208   'Pretty Dick': *Colonial Monthly*, April 1869, 128–41, reprinted in *Holiday Peak*.

p. 209   on that trip: an outing to Ferntree Gulley with Myers.

p. 209   six months after the receipt of the letter: the letter is dated by BE as 1873, the year
when 'La Béguine' was written (BE 10).

p. 209   Bentley: the English publishing house founded by Richard Bentley (1794–1871) and
continued by his son George Bentley (1828–95). They published the first English
edition of *HNL* in 1875, and continued to reissue it; they were acquired by Macmillan
in 1897, who published subsequent editions of *HNL*. See Ian F. McLaren, 'Richard
Bentley and the Publication of *His Natural Life*', *Bibliographical Society of Australia and
New Zealand Bulletin*, 4, 1, 1982, 3–21, and McL 2047, 3383.

p. 209   'La Béguine' is the best story: nonetheless, Mackinnon omitted it from his two
anthologies of Clarke.

p. 210   Mrs. Cashel Hoey (1830–1908); her husband was a close associate of Charles Gavan
Duffy, the Irish nationalist whom Clarke knew in Victoria, and to whom he dedicated
HNL. She was instrumental in the publication of 'An Australian Mining Township'
in *All the Year Round*, 22 February 1873, 352–7, and was involved in editing the
English edition of *HNL* (1875). See P. D. Edwards, *Frances Cashel Hoey (1830–1908): A
Bibliography* (1982). Mackinnon quotes her piece in the *Australasian* on Clarke's death.
She was a cousin of George Bernard Shaw.

p. 210   *Felix and Felicitas*: see note to Preface and to Ch. 23 (ii).

p. 210   Arthur Patchett Martin: 'An Australian Novelist', *Temple Bar*, 71, May 1884, 104.

p. 210   the Public Library of Melbourne: the Melbourne Public Library opened its doors in
1856 and expanded its activities to include a Museum and a Fine Art collection. In
1869 the Public Library, Museum and National Gallery of Victoria were incorporated
under the general supervision of the Trustees. Clarke was appointed Clerk to the
Trustees of the Library on 10 June 1870 at a salary of £175 p.a.. His duties included
being secretary to the Fine Arts Board responsible for the National Gallery of Victoria.
In September 1873 he was promoted to sub-librarian, when Henry Sheffield was
appointed Chief Librarian following the death of the founding Librarian, Augustus
Tulk. In October 1880 Clarke applied unsuccessfully for the post of Librarian. Having
borrowed money on the expectation of becoming Librarian, in June 1881 he was
declared bankrupt for a second time. His insolvency, together with the controversy
with the Bishop of Melbourne over his article 'Civilisation without Delusion', and
his adaptation, with R. P. Whitworth, of Gilbert A'Beckett's *The Happy Land* (1880)
(adapted in its turn from W. S. Gilbert's *The Wicked World*), a political farce satirising
the Berry government, ruled out his chances of promotion to Librarian. He resigned
from the Library in July 1881. He died the following month, 2 August 1881. See BE
247–52, and John Arnold, 'Marcus Clarke Joins the Public Library, Museum and
National Gallery of Victoria', *Margin*, 40, November 1996, 19–21. Correspondence
involving Clarke and the Library survives in SLV (McL 229).

p. 210   the writer in the Sydney *Bulletin*, previously mentioned: Frank Myers, see note above.

p. 210   on the other hand, Mr. Hamilton Mackinnon: *MV* 57. CH is repeating himself from Ch.
          23 (ii), possibly suggesting that the final chapters, some of which contain repetition, may
          have been written at a later date. See note to Ch. 23 (ii) re Mackinnon's comments.

p. 211   In the MS the chapter concluded with the following passage, which was later crossed
          out: 'Perhaps the better plan will be to introduce at this point of my narrative the
          fragment of *Felix and Felicitas* in question in order to give the reader an opportunity of
          judging of its merits.' The fragment of the novel is not included in Hopkins' MS at this
          or any other point.

Chapter 25

p. 212   *Chidiock Tichbourne or the Babington Conspiracy*, serialised in the monthly *Australian
          Journal*, September 1874 – March 1875. It was published posthumously in book form
          as *Chidiock Tichbourne or the Catholic Conspiracy* (Eden Remington, London, 1893).
          It is an historical novel set in Elizabethan England, and deals with the Babington
          conspiracy to set Mary, Queen of Scots, on the English throne. One of the characters
          is called Gerard, another Hopkins, allowing the possibility that Clarke is at some level
          playing with the name of his former school-friend now become a Roman Catholic
          convert, GMH. See Michael Wilding, 'Marcus Clarke's *Chidiock Tichbourne*', *ALS*,
          6, 1974, 381–93. Clarke drew on the contemporary Tichborne case, in which Arthur
          Orton claimed to be the missing heir Roger Tichborne, for John Rex's imposture in
          HNL. With *Chidiock Tichbourne* Clarke exploited the notoriety of the name. GMH
          wrote about the Tichborne case to his mother, and in 1873 attended Lord Chief Justice
          Cockburn's summing up (Abbott, ed., *Further Letters of Gerard Manley Hopkins*, 60,
          117–8, 123, 236; R. B. Martin, 229).

p. 213   the 'Noah's Ark' papers: 'Noah's Ark. By Marcus Clarke', the column in the weekly
          Australasian, 18 May 1872 – 13 September 1873.

p. 213   republished in volume form: a selection of 'The Peripatetic Philosopher' column was
          republished in volume form in 1869, but not 'Noah's Ark'.

p. 213   Robert Percy Whitworth (1831–1901), born England. A journalist in Sydney and,
          after 1864, in Melbourne for the *Age, Argus* and *Punch*, and *Town Talk* of which he
          was proprietor and editor. He completed Clarke's drama *Reverses* (Clarson, Massina,
          Melbourne, 1876) and collaborated with Clarke on research for the *History of the
          Continent of Australia and the Island of Tasmania* (F. F. Baillière, Melbourne, 1877)
          which Clarke edited, and on adapting *The Happy Land* (1880), a political farce
          satirising the Berry government. His *Mary Summers: A Tale of the Bush* (1868) is a
          bushranger tale with an early detective motif. *LMC* lists *Round the Camp Fire* by R. P.
          Whitworth.

p. 213   just as he had done in his earlier letters: only one is cited above.

p. 213   'On Female Education': 'Noah's Ark', *Australasian*, 18 May 1872, 615.

p. 213   'Bullocktown': published as 'An Up-country Township' in the *Australasian*, 6 August
          1870, 170, reprinted in *Holiday Peak*. MS has 'Bullock Town'.

p. 213   physical characteristics of Australia: 'Noah's Ark', *Australasian*, 18 May 1872, 615,
          reprinted *CC*.

p. 213   'Pure the air and light the soil': from *Paradise Regain'd* (4.239) by John Milton (1608–
          74), referring to Athens.

p. 214   aeronaut: balloonist. For an account of the first ascent of a manned balloon in
          Melbourne on 1 February 1858, see Harold Love, *James Edward Neild: Victorian
          Virtuoso*, 1989, 57–9

p. 214   favourite poet: Milton's *Paradise Lost* (1667) is quoted above, Ch. 8, and in *HNL*.

p. 214   'L'Allegro': poem by John Milton, also referred to by Clarke in *Photographs of the
          Pictures in the National Gallery, Melbourne*, quoted in Ch. 26. The passage comes from
          'Noah's Ark. By Marcus Clarke', *Australasian*, 12 July 1873, 43–4, reprinted *CC*.

p. 214   Ruysdael: (c. 1602–70), Dutch landscape painter.

p. 214   secular or religious education: *Australasian*, 18 May 1872, 615, reprinted *CC*.

p. 214   Hugh Latimer (?1492–1555), English Protestant divine, bishop of Worcester, burnt at the stake as a heretic in Mary Tudor's reign.

p. 214   Aphra Behn (1640–89), English writer, author of the novel *Oroonoko* (1688), based on her visit to Surinam in 1663, and some fifteen plays including *The Forced Marriage* (1670) and *The Rover* (1677, 1681). She is referred to in Clarke's story 'La Béguine', *Australasian*, 8 February 1873, 166.

p. 215   Bacon–Shakespeare controversy: 'There is a theory, you know, that Bacon wrote Shakespeare's plays', 'Noah's Ark', *Australasian*, 18 May 1872, 615, reprinted *CC*. The Melbourne doctor William Thomson 'devoted a large monograph and several pamphlets' to advocating the theory at this time (Love 147).

p. 215   *Erewhon*: a satirical utopia (1872) by Samuel Butler (1835–1902), English writer, which draws on his years in New Zealand from 1859 to 1864; author of the autobiographical *The Way of All Flesh* (1903).

p. 215   Sheridan Le Fanu (1814–73): Irish writer, author of *Uncle Silas* (1864) and other novels and the collection of ghost and horror stories *In a Glass Darkly* (1872), which includes 'Green Tea'. Green tea here is unoxidised Chinese tea. Clarke refers to smoking green tea, or, rather, denies doing so, in 'A Quiet Club', *Australasian*, 9 May 1868, 593, reprinted *PP*. But this may have been marijuana – 'tea' was nineteenth- and twentieth-century slang for marijuana. See Wilding, 'Marcus Clarke: Australia's First Drug Writings', *Australasian Weed*, 1, May 1977, 14—15, and 'Weird Melancholy', *Studies in Classic Australian Fiction*, 26.

p. 215   Spaniard's tavern: Clarke used the Spaniard's inn as a setting in the prologue added to the revised version of *HNL*.

p. 215   'Ancient Mariner': Clarke refers to *The Rime of the Ancient Mariner* (1798) in 'An Australian Crusoe' in *OT* and in his comments on Rabelais in his essay 'Balzac and Modern French Literature', *Australasian*, 3 August 1867, 136. On Coleridge, see note to Ch. 5.

p. 216   *The Mystery of a Hansom Cab* (Melbourne, 1886), best-selling crime novel by Fergus Hume (1859–1932) which 'owed so much to Clarke' (Andrew McCann, *Marcus Clarke's Bohemia: Literature and Modernity in Colonial Melbourne*, 2004, 230). Born in London to Scots parents and taken to New Zealand as a child, he qualified as a barrister there. He lived in Melbourne, where the novel is set, from 1885 to 1888, before returning to England and writing some 150 further novels.

p. 216   Albunazar, or Abu Mashar (781–885), astronomer and astrologer, born in Balkh, Afghanistan, spent much of his life in Baghdad. Known primarily for his theory that the world, created when the seven planets were in conjunction in the first degree of Aries, will come to an end at a like conjunction in the last degree of Pisces.

p. 216   Arnaud de Villeneuve (1235?–1312), physician, alchemist and astrologer, probably of Spanish (Catalan) origin. Taught at Paris and Barcelona.

p. 216   Regiomontanus (1436–76), the name given to Johannes Müller, from his Franconian birthplace, Königsberg (Mons Regius). German mathematician and astronomer. His *Ephemerides 1475–1506* was published in 1473.

p. 216   Fra Girolamo Savonarola (1452–98), Florentine Dominican monk, executed as a heretic.

p. 217   Was Poe a plagiarist?: 'American Literature', 'Noah's Ark', *Australasian*, 25 May 1872, 648. Before leaving London, Clarke gave his copy of Poe's poems to GMH. See note to Ch. 2.

p. 217   'The Haunted Author': 'Hunted Down', *Australasian*, 6 May 1871, 550, reprinted in *MV* as 'The Haunted Author', quoted in Ch. 25. The story is interesting as an early send-up of stereotypes in Australian literature.

p. 217   Frank Fowler (1833–63), English writer, lived in Australia 1855–8. He edited the
          Month, 1857–8. Author of *Southern Lights and Shadows* (Sampson Low, London,
          1859), *Dottings of a Lounger* (1859) and *Last Gleanings* (1864).

p. 217   Orion Horne: Richard Hengist Horne, see note to Ch. 22 (i).

p. 217   Kingsley: Henry Kingsley: see note to Preface.

p. 217   Howitt: William Howitt (1792–1879), English author and traveller, visited Australia
          1852–54, author of *Land, Labour and Gold, or Two Years in Victoria* (1855), *The History
          of Discovery in Australia, Tasmania and New Zealand* (1865) etc.

p. 217   Thatcher: Charles Thatcher (1831–78), English-born flautist, came to Australia in
          1852. Failing as a digger, he became a popular goldfields entertainer, publishing
          Thatcher's Victorian Songster (1855), *Thatcher's Colonial Songster* (1857) and *Thatcher's
          Colonial Minstrel* (1859).

p. 219   E. W. Hornung (1866–1921), English novelist. He lived in Australia in the Riverina
          in the early 1890s, before returning to the UK and writing the Raffles stories. *The
          Unbidden Guest* was published by Longman, London and New York, 1894. Hornung's
          The Rogue's March (Cassell, London; Scribner, New York, 1896) is a 'highly competent
          sub-Clarke convict novel' that is 'largely imitating the structure' of *HNL* – Stephen
          Knight, *Continent of Mystery: A Thematic History of Australian Crime Fiction* (1997) 49,
          148.

p. 219   Norfolk Island: infamous place of secondary punishment for convicts; used as a setting
          in *HNL*.

p. 220   Marcus Clarke follows up the story … with one … entirely different: it was not Clarke
          but Hamilton Mackinnon who followed 'The Haunted Author' with 'A Christmas Eve
          Watch' in *MV* and *AE*. Clarke originally published the stories in the *Australasian*, 6
          May 1871 and 28 December 1872.

p. 220   'A Christmas Eve Watch': 'A Watch on Christmas Eve', *Australasian*, 28 December
          1872, 808, reprinted as 'A Christmas Eve Watch' in *MV* and as 'A Sad Christmas Eve
          Retrospect' in *AE*, BW, *ST*.

p. 220   'The Poor Artist': *Australasian*, 13 July 1872, 40, collected by Clarke in *Four Stories
          High*, 1877. Cyril paraphrases this story, rather than quotes.

Chapter 26

p. 223   letterpress he contributed to the illustrated catalogue: Marcus Clarke, ed., *Photographs
          of Pictures in the National Gallery, Melbourne* (F. F. Baillière, Melbourne, 1874).
          Originally published in eighteen monthly parts, October 1873 – March 1875. See note
          to Preface above on Adam Lindsay Gordon and to Ch. 2 on Edgar Allan Poe.

p. 223   Eugene Ernest Hillemacher (1818–87). His 'Psyche aux Enfers' is the third of the
          Pictures in the National Gallery Melbourne, Reproduced in Photography, February 1874,
          to which Clarke contributed the accompanying text.

p. 224   Apuleius (fl. 150 AD), North African author of *Metamorphoses* or *The Golden Ass*,
          which includes the story 'Cupid and Psyche'.

p. 224   Plato (c. 428–348 BC), Greek philosopher. Clarke refers to him in the *Age*, 23 March
          1880, reprinted *CC*.

p. 224   Plotinus (c. 203–62 AD), Greek Neoplatonic philosopher. Clarke refers to
          Neoplatonism in *LO*.

p. 224   Synesius (c. 375–413 AD), Greek philosopher and Neoplatonic poet, Bishop of
          Ptolemais.

p. 224   Edwin Long (1829–91), English painter. His *The Dancing Girl or, A Question of
          Propriety* was the first of the *Pictures in the National Gallery Melbourne, Reproduced in
          Photography*, October 1873, to which Clarke contributed the accompanying text.

p. 224   Henry Wadsworth Longfellow (1807–82), American poet, author of *The Song of
          Hiawatha* (1858) etc. *The Spanish Student*, a comic drama, published in 1842/43.

Clarke refers to him in *LO* and his discussion of American literature in 'Noah's Ark', *Australasian*, 25 May 1872, 648. *LMC* lists Longfellow's *New England Tragedies*.

p. 225   Frederick Richard Lee (1799–1879), English painter. His *River, Mill and Farm* was the fourth of the *Pictures in the National Gallery Melbourne, Reproduced in Photography*, December 1873, to which Clarke contributed the accompanying text.

p. 225   Milton: *L'Allegro*, 71–2.

p. 225   Charles Meer Webb (1830–95), English painter. His *Checkmate* was the fifth of the *Pictures in the National Gallery Melbourne, Reproduced in Photography*, November 1873, to which Clarke contributed the accompanying text.

p. 225   Michael Angelo Titmarsh: pseudonym used by Thackeray in his early journalism for *Fraser's Magazine* (1830–82). *LMC* lists Thackeray's *Titmarsh*.

p. 226   The story is told in words scarcely less simple than those chosen by the historical knife-grinder of Mr. Canning: 'The Friend of Humanity and the Knife Grinder', by George Canning and John Hookham Frere, *Anti-Jacobin Review*, reprinted in G. Canning and J. H. Frere, eds, *Poetry of the Anti-Jacobin* (1799) 10. George Canning (1770–1827), English politician and Prime Minister, poet and a founder of the *Quarterly Review* in 1808. *Collected Poems* (1823), *Collected Speeches* (1828). First stanza runs (speaker is the Friend of Humanity):

> Needy knife-grinder, whither are you going?
> Rough is the road, your wheel is out of order;
> Bleak blows the blast, your hat has got a hole in't;
> So have your breeches!

The Knife-Grinder proves quite indifferent to his would-be patron's enthusiasm for the Jacobin cause, and this finally earns him a kicking.

p. 226   Samuel Bough (1822–78), English painter. His painting *The Weald of Kent* is the second of the *Pictures in the National Gallery Melbourne, Reproduced in Photography*, January 1874, to which Clarke contributed the accompanying text.

p. 226   well-known introduction: Clarke's preface to Adam Lindsay Gordon's poems *Sea Spray and Smoke Drift* (1876), frequently reprinted in successive editions of Gordon *Poems* (1880). It is reprinted in *BW* and *MC*. It incorporated material that Clarke previously published in *Photographs of Pictures in the National Gallery, Melbourne*. On Gordon, see note to Preface.

p. 226   Lord Lytton: see note to Preface.

p. 226   'The Sick Stockrider': first published in the *Colonial Monthly*, 5, January 1870, 342–4 and reprinted in the *Australasian*, 15 January 1870, 71.

p. 228   Wrapped in the mists of early morning: Clarke's original text to Buvelot's painting reads 'mists'; the Preface text reads 'midst' which CH follows, but this is most likely a misprint for 'mists'.

p. 229   *The New Nation*: the quotation is from the book of that name by Percy Rowland (Smith, Elder, London, 1903) 248.

p. 229   Wallace Nelson (1856–1943), *Foster Fraser's Fallacies, and Other Australian Essays* (Gordon and Gotch, Sydney, 1910) 151. It includes brief sketches of Marcus Clarke, Henry Kendall, Alexander Sutherland, Arthur Bayldon and others.

p. 229   the contrast between the ideal delights of a drover's life: this is said to have been a staged debate in the *Bulletin*, see Denton Prout, *Henry Lawson* (1963) 100–3.

p. 230   John Foster Fraser, *Australia: The Making of a Nation* (Cassell, London, 1910) 77–8.

p. 230   H. M. Hyndman: *The Record of an Adventurous Life* (1911) 112–13.

p. 231   Mrs. Campbell Praed: *My Australian Girlhood: Sketches and Impressions of Bush Life* (1902), 9, 42–3.

p. 232   Marcus Clarke's preface: to Gordon's poems.

p. 232   description of a native corroboree: Praed 91–2.

p. 232   William Moore (1868–1937); after experience as an actor in the USA and England, he returned to Melbourne in 1909 and encouraged Australian drama. Later art critic for the Melbourne *Herald* and the Sydney *Daily Telegraph* and author of *City Sketches*

(Melbourne, 1905) and *Studio Sketches* (Melbourne, 1906), both books presenting aspects of Bohemian life in Melbourne, and of *The Story of Australian Art*, 2 vols, 1934.

p. 233   Bernard O'Dowd (1866–1953), Australian poet of radical political views, editor of *Tocsin*.

p. 233   Richard Strauss (1864–1949), German composer.

p. 234   Barcroft Boake (1866–92), Australian poet of radical politics, author of *Where the Dead Men Lie* (1897). Hanged himself with his stock-whip after financial and personal difficulties.

p. 234   Ernest Henry Clarke: third son of Marcus Clarke, known as 'Rowley'. Hopkins met him twice in the UK and got to know him 'more intimately' than other members of the Clarke family (see Hopkins' letter to Ethel Marion Clarke, Marcus's daughter, 19 December 1926, MS ML). Ernest may have sent Hopkins copies of the newspaper items mentioned in this chapter.

p. 235   William Wordsworth (1770–1850), English poet. *LMC* lists Wordsworth's *Poems*.

p. 235   'The Solitude of Alexander Selkirk', by the English poet William Cowper (1731–1800), beginning 'I am monarch of all I survey' and including the lines beginning 'O Solitude! where are the charms …?' The poem is based on the life of Alexander Selkirk (1667–1721), Scots seaman on whom Defoe based *Robinson Crusoe*.

p. 237   Dmitrii Demetrius Grigorovich (1822–99), Russian novelist, whose tales *The Village* (1846) and *Anton Gorenykan* (1847) were famous for their sympathetic depiction of the miseries of peasant life. Beatrice Tollemache translated *Russian Sketches, Chiefly of Peasant Life, by Various Authors* (Smith Elder & Co, London, 1913). MS has 'Gregorovitch' and 'Tollemach'.

Chapter 27

p. 238   Andrew Lang: see note to Ch. 2. He was a friend of Robert Louis Stevenson.

p. 238   *The Wrecker* (1892), a novel written by Robert Louis Stevenson in collaboration with his stepson Lloyd Osbourne. It is set partly in Australia.

p. 238   a letter dated June 1874: BE remarks of this letter 'the date Hopkins gives it, June 1874, seems too early for some of its details and too late for others. Two or three letters seem to have been inadvertently telescoped, but they belong to much about the same time …' (171).

p. 239   Gisborne: a town in the Mount Macedon Hills, 54 km north-east of Melbourne, where early prospectors rested overnight on their way to the goldfields.

p. 239   two drunken diggers: BE inaccurately transcribes this as 'two drunken niggers' (172).

p. 239   librarian to the Public Library: Clarke was appointed secretary to the Trustees of the Public Library, June 1870; in September 1873 he became sub-librarian on the death of the first Librarian, Augustus Tulk, and Henry Sheffield was promoted to Librarian. On Clarke's work at the Library, see BE 167–83; E. La Touche Armstrong, later Chief Librarian at the Melbourne Public Library, quoted in E. Morris Miller, 'Some Public Library Memories', ed. Derek Drinkwater, *La Trobe Library Journal*, 9, 35, 1985, 64; John Arnold, 'Library Profile: Edward La Touche Armstrong', *La Trobe Library Journal*, Spring 2003, 80–4; Sandra Burt, 'Marcus Clarke at the Public Library', *La Trobe Library Journal*, 67, 2001, 55–60; and David McVilly, 'Personalities from the Past: Marcus Clarke, Librarian', *Australian Library Journal*, March 1975, 70–1. McL reprints minutes relating to Clarke at the Library, 242–5.

p. 239   two hundred thousand volumes: Anthony Trollope estimated the figure at 60,000 in 1870, and Sir Archibald Michie suggested 'upward of 100,000' in 1879 (BE 172, 175). It had certainly expanded considerably from the 'strangely unfit' condition in which Sir Charles Gavan Duffy found it on his arrival in Melbourne in 1856 (*My Life in Two Hemispheres*, 2, 134–5).

<table>
<tr><td>p. 239</td><td>five hundred a year: according to BE (175), 'His salary is also overstated, unless he had perquisites which augmented his official figure, which never rose above £450.'</td></tr>
<tr><td>p. 239</td><td>written two novels: Long Odds (1869) and His Natural Life (Melbourne, 1874; London, 1875).</td></tr>
<tr><td>p. 239</td><td>which I had hoped might meet with notice in London: LO received excellent reviews, quoted in Samuel R. Simmons, A Problem and a Solution: Marcus Clarke and the Writing of "Long Odds", 1946, when reissued as Heavy Odds (1896). Excellent notices of HNL are quoted in Mackinnon's biography in MV and AE. See also L. T. Hergenhan, 'The Contemporary Reception of His Natural Life', Southerly, 31, 1971, 50–63.</td></tr>
<tr><td>p. 239</td><td>I became insolvent: see BE 122–3, 172–7, 249.</td></tr>
<tr><td>p. 239</td><td>a little farm of eight hundred acres: Clarke's cousin, Sir Andrew, gave Clarke power of attorney over his Melbourne property. See BE 177–82 and text below.</td></tr>
<tr><td>p. 239</td><td>waging war against the piratical chiefs: cf. Clarke's letter to Sir Charles Gavan Duffy, 10 April 1875: 'I suppose you know that my cousin Andrew Clarke, after generally slaughtering pirates in the Malay Peninsula, has been named Minister of Public Works in India at £9,600 a year. Lucky fellow he is, to be sure. I would take his work for half the money, and sustain the dignity as royally as in me lies' (Duffy, 2, 367).</td></tr>
<tr><td>p. 240</td><td>Petshorin: a character in Lermontov's novel A Hero of Our Times (1840): see note to Ch. 17.</td></tr>
<tr><td>p. 240</td><td>alluding to Clarke's insolvency Mr. Hamilton Mackinnon writes: MV 47–8.</td></tr>
<tr><td>p. 240</td><td>A. B. Paterson: 'Introductory Memoir', For the Term of His Natural Life (Angus & Robertson, Sydney, 1899).</td></tr>
<tr><td>p. 242</td><td>His Natural Life, published by Richard Bentley in three volumes, September 1875 (McL 312–25).</td></tr>
<tr><td>p. 242</td><td>a recent writer in the Sydney Bulletin: Frank Myers, red page, Bulletin, 26 November 1903.</td></tr>
<tr><td>p. 243</td><td>the Daily Telegraph people: the London Daily Telegraph was founded in 1855; within twenty years it was claiming the 'largest circulation in the world'. Mackinnon quotes a letter from Lawson Levy inviting Clarke to contribute: 'I have read your books with very great pleasure, and it has occurred to me that you possess most of the qualifications for journalism of the highest order. Has the idea ever occurred to you of adopting this branch of literature, and would it suit your views to come to England?' (MV, 51). McL (3144 and 3145) refers to two letters from Edward Lawson and three from John Le Sage (3149–52) of the Daily Telegraph about two published articles, 'The Turf at the Antipodes' and 'Democracy in Australia' (see below) but declining 'the bush-ranging' article. There is some variation on the name of Clarke's correspondent at the Telegraph: Mackinnon and BE have Lawson Levy, McL has Edward Lawson, Google gives Edward Levy-Lawson. Two letters from Edward Lawson to Clarke inviting him to join the London Daily Telegraph are held in ML (McL 3144–3145).</td></tr>
<tr><td>p. 243</td><td>Clarke's articles in the London Daily Telegraph listed in McL (881–7) are: 'Democracy in Australia', part 1, 4 September 1877, part 2, 6 September 1877 (both reprinted CC); 'The Turf at the Antipodes', 23 April 1878; 'Beaconsfield', 1 April 1879; 'McMillan and Gippsland', 10 June 1879; 'Captain Moonlite', 28 November 1879; 'The Melbourne Exhibition', 16 November 1880.</td></tr>
<tr><td>p. 243</td><td>the 'good news' that I had to tell you: the following quotations from this letter are cited by BE, who comments: 'Since this letter is quoted with interruptions it too may be a patchwork of two or three' (182).</td></tr>
<tr><td>p. 244</td><td>there is no society in Melbourne: Clarke apparently maintained some upper middle-class consciousness, derived from his youth in England, throughout his Melbourne days, though he could alternate it with the democratic, radical views that inform his writings. The latter was a side of himself he was less likely to talk about with Cyril because, as in these last letters to him, dated January 1877 (BE 179), Clarke did not want to give the appearance of having come down in the world, concentrating instead on his achievement and social standing. Clarke was scathing about the pretensions and materialism of the</td></tr>
</table>

wealthy in post gold-rush Melbourne, as in his satire, 'Nasturtium Villas', from his
Wicked World series, *Weekly Times*, 14 February 1874, 9, reprinted *CC*.

p. 244   *Once a Week*: see note to Ch. 5.

p. 244   How did you like *His Natural Life*, I mean *really* you know: Clarke here spells out the
          irony of the title and reveals his desire for the novel to be recognised in Britain. The MS
          has 'really' strongly underlined.

Chapter 28

p. 245   H. G. Turner: 'Marcus Clarke', *Melbourne Review*, 7, 25 (January 1882), 4.

p. 245   Patrick Moloney: see note to Preface. Clarke's posthumously published *The Mystery of
          Major Molineux and Human Repetends* was dedicated to Moloney 'at the express wish
          of the late Marcus Clarke'. On Moloney, see Hugh McCrae, *My Father and My Father's
          Friends* (1935), 56–9.

p. 245   Garton's hotel: situated in Swanson Street, Melbourne. Mentioned in 'New Chums',
          Australasian, 10 October 1868, 465, and 'A Fast Sporting Man's Melbourne',
          Australasian, 4 January 1868, 17, both reprinted *PP*, *CC*, see notes *CC* 414.

p. 246   undiscovered country from whose bourn no traveller returns: Shakespeare, *Hamlet*,
          3.1.81–2.

p. 246   a bailiff had been sent to his house: BE devotes an appendix, 'Marcus Clarke and the
          Bailiff' to this story (262–5), comparing it with the plot of Clarke's farce, *Baby's Luck*.
          According to CH, 'the incident actually occurred within some months of his [Clarke's]
          death' in 1881, but BE points out that as the farce 'was produced in March 1879, it
          is possible that fact and fiction have been confused' (264). BE concludes: 'In fine,
          whether this story is a version of *Baby's Luck*, or *Baby's Luck* is a version of this, or both
          are highly decorated versions of some actual incident, is a problem which can hardly
          be decided without further evidence' (265). *Baby's Luck*, alternatively titled *A Man in
          Possession*, was, according to McL (1159), an 'original comedietta, 1878, adapted from
          Christmas in Possession by Mary Clarke … Text not seen.' Eric Irvin comments that the
          work 'was said by one critic to have been adapted from a story by the English novelist
          Mary (M. E.) Braddon and by another from a story by Dickens', *Australian Melodrama*
          (1981) 36. Clarke refers to Braddon in his essay 'Charles Dickens', *Argus*, 8 July 1870,
          reprinted *CC*, *MC*. *LMC* lists Braddon's *Charlotte's Inheritance*.

p. 248   E. La Touche Armstrong's contention: Edmund La Touche Armstrong, *The Book of
          the Public Library, Museums, and National Gallery of Victoria, 1856–1906* (Ford & Son,
          Melbourne, 1906) 118–20. BE comments: 'Estimates of his [Clarke's] efficiency as a
          librarian vary and are not very reliable' (171).

p. 248   Sir Redmond Barry: see note to 'Sir Harry Bedmont', Ch. 8.

p. 248   Francis Adams, 'Two Australian Writers', *Fortnightly Review*, 309, 1 September 1892;
          reprinted in Francis Adams, *The Australians* (1893) 106.

p. 248   Walter Murdoch, 'Marcus Clarke', *Argus*, 22 October 1904, 4; collected in Murdoch,
          Loose Leaves (George Robertson, Melbourne, 1910) 50–5, with 'such as we can
          reasonably be asked to admire' replacing 'such as Dr. Smiles' … chronicle'.

p. 249   Henry Fielding (1707–54), English novelist, author of *The History of Tom Jones* (1749).
          Clarke mentions him in 'Of French Novels', *Argus*, 2 February 1872, 6, and his *Tom
          Jones* in 'Charles Dickens', *Argus*, 8 July 1870, 7, and in 'Noah's Ark', *Australasian*, 27
          July 1872, all reprinted *CC*; it is one of the books that Sylvia reads in *HNL*. He refers
          to Fielding in his story 'La Béguine', *Australasian*, 8 February 1873.

p. 249   Leslie Stephen on R. L. Stevenson; *National Review*, 38, January 1902, 725–43; the
          essay is reprinted in vol. 9 of *The Works of R. L. Stevenson*, ed. Charles Curtis Bigelow
          and Temple Scott (New York, 1906).

p. 249   Adams 115.

p. 249   of the former that a certain classical sense saved him from Balzac's pedantry, if he was
          unable to fathom Balzac's profundity, adding: this passage is crossed out in MS.

p. 250   Arthur Patchett Martin, 'An Australian Novelist', *Temple Bar*, 71, May 1884, 108–9.
          Cyril has reordered the sequence of paragraphs.

p. 250   'Narrowing Envy': Tennyson, 'Lucretius' 210–12: ' I thought I lived securely as
          yourselves / No lewdness, narrowing envy, monkey-spite, / No madness of ambition,
          avarice, none'.

p. 250   Tasma: see note to Ch. 7.

Bibliography

1 Marcus Clarke: Books

Clarke, Marcus, *About Gardens and Flowers*, Mulini Press, Canberra, 1996. Reprinted from
    Mackinnon's *Memorial Volume*

Clarke, Marcus, *Australian Tales*, A. W. Bruce, Melbourne, 1896, reprinted as *Australian Tales of
    the Bush*, George Robertson, Melbourne, 1897, both reissues of Mackinnon's *Austral
    Edition*, part II, 'Australian Tales and Sketches'

Clarke, Marcus, *Chidiock Tichbourne or the Babington Conspiracy*, serialised in the *Australian Journal*,
    September 1874 – March 1875; published in book form as *Chidiock Tichbourne or the
    Catholic Conspiracy*, Eden Remington, London, 1893

Clarke, Marcus, *Civilisation without Delusion*, F. F. Baillière, Melbourne, 1880, reprinted with
    changes as *What Is Religion?*, Robert Barr, Fitzroy, 1895

Clarke, Marcus, *The Future Australian Race*, F. F. Baillière, Melbourne, 1877, reprinted in *MV, AE,
    AT, ST*

Clarke, Marcus, *Four Stories High*, A. H. Massina, Melbourne, 1877

Clarke, Marcus, *His Natural Life*, serialised in the *Australian Journal*, March 1870 – June 1872; ed.
    Stephen Murray-Smith, Penguin, Ringwood and Harmondsworth, 1970

Clarke, Marcus, *His Natural Life*, George Robertson, Melbourne, 1874; Richard Bentley, London,
    1875. Re-titled *For the Term of His Natural Life* in 1882.

Clarke, Marcus, ed., *History of the Continent of Australia and the Island of Tasmania*, F. F. Baillière,
    Melbourne, 1877

Clarke, Marcus, *Holiday Peak and Other Tales*, George Robertson, Melbourne, 1873

Clarke, Marcus, *Long Odds*, Clarson, Massina, Melbourne, 1869; the unrevised serial text, *Colonial
    Monthly*, March 1868 – July 1869, was reissued as *Heavy Odds*, Hutchinson, London,
    and J. B. Lippincott, Philadelphia, 1896

[Clarke, Marcus], *Mark Forrester's Trial*, Mulini Press, Canberra, 2007. First published anonymously
    Australian Monthly Magazine, September 1865 – February 1866. Introduction by
    Lurline Stuart argues for Clarke's authorship.

Clarke, Marcus, *The Mystery of Major Molineux and Human Repetends*, Cameron, Laing & Co,
    Melbourne, 1881, introduction by R. P. Whitworth. Facsimile reprint of *Major
    Molineux* alone, Mulini Press, Canberra, 1996.

Clarke, Marcus, *Old Tales of a Young Country*, Mason, Firth & McCutcheon, Melbourne, 1871;
facsimile reprint, introduced by Joan Poole, Sydney University Press, Sydney, 1972.
Originally, fourteen of the fifteen tales were published as 'Old Tales Retold' in the
Australasian, 19 February 1870 – 24 June 1871.

[Clarke, Marcus], *The Peripatetic Philosopher by 'Q'*, George Robertson, Melbourne, 1869. A
selection from Clarke's column in the weekly *Australasian*, 23 November 1867 – 17
April 1869.

Clarke, Marcus, ed., *Photographs of Pictures in the National Gallery*, Melbourne, F. F. Baillière,
Melbourne, 1874. Originally published in eighteen monthly parts, October 1873
– March 1875.

Clarke, Marcus, *Reverses*, completed by R. P. Whitworth, Clarson, Massina, Melbourne, 1876; ed.
Dennis Davison, English Department, Monash University, 1981

Clarke, Marcus, *Stories of Australia in the Early Days*, Hutchinson, London, 1897. A reissue of the
'Biography' and Mackinnon's *Austral Edition*, part I; comprising *Old Tales of a Young
Country* with five additional historical essays.

Clarke, Marcus, *Sensational Tales*, Australian Shilling Series, M'Carron, Bird & Co, Melbourne, 1886

Clarke, Marcus, *Stories*, introduction by Michael Wilding, Hale & Iremonger, Sydney, 1983.
Reissue of Mackinnon *Austral Edition*, part II, 'Australian Tales and Sketches' and
Austral Edition, part III 'Stories – Imaginative and Fanciful'.

Clarke, Marcus, *'Twixt Shadow and Shine*, George Robertson, Melbourne, 1875; Swann
Sonnenschein, London, 1893

2 Marcus Clarke: Stories, essays, poems etc.

'Ad Barinem': Horace, Lib. II, Car. 8; *Colonial Monthly*, May 1868, 192–3.

'American Literature', 'Noah's Ark', *Australasian*, 25 May 1872, 648, reprinted *CC*.

'Arcades Ambo', *Australasian*, 26 February 1870, 273, reprinted *Holiday Peak* and *CC*, and as
'Squatters Past and Present', *MV, AE, AT, ST*.

'Austin Friars', *Australian Monthly Magazine*, May 1866, 199–209, reprinted *MV, CC* (under the
pseudonym of Mark Scrivener)

'Balzac and Modern French Literature', *Australasian*, 3 August 1867, 136, reprinted in *MV, AE,
BW, MC*

'The Brief Experiences of Mr. Thomas Twopenny', 'The Wicked World', *Weekly Times*, 14 March
1874, 9, reprinted *Australian Letters*, 1 November 1958, 5–9, *CC*

'The Café Lutetia', 'The Wicked World', *Weekly Times*, 28 February 1874, 9, reprinted *CC, MC*.

'Cannabis Indica – a Psychological Experiment', *Colonial Monthly*, 1, 6, February 1868, 454–68,
reprinted in *MV* and *MC*, and as 'A Haschich Trance' in *AE* and *ST*

'Charles Dickens', *Argus*, 8 July 1870, 7, reprinted *CC, MC*

'A Cheap Lodging-House', Lower Bohemia – 5, *Australasian*, 31 July 1869, 136, reprinted *CC*

'The Chinese Quarter', Night Scenes in Melbourne – 3, *Argus*, 9 March 1868, 5–6, reprinted *CC*

'Civilisation without Delusion', *Victorian Review*, 1, 1, November 1879, 65–75, reprinted *MC*.
Together with Bishop Moorhouse's reply and Clarke's rejoinder, the whole controversy
was collected in book form as *Civilisation without Delusion*, F. F. Baillière, Melbourne,
1880, and reprinted with changes as *What Is Religion?*, Robert Barr, Fitzroy, 1895.

'The Curious Experience of Anthony Venn', *Australasian*, 27 September, 389, 18 October, 485, 1
November 1873, 549, reprinted as 'The Mind Reader's Curse', *Sensational Tales, AE,
AT, ST*

'The Doppelgänger', *Australian Monthly Magazine*, July and August 1866, 363–74, 433–40,
reprinted as 'The Dual Existence', *Sensational Tales, AE* and *ST*

'Glycera', *Humbug*, 22 December 1869, 6, reprinted *Australian Journal*, January 1870, 309–10, *MV*
and *CC*

'The Gypsies of the Sea, or the Island of Gold', Melbourne *Herald*, 24–31 December 1874, 4,
reprinted *Sensational Tales*, and as 'A Modern Eldorado' in *AE* and *ST*

'A Hero of Romance', *Colonial Monthly*, October 1868, 147–57, November 1868, 215–30
'Holiday Peak', *Australasian*, 18 January 1873, 72; 25 January, 104, reprinted in *Holiday Peak and
    Other Tales*, George Robertson, Melbourne, 1873, *AE, AT, MC* and *ST*; excerpted by
    Mackinnon as 'A Night in the Bush' in *MV*
'Human Repetends', *Australasian*, 14 September 1872, 326, reprinted in Marcus Clarke, *The Mystery
    of Major Molineux and Human Repetends*, Cameron, Laing & Co, Melbourne, 1881,
    and in *MC*, and, as 'A Mysterious Coincidence' in *Sensational Tales*, *AE* and *ST*
'Hunted Down', *Australasian*, 6 May 1871, 550, reprinted as 'The Haunted Author', *MV*, and as
    'The Author Haunted by His Own Creations', in *AE, BW, ST*
'In a Bark Hut', *Australasian*, 17 May 1873, 616, reprinted in *Australasian Sketcher*, 17 May 1873,
    26, and *MV*, and as 'Learning "Colonial Experience"' in *AE, AT, BW, ST*
'In Outer Darkness', Lower Bohemia – 6, *Australasian*, 21 August 1869, 232, reprinted *CC, MC*
'King Billy's Breeches', *Australasian*, 12 August 1871, 197, reprinted in *Four Stories High, AE, AT, ST*
'La Béguine', *Australasian*, 8 February 1873, 166, reprinted in *Four Stories High*, A. H. Massina,
    Melbourne, 1877, and *MC*
'The Lady of Lynn', *Colonial Monthly*, March 1868, 15–17, reprinted *MV*
'The Language of Bohemia', Lower Bohemia – 4, *Australasian*, 17 July 1869, 72, reprinted *CC*
'Le roi s'amuse', *Australasian*, Lower Bohemia – 2, 19 June 1869, 776, reprinted *CC*
'Letters from Home', *Australasian*, 28 November 1868, 689, reprinted *PP, MV, AE, BW, CC*
'The Luck of Roaring Camp', *Australian Journal*, March 1871, 389–90, reprinted *CC* and *MC*
'The Mantuan Apothecary: A Picture in Two Panels', *Australian Monthly Magazine*, 2, March 1866,
    51–6
'Mark Clancy's Leap', *Humbug*, 22 December 1869, 11, reprinted *Australian Journal*, January 1870,
    309–10, *MV* and *CC*
'A Melbourne Alsatia', *Colonial Monthly*, February 1869, 473–9, reprinted *CC*
'Melbourne Streets at Midnight', Night Scenes in Melbourne – 1, *Argus*, 28 February 1868,
    reprinted *CC*
'A Mining Township', *Australasian*, 5 November 1870, 582, reprinted as 'An Australian Mining
    Township', *All the Year Round, incorporating Household Words*, 22 February 1873, 352–
    7, and as 'Grumbler's Gully', *Holiday Peak, AE, AT* and *ST*
'The Monster Nugget', *Australasian*, 13 February 1869, 209, reprinted *PP*
'The Mystery of Major Molineux', the *Campbelltown Herald* (Victoria), July 1881; collected
    posthumously in Marcus Clarke, *The Mystery of Major Molineux and Human Repetends*,
    Cameron, Laing & Co, Melbourne, 1881, with an introduction by R. P. Whitworth.
    Facsimile reprint of 'The Mystery of Major Molineux', Mulini Press, Canberra, 1996.
'New Chums', *Australasian*, 10 October 1868, 465, reprinted *PP, MV, AE, CC*
'A Night at the Immigrants' Home', Lower Bohemia – 1, *Australasian*, 12 June 1869, 762–3,
    reprinted *CC, MC*
'A Night with Horace', *Australasian*, 22 July 1871, 101, reprinted *Holiday Peak*, and as '"Horace" in
    the Bush' in *AE, AT* and *ST*
'Noah's Ark. By Marcus Clarke', *Australasian*, weekly from 18 May 1872 to 13 September 1873. It
    included stories, poems, essays, sketches and dialogues. A selection is reprinted in *CC*,
    275–81. Some of the stories were collected in *Holiday Peak and Other Tales* (1873).
'Of French Novels', The Buncle Correspondence, *Argus*, 2 February 1872, 6, reprinted *CC*
'Old Tales Retold', *Australasian* at irregular intervals 19 February 1870 to 24 June 1871; collected
    with a fifteenth article, 'The Rule of the Bushranger', in *Old Tales of a Young Country*,
    Mason, Firth & McCutcheon, Melbourne, 1871; facsimile reprint, introduced by Joan
    Poole, Sydney University Press, Sydney, 1972. Mackinnon reprinted the fifteen essays
    of the book together with five additional historical essays as Part I of *The Austral Edition
    of the Selected Works of Marcus Clarke*; this section of *AE* was later published separately
    as *Stories of Australia in the Early Days*, Hutchinson, London, 1897.
'On Business Men', *Humbug*, 3 November 1869, 6, 11, reprinted in *MV, BW, CC*
'On the Pursuit of Pleasure', *Australasian*, 18 April 1868, 497, reprinted *PP*, and *CC* as 'Colonial
    Holiday Making'

'Our Glorious Climate', *Humbug*, 12 January 1870, 5, reprinted *Australian Journal*, February 1870, 355, *MV*, *AE*

'A Pawnbroker's Shop on a Saturday Night', Night Scenes in Melbourne – 2, *Argus*, 6 March 1868, 6, reprinted *MV*, *CC*

'The Peripatetic Philosopher': a weekly column, *Australasian*, 23 November 1867 – 11 June 1870, signed 'Q'; a selection reprinted in volume form in *PP – The Peripatetic Philosopher by 'Q'*, George Robertson, Melbourne, 1869; selections in *MV*, *AE*, *CC*

'Playing with Fire', *Colonial Monthly*, November 1867, 168–84, reprinted *Australian Journal*, February 1871, 326–30

'The Poor Artist', *Australasian*, 13 July 1872, 40, collected by Clarke in *Four Stories High*, 1877

'Poor Jo', *Australasian*, 15 April 1871, 453, reprinted *Holiday Peak*, *AE*, *AT*, *MC* and *ST*

'Popular Art and Gustave Doré', *Australasian*, 28 September 1867, 392, reprinted as 'Modern Art and Gustave Doré' in *MV*, *AE*

'Preface', to Adam Lindsay Gordon, *Sea Spray and Smoke Drift*, Clarson, Massina, Melbourne, 1876, reprinted in the collected *Poems of the Late Adam Lindsay Gordon*, A. H. Massina, Melbourne, 1880, and in successive editions. Reprinted in BW and *MC*. Shorn of the specific references to Gordon, it is reprinted as 'Australian Scenery' in *MV*, *AE*, *AT* and *ST*, and in various anthologies subsequently. It incorporated in its concluding two-fifths material Clarke had previously written to accompany the photographic reproduction of Louis Buvelot's *Waterpool near Coleraine* and Nicholas Chevalier's *The Buffalo Ranges* in *Photographs of Pictures in the National Gallery, Melbourne*, ed. Marcus Clarke, F. F. Baillière, Melbourne, 1874, reprinted in *CC*.

'The Puff Conclusive', *Melbourne Punch*, 19 November 1863, 162

'A Quiet Club', *Australasian*, 9 May 1868, 593, reprinted *PP*

Review, Bret Harte's poems, *Australian Journal*, July 1871, 645

'Speech Days and School Days', *Australasian*, 28 December 1867, 817, reprinted *PP*

'The Sphinx-Riddle', translation from Heinrich Heine, *Australasian*, 7 September 1872, 296, reprinted *MV*, *AE*

'A Sunday at Farnham Rectory', *Leader* supplement, 24 April 1880, 1

'The Traveller of the Period', *Argus*, 13 April 1872, 6, reprinted *CC*

'Alfred Telo: a reminiscence', *Leader*, 11 October 1879, 18–19, reprinted *CC*

'An Up-country Township', *Australasian*, 6 August 1870, 170, reprinted in *Holiday Peak and Other Tales* and *MC*, and as 'Bullocktown' in *MV*, *AE*, *AT* and *ST*

'A Very Tough Subject', *Australian Monthly Magazine*, July 1867, 321–31, published under the pseudonym 'Mark Scrivener'

'What to Do with Our Boys', *Australasian*, 5 March 1870, 305, reprinted *PP*, *CC*

'The Working Man from His Own Point of View', *Australasian*, 26 March 1870, 401, reprinted *PP*, *CC*

3 Secondary materials

Abbott, Claude Colleer, ed., *Further Letters of Gerard Manley Hopkins including his correspondence with Coventry Patmore*, Oxford University Press, London, 1956, 2nd edn 1970

Abbott, C. C., ed., *The Letters of Gerard Manley Hopkins to Robert Bridges*, Oxford University Press, London, 1970

Abbott, C. C., ed., *The Correspondence of Gerard Manley Hopkins and Richard Watson Dixon*, Oxford University Press, London, 1970

Abbott-Young, Wendy, 'The Felix and Felicitas Papers of Marcus Clarke: An Annotated Edition with an Introduction', unpublished MA thesis, University of Adelaide, 1987

Abraham, Lyndy, 'The Australian Crucible: Alchemy in Marcus Clarke's *His Natural Life*', *Australian Literary Studies*, 15, 1991–92, 38–55

Abraham, Lyndy, *A Dictionary of Alchemical Imagery*, Cambridge University Press, Cambridge, 1998

Ackland, Michael, *Henry Kendall: The Man and the Myths*, Miegunyah Press, Melbourne, 1995

Ackland, Michael, ed., *Henry Kendall: Poetry, Prose and Selected Correspondence*, Australian Authors series, University of Queensland Press, St Lucia, 1993

Adams, Francis, 'The Prose Work of Marcus Clarke', *Sydney Quarterly Magazine*, 4, 2, 1887, 115–35

Adams, Francis, 'Two Australian Writers', *Fortnightly Review*, 52 n.s., 309, 1 September 1892, 352-65

Adams, Francis, *The Australians*, Unwin, London, 1893

Adams, Jad, *Hideous Absinthe: A History of the Devil in A Bottle*, I. B. Tauris, London, 2004

Albinski, Nan Bowman, 'Marcus Clarke's First Australian Publication', *Margin*, 21, 1989, 1–10

Allsopp, Michael, 'Hopkins at Highgate: Biographical Fragments', *Hopkins Quarterly*, 6, 1, Spring 1979, 3–10

Arnold, John, 'Marcus Clarke Joins the Public Library, Museum and National Gallery of Victoria', *Margin*, 40, 1996, 19–21

Aubrey, Philip, *Mr Secretary Thurloe: Cromwell's Secretary of State, 1652–1660*, Athlone Press, London, 1990

Birns, Nicholas, 'Receptacle or Reversal? Globalization Down Under in Marcus Clarke's *His Natural Life*', *College Literature*, 32, 2, April 2005, 127–45

Boehm, Harold J., '*His Natural Life* and Its Sources', *Australian Literary Studies*, 5, 1971, 42–64

Bottigheimer, Karl, *English Money and Irish Land*, Clarendon Press, Oxford, 1971

Bright, Charles, 'Marcus Clarke', *Cosmos*, 30 April 1895, 418–22

Brodzky, Maurice, 'A Biographical Study of Marcus Clarke' (1904), Mitchell Library, MSS 6176

Burt, Sandra, 'Marcus Clarke at the Public Library', *La Trobe Library Journal*, 67 (2001), 55–60

Byrne, Desmond, *Australian Writers*, Richard Bentley, London, 1896

Cantrell, Leon, ed., *A. G. Stephens: Selected Writings*, Angus & Robertson, Sydney, 1977

Carrington, F. T. D. and Watterson, D., *The Yorick Club: Its Origin and Development, May 1868 to December 1910*, Atlas, Melbourne, 1911

Denholm, Decie, 'The Sources of *His Natural Life*', *Australian Literary Studies*, 4, 1969, 174–8

Drabble, Margaret, ed., *The Oxford Companion to English Literature*, Oxford University Press, Oxford, 1985

Duffy, Sir Charles Gavan, *My Life in Two Hemispheres*, 2 vols, T. Fisher Unwin, London, 1898; facsimile reprint, Irish University Press, Shannon, 1969

Edwards, P. D., 'The English Publication of *His Natural Life*', *Australian Literary Studies*, 10, 1982, 520–6

Edwards, P. D., *Frances Cashel Hoey (1830–1908): A Bibliography*, Victorian Fiction Research Guides, No. 8, Department of English, University of Queensland, St Lucia, 1982

Elliott, Brian, 'Gerard Hopkins and Marcus Clarke', *Southerly*, 8, 1947, 218–27

Elliott, Brian, *Marcus Clarke*, Clarendon Press, Oxford, 1958

Gaunt, William, *Kensington*, B. T. Batsford, London, 1958

Gelder, Ken, 'Australian Gothic', in Catherine Spooner and Emma McEvoy eds, *Routledge Companion to Gothic*, Routledge, New York, 2007

Gibbs, A. M., *Bernard Shaw: A Life*, University Press of Florida, Gainesville, 2005

Gordon, Adam Lindsay, *The Poems of Adam Lindsay Gordon*, ed. Frank Maldon Robb, Oxford University Press, London, 1912

Hadgraft, Cecil, ed., *The Australian Short Story Before Lawson*, Oxford University Press, Melbourne, 1986

Hayter, Alethea, *Opium and the Romantic Imagination*, Faber & Faber, London, 1968

Henderson, Ian, '"There Are French Novels and There Are French Novels": Charles Reade and the "Other Sources" of Marcus Clarke's *His Natural Life*', *JASAL*, 1 (2002), 51–66

Hergenhan, L. T., *A Colonial City: High and Low Life. Selected Journalism of Marcus Clarke*, University of Queensland Press, St Lucia, 1972

Hergenhan, L. T., 'The Contemporary Reception of *His Natural Life*', *Southerly*, 31, 1971, 50–63

Hergenhan, L. T., 'The Corruption of Rufus Dawes', *Southerly*, 29, 1960, 211–21

Hergenhan, L. T., 'English Publication of Australian Novels: The Case of *His Natural Life*' in Leon Cantrell ed., *Bards, Bohemians and Bookmen: Essays Presented to Cecil Hadgraft*, University of Queensland Press, St Lucia, 1976, 56–71

Hergenhan, Laurie, 'Literary New Chums: Michael Wilding and Marcus Clarke', in *Running Wild: Essays, Fictions and Memoirs Presented to Michael Wilding*, ed. David Brooks and Brian Kiernan, Sydney Studies in Society and Culture, no. 22, Manohar, New Delhi, 2004, 223–32

Hergenhan, L. T., ed., *Marcus Clarke: A Checklist*, Wentworth Books, Sydney, 1976

Hergenhan, L. T., 'Marcus Clarke and the Colonial Landscape', *Quadrant*, 13, 1969, 31–51

Hergenhan, L. T., 'The Redemptive Theme in *His Natural Life*', *Australian Literary Studies*, 2, 1965, 32–49

Hergenhan, L. T., *Unnatural Lives: Studies in Australian Fiction About the Convicts*, University of Queensland Press, St Lucia, 1983

Hergenhan, L. T., ed., *The New Penguin Literary History of Australia*, Penguin, Ringwood, 1988

House, Humphrey, ed., *The Note-Books and Papers of Gerard Manley Hopkins*, Oxford University Press, London and New York, 1937

House, Humphrey and Storey, Graham, *The Journals and Papers of Gerard Manley Hopkins*, Oxford University Press, London, 1959

Howarth, R. G., 'Marcus Clarke's *For the Term of His Natural Life*', *Southerly*, 15, 1954, 268–76

Hutton, Geoffrey, *Adam Lindsay Gordon: The Man and the Myth*, Faber & Faber, London, 1978; Melbourne University Press, Melbourne, 1996

Hyndman, H. M., *The Record of an Adventurous Life*, Macmillan, London, 1911

Irvin, Eric, 'Marcus Clarke and the Theatre', *Australian Literary Studies*, 7, 1975, 3–14

Irvin, Eric, *Australian Melodrama*, Hale & Iremonger, Sydney, 1981

Kelly, Veronica, *Annotated Checklist of Comments on the Performance and Banning of Marcus Clarke's* The Happy Land *in Melbourne and Sydney*, Monash Bibliographical Series, Monash University, 1985

Kelly, Veronica, 'The Banning of Marcus Clarke's *The Happy Land*: Stage, Press and Parliament', *Australasian Drama Studies*, 2 (1983–84), 70–111

Kelly, Veronica, 'Colonial "Australian" Theatre Writers: Cultural Authorship and the Case of Marcus Clarke's "First" Play', *Australian Literary Studies*, 18 (May 1997), 31–44

Kelly, Veronica, 'Early Australian High Comedy to 1890: Performing the Colonial Bourgeois Self', *Southerly*, 64, 2004, 58

Kiernan, Brian, *Criticism* (Australian Writers and Their Work), Oxford University Press, Melbourne, 1974

Kiernan, Brian, *Studies in Australian Literary History*, Sydney Studies in Society and Culture, Sydney; Shoestring Press, Nottingham, 1998

Knight, Stephen, *Continent of Mystery: A Thematic History of Australian Crime Fiction*, Melbourne University Press, Melbourne, 1997

Kramer, Leonie, 'The Literary Reputation of Adam Lindsay Gordon', *Australian Literary Studies*, 1, 1963, 42–56

Kramer, Leonie and Hope, A. D. ed., *Henry Kendall*, Colonial Poets series, Sun Books, Melbourne, 1973

Love, Harold, *James Edward Neild: Victorian Virtuoso*, Melbourne University Press, Carlton, 1989

Love, Harold, ed., *The Australian Stage: A Documentary History*, New South Wales University Press, Sydney, 1984

McCann, Andrew, 'Colonial Gothic: Morbid Anatomy, Commodification and Critique in Marcus Clarke's The Mystery of Major Molineux', *Australian Literary Studies*, 19, 2000, 399–412

McCann, Andrew, *Marcus Clarke's Bohemia: Literature and Modernity in Colonial Melbourne*, Melbourne University Publishing, Melbourne, 2004

McCrae, Hugh, *My Father and My Father's Friends*, Angus & Robertson, Sydney, 1935, reprinted in Hugh McCrae, *Story Book Only*, Angus & Robertson, Sydney, 1948

McDermott, John, *A Hopkins Chronology*, St Martin's Press, New York, 1997

Mackinnon, Hamilton, ed., *The Austral Edition of the Selected Works of Marcus Clarke*, Fergusson and Mitchell, Melbourne, 1890

Mackinnon, Hamilton, ed., *The Marcus Clarke Memorial Volume*, Cameron, Laing & Co, Melbourne, 1884

McLaren, Ian F., *Marcus Clarke: An Annotated Bibliography*, Library Council of Victoria, Melbourne, 1982

MacRae, C. F., *Adam Lindsay Gordon*, Twayne, New York, 1968

Martin, Arthur Patchett, 'An Australian Novelist', *Temple Bar*, 71, May 1884, 96–110

Martin, Arthur Patchett, *The Beginnings of an Australian Literature*, Henry Sotheran, London, 1898

Martin, Robert Bernard, *Gerard Manley Hopkins: A Very Private Life*, Putnam, New York; HarperCollins, London, 1991

Moore, Tony, 'The Urban Iconoclast' (Marcus Clarke), *Meanjin*, 64, 2005, 204

Morris, Edward E., *Austral English: A Dictionary of Australasian Words, Phrases and Usages*, Macmillan, London, 1898, reissued Sydney University Press, Sydney, 1972

Pearl, Cyril, *The Three Lives of Gavan Duffy*, University of New South Wales Press, Kensington, 1979

Phare, E. E., *Gerard Manley Hopkins*, Cambridge University Press, Cambridge, 1933

Phillips, Catherine, ed., *Gerard Manley Hopkins*, Oxford University Press, New York, 1995

Robb, Graham, *Balzac: A Biography*, Picador, London, 1994

Ruggles, Eleanor, *Gerard Manley Hopkins: A Life*, W. W. Norton, New York, 1944; John Lane, London, 1947

Shakespeare, William, *The Complete Works*, ed. Stanley Wells and Gary Taylor, Clarendon Press, Oxford, 1988

Simmons, Samuel R., *A Problem and a Solution: Marcus Clarke and the Writing of "Long Odds"*, The Simmons Press, Melbourne, 1946

Stewart, Annette, 'The Design of *For the Term of his Natural Life*', *Australian Literary Studies*, 6, October 1974, 394–403

Stewart, Ken, *Investigations in Australian Literature*, Sydney Studies in Society and Culture, Sydney; Shoestring Press, Nottingham, 2000

Stewart, Ken, 'Sylvia's Books: Literature, Civilisation and *His Natural Life*', in *'And What Books Do You Read?' New Studies in Australian Literature: a Festschrift for Laurie Hergenhan*, ed. Martin Duwell and Irmtraud Petersson, University of Queensland Press, St Lucia, 1996, 1–14, reprinted in Stewart, Ken, *Investigations in Australian Literature*, 89–102

Stuart, Lurline, *Australian Periodicals: An Annotated Bibliography*, Hale & Iremonger, Sydney, 1979

Stuart, Lurline, *Australian Periodicals with Literary Content 1821–1925*, Australian Scholarly Publishing, Melbourne, 2001

Stuart, Lurline, *James Smith: The Making of a Colonial Culture*, Allen & Unwin, Sydney, 1989

Stuart, Lurline, ed., Marcus Clarke, *His Natural Life* (Academy Editions of Australian Literature), University of Queensland Press, St Lucia, 2001

Turner, H. G., 'Marcus Clarke', *Melbourne Review*, 7, 25, January 1882, 1–15

Turner, H. G., 'Marcus Clarke', *Once a Month* 3, 4, October 1885, 241–6

Turner, H. G. and Sutherland, Alexander, *The Development of Australian Literature*, Longmans, London, 1898, 300–43

Vetch, R. H., *General Sir Andrew Clarke*, John Murray, London, 1905

Wannan, Bill, ed., *A Marcus Clarke Reader*, Lansdowne Press, Melbourne, 1963

White, Norman, *Hopkins: A Literary Biography*, Clarendon Press, Oxford, 1992

White, Norman, 'Gerard Manley Hopkins', *Oxford Dictionary of National Biography*, Oxford University Press, Oxford, 2004, vol. 28, 54–8

Wilding, Michael, edited with an introduction, *Marcus Clarke* (Portable Australian Authors), University of Queensland Press, St Lucia, 1976, 2nd edn (Australian Authors), 1988

Wilding, Michael, *Marcus Clarke* (Australian Writers and Their Work), Oxford University Press, Melbourne, 1977

Wilding, Michael, 'Marcus Clarke: Australia's First Drug Writings', *Australasian Weed*, 1 (1) May 1977, 14–15

Wilding, Michael, 'Marcus Clarke, Bohemian', *Hemisphere*, 26, 1981, 148–51, reprinted in *Hemisphere Annual*, 3, Canberra, 1981

Wilding, Michael, 'Marcus Clarke in the Colonial City', *Southerly*, 33, 1973, 441–50

Wilding, Michael (with Poole, Joan), 'Marcus Clarke's Contributions to *Notes & Queries*', *Australian Literary Studies*, 6, 1973, 186–9

Wilding, Michael, 'Marcus Clarke's *Chidiock Tichborne*', *Australian Literary Studies*, 6, 1974, 381–93

Wilding, Michael, 'Marcus Clarke's *His Natural Life*', in W. S. Ramson, ed., *The Australian Experience: Critical Essays on Australian Novels*, Australian National University Press, Canberra, 1974, 19–37

Wilding, Michael, 'Marcus Clarke's *Old Tales of a Young Country*', *Southerly*, 33, 1973, 394–408

Wilding, Michael, 'The Short Stories of Marcus Clarke' in Leon Cantrell, ed., *Bards Bohemians and Bookmen: Essays in Australian Literature* (Essays presented to Cecil Hadgraft), University of Queensland Press, St Lucia, 1976, 72–97. Reprinted in Janet Mullane, ed., *Nineteenth-Century Literature Criticism*, Gale Research, Detroit, 1989

Wilding, Michael, *Studies in Classic Australian Fiction*, Sydney Studies in Society and Culture, Sydney; Shoestring Press, Nottingham, 1997

Wilding, Michael, 'Weird Melancholy: Inner and Outer Landscapes in Marcus Clarke's Stories', in P. R. Eaden and F. H. Mares, ed., *Mapped But Not Known: The Australian Landscape of the Imagination*, (Essays presented to Brian Elliott), Wakefield Press, Adelaide, 1987, 128–45. Reprinted in Wilding, *Studies in Classic Australian Fiction*, 9–31, and in *Nineteenth-Century Literature Criticism*, vol. 124, Gale Research, Detroit, 2003

Wilkes, G. A., *A Dictionary of Australian Colloquialisms*, Sydney University Press, Sydney, 1985